Oliver Edwards'

FLYTYER'S MASTERCLASS

Oliver Edwards' FLYTYER'S MASTERCLASS

Written & illustrated by Oliver Edwards
with new colour photographs by Terry Griffiths

Coch-y-Bonddu Books
2009

Oliver Edwards'
FLYTYER'S MASTERCLASS

First published in 1994 by Merlin Unwin Books, Ludlow
New edition published by The Flyfisher's Classic Library in 2009
This spiral-bound "Flytyer's Edition" is published in 2009 by Coch-y-Bonddu Books Ltd

Photographs by Terry Griffiths

An imprint of
Coch-y-Bonddu Books Ltd, Machynlleth, Powys SY20 8DG
01654 702837
www.ffcl.com *www.anglebooks.com*

ISBN 978 1 904784 21 0

Contents

ACKNOWLEDGMENTS

Although this book is the result of my own efforts with pen and pencil, there are several people who have, over the years, helped me bring it to publication.

First, I would like to thank Roy Eaton, former editor of *Trout & Salmon* magazine. Roy gave me my first writing and drawing assignment for *Trout & Salmon* and he also gave me the idea for this book, as a result of those first articles. Several American flyfishers, flytyers and authors deserve special mention, especially Gary Lafontaine for his incredible book, *Caddisflies* - essential reading for any serious flyfisher. I have quoted Gary in my chapter on the post-ovipositing behaviour of certain caddisflies. *The Caddis and the Angler* by Larry Solomon and Eric Leiser is a gem of a book, and again I am grateful to have quoted from it.

American flytyers have been a great influence on me over the past 20 years, none more so than Poul Jorgensen, Dave Whitlock, Darrel Martin and my friends in the Federation of Fly Fishers. Poul Jorgensen is one of the guest tyers in this book. His Cut-Wing Dun is a pattern I have used to great effect ever since I purchased his book *Modern Fly Dressings for the Practical Angler* in 1977.

The other guest tyer in this book is a Dutchman, and the scourge of grayling everywhere - Hans van Klinken. Hans is the creator of the Klinkhamer Special and the Leadhead Grayling Bug. The weighting system on the latter pattern finally unlocked the door to success for my own Peeping Caddis. Hans supplied me with much background information on both of his patterns. A big 'thank you' is also due to another Dutchman, Hans P.C. (burn 'em in the vice) de Groot. Hans not only creates stunning fully-dressed salmon flies (which he has been known to torch if they do not match up to his exacting high standards). He is also the originator of Flexibody, a material which has revolutionised many of my nymphs.

I would also like to thank my good pal, Davy Wotton, master of materials and the neatest, swiftest flytyer I have ever seen. Davy has produced the blends of dubbing used in this book using his high glint Finesse, thus saving me hours of blending myself.

The British hook-makers Partridge of Redditch deserve a very special 'thank you' from me, particularly their Managing Director, Alan Bramley. Alan's support over the past 15 years has been tremendous. He has a knack of making things happen and through him I have had the privilege of meeting and working with many world class tyers.

Finally, I would like to thank two fellow Yorkshiremen. While neither have contributed directly to this book their contribution is no less real. First, John Roberts, a man equally skilled with rod and pen. John's contribution was encouragement and inspiration. Secondly, my fishing partner of more than 30 years, Bernard Benson of Rothwell near Leeds. Bernard and I go to, and leave the river together, but see little of each other while actually fishing unless we're working on a particular problem. He is the perfect fishing mate. Bernard was also an early guinea pig for my Rhyacophila Larva and Popa Caddis.

Introduction to the 2009 Edition

"A fly fisherman must always be picturing to himself what is going on under the water; he must try to understand what his fly means to the fish and so he must choose it or tie it with meaning. He must look for new ideas, try them out when they come to him and watch closely to see their effect and find others."

Roderick Haig-Brown, *A River Never Sleeps*, 1948.

Oliver Edwards began demonstrating fly-tying at Fairs and Shows during the early 1980s, and was witness to the end of the insular nature of fly-tying. Up until then fly-tying and fly-fishing had mainly been local pastimes. When Oliver first picked up a fly-rod at the age of fifteen in 1953 to serve his apprenticeship on the Wharfe and other Yorkshire streams, he began with the traditional North Country spider patterns made famous by men like T.E. Pritt (a Lancastrian!), F.M. Walbran, H.H. Edmonds and N.N. Lee. So did I, and so did every North Country lad who wanted to fly-fish for trout and grayling up to the 1980s, before the advent of ponds stuffed full of naive stew-pond rainbow trout.

Oliver had not been fishing for very long when he noticed something that previous fly-fishers in our region had overlooked. The brown trout and grayling that he took home and cleaned for the table had in their stomachs creatures that looked nothing like the Partridge & Orange, Waterhen Bloa, and Snipe & Purple that he had used to catch them. One frequently found nymph had a flattened shape, broad shoulders and very stout limbs, whilst a commonly found larva was a green caddis grub. No one had attempted to imitate them. Why not? Even some fairly common food items such as the freshwater shrimps had no good practical imitations at that time. And whilst Sawyer's Pheasant Tail Nymph caught trout that could be seen in clear chalkstreams taking olive nymphs swimming to the surface to hatch, it was pretty useless when trout and grayling were feeding on real olive nymphs close to the bottom of dark northern rivers.

And so Oliver turned to his fly-vice and slowly, over many years, with much observation, trial and testing, devised imitative flies that had trout and grayling licking their lips in gustatory anticipation. During this period he became one of the world's greatest fly-dressers; in 1980 and 1981 he won the Fly-Tyer of the Year competition, and in 1982 was invited to join the judging panel!

I first met Oliver at Chatsworth Angling Fair, where Alan Bramley, Managing Director of hookmakers Partridge of Redditch, invited fly-tyers to demonstrate their skills on his stand. In all Oliver appeared at 26 Chatsworths; I enjoyed 21. So when I joined the Partridge Family, Oliver was already an old hand. I found it strange at first, tying flies with the public watching, sitting alongside Oliver. And not only Oliver, for Alan brought people from around the world to the show; Theo Bakelaar, Hans de Groot, Hans van Klinken and Roman Moser from mainland Europe, and Ed Jaworowski, Poul Jorgensen, Lefty Kreh, Darrel Martin and Dave Whitlock from the USA. The effect of this was to break down the boundaries between the different schools of fly-tying, and to make the subject truly international. Oliver was invited to demonstrate at the Dutch Flyfair in 1988, and subsequently at the Federation of Fly Fishers Conclave in West Yellowstone in 1990.

Then, one Monday morning in 1991, he arrived at work (he was a senior design draughtsman) to find a brown envelope on his desk informing him that he was redundant forthwith. Aged 53, how was he going to survive financially?

Encouraged by his wife Hazel and Alan Bramley, Oliver phoned me. After a brief natter we came up with the idea of doing 'hands-on' fly-tying weekends. We would book a hotel, which would provide accommodation and meals for us and the paying guests, and rooms where we could teach fly-tying. Then we were invited to teach fly-tying and fly-fishing at consecutive Glenmorangie Festivals on the Shetland Isles, and Shetland Anglers did us proud, for we also fished some of their superb lochs, including the fabulous Spiggie.

For many years John Norris had a show at Penrith that ran six days from Easter Tuesday to the following Sunday. There we tied flies and put the fly-tying and fly-fishing world to rights. I think that this is where I saw Oliver at his best. When demonstrating a particular technique, such as tying off a Klinkhamer, or spinning deer hair, or using foam to tie a beetle imitation, his handling of the tying thread and materials was accompanied by a perfect commentary, so that when he had finished, further questions were superfluous.

Many great fly-tyers are, it has to be admitted, not the greatest fly-fishers (just as some of the greatest fly-fishers are pretty scruffy when it comes to the flies they tie). Oliver Edwards, though, can tie flies and catch fish. The best illustration of his ability was in the Foot-and-Mouth Year of 2001 when Chatsworth Angling Fair was postponed to October. Each day the Show ended with what was known as the 'Fly versus Maggot Competition', in which Ian Heaps and Bob Nudd would fish their maggots on their long poles and (in this case) three fly-fishers would fish their flies in front of a crowd of many hundreds, crammed into riverside grandstands. My job was to commentate. That day, as we got ready to start, Oliver and I noticed a few grayling rising steadily to a grand hatch of large dark olives. Oliver waded to a point opposite my commentary position on the platform close to the coarse fishermen. The competition started. Oliver caught a fish, then another, then another. Messrs Heaps and Nudd occasionally caught a fish on their maggots, but the wild groundbait of the olive duns kept the fish looking up. Then I thought it would be a good idea to bring the great audience into play. I pointed to a rising fish and told the throng to watch the tip of Oliver's floating fly-line as his flies drifted over it. The line moved as a fish took. Oliver lifted his rod and set the hook, and the gathering cheered. This happened time after time in the hour the event lasted. At the end Messrs Heaps and Nudd joined the crowd in applauding Oliver's performance. What was especially interesting is that the other fly-fishing participants were well and truly water-licked by a Master!

For many years Oliver and I ran what were called 'River Walks' at Chatsworth Angling Fair, which involved showing fly-fishers how to sample river invertebrates and identify trout foods, and ways of imitating those foods. Many consider those events to be the beginning of the recent upsurge in interest in aquatic entomology, for subsequently we were both asked to do similar demonstrations in other parts of the world. Oliver has travelled throughout Europe and the USA with his fly-tying kit, demonstrating how to tie his flies. For twelve years (1995-2006) he also ran the Orvis Fly-Fishing Schools in Yorkshire with Peter Moore and on the Test in Hampshire with Robin Gow.

Oliver had written articles for fly-fishing magazines for some years. In some he had described his own flies and illustrated his articles with precise drawings of his tying techniques. In 1994 Merlin Unwin published this book, *Flytyer's Masterclass*, that brought together the tying of his own flies and some great patterns designed by others. It was an immediate success. The English edition was quickly followed by editions in the USA, the Czech Republic, Italy, Norway, Finland, Germany and, more recently, Russia. It is now a classic. In 2000 Oliver began to make a wide-ranging series of films on fly-tying and fly-fishing under the title *Essential Skills*. These DVDs are the best on the market and should you, who have just purchased this book, be a relative beginner, let me urge you to invest in them as well.

Oliver Edwards is officially retired but you may still encounter him wading deep in a river somewhere, if not his beloved Wharfe or Ure then Iceland is a particular favourite, and in the first weekend of November, he will be at the *British Fly Fair International*, tying his flies and nattering with me about the good old days.

Malcolm Greenhalgh
June 2009

AUTHOR'S INTRODUCTION FROM THE 1994 EDITION

From my earliest days as a flyfisher, I have had a very keen interest in the food that trout and grayling eat. It soon became obvious to me that these fish, with a few noteworthy and seasonal exceptions, fed on quite small and, in many cases, distinctly shaped insects. What also became apparent was that it was impossible to find published dressings which would copy - to my satisfaction - those naturals. Any patterns I did discover appeared either far too bulky or totally ignored the all-important 'silhouette trigger'. I knew then that quite a large gap existed in the flyfisher's arsenal, since the fish I caught - or tried to catch - were no different to the rest!

All that was about thirty years ago. However, I was, by then, on tramlines with only one direction to go. I started developing my own patterns and, during the ensuing years, there have been many, many attempts at copying specific insects - a great many have had the razor blade through them! Collecting insect specimens is a fascinating and very important sideline to flyfishing. We flyfishers should be keenly interested in the creatures upon which our quarry feeds. It is quite simply the fundamental part of our sport - higher in the list of priorities, in my opinion, than being able to cast well! Stomach samples - autopsies - are particularly important since they prove what you may have only suspected. My life-long interest in the natural world was a great help to me in this regard and I have never failed to be fascinated by what my eager three-quarter pounder ate before he made his mistake!

Within a few years, I had made sufficient autopsies to give me a good idea of what I could expect trout and grayling to be feeding on at any given time of the year. So a very important picture was developing, a seasonal chart if you like. Remember, this was almost thirty years ago, Grafham hadn't opened yet, and the stillwater scene was in its infancy.

One thing above all others, though, shouted at me when I was dabbling in stomach contents. I found that by far the most common food organisms throughout the season were the aquatic stages of the insect's life cycle - larvae and pupae. Even fish caught during a prolific hatch would still show no strong bias towards the winged adults. In fact, very often, there would be a large proportion of those insects at the very act of eclosion - the now-popular 'emergers'.

As the years rolled by, my flydressing skills improved, and so also did the materials I was working with. Modem synthetics have made a tremendous difference. Now, the task of producing, for example, a slim tapering translucent segmented abdomen, is child's play. It is these last ten years of my flytying which have seen the greatest strides towards my own personal satisfaction.

Now I have been given the task of setting out in words and illustrations twenty of my most successful patterns. Just two are guest patterns. I make no apologies for the self indulgence, it is a rare privilege. All the patterns are straight out of my own fly box and while three have been in print previously (in *Salmon, Trout and Seatrout* magazine), they have had subsequent improvements.

The rationale behind these twenty patterns is simple. I have imitated only those food items which are regularly and reliably devoured by trout and grayling over a full season (which includes the winter months for us masochistic grayling fishers). The patterns cover what I have found to be generically the most important groups of insects - mayflies, caddisflies, stoneflies and land-bred flies - the terrestrials - plus that ever popular crustacean, the freshwater shrimp. The patterns have how had many years of trial: all are well tried and proven on many waters of the UK. Some have even received the seal of approval from the wild trout of Montana USA. Each one is a tremendous fish deceiver. However, like all imitive patterns, they should be used at the correct time and properly presented.

Two of these patterns, the stone-clinging Heptagenid nymph and the free-living Rhyacophila caddis larva, have been particularly exciting for me, not simply because they are 'firsts' in the UK but also because they are devastatingly effective.

Some flydressers accuse me of tying super-realistic flies (the implication being that they are no good for fishing). Super-realism was never my real goal. My true goal has been to give every pattern the best possible 'silhouette trigger'.

Although I have illustrated these fly patterns showing barbed hooks, I do however recommend that the barbs are crushed down before tying and fishing.

Finally, none of the patterns featured in this book are difficult, they are merely construction jobs. Just follow the sequence drawings, fix the route in your mind, have the correct materials to hand and - with a little practice - you'll produce flies identical to the ones in my box. Then go out and catch lots of trout with them.

Oliver Edwards,
Carlton, Wakefield,
West Yorkshire,
England.

1. The Baetis Nymph

Mayflies belonging to the family Baetidae are widespread throughout the British Isles, USA and Western Europe. In Britain there are four genera producing a total of 14 species. These are the famous 'duns' and 'olives' of the British fly fisherman.

Of the 14 species, only two are stillwater (or slow water) insects. These are the pond olive (*Cloeon dipterum*) and the lake olive (*Cloeon simile*).

The remaining 12 species are found mainly in running water, often in swift, broken water. Caution is necessary, however, when identifying species by habitat. Slow-flowing rivers, or even large, slow pools on fast rivers, if rich in vegetation, can provide an ideal habitat for the pond olive. Similarly, exposed lakes which have wave-crashed shores, can have shorelines which are high in oxygen, conditions not dissimilar to a good stream riffle. Such shores may also provide a home for some of the stream species.

The running-water species favour a rough stream bed with random-sized rocks, stones, gravel and sand. The underside of these rocks will have countless tiny nooks and crannies, with the surrounding water highly charged with oxygen. The current two inches away from the nymph might be a tearing 4ft (1.2 metres) per second but these tiny pockets and crevices will provide shelter. In rough streams the nymphs of the Baetidae will flourish and may be very numerous indeed since they will be reasonably safe from most predators. Their main threat will be 'free-living' caddis larvae, particularly the prowling rapacious larvae of the Rhyacophilidae.

Most nymphs of the Baetidae thrive in neutral to slightly acidic waters. The freestone rivers of upland areas of the UK usually have good populations of several species. There are, however, some species which have a liking for calcareous water, the chalk and limestone streams. On such waters, aquatic weed is usually rampant, and it can house quite staggering numbers of baetis nymphs.

Although commonly labelled as 'swimmers' or 'swimmer/climbers', I think a more apt description would be 'darters' since their usual movement is only over short distances. When disturbed, say by an angler wading through a weedy stream, they flee in short darting spurts, quickly seeking cover again.

When looking at a mature specimen of one of the swimmers, say the nymph of the large dark olive (*Baetis rhodani*), you recognize immediately that it is designed perfectly for quick starts and short sprints. It is the perfect streamlined shape, a slimmed-down 'indian club'. The tails are minutely but very densely clothed with tiny hairs, the inner tail clothed along both edges, the outer tails along their inside edges only. The entire unit is a highly efficient paddle which beats up and down in the dorso-ventral plane at such a rapid rate that it becomes a blur.

All the nymphs of the Baetidae have three tails, an exception being the American genus Pseudocloeon. This has just two tails (there may be a hint of a vestigial central third tail). Most species have tails which are well equipped with hairs along their edges.

Baetis nymphs feed by scraping microscopic algae and organic detritus from the rocks and stones on the stream bed. They are always well hidden from view by day - a survival strategy.

There can be confusion between the nymphs of the Baetidae and those of the Ephemerellidae. The Ephemerellidae (see p16) of the UK amount to only two species. Of those two, it is the very common and widespread blue winged olive (*Ephemerella ignita*) which the flyfisher frequently encounters. The nymphs of this species and those of some Baetis species are quite similar at a glance, and I can understand the confusion. Nevertheless, with a bit of practice they can be distinguished. Baetis nymphs are significantly more streamlined than those of the Ephemerella (particularly when comparing American species). The Baetis nymph's abdomen can be a taper (when viewed from above) from first (nearest the thorax) to tenth segment. On some species the abdomen is parallel-sided from segments 1 to 3, or 4 then tapers evenly to the tails. There is never a widening then reducing, just a gradual, even taper from thorax to tail.

The abdomen of the Ephemerella nymph, on the other hand, increases in width from the end of the thorax to the third or fourth segment - the widest point. It then reduces in width, in a curve, to the base of the tail. This swelling gives the Ephemerella nymph an altogether more tubby appearance.

Another useful comparison between the two is the position of the tips of the wing buds on the mature nymphs, relative to the nymph's overall length. On the Baetis nymph, the wing bud tips rarely reach the half way point along the entire body. On the Ephemerella nymph, the wing bud tips extend past the half way point, on some American species well past.

With practice, these differences are soon spotted. In the UK we need only concern ourselves with the blue winged olive nymph v. the Baetidae nymphs, since our other Ephemerella, the yellow evening dun (*E. notata*), is now very rare and localised.

Baetis body colour varies from species to species. It may be a pale almost transparent, olive-green to a yellow-olive or an olive-brown. The tails and legs are never barred, being a plain colour and usually paler than their bodies.

In North America, the flyfisher has considerably more species of the Baetidae to contend with. Nevertheless, a Baetis nymph is a Baetis nymph, and the physical characteristics of the Baetidae from both sides of the Atlantic are remarkably similar.

In recent times, some American entomologists have added the genera Isonychia and Siphlonurus to the family Baetidae. However in the UK the Siphlonurus mayflies have been separated from the Baetidae and awarded a distinct family - the Siphlonuridae.

The Isonychia and Siphlonurus nymphs are similar yet larger than the Baetis nymphs. Both species have the three powerful tails, with the same hair fringing as the Baetis nymph. Both species also display the same clean lines of the Baetidae, suggesting that we are again looking at efficient swimmers, which they most certainly are.

If there is one very distinct difference between these nymphs and the Baetidae - disregarding size - it is the abdominal gilling. The Isonychia and Siphlonurus nymphs are very heavily gilled, from segments one to seven, each gill being a blunt petal shape and slightly overlapping each other, giving the appearance of an almost continuous frill down both sides of the abdomen. This is reminiscent in some ways of the gilling on the stone-clinging nymphs of the Rhithrogena.

It is now accepted that aquatic nymphs and pupae generate a kind of body gas immediately prior to emergence. This gas has the function of being the separator of the old outer skin of the nymph from the new skin of the winged adult. In other words, this gas is blown between the two skins, making the act of eclosion possible. Given that this gas is less dense than water, then the envelope of gas within the nymph will presumably assist the nymph towards the surface - gas bubbles rise in water, however microscopic.

So, with a combination of a gas-lined outer skin and the powerful sculling action of its tail unit, our ripe Baetis nymph propels itself towards the surface. Unfortunately, during heavy hatches and often when stream conditions make high

BAETIS NYMPHS

(From top clockwise) Large Dark Olive (underside) - Large Dark Olive
Iron Blue - Pond/Lake Olive - Pale Watery/Spurwing - Medium Olive

surface tension, many nymphs, already weakened by the journey to the surface, cannot muster the energy necessary to push the upper side of their mesothorax through the stream's surface, the necessary first stage of emergence. They appear to take a breather and drift away seemingly glued to the underside of the meniscus. Their legs, instead of tucked smoothly to the sides of their bodies, as when they were shooting up to the surface to emerge, are now held outstretched, clearly visible. The three tails also relax and spread more widely.

Many of these failed nymphs are nabbed at the surface. Those which escape the immediate attention of trout and grayling float away, to be jostled and churned about by the next downstream section of riffle. Despite their gas-lined jackets, these casualties can be found anywhere in the water column, an easy target for trout. Some expire totally, due to the stress of emergence, while others recover, gain a second wind, re-orientate themselves and scoot off to the surface again.

My pattern is meant to copy these prostrate exhausted emergers. It is a dead drifter, fished upstream, and given free rein at the whim of the current, no tethering, no pulling, just absolutely free drift.

There is nothing new, of course, about Baetis nymph patterns. G.E.M. Skues had a pattern which very neatly copied the salient features. Frank Sawyer's famous Pheasant Tail nymph, a masterpiece of simplicity, (rarely dressed slim enough these days) highlighted the 'indian club' profile and distinct tails. Sawyer's pattern, it must be remembered, copied the natural as it swam to the surface just prior to emergence so it didn't require legs. This is simulated effectively by his 'induced take' method. Sawyer was fishing to sighted fish in clear water. He could actually see the nymph and knew just when to lift, to induce, to kid the fish that here was another nymph going to the surface. I've fished the Avon many times and I know how effective this method is. Sawyer's nymph is lethal as an inducer. As a drifting pattern, I find it much less effective.

The pattern I am about to describe is one of

SOME NATURALS APPROPRIATE TO THIS PATTERN

BRITISH GENERA:
Baetis, Centroptilum, Cloeon, Procloeon

BRITISH SPECIES:
Large Dark Olive or Spring Olive *Baetis rhodani*
Small Dark Olive or July Dun *Baetis scambus*
Medium Olive or Blue Dun *Baetis vernus*
Medium Olive or Blue Dun *Baetis buceratus*
Pale Watery *Baetis fuscatus*
B. digitatus - no known popular name
Dark Olive *Baetis atrebatinus*
Iron Blue
or Dark Watchet (N. England) *Baetis niger*
Iron Blue
or Dark Watchet (N. England) *Baetis muticus*
Small Spurwing
or Pale Watery *Centroptilum luteolum*
Large Spurwing
or Pale Watery *Centroptilum pennulatum*
Pond Olive *Cloeon dipterum*
Lake Olive *Cloeon simile*
Pale Evening Dun
or Pale Watery *Procloeon bifidum*

NORTH AMERICAN GENERA:
Baetis, Callibaetis, Cloeon, Pseudocloeon, Siphlonurus, Isonychia

NORTH AMERICAN SPECIES:
Little Western Iron Blue Quill *Baetis parvus*
Little Iron Blue Quill or BWO *Baetis vagans*
Little Slate Winged Brown Quill or BWO *Baetis hiemalis*
Blue Winged Olive
or Little Western Iron Blue Quill *Baetis tricaudatus*
Little Speckle Wing Quill
or Speckled Dun *Callibaetis coloradensis*
Dark Speckle Wing Quill
or Speckled Dun *Callibaetis nigritus*
Tiny Grey Winged Sepia Quill *Cloeon simplex*
Tiny Grey Winged Olive Quill
or Tiny Blue Winged Olive *Cloeon implicatum*
Tiny Grey Winged Olive
or Tiny Blue Winged Olive *Pseudocloeon anoka*
Great Drake or Gt Summer Drake *Siphlonurus ocidentalis*
Grey Drake/Eastern Brown Quill *Siphlonurus quebecensis*
Dark Mahogany Dun or Great Leadwing Drake
Isonychia bicolor

my all-time high scorers. It is a tremendous fish fooler and has taken countless numbers of trout and grayling throughout every season since its inception, some 15 years ago. It has also worked effectively on the beautiful rivers I fished in Montana in 1991.

It is particularly deadly in Britain when the large dark olive (*Baetis rhodani*) hatches in spring. Later on, I fish a smaller size to represent the medium olive (*Baetis vernus*) and I lighten the body colour to copy the nymphs of the pale wateries. I revert to the larger type when fishing the late autumn/early winter hatch of the second brood of the large dark olive.

NOTES ON MATERIALS AND TYING

I am a strong advocate of incorporating prominent or characteristic features of the natural nymph into my artificials, even to the extent of slightly exaggerating them. We have already discussed the hair-fringed tails on the natural. Cock pheasant tail barbs are therefore a good choice. They make lovely tails. I have just one complaint: I find that they're too weak, and won't stand up to the maulings of trout.

So my recommendation is to use any stout, straight animal hair which tapers to a fine point. I always tie in three, as on the natural, and I fix the two outer tails so that they are nicely splayed outwards and remain permanently fixed thus. Such splayed tails are instantly recognised by fish; there's no doubt in my mind that they are an important trigger. My favourite for Baetis nymph tails are pale olive dyed bristles from a good quality shaving brush. They make excellent tails, well defined, and strong. The white tips can be dyed any colour.

Outstretched legs are another prime trigger on my nymphs and for these legs I love the mottled effect on the back and breast feathers of the English partridge. I dye the grey ones all shades of olive, in fact, I dye entire skins. Partridge breast and back hackle barbs have that all-important width, with an abrupt taper to a fine point. I know that the legs of Baetis nymphs have no barring but the fish don't seem to mind the mottled effect of

BAETIS NYMPH DRESSINGS

1. LARGE DARK OLIVE NYMPH
Hook: Medium wire 2x to 3x long or curved shank. Suggest Partridge 'Capt. Hamilton Nymph' Code H1A size 16 or Partridge 'Oliver Edwards Nymph/Emerger' Code K14ST size 16.
Weight: Strip of wine bottle lead foil.
Thread: Danville's 'Spider Web'.
Cement: Dave's Flexament (USA) or Floo Gloo (UK)
Tails: Tapering, white animal bristle, from good quality shaving brush. Dyed yellow-olive.
Abdomen: Polythene 0.008" (0.2mm) or Flexibody, dyed olive-brown. Dorsal tint: light brown felt pen. Ventral tint: fluorescent yellow highlighter pen.
Thorax: Fine synthetic dubbing, brown-olive or green-olive, eg. Davy Wotton Finesse Masterclass MC1 or 2.
Legs: Light partridge hackle or light grey hen saddle hackle dyed pale yellow.
Wing buds: Black quill feather section, natural or dyed.

2. MEDIUM OLIVE NYMPH
As for No.1 above, except for:
Hook: Size 18, both codes.
Abdomen: Yellow-olive Flexibody, tints as No.1.
Thorax: Yellow-olive dubbing, eg. Wotton MC3.

3. IRON BLUE NYMPH
As for No.1 above, except for:
Hook: Standard dry fly, size 20. eg. Partridge code L3A
Tails: Dyed grey.
Abdomen: Medium grey Flexibody. Tint: dark brown (dorsal), ventral as No.1
Thorax: Very dark grey green, eg. Wotton MC4.
Legs: black hackle from elbow of starling wing

4. PALE WATERY AND SPURWING NYMPHS
As for No.1 above, except for:
Hook: Standard dry fly, size 18 or 20, eg. Partridge L3A.
Abdomen: clear Flexibody. Tint: light brown.
Abdomen tint: Light fawn waterproof felt pen all over.
Thorax: Pale sandy olive, eg. Wotton MC5.
Legs: Light grey hen saddle hackle dyed olive.

5. POND AND LAKE OLIVE NYMPHS
As for No.1 above, except for:
Hook: Size 18.
Tails: Three barbs from the smallest Lady Amherst pheasant tippet feather, dyed medium olive.
Abdomen: Dyed green-olive Flexibody, tint as for No.1.
Thorax: Green olive dubbing, eg. Wotton MC2.
Legs: Dyed green-olive.

partridge hackle barbs and, suitably dyed, they make beautiful and effective legs.

For years, I fashioned the abdomens of small nymphs from dyed polythene of 0.004" (0.1mm) to 0.008" (0.2mm) thickness. The problem with narrow strips of polythene, though, is the sudden way it stretches - it just gives, almost without warning, and doesn't recover afterwards.

Then, in 1988, I was introduced to the perfect alternative. Hans P.C. de Groot, the Dutch salmon fly maestro, showed me a packet of multi-coloured Flexibody, a material he had developed. Flexibody is a plastic; it is softer than polythene, dyed colourfast, beautifully translucent, stretches without any hint of sudden collapse, and recovers about 65% of the stretched distance. Each coloured piece is backed by a sheet of white card to make cutting easy. So, you simply cut a strip, peel off the backing, offer it up and tie it in. Lovely stuff! It has another advantage over polythene, it has a soft almost waxy feel, so that when you wind on the strip to form a segmented abdomen, each turn grips the previous one, instead of always tending to slip off as polythene does. Hans also showed me how to further enhance the segmented appearance. Before cutting, he wipes all along the edge of the strip with a dark permanent felt marker pen.

I have developed a method of making two wing buds with a separate mid-thorax (the mesothorax). I've never liked the single large pad of black feather fibre as popularly featured on many patterns. My method takes a little longer but produces a tremendous effect. Remember, a nymph tumbling at the mercy of the current may be viewed from any angle.

Also, a large dark olive nymph, even in fairly fast water, will appear to a 10" trout much as a currant bun does to us, and we can spot the currants in the bun, in the baker's window, from across the street, yes, even when passing in a car!

Finishing the pattern by folding back the Flexibody at the front is just a neat solution. The fact that it also makes a rather distinct head is a bonus, as are the tag ends of the wing buds for eyes. A head so-produced leaves a very clean 'front end' with no ragged cut ends to interfere with the hook eye.

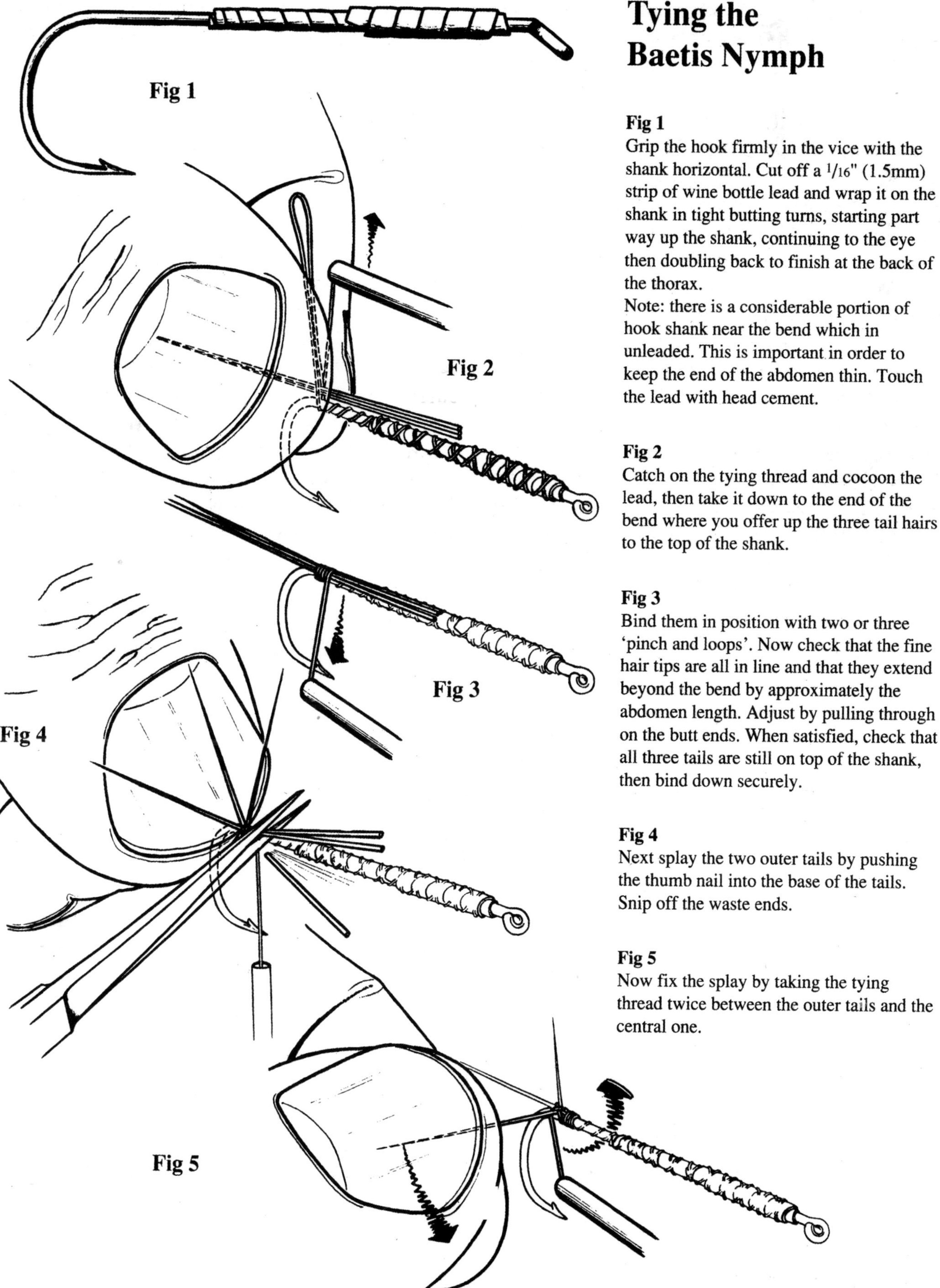

Tying the Baetis Nymph

Fig 1
Grip the hook firmly in the vice with the shank horizontal. Cut off a 1/16" (1.5mm) strip of wine bottle lead and wrap it on the shank in tight butting turns, starting part way up the shank, continuing to the eye then doubling back to finish at the back of the thorax.
Note: there is a considerable portion of hook shank near the bend which in unleaded. This is important in order to keep the end of the abdomen thin. Touch the lead with head cement.

Fig 2
Catch on the tying thread and cocoon the lead, then take it down to the end of the bend where you offer up the three tail hairs to the top of the shank.

Fig 3
Bind them in position with two or three 'pinch and loops'. Now check that the fine hair tips are all in line and that they extend beyond the bend by approximately the abdomen length. Adjust by pulling through on the butt ends. When satisfied, check that all three tails are still on top of the shank, then bind down securely.

Fig 4
Next splay the two outer tails by pushing the thumb nail into the base of the tails. Snip off the waste ends.

Fig 5
Now fix the splay by taking the tying thread twice between the outer tails and the central one.

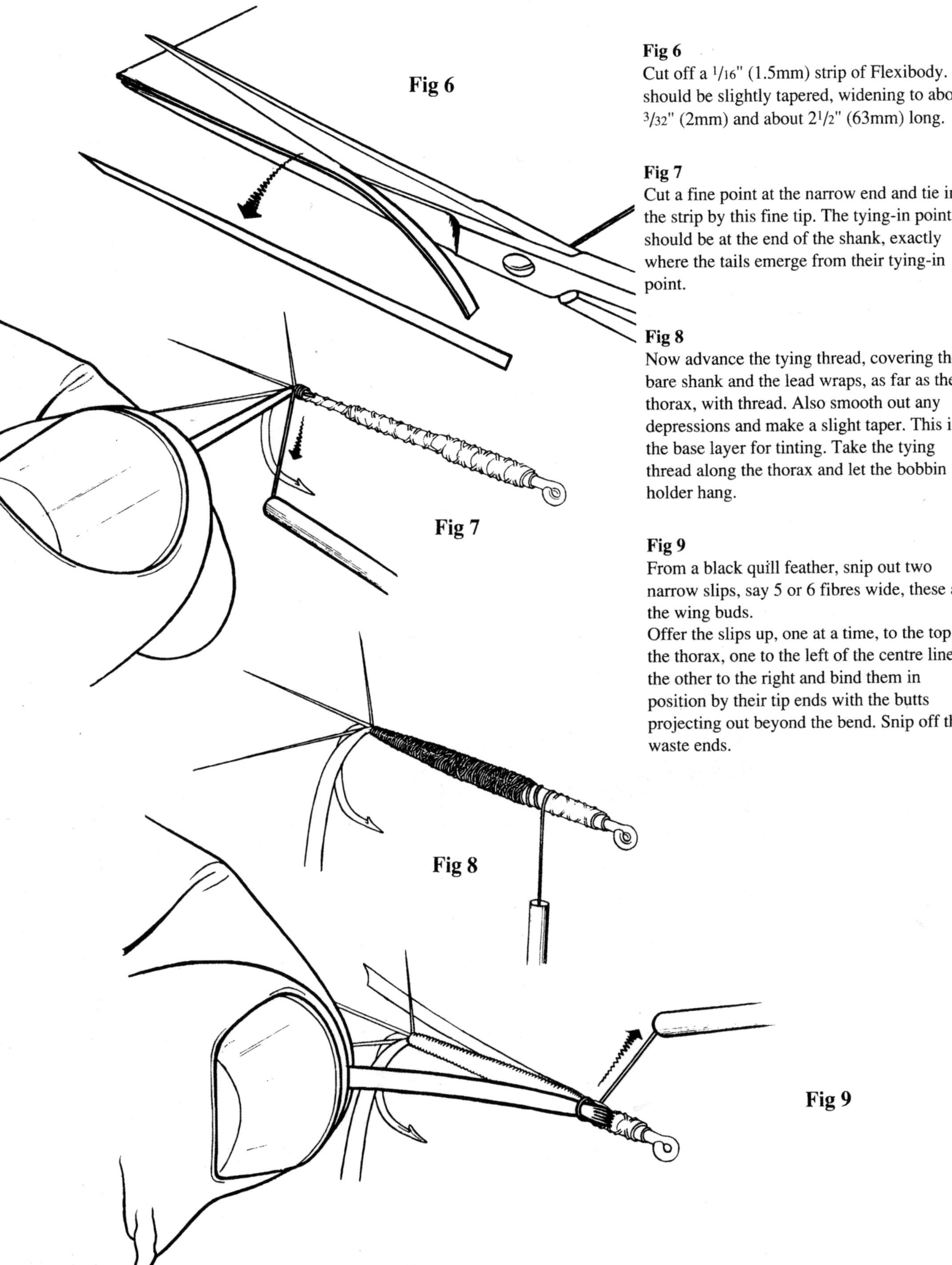

Fig 6
Cut off a 1/16" (1.5mm) strip of Flexibody. It should be slightly tapered, widening to about 3/32" (2mm) and about 2 1/2" (63mm) long.

Fig 7
Cut a fine point at the narrow end and tie in the strip by this fine tip. The tying-in point should be at the end of the shank, exactly where the tails emerge from their tying-in point.

Fig 8
Now advance the tying thread, covering the bare shank and the lead wraps, as far as the thorax, with thread. Also smooth out any depressions and make a slight taper. This is the base layer for tinting. Take the tying thread along the thorax and let the bobbin holder hang.

Fig 9
From a black quill feather, snip out two narrow slips, say 5 or 6 fibres wide, these are the wing buds.
Offer the slips up, one at a time, to the top of the thorax, one to the left of the centre line, the other to the right and bind them in position by their tip ends with the butts projecting out beyond the bend. Snip off the waste ends.

Fig 10
Now run the tying thread to the centre of the thorax, fold over both feather slips and hang the thread over them. This simply keeps them both out of the way while you complete the abdomen.

Fig 11
At this stage, you can use your artistic licence and tint the tying thread which completely covers the abdomen (hence the use of the white thread). A yellow felt pen gives a nice abdomen colour when used in conjunction with olive-brown Flexibody. If you really want to be artistic, you can wipe along the top edge of the abdomen with a darker pen to produce the natural shading effect which all nymphs have.

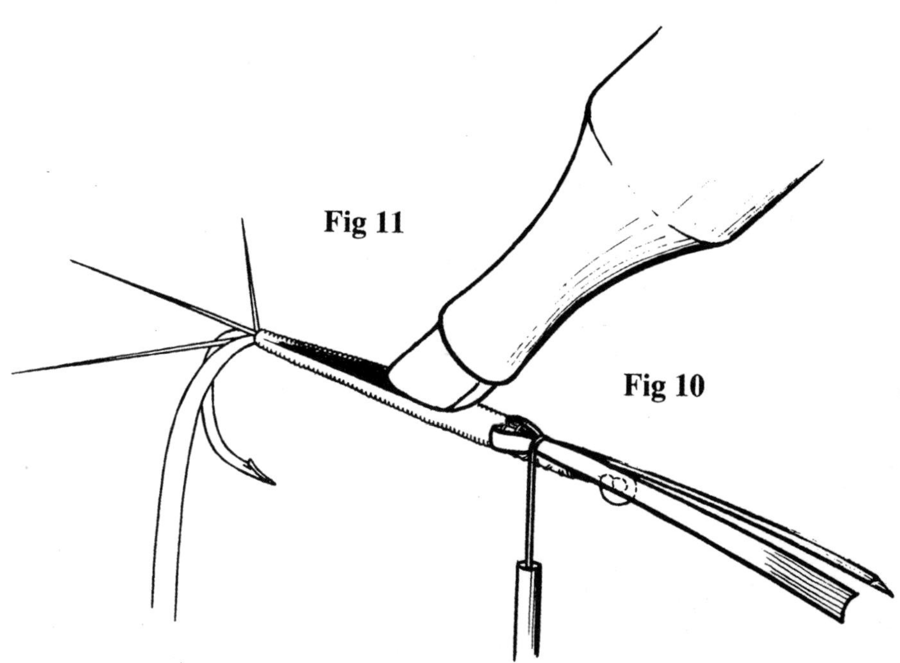

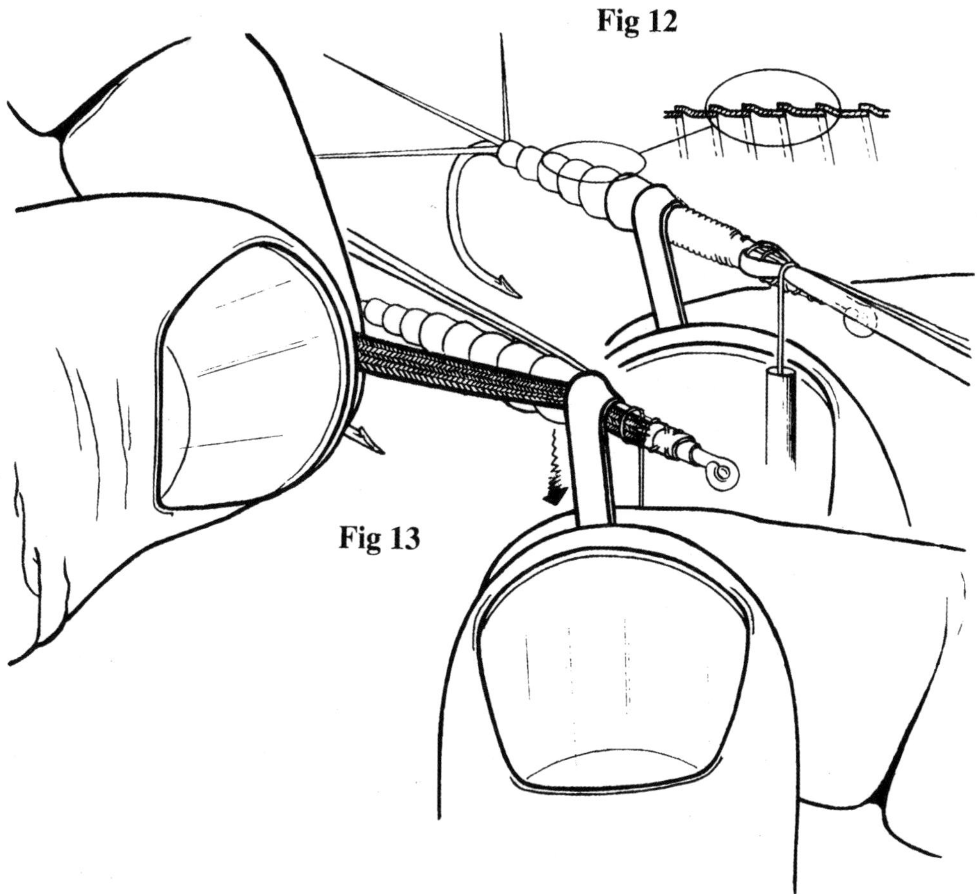

Fig 12
Now form the translucent abdomen. Take hold of the Flexibody strip and wrap it all the way up the abdomen. Stretch it a little to start with, then keep that same tension as you wrap on. As you progress along the shank, ensure that each new turn slightly overlaps the previous one.

Fig 13
Continue wrapping on the Flexibody strip, then, as you approach the two black quill slips, lift off the turn of thread which is holding them forward and allow them to flip back over. Now make a turn of the Flexibody strip over the two backward-facing black quill slips, tightly trapping them down. As you trap the pair down, make sure that each one is separated from the other.

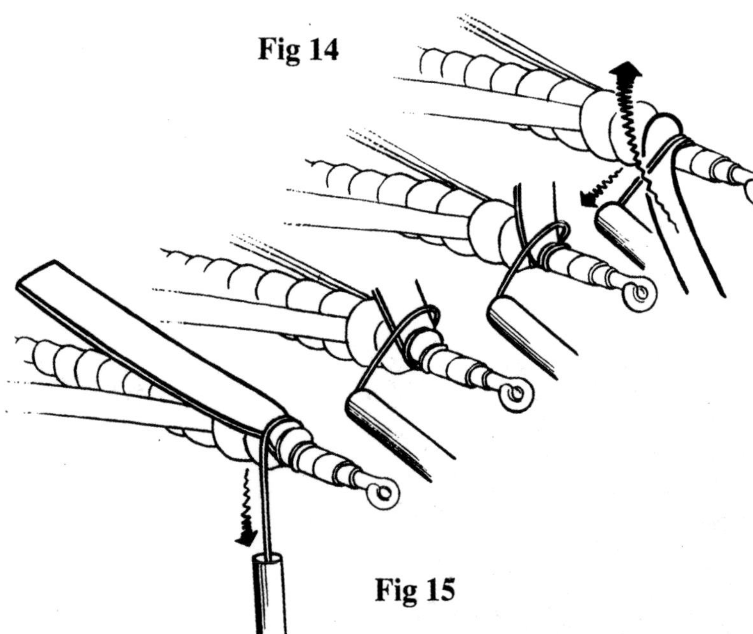

Fig 14

Fig 15

Fig 14
Make another full turn of the Flexibody strip, then tie it off very securely on top of the thorax.

Fig 15
Now, instead of trimming off the Flexibody, fold it over and manoeuvre the tag end so that it lies in line with the abdomen, projecting out towards the tails. When in this position, take several wraps of thread over the folded portion, thus holding it down. Let the bobbin holder hang.

Fig 16
Take one of the partridge breast or back feathers, strip off the lower fluff, then go to the very tip and coax back the hackle barbs on both sides of the central quill, almost to the tip.

Fig 16

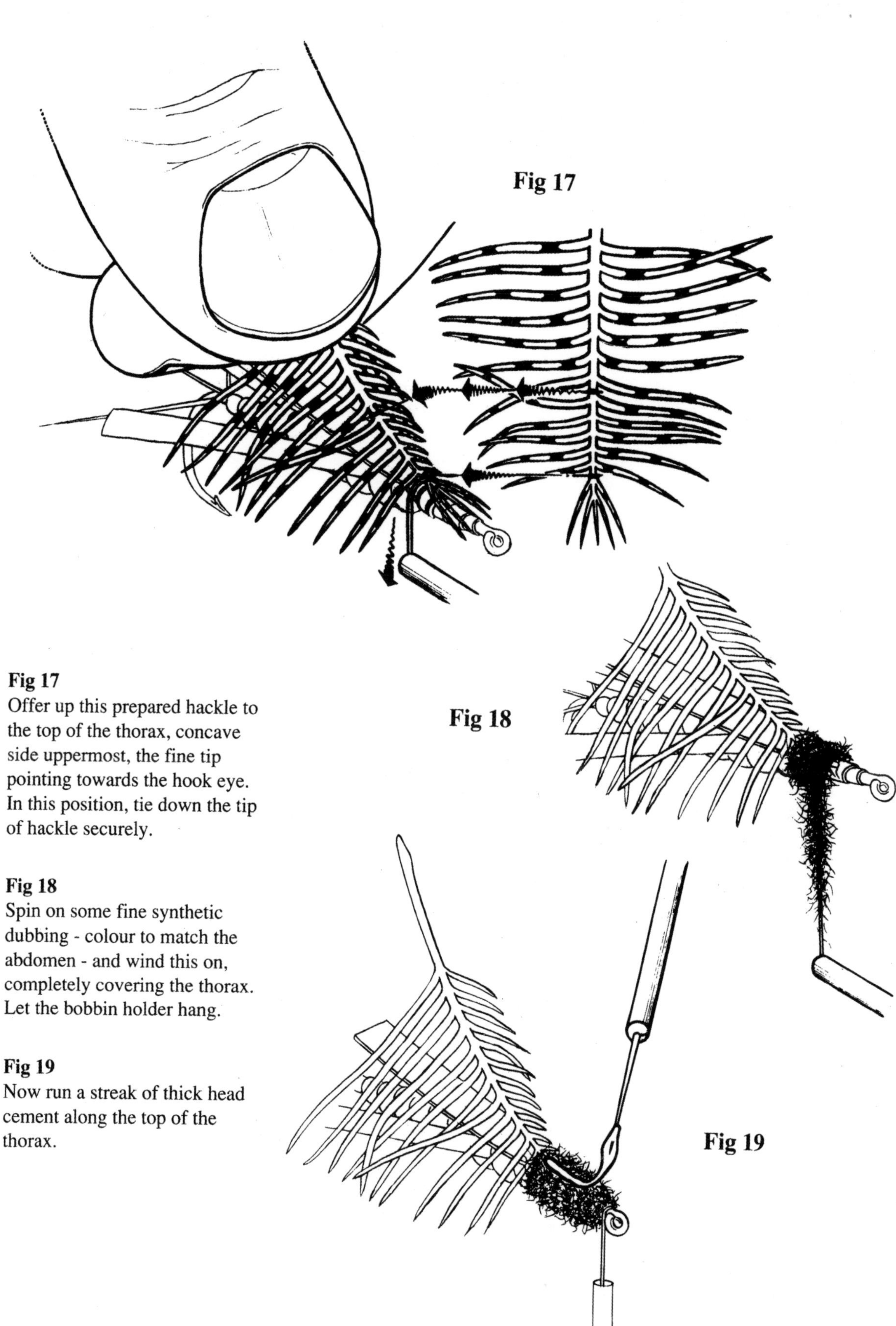

Fig 17
Offer up this prepared hackle to the top of the thorax, concave side uppermost, the fine tip pointing towards the hook eye. In this position, tie down the tip of hackle securely.

Fig 18
Spin on some fine synthetic dubbing - colour to match the abdomen - and wind this on, completely covering the thorax. Let the bobbin holder hang.

Fig 19
Now run a streak of thick head cement along the top of the thorax.

Fig 20
Carefully pull over the hackle, press it lightly into this thick cement and bind it down. Let the bobbin hang. Snip off the waste hackle.

Fig 21
The next to be formed are the distinctive wing buds. Take hold of the far slip of black quill and pull it forward over the thorax, over the projecting legs, crossing it to the near side just behind the hook eye, at which point you bind it down securely. Follow this by repeating the process with the nearside quill slip.

Fig 22
Apply another thin streak of the head cement to the pulled over hackle quill.

Fig 23
The last item to be manoeuvred is the tag of Flexibody. Pull it over and bind it down securely just behind the eye, gently easing the two projecting black quill slips out at right angles.

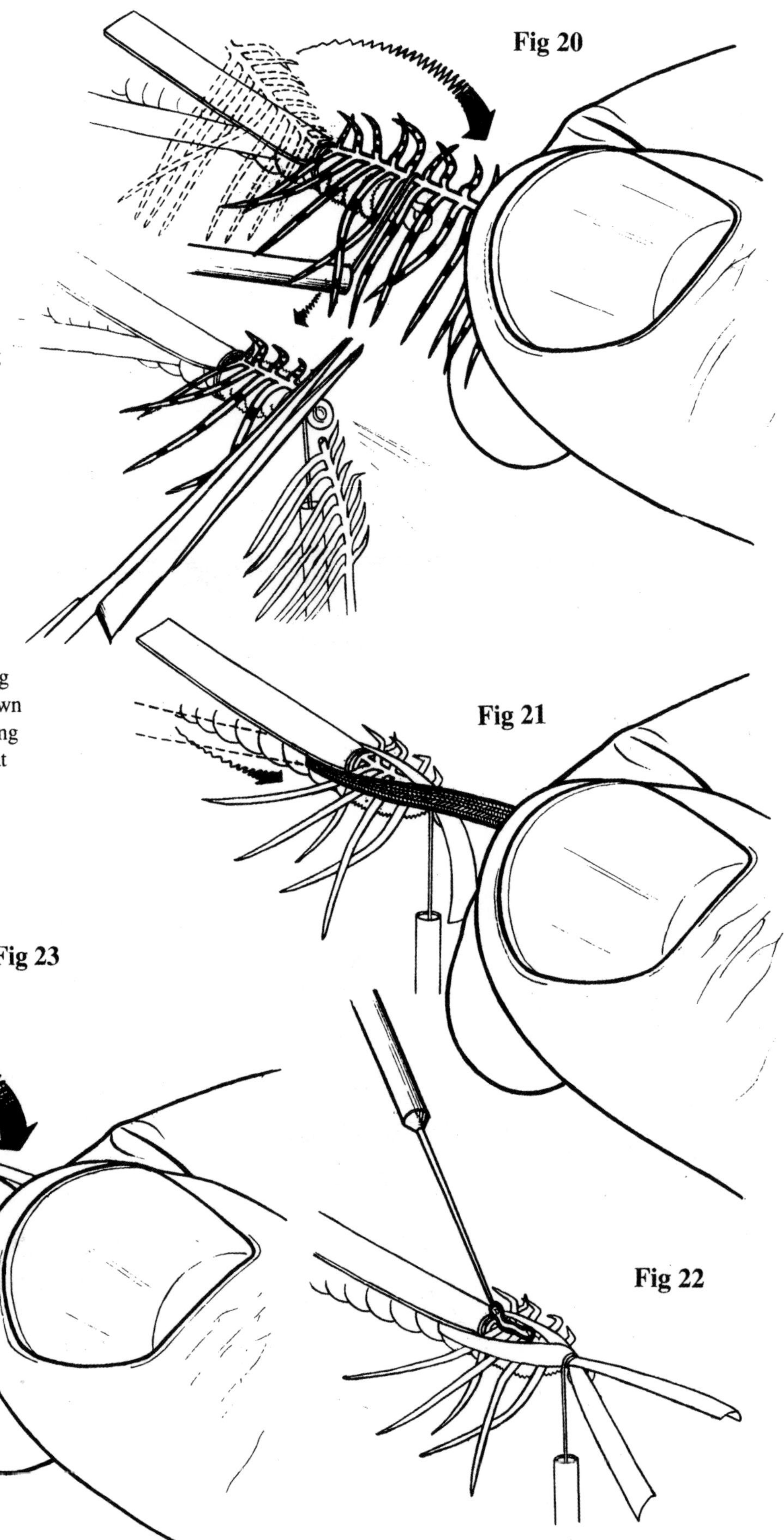

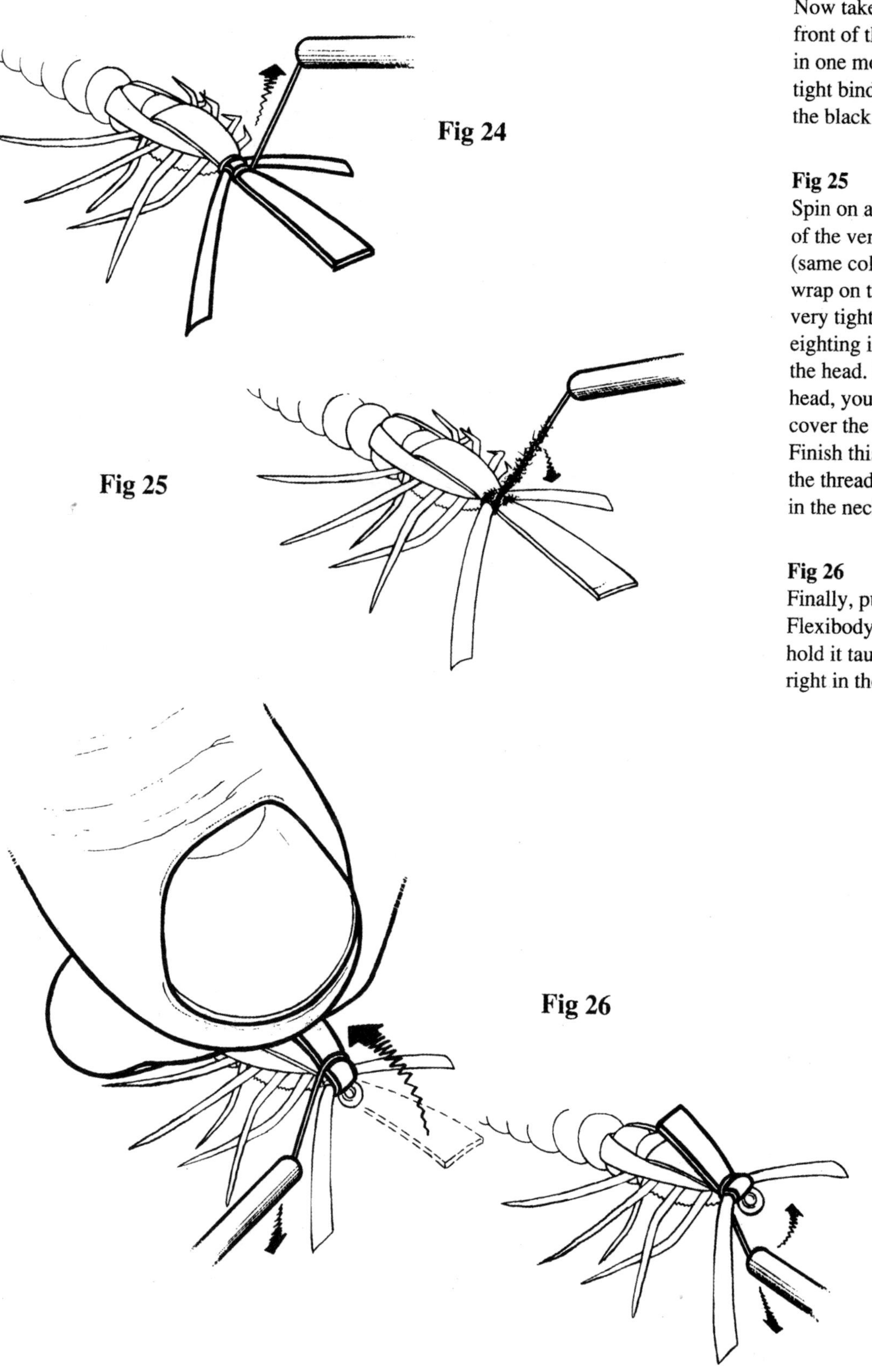

Fig 24
Now take the tying thread in front of these two black slips in one move and make a very tight binding, thus trapping the black quill slips.

Fig 25
Spin on a very small amount of the very finest dubbing (same colour as before) and wrap on this dubbing spindle very tightly, figure-of-eighting it around and across the head. Don't make a large head, you only need really to cover the thread wraps. Finish this manoeuvre with the thread behind the head - in the neck.

Fig 26
Finally, pull back the tag of Flexibody, stretch it slightly, hold it taut and bind it down, right in the neck.

Fig 27
Whip finish in the neck and snip off the tying thread, the Flexibody excess and the two black quill slips, leaving each 'eye' projecting about 1/64" (0.5mm).

Fig 28
Touch the entire top side of the head, and the thread wraps in the neck with head cement - and that's it.

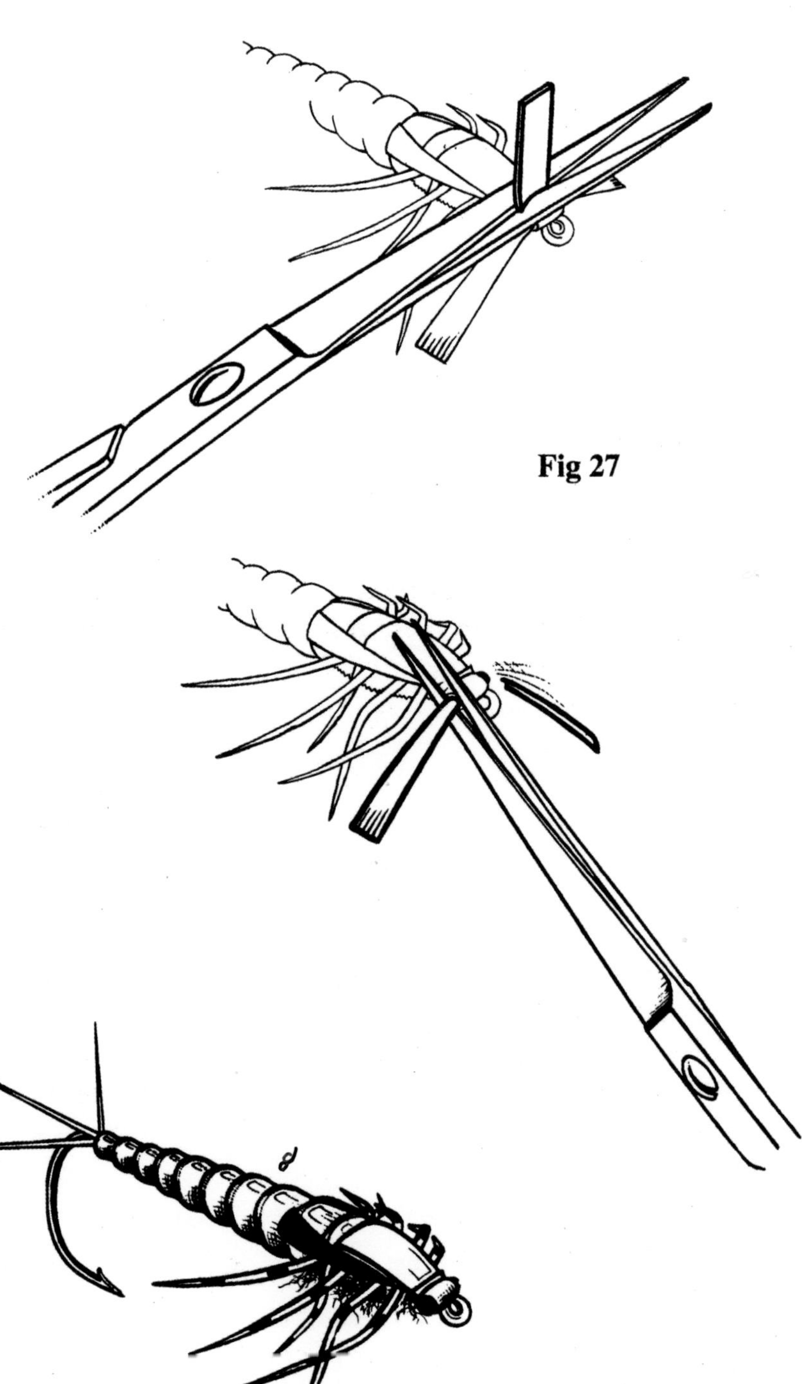

Fig 27

Fig 28

2. The Ephemerella Nymph

This family of mayflies is of supreme importance to the American flyfisher, since the number of species within the family is far greater in North America than in the UK.

In North America, this one genus produces a staggering number of individual species, at least 17 of which are of great interest to the flyfisher. Several species are known to hatch in such prolific quantities (often over many hours and for several weeks) as to qualify for the status of 'super hatches'. These include such legendary flies as the Hendricksons, sulphur duns, pale morning duns, western green drakes, etc. Names guaranteed to raise the pulse of every serious American flyfisher!

In complete contrast, the rivers and streams of Britain can boast only two species and, of these, only one, the blue winged olive (*Ephemerella ignita*), is worthy of consideration since hatches are often very heavy, and the nymph, dun and spinner are taken with great relish whenever they appear. It is, however, a most frustrating fly because its typical emergence period is often very late in the evening (the warmer the weather, the later they seem to emerge).

In the drought-stricken summer of 1989, for example, my local rivers were at a dangerous level by July. Water temperature was a major problem, peaking one week at 78°F! Yet that summer, I witnessed some of the heaviest hatches of the blue winged olive I have ever seen. Unfortunately for me, it was always almost dark when the first duns appeared. On one occasion, as the hatch was increasing, I fished on into the dark as rising fish appeared everywhere from what had been a very dour river an hour earlier. All this activity started at 10.45pm and was still going strong when frustration drove me from the bank at midnight. Many duns hitched a ride home with me that evening as the walls of my kitchen testified the next morning.

The other species, the yellow evening dun (*Ephemerella notata*), although a most attractive fly, is not of much angling value, since it is very locally distributed and I have yet to read of anyone actually fishing a hatch.

The nymphs of the two British species are classified as 'sprawlers' by the entomologists. However, the alternative label 'moss creeper' seems more apt since these nymphs appear to have a definite liking for moss-felted rocks and stones. But you may come across them in just about any running water habitat - weedbeds, under stones, rocks and dead logs, etc. They are also reputed to have a liking for decaying vegetation, particularly below fast runs. In fact, the nymphs of these two British species are more likely to be encountered away from the really swift water of riffles and stickles, preferring the steadier glides and pool tails.

The nymphs of the many North American species have a more catholic taste when it comes to habitat. The stream species, for instance, can be found in virtually all current speeds. Nevertheless, it is probably fair to say that more species are found in moderately-paced water than in any other type. Their micro-habitat too is wide ranging - rocks, stones, gravel, weedbeds, in fact just about anywhere in the stream where the substrate offers food, protection and shelter.

The American nymphs, as you would expect,

have a much wider size range than the two UK species. At the upper end of the scale there is the western green drake (*Ephemerella grandis*) a large nymph with thick femurs, requiring a size 10 hook on which to dress the pattern, while a size 18 hook would be more appropriate for the nymph of the pale morning dun (*Ephemerella inermis*).

The main features of the Ephemerella nymph are: stocky thorax, wide abdomen, stout legs and very prominent eliptical head. If the nymph possesses all the above and also has ripe wing buds whose tips reach more than halfway along the body (tails excluded of course), then it is more than likely to be an Ephemerella nymph.

The nymph of the common UK species, the blue winged olive (*Ephemerella ignita*), is one of the easiest of all to identify. Its legs and tails are always a heavily-barred dark brown (almost black) giving the legs a most obvious striped effect. Even on the very dark specimens, the barring is evident. This same barring of the legs and tails also seems to be a common feature of the North American nymphs, although on many species the leg bars are more widely spaced.

NOTES ON MATERIALS AND TYING

With this nymph I'm going to show you a different method of making an abdomen, one that produces a nice segmented effect. You could, of course, tie this nymph with an abdomen of Flexibody, just as we did for the Baetis nymph. However, this is a good opportunity to illustrate another method of making a segmented abdomen using a different material. Furthermore for this nymph, the Antron Sparkle Yarn does seem to be a little more attractive than the Flexibody abdomen.

Ephemerella nymphs are usually well hidden in their mossy jungle, safe from the eyes of trout. As such, they are only available in quantity during a hatch (remember it is quantity which produces real fish activity) when they leave the security of their hideaways and make the perilous journey to the surface. Some of the nymphs within this genus shed their shucks before actually reaching the surface. The European blue winged olive can apparently do so. It is conceiveble that during a heavy hatch (and often they are very heavy) fish will not always be seeing organised symmetrical shapes. The general outline of the nymph will of course still be present, but now other features will be starting to appear. The sub-imago struggles free of its nymphal shuck as the surface is approached and I can well imagine that in such situations an artificial nymph with a slightly roughened surface, with many 'fly away' filaments may convey a split-second illusion of movement, limbs pulling clear of the shuck, etc. The Antron Sparkle Yarn with its reflective tri-lobal filaments gives the illusion of a gas-filled nymph just prior to emergence.

To copy the barred legs and tails of these nymphs, the tyer is spoiled for choice. However, these choices are all feather fibre: partridge, grouse, mallard, wood duck, etc. But, feather fibre, as we all know, is not all that tough. I've searched for a finely-barred, tough animal hair but so far I've drawn a blank. It's not difficult to find animal hair which is barred, you understand. However, you invariably find that the barrings are far too widely spaced. I'm looking for hair which is stout, tapers to a fine point, is sandy brown in colour and has at least five very dark bars over the last 5 or 6mm. Mission impossible!

So, I have settled for good old partridge and

SOME NATURALS APPROPRIATE TO THIS PATTERN

BRITISH GENUS: Ephemerella
BRITISH SPECIES: *Ephemerella ignita, E. notata.*
BRITISH FISHING NAMES: Blue Winged Olive, Yellow Evening Dun.

NORTH AMERICAN GENUS: Ephemerella.
NORTH AMERICAN SPECIES: *Ephemerella subvaria, E. lata, E attenuata, E flavilinea, E dorothea, E infrequens, E grandis.*
NORTH AMERICAN FISHING NAMES: Hendricksons, Slate Winged Olives, Sulphur Duns Pale Morning Duns (several species in each case), Western Green Drake.

THE EPHEMERELLA NYMPH DRESSING

Hook: Medium or fine wire 2x long or curved shank. Suggest Partridge 'Capt. Hamilton' Standard Dry Fly, Code L3A, size 20; or Partridge 'Oliver Edwards Nymph/Emerger' Code K14ST, size 18 or 20; or Partridge 'Hooper' l/s Dry Fly, Code.E1A, size 18.
Weight: Very fine copper wire.
Thread: Danville's 'Spider Web'.
Cement: Dave's Flexament (USA) or Floo Gloo (UK).
Tails: 4 dark, speckled barbs from a partridge's tail quill (common or grey partridge, not red-legged).
Abdomen: 4-ply knitting yarn, 100% synthetic fibre, or synthetic and natural fibre blend, preferably with the addition of Antron or other reflective sparkle fibres. Colours: medium brown or dark brown both with a reddish tinge.
Thorax: As abdomen.
Legs: Dark, speckled barbs from a partridge's tail quill.
Wing buds: Black quill feather section, natural or dyed.
Head (optional): 2 ruddy barbs from a common cock pheasant (ringneck, USA).

the best barbs to use, for both legs and tail, are from a dark, speckled tail quill. These barbs are much more robust than barbs taken from the back hackle. They are reasonably tough (but nowhere near as tough as animal hair). So when I tie in the tails, I play safe and tie in four! Another point to bear in mind is that, when you attempt to splay them - as detailed in the diagrams - you rarely get the same neat spread of fibres that you do with stiff animal hair. It's a compromise. However, if the end result looks a little scruffy, don't be put off, press on.

The method of producing the segmented abdomen, familiar to American flydressers, is known as 'cording' or 'roping'. It is similar to the 'noodle' method of producing soft segmentations. However, the noodle method popularised by Andre Puyans, is a true dubbing 'rope' whereas the method discussed here uses a factory-spun yarn and will be seen by some flydressers as anathema. However, tapered correctly it makes a very attractive abdomen.

EUROPEAN BLUE-WINGED OLIVE NYMPHS

Usually very dark brown or dark brownish olive but rusty specimens are encountered.

Tying the Ephemerella Nymph

Fig 1

Grip the hook firmly in the vice and wrap on the fine copper wire to form the correct foundation shape. Note the taper of the abdominal portion and the slight 'necking in' before the thorax. Flood the copper wrappings with head cement.

While cement is still wet, wrap tying silk over the foundation shape, criss-crossing it backwards and forwards so as to cocoon it. Let the bobbin holder hang at the bend.

When making this body shape on hooks size 16 and smaller it is impractical to construct both abdomen and thorax from copper wire. I find that the tapered abdomen shape is best formed with tying thread, and only the thorax formed with copper wire.

Fig 2

Now we come to the tails, and this time we have rather a tricky feather fibre to contend with. This material will not readily respond to the jamming method to splay the tails (as used on animal hair), so we use a totally different method to spread the tail fibres. The principle is simple - forcing apart the fibres against a fixed abutment or shoulder. With the tying thread now hanging at the end of the shank, spin on a tiny amount of fine dubbing to make a small 'button'. Spin it on very tight. This is important! Finish with the tying thread hanging on the hook eye side of the 'button'.

Fig 3

Now for the tails. Tweak out two speckled barbs from a partridge tail quill, offer these up together, on the far side of the shank, and catch them down.

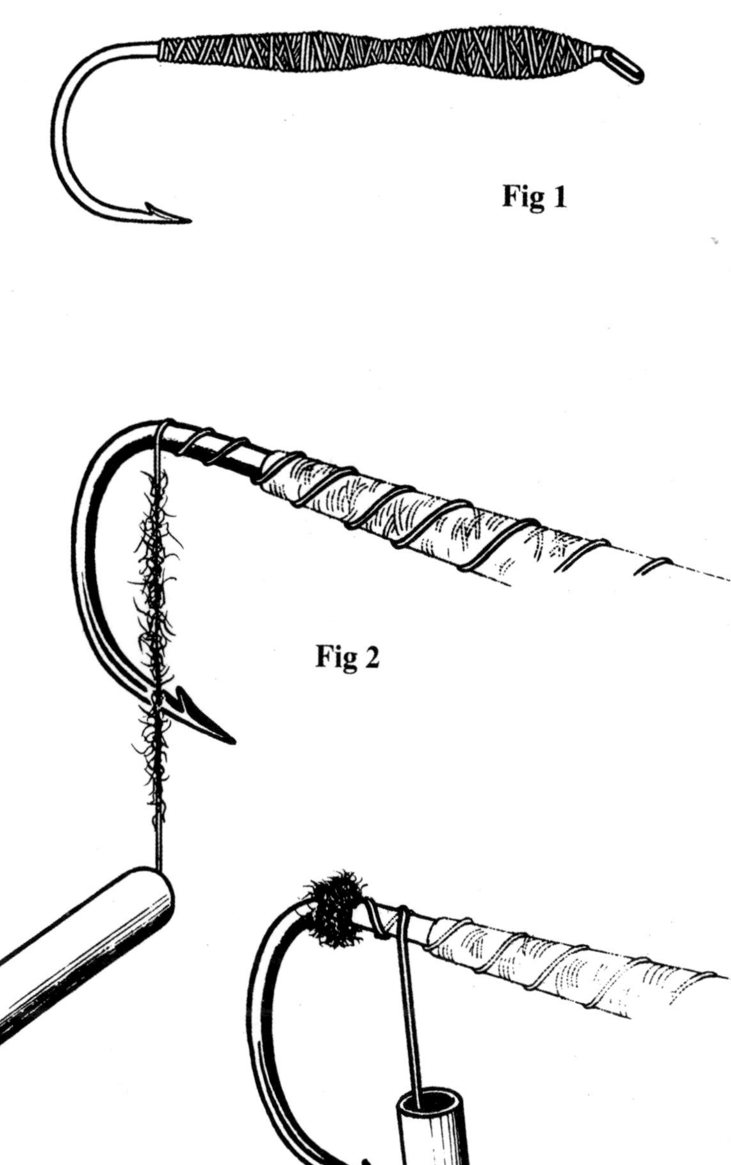

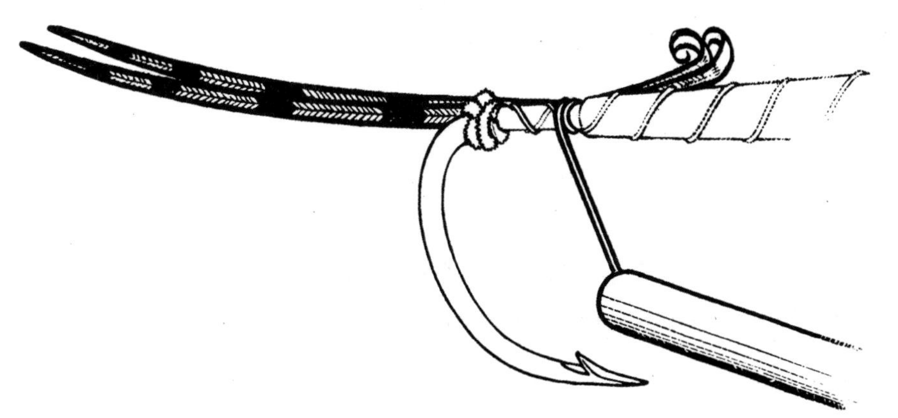

Fig 3

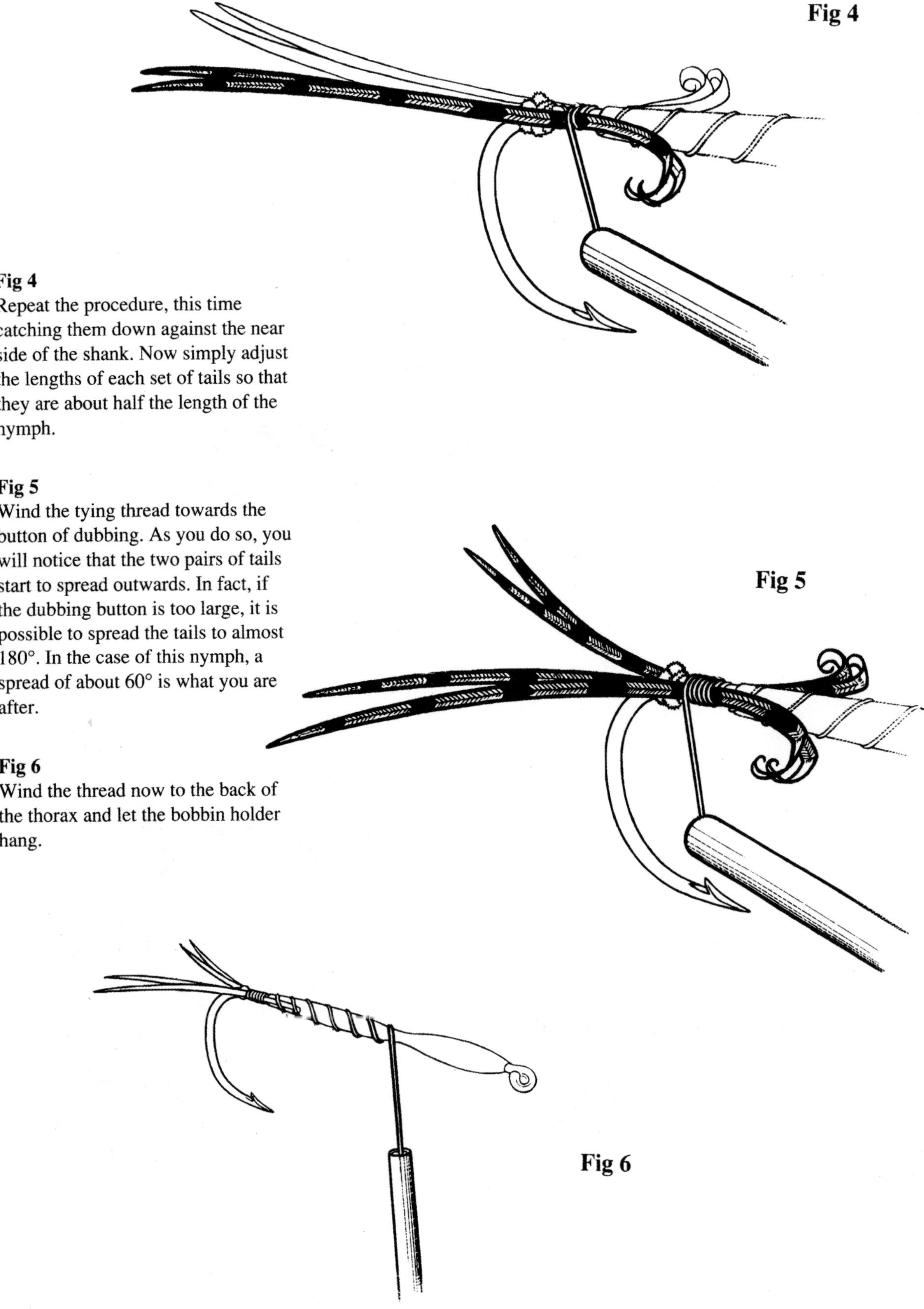

Fig 4
Repeat the procedure, this time catching them down against the near side of the shank. Now simply adjust the lengths of each set of tails so that they are about half the length of the nymph.

Fig 5
Wind the tying thread towards the button of dubbing. As you do so, you will notice that the two pairs of tails start to spread outwards. In fact, if the dubbing button is too large, it is possible to spread the tails to almost 180°. In the case of this nymph, a spread of about 60° is what you are after.

Fig 6
Wind the thread now to the back of the thorax and let the bobbin holder hang.

Fig 7
Now snip off a 3" (75mm) piece of Antron yarn of the desired colour to match the Ephemerella nymph you wish to copy. (Remember, though, to choose the colour when wet). From the piece of yarn, strand out two of the plys - my yarn is 4-ply. Now, holding the two plys together, 'shave down' one end by stripping out fibres using index finger and thumb nail. Don't be afraid of it, attack it vigorously! The idea is to taper down the last 1/4" (6mm) of the yarn.

Fig 7

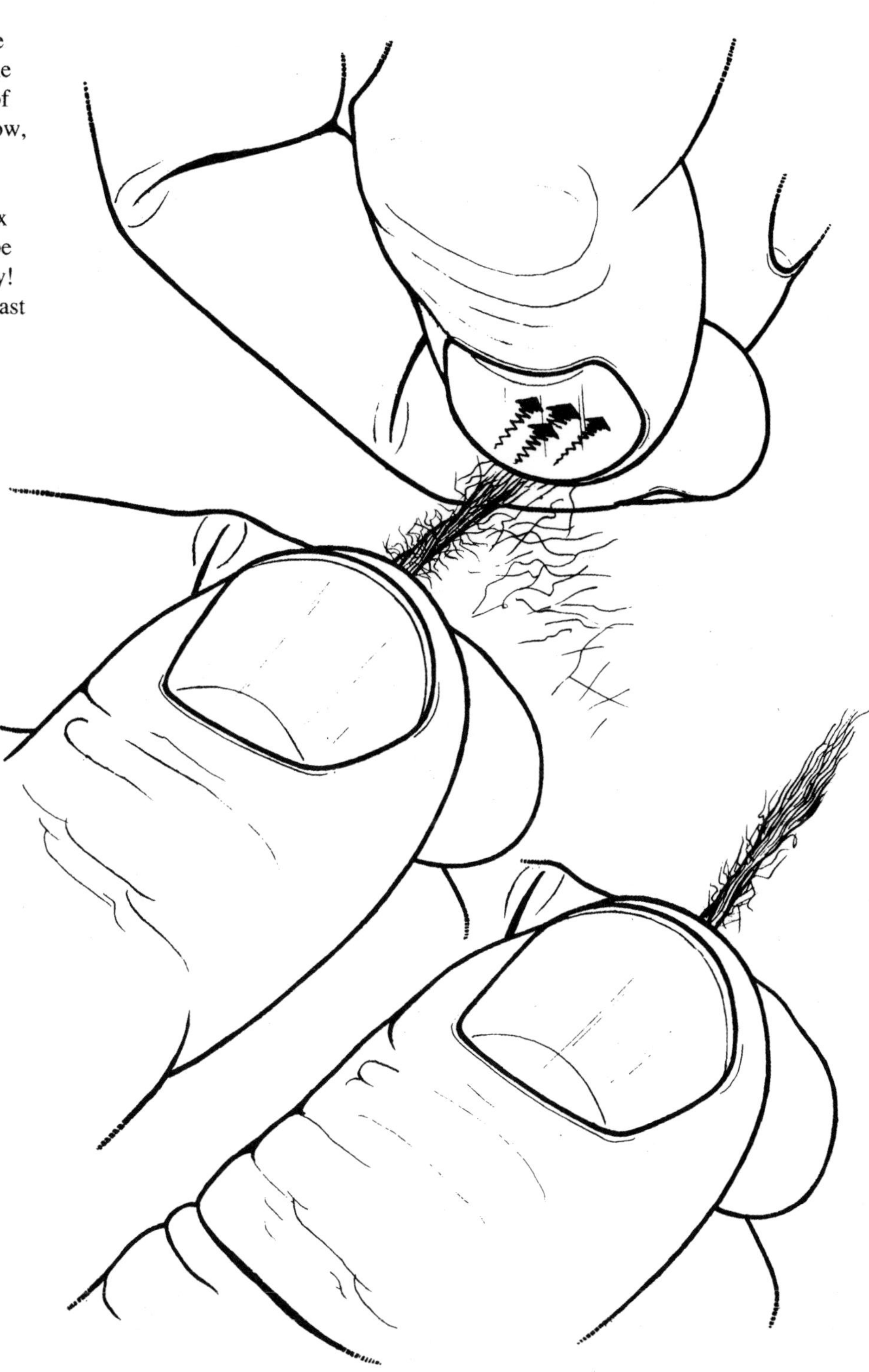

Fig 8
Offer this piece of yarn (both plys together) to the hook shank and circle around it with the tying thread. Wind the tying thread towards the tails, binding the yarn to the hook shank with fairly light tension. As you do so, start pulling the yarn through the turns of tying thread. Continue 'chasing' the advancing turns of thread with the tapering portion of yarn, until you arrive at the start of the tails with the tying thread. Finish by binding it tightly to the hook shank at the very tip of the tapered end of yarn. It has been a little difficult to explain what I am doing here. Essentially this is a simple technique to ensure that you gather up, and bundle together, all or most of the frayed fibres in the 'shaven' portion.

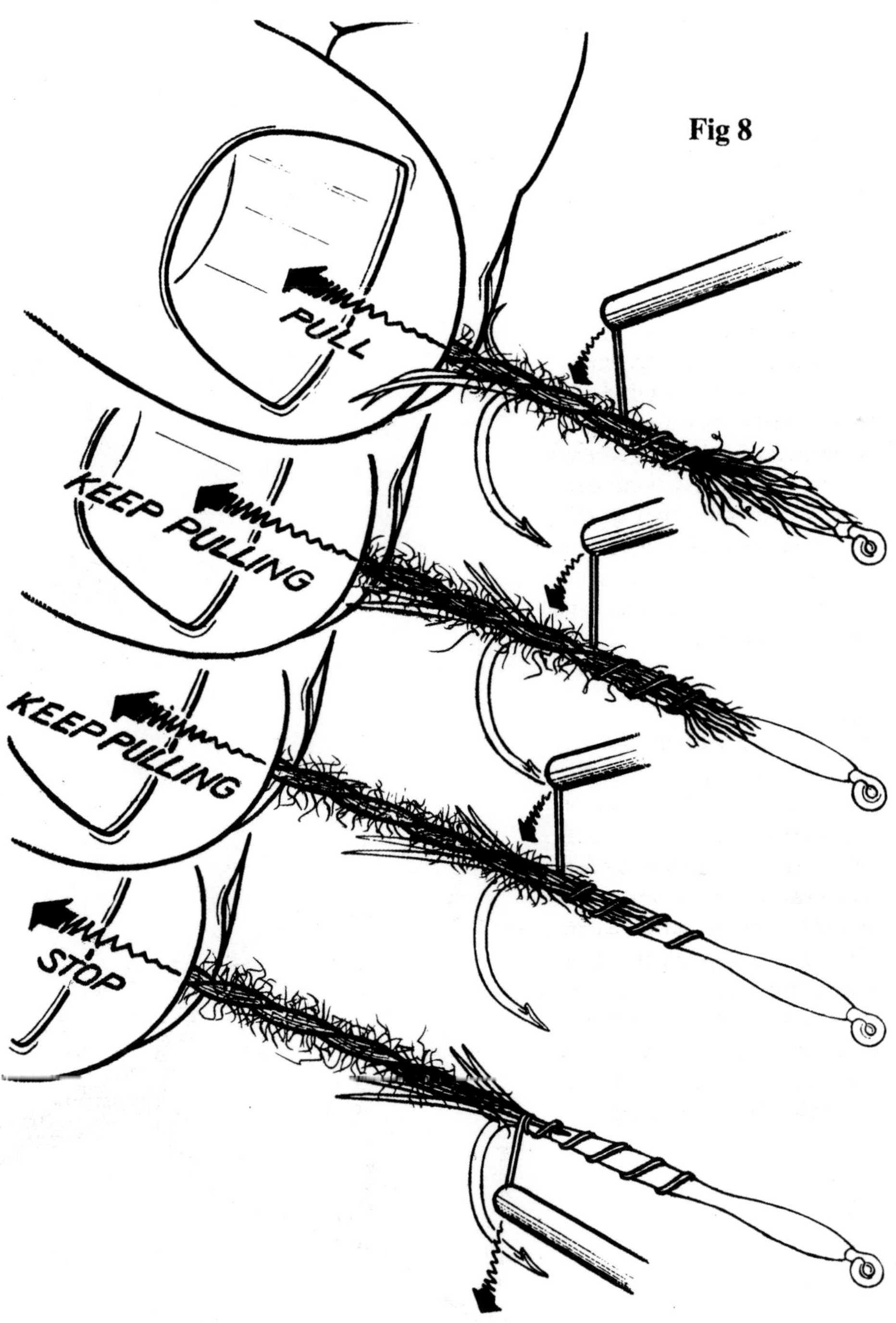

Fig 8

Fig 9
Now wind the tying thread back along the shank to a position just on the back taper of the thorax. Let the bobbin holder hang.

Fig 10
Take a firm grip of the free end of the yarn and start twisting it, making a tight rope.

Fig 11
Once the yarn is twisted, you simply wrap it around the hook shank, advancing towards the thorax. When you reach the start of the thorax, tie it down securely but don't snip off the waste end. Make sure that the direction of twist continues tightening as you wind it on. If the cording untwists then you have to wrap it on in the opposite direction.

Fig 12
The wing buds are next. The material I use is black feather fibre from a quill. The choice is wide - crow, rook, turkey, etc. Cut off two sections of black feather fibre - say 4-5 fibres. Remember they will compress when tied in. Tie in both clumps on the upper sides of the thorax. Tie them in by the tips at the back of the thorax bulge, then wind the tying thread forwards to just short of the eye. Let the bobbin holder hang.

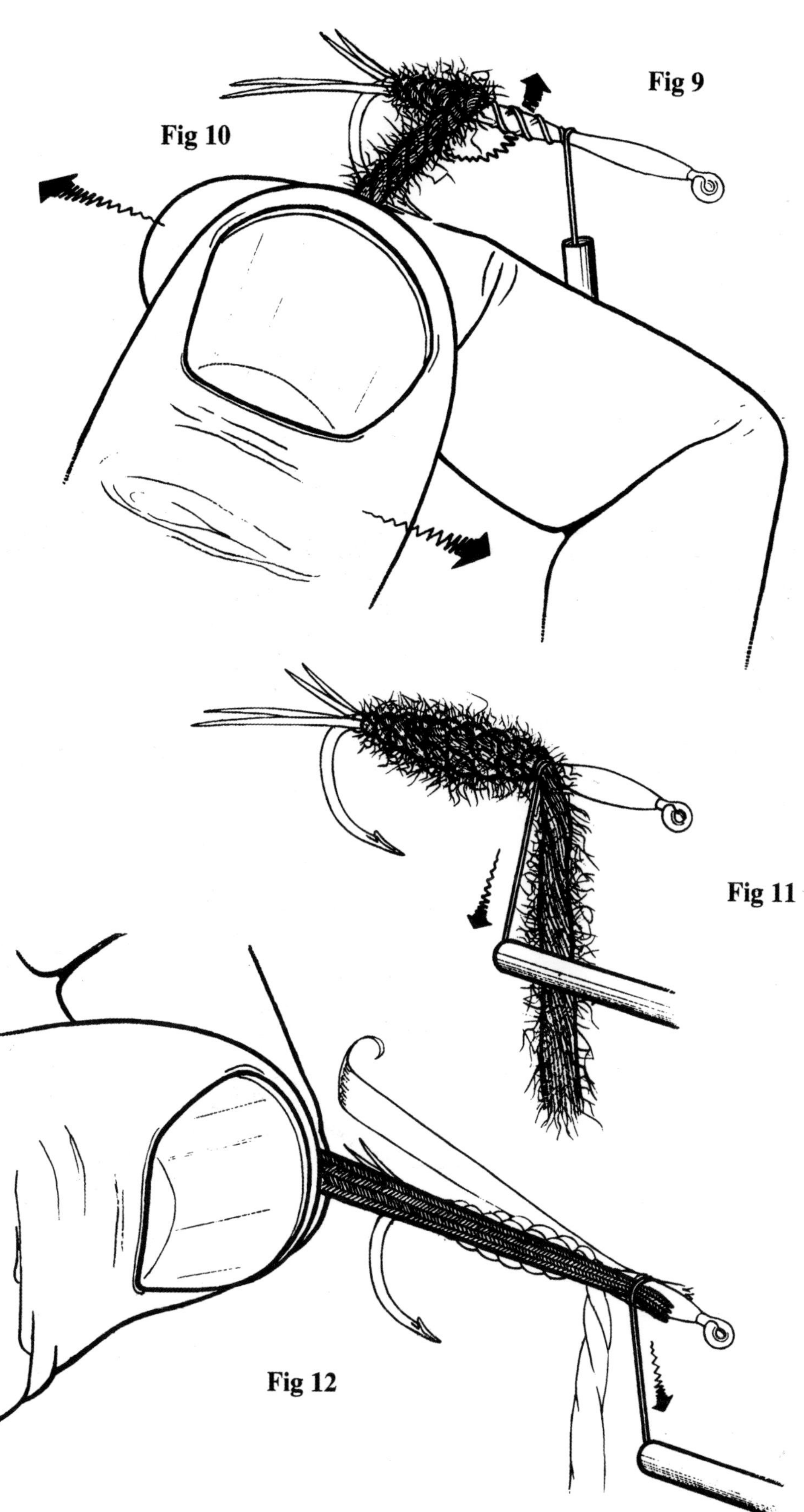

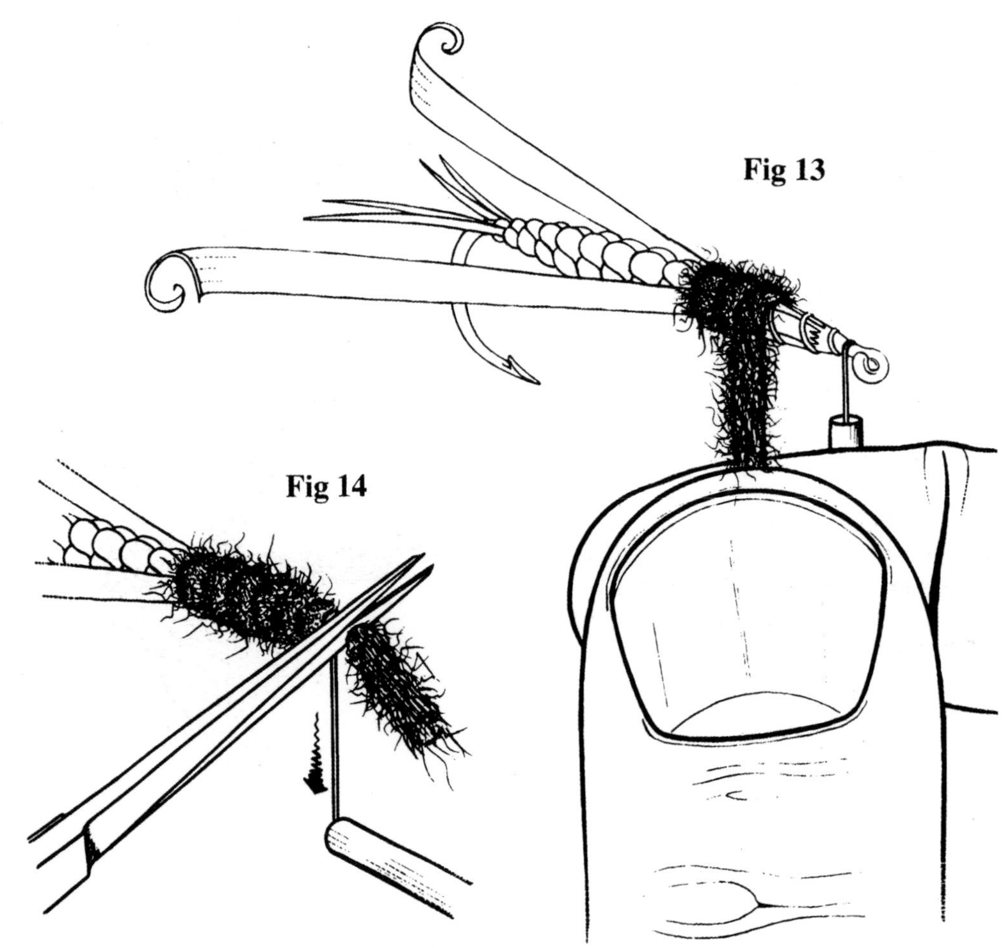

Fig 13
Next take up the waste end of yarn. It will have lost the tight twist now - this is exactly what you want - and wrap it towards the hanging bobbin holder, entirely covering the thorax bulge.

Fig 14
When you reach the waiting tying thread, tie off the yarn and snip off its waste end.

Fig 15
Bring forward the two black feather fibre clumps and tie them down. I prefer to make the two clumps converge so that they touch at the tying-off point.

Fig 16
Snip off the waste fibre.

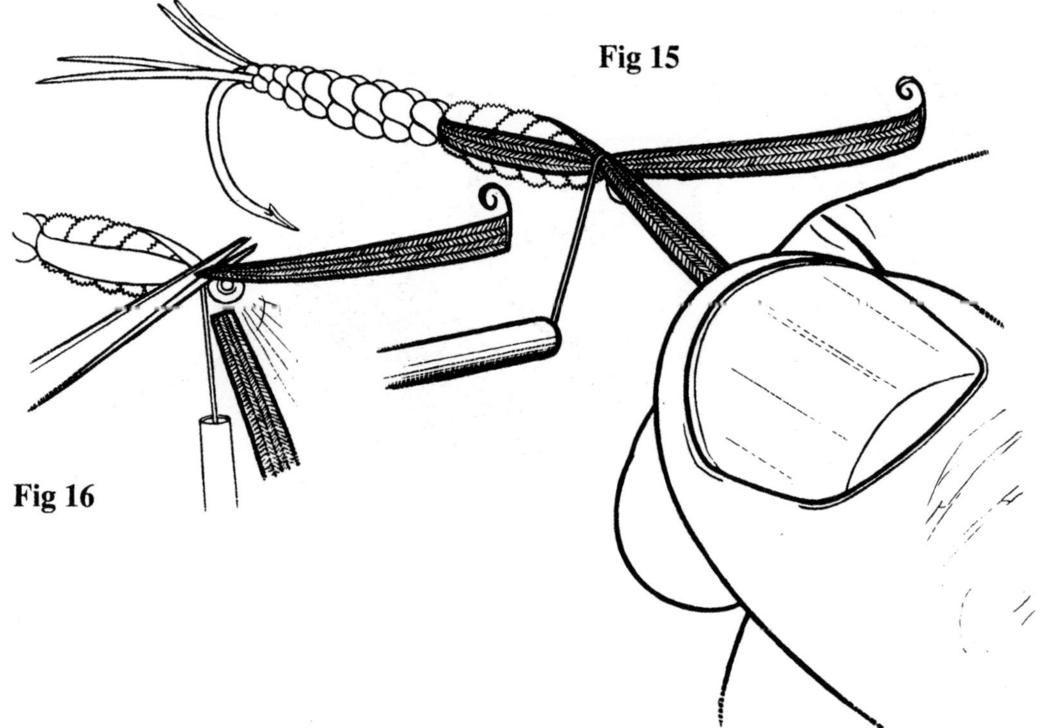

Fig 17
Now for the legs. Take a dark, well-speckled, partridge tail quill feather, one with an equal amount of barb on either side of the centre quill. Snip out and discard a small section near the tip by cutting through the centre quill.

Fig 18
Stroke back all the barbs except the last four or five pairs.

Fig 19
Now offer up this prepared feather to the underside of the nymph. Holding the feather barbs in position, by pressing both clumps against the respective sides of the thorax, take a turn or two of tying thread around the centre quill, binding it to the underside of the hook shank just in front of the thorax.

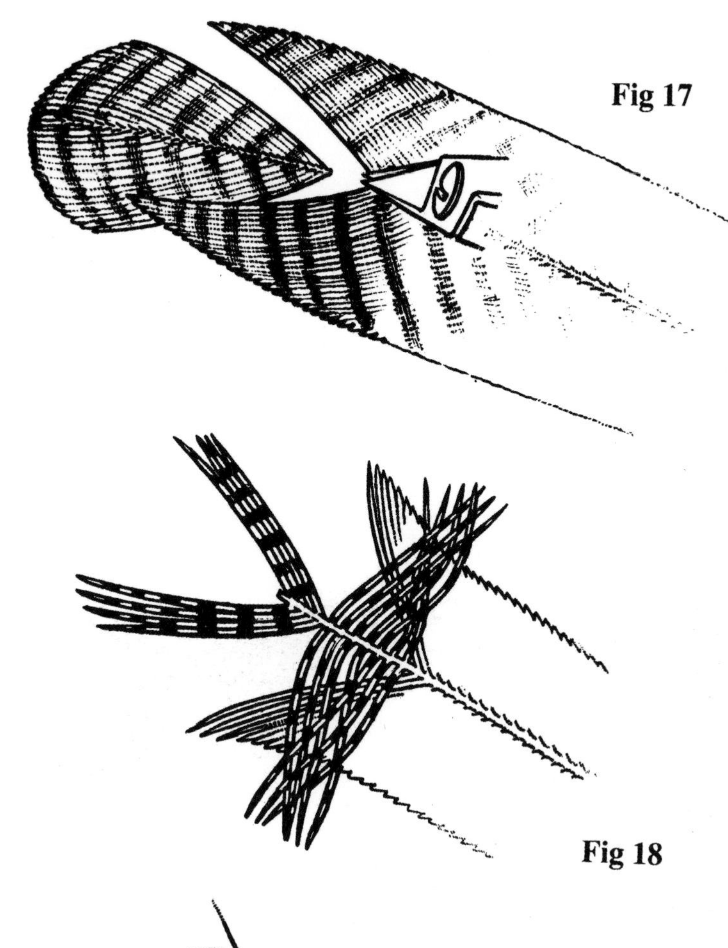

Fig 17

Fig 18

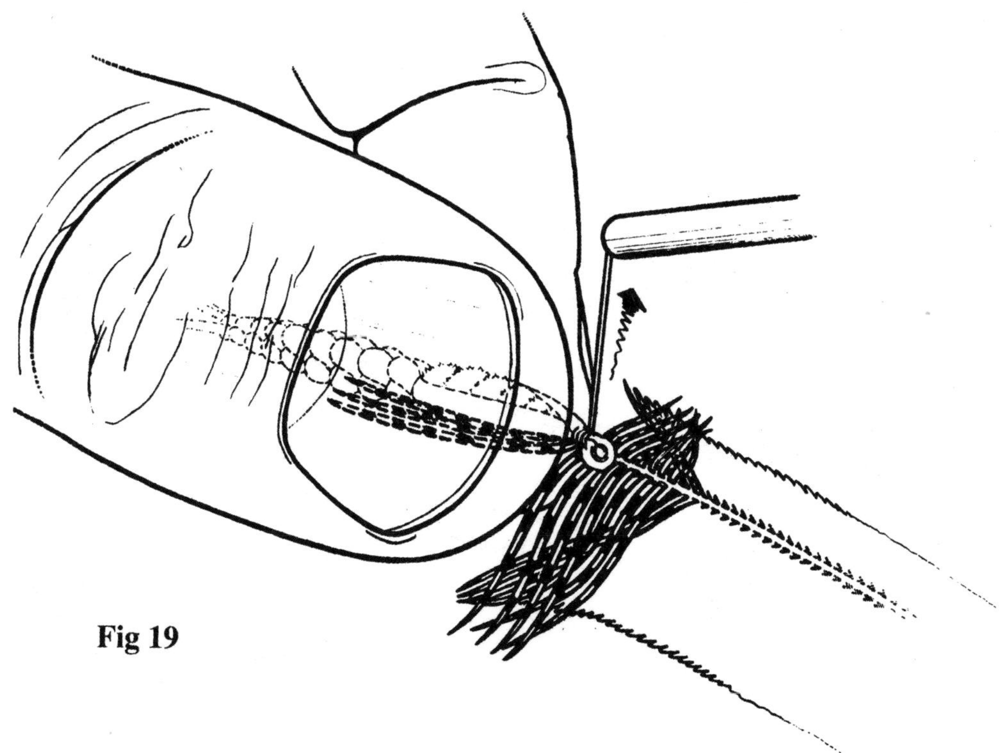

Fig 19

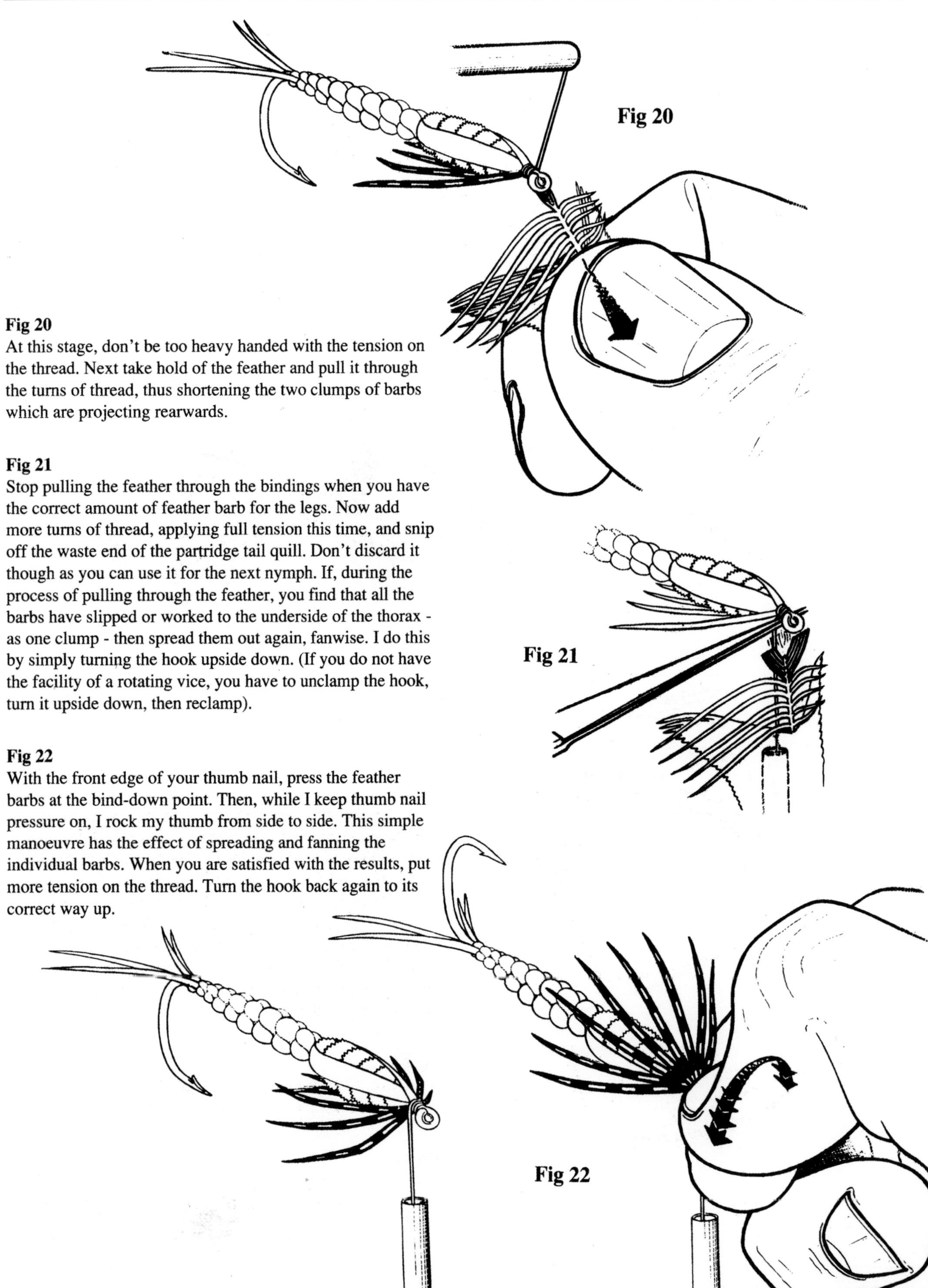

Fig 20

At this stage, don't be too heavy handed with the tension on the thread. Next take hold of the feather and pull it through the turns of thread, thus shortening the two clumps of barbs which are projecting rearwards.

Fig 21

Stop pulling the feather through the bindings when you have the correct amount of feather barb for the legs. Now add more turns of thread, applying full tension this time, and snip off the waste end of the partridge tail quill. Don't discard it though as you can use it for the next nymph. If, during the process of pulling through the feather, you find that all the barbs have slipped or worked to the underside of the thorax - as one clump - then spread them out again, fanwise. I do this by simply turning the hook upside down. (If you do not have the facility of a rotating vice, you have to unclamp the hook, turn it upside down, then reclamp).

Fig 22

With the front edge of your thumb nail, press the feather barbs at the bind-down point. Then, while I keep thumb nail pressure on, I rock my thumb from side to side. This simple manoeuvre has the effect of spreading and fanning the individual barbs. When you are satisfied with the results, put more tension on the thread. Turn the hook back again to its correct way up.

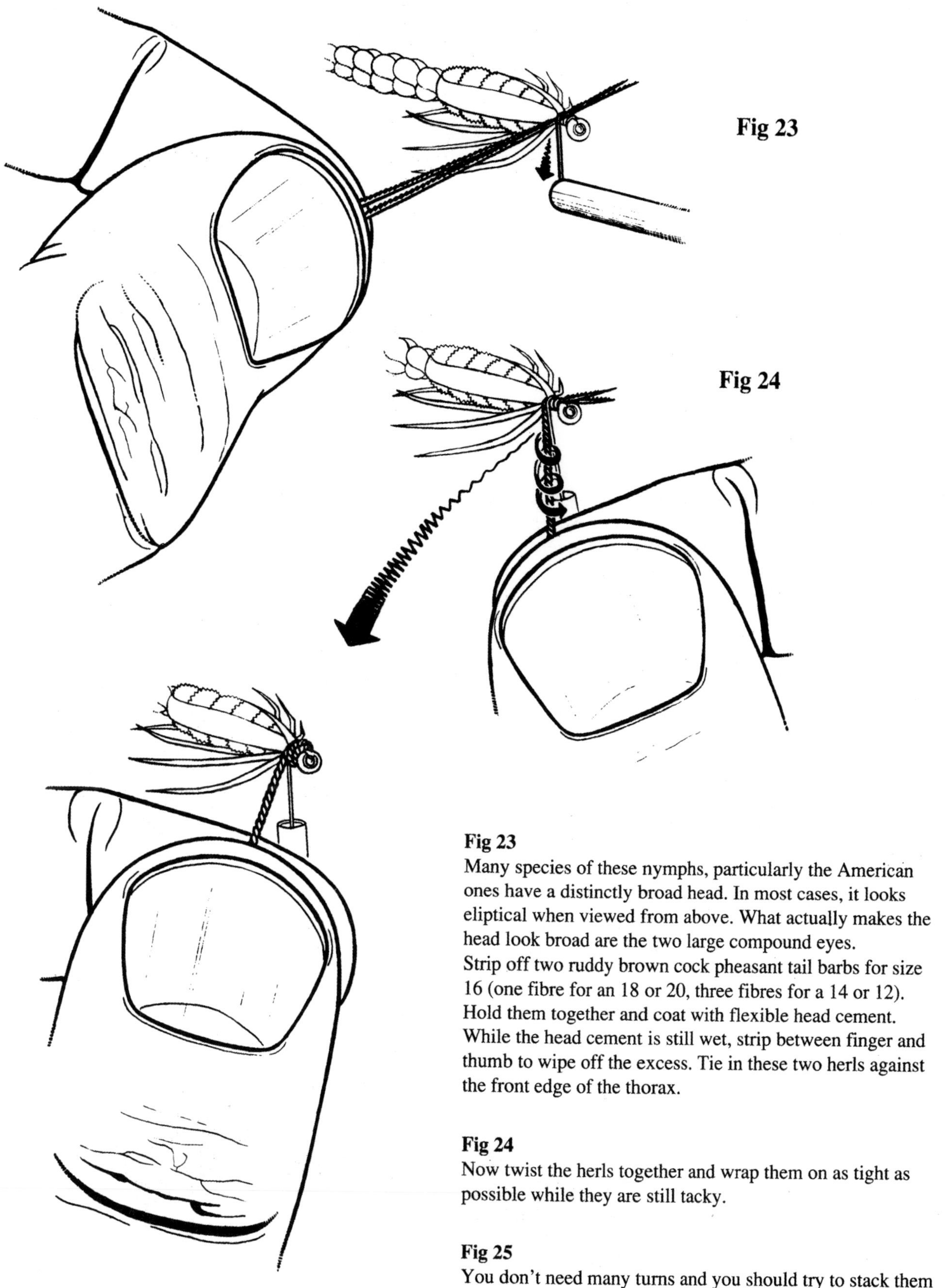

Fig 23
Many species of these nymphs, particularly the American ones have a distinctly broad head. In most cases, it looks eliptical when viewed from above. What actually makes the head look broad are the two large compound eyes.
Strip off two ruddy brown cock pheasant tail barbs for size 16 (one fibre for an 18 or 20, three fibres for a 14 or 12). Hold them together and coat with flexible head cement. While the head cement is still wet, strip between finger and thumb to wipe off the excess. Tie in these two herls against the front edge of the thorax.

Fig 24
Now twist the herls together and wrap them on as tight as possible while they are still tacky.

Fig 25
You don't need many turns and you should try to stack them on top of one another, rather than travelling along the hook shank.

Fig 26
Having formed a broad head, tie off the herls behind the head, where you originally tied them in.

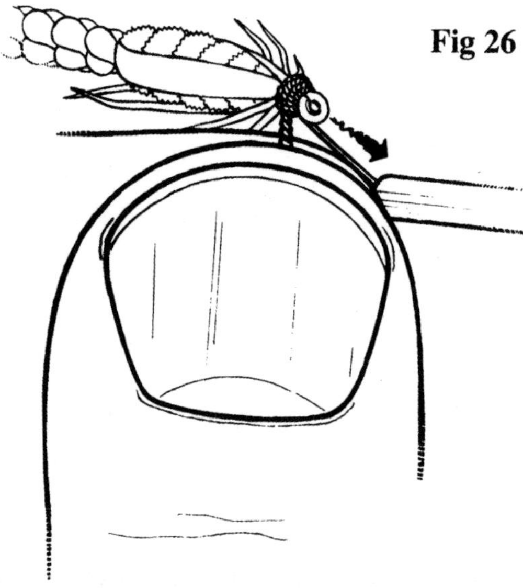

Fig 26

Fig 27
The fly is now complete. If you wish to roughen it up a little, just give a light once-over with your Velcro lolly-pop stick.

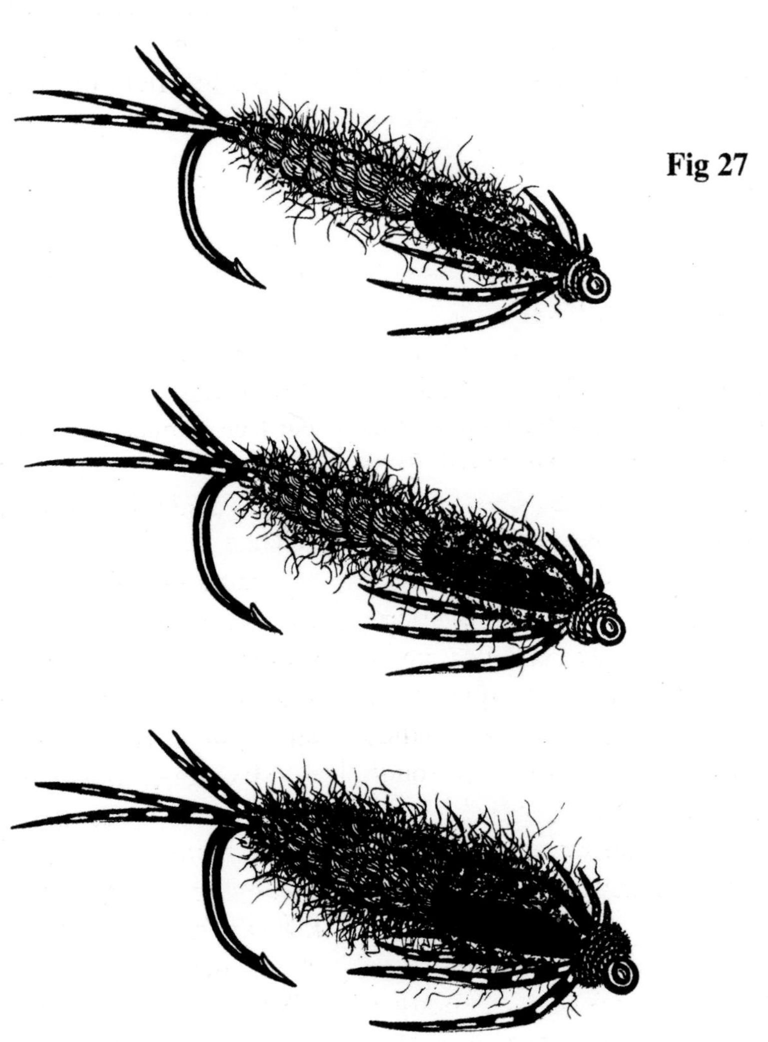

Fig 27

3. The Heptagenid Nymph

Of all the nymphs of the Ephemeroptera, the family Heptageniidae continues to be the most neglected - particularly from the flytying point of view.

Not only have these nymph patterns rarely appeared in our fly boxes, but the presence of the actual nymphs in our trout streams has been virtually overlooked. I bet that less than 10% of regular river flyfishers know with reasonable accuracy what one of these mayfly nymphs looks like, even though their shape is quite unique and unmistakeable.

The reason for this lack of interest is easy to explain. River flyfishing in Britain has been very strongly influenced by the famous flyfishing authors of a century ago. They fished the chalkstreams of Wessex and naturally their studies of aquatic insects took them no farther afield. Even in more modern times, angler/entomologist writers have, it seems, hailed from the south, where the chalkstreams again have received the lion's share of attention. On the chalkstreams it is the Baetidae, Ephemerellidae and Ephemeridae families which form the mainstay mayfly hatches. Chalkstreams are *not* the haunt of the Heptageniidae, since chalkstreams lack the rocky substrate and rough water which is the preferred habitat of the heptagenid nymph. The one exception is the yellow may dun which is fairly common in some chalkstreams.

All this has meant that no one has ever bothered to set about the task of devising a reasonably accurate artificial to represent this family. 'Not so!' you may well say. 'What about the march brown? That's a Heptagenid!'

It is a fact that there are several patterns for this nymph. Courtney Williams' *A Dictionary of Trout Flies* lists two standard dressings, one being from the pen of G.E.M. Skues no less. It is true, of course, that nymph patterns of the March Brown have been around for years. However, it has to be said that they look nothing like the real thing, not even superficially. They all lack the one most important feature, the unique distinctive silhouette. It is this above everything else which is, I believe, the trigger.

In the northern counties of England, the South-West, the Border regions and Scotland generally, there are very many classic rainfed (freestone) rivers, with stretches of rushing white water, dancing stickles and boulder-strewn beds - the true habitat of the Heptagenid. Most of these rivers have tremendous populations of Heptagenids; in some instances they eclipse the Baetids.

In these regions, the serious nymph fisherman would do himself a favour if he were to familiarise himself with these nymphs and their potential. He should certainly have a good pattern in sizes 16,14, and 12 in his fly box!

Evidence that trout and grayling feed on Heptagenid nymphs is easily missed since one rarely finds intact specimens in autopsies. But examine the stomach contents of a summer-caught fish carefully with a x10 or x20 lens, and evidence of feeding on these nymphs can often be found. What one finds are the less easily digestible chitinous femurs, plus the head capsule. These tough remains are often found packed towards the posterior end of the stomach, suggesting that the nymphs were eaten during the previous evening or night, hours before the trout's daytime capture. Once ingested, the soft parts of these nymphs are assimilated quite quickly. This fits in well with what we know of prey and predator in this instance. Heptagenid nymphs, tucked safely out of sight during the day on the underside of rocks and stones, venture to the exposed upper surfaces of these rocks at dusk and night to graze. And when do brown trout feed most actively during summer? At dusk and the first few hours of darkness. Nevertheless, trout are known opportunist feeders and will feed anytime on a loose 'drifter'.

In North America, the popularity of Heptageniidae with both fish and fishermen cannot be over-emphasised; with five important genera and at least 16 species which produce good rises. Happily for the American river nymph fisherman many Heptagenids are open water emergers giving trout a tremendous opportunity to gorge. Despite this, America still does not have a Heptagenid nymph pattern with the correctly 'triggered' silhoette.

Heptagenid nymphs spend most of their lives on the underside or downstream faces of rocks and stones on the stream bed, where they feed by scraping away at the fine algae and detritus covering their surfaces. These nymphs prefer the swifter parts of the river. Some species can even be found right at the edges of 'white water'.

To enable the nymph to withstand the tearing force of the current they have perfect physical adaptations. For a start they are flattened, offering the smallest possible frontal area to the force of the current. Their underside is quite flat, allowing the nymph to squat low to the rock surface, almost sealing itself all round.

Even the legs have special adaptations to assist in keeping these nymphs 'glued' down. Each femur is very broad and flattened, and set at an angle. When viewed from the side the leading edge of each femur is lower than the back or trailing edge. When held together - three legs down each side - these femurs form an almost continuous sloping face, sloping upwards that is, from front to rear. Thus when facing the flow, a downward pressure is produced by the current.

However, the most dramatic feature of this nymph is its head, which has a grotesque, almost sci-fi, appearance, being twice as wide as long. Someone once suggested that we should imagine a saucer broken in half, the front of the nymph's head being the smooth curved rim of the saucer; also imagine the broken saucer turned upside down so that it sits on its rim. Now you have a good picture of the head of a Heptagenid nymph. No current can possibly go underneath the nymph. Instead, it passes over the head, pressing it to the rock.

These nymphs cope very well in what appears to us a very hostile environment, rarely dislodged and swept away.

If the shape of these nymphs seem strange, then their emergence behaviour is no less strange, since within this single family, all three methods of emergence are used. This is unique among the Ephemeroptera.

The three methods of emergence are:

a) Emergence at the surface.

b) Emergence on dry land, the nymph having crawled out on to a bankside rock or stone or other

SOME NATURALS APPROPRIATE TO THIS PATTERN

BRITISH GENERA:
Rhithrogena, Heptagenia, Ecdyonurus.
BRITISH FISHING NAMES: March Brown, Olive Upright, Dusky Yellowstreak, Yellow May Dun, Autumn Dun, Late March Brown, Large Brook Dun, Large Green Dun.

NORTH AMERICAN GENERA:
Rhithrogena, Heptagenia, Stenonema, Epeorus, Cinygmula.
NORTH AMERICAN FISHING NAMES:
Slate Grey Dun, Light Cahill Grey Fox, Quill Gordon, Slate Brown Dun, American March Brown.

HEPTAGENID NYMPHS

(Top three) copying the larger Ecdyonurus species – Large Brook Dun, False March Brown, etc.
(Bottom three) copying the Heptagenia and Rhithrogena species – Olive Upright, Yellow May, etc.

projecting object.

c) Emergence underwater from a rock or stone on the stream bed. Here the phyrate subimago (dun) either swims, is buoyed by internal gas to the surface, or is propelled by a combination of both.

This last method of emergence is reputedly peculiar to the genus Heptagenia and to one particular species, the dusky yellowstreak (*Heptagenia lateralis*) However, I have strong evidence that at least one other member of the genus also uses this method: the yellow may dun (*Heptagenia sulphurea*). On one of my local rivers, the trout specialise in taking these 'emergers' with their stumpy, embryonic wings. Time after time, my autopsies have shown them to be a popular food item in June and July.

However, professional entomologists cannot all agree. Some say that heptagenid nymphs emerge on the surface, others say from the stream bed. Clearly there is still much to be learned about the Heptageniidae.

The following summary groups the important British Heptageniidae according to their three types of emergence.

a) EMERGENCE AT THE SURFACE:
 Rithrogena species: march brown, olive upright
 Heptagenia species:
  Dusky yellowstreak
 Ecdyonurus species:
  August dun, late march brown.

b) EMERGENCE ON DRY LAND:
 Ecdyonurus species (of less importance to the fly fisherman): Late march brown, large brook dun, august dun.

c) FROM UNDERWATER:
 Heptagenia species: Dusky yellowstreak, yellow may dun.

Apart from possibly the North American genus Epeorus, these nymphs look sufficicently similar to be copied by one design. Therefore all the flytyer has to vary is size, with maybe some changes of colour.

This pattern is my mainstay summer fly - it has been a very consistent fish fooler and has given me many 20+ days, with one single nymph once taking 15 fish. It is a robust artificial! I fish it upstream, dead drift, searching carefully through brisk riffles and boisterous pocket water, usually as a single fly on a tippet of 2-3 lb BS.

NOTES ON MATERIALS AND DESIGN

When starting out to develop this nymph pattern, the single most difficult tying problem I had was how to produce the short, but very broad, oval head, which is the characteristic feature of the nymphs of this family. A second problem was how to make those awkward yet distinctive legs which, are very obvious and pronounced on the natural.

The heads on my earliest nymphs were fine copper wire which I wrapped on many turns then used snipe-nosed pliers to flatten to shape. The results, I have to admit, were mixed!

Then, one day, when I was making some heat-balled eyes out of thick monofilament for a Damsel Nymph, it came to me in a flash and I could see the solution to my wide head problem. Simply lash on to the shank - at right angles - a stout piece of flat nylon mono. If this is then trimmed down with scissors to leave two short stumps - one on either side - and the sharp edges rounded off with a lighter flame, it is now easy to make the correctly-shaped head capsule every time. Copper wire is then wrapprd around the two stumpy mono extensions with criss-crossing turns as the wire is taken from one side to the other. Finally, it is smoothed out with soft dubbing. Hey presto!

On my earlier patterns, I used partridge hackles to simulate the legs: not robust enough and lacking definition. I was looking for something more chunky in appearance. So I decided to try guinea fowl underwing coverts, and they are by far the best feather, well marked and with distinctive light patches not dissimilar to the legs of the natural.

Pheasant tail fibres, I have now decided, are much too weak for nymph tails because they will not withstand the repeated maulings of trout, nor permanently hold the well-splayed position, which I believe is important on this pattern since it is another trigger. I finally settled for those lovely long, tapering hairs from a moose's mane. The individual hairs are very tough, although they appear not to be so, as they can be tweaked off the hide very easily. However the main shaft of the hair is very strong and it holds the splay well.

The abominal gills on all Heptagenids are leaf-shaped projections down each side of the abdomen, arising from the segment junctions (the last two tail-end junctions are without gills). Of the European Heptagenids, the genus Rhithrogena has the most obvious gills, quite large, and arranged down the side of the abdomen with a curious overlap - imagine a row of roof tiles - making what amounts to a continuous frill. These particular gills appear to have a dual function: a respiratory organ, and also a kind of continuous suction device.

This highly specialised gill arrangement is also evident on the nymphs of the North American Rhithrogena species. However, in North American trout streams there is one Heptagenid whose nymphs have abdominal gills modified to perfection. These are the nymphs of the Epeorus genus and they have quite incredibly large gills, each one dished like a miniature mouse's ear. These gills are also used as suction discs. The broad flattened head of an Epeorus nymph now looks more in proportion with the abdomen with its double row of 'mouse's ears'. Because of these appendages, the abdomen has more of an oval shape.

Imitating the gills of Heptagenid nymphs is a problem for the flydresser. Trying to imitate gill shape is impractical - and unnecessary - but the beating movement of the gills can, with a little imagination, be simulated. I favour dyed, long-flued ostrich herl which moves with the slightest current.

But when it comes to the nymphs of the North American Epeorus, ostrich herl, to represent gills, seems totally inappropriate. For these nymphs, something far more obvious is required. One suggestion is to change the construction completely and see what can be achieved by the use of dyed deer hair, trimmed to the flattened ovoid shape.

HEPTAGENID NYMPH DRESSING

Hook: Medium wire 2x to 3x longshank. Suggest Partridge 'Capt. Hamilton' Nymph Code H1A sizes 14,16,18; or Partridge 'Hooper' l/s 4x Fine Dry Code E1A sizes 14,16,18.
Weight: Narrow strip of wine bottle lead foil or fine copper wire.
Thread: Danville's 'Spider Web'.
Cement: Dave's Flexament (USA) or Floo Gloo (UK).
Tails: Tapering, white animal bristle from good quality shaving brush, dyed yellow-olive, or moose hairs dyed to match natural.
Abdomen: Thick polythene 0.008" (0.2mm) dyed yellow-olive, or yellow-olive Flexibody. Optional extra: brown or black waterproof felt pen dorsal side.
Abdomen gills: Ostrich herl dyed yellow-olive.
Thorax and head capsule: Fine synthetic dubbing, golden yellow olive eg Davy Wotton Finesse 'Masterclass' Blend Mc 6.
Head capsule cover: Brown Raffene strip.
Legs: Guinea fowl undercover or flank hackle dyed yellow olive.
Wing buds: Dark, brick red, grouse hackle coated with flexible head cement or clear flexible adhesive.

Tying the Heptagenid Nymph

Catch the tying thread behind the eye and run it down the shank to the start of the bend in open turns. Let the bobbin holder hang. Tweak out three individual hairs from a moose's mane. Tie these hairs in - as a bundle - and even up the tips. Adjust them so they extend about the total length of the hook. Next, widely splay the two outer hairs to 90°. For the method of tying in and splaying these tails see p7.
Run the tying thread to the back of the hook eye.

Fig 1
Snip off a 1" (25mm) length of mid-brown raffene, open it out fully then cut off a strip approximately 5/16" (6-7mm)wide.

Fig 2
Gather in one end to form a taper. Tie in by this tapered end on top of the shank. Ensure it is tied in hard up to the back of the eye - this is important. The Raffene should now project over the hook eye and should be gathered in, neatly, evenly and tightly, with the hook eye central when viewed from above.

Fig 3
Next to be tied in is the short nylon stump on which the head is formed. Cut off a 1/2" (12mm) length of thick flat monofil (I use black Amnesia shooting head backing). Bind this very securely on top of the shank at right angles to it, making a cross. Use figure-of-eight binding.

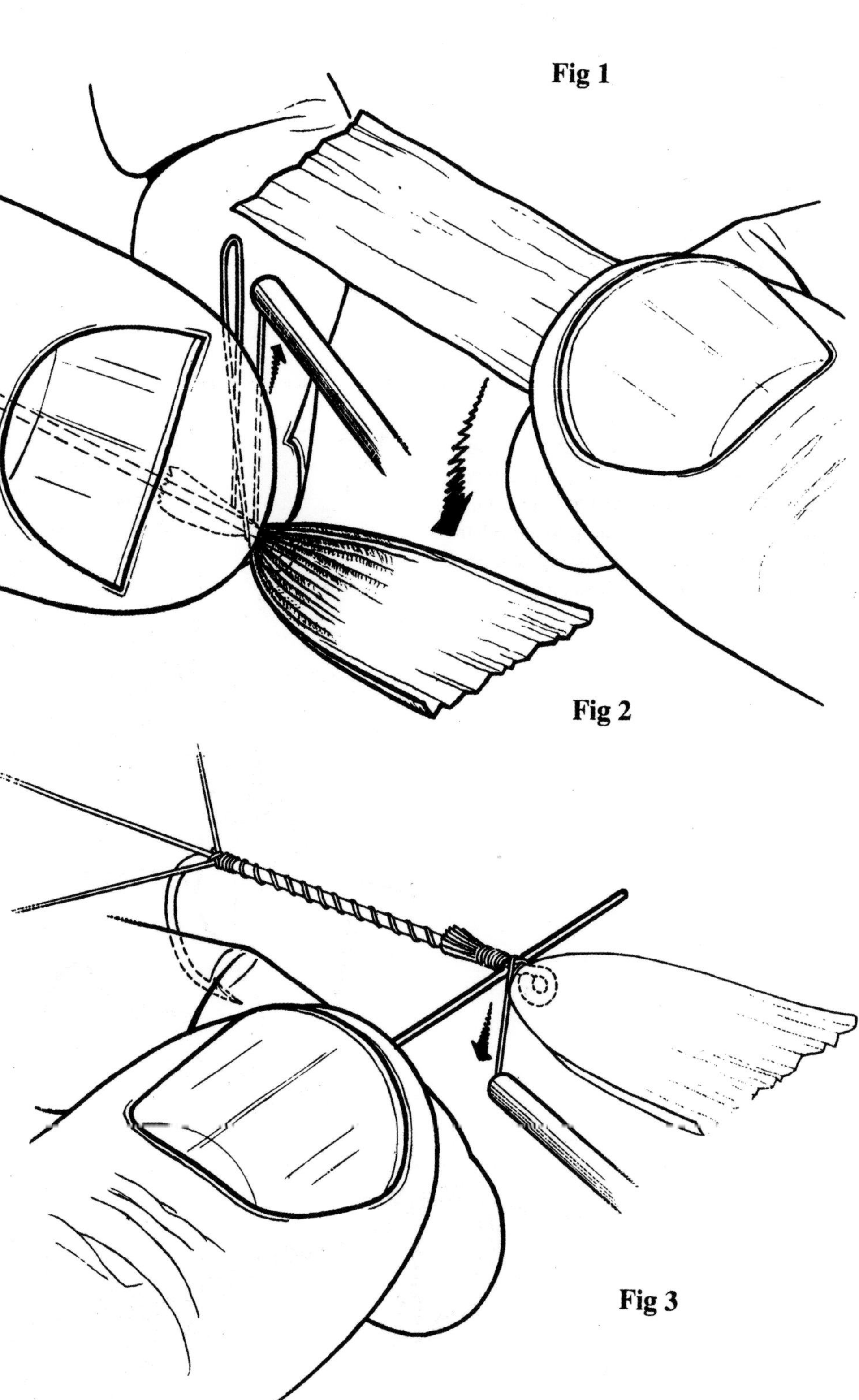

Fig 1

Fig 2

Fig 3

Fig 4

Fig 4
The position of this nylon stub should be just back from the eye. Trim both ends of nylon, so that each one is about 1/10" (2mm) long.

Fig 5
Very carefully, with the edge of a lighter flame, melt both ends so they are smooth and rounded. It helps if they become slightly balled.

Fig 6
Run the tying thread almost to the tails and let the bobbin holder hang. Take a 4" (100mm) length of fine copper wire and catch it in just behind the nylon stumps. Wind the wire tightly around the stumps. Criss-cross from one stump to the other at fairly regular intervals, making as many criss-crosses underneath as on top.

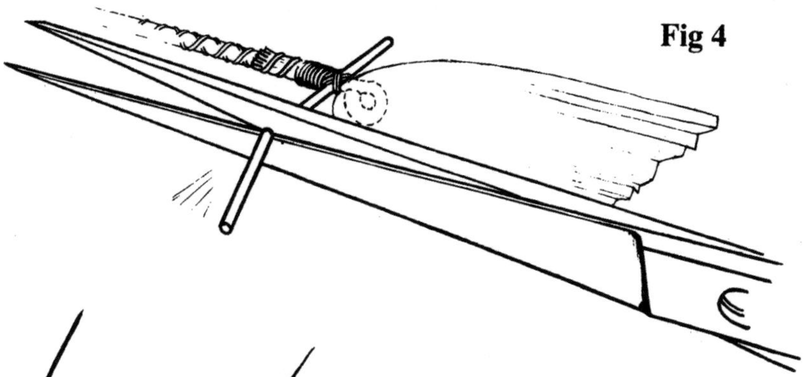

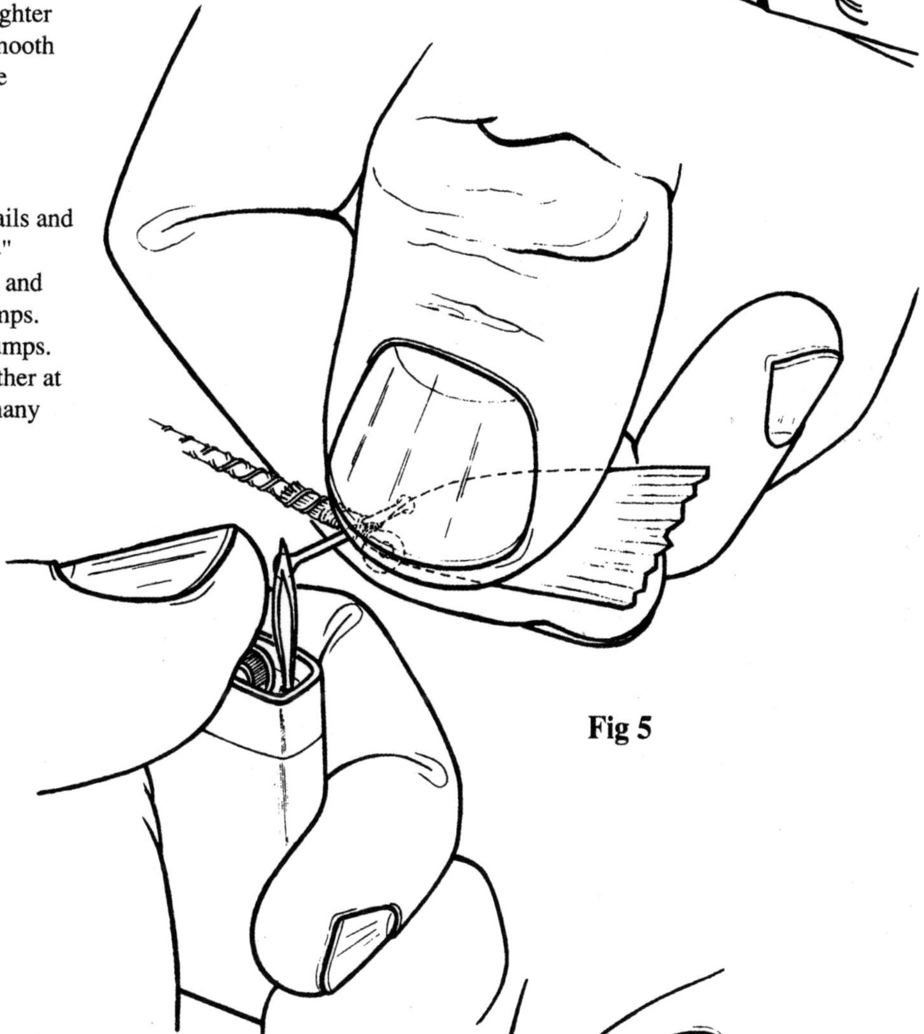

Fig 5

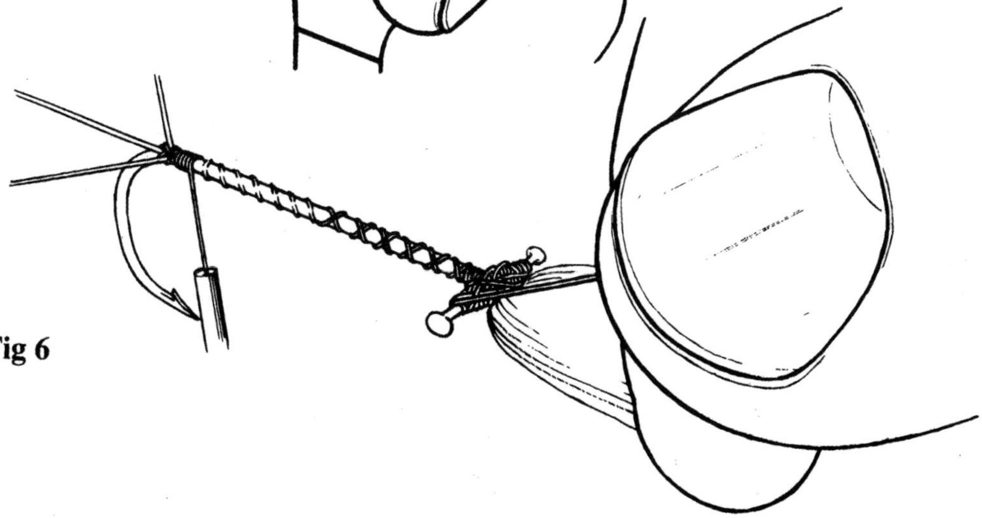

Fig 6

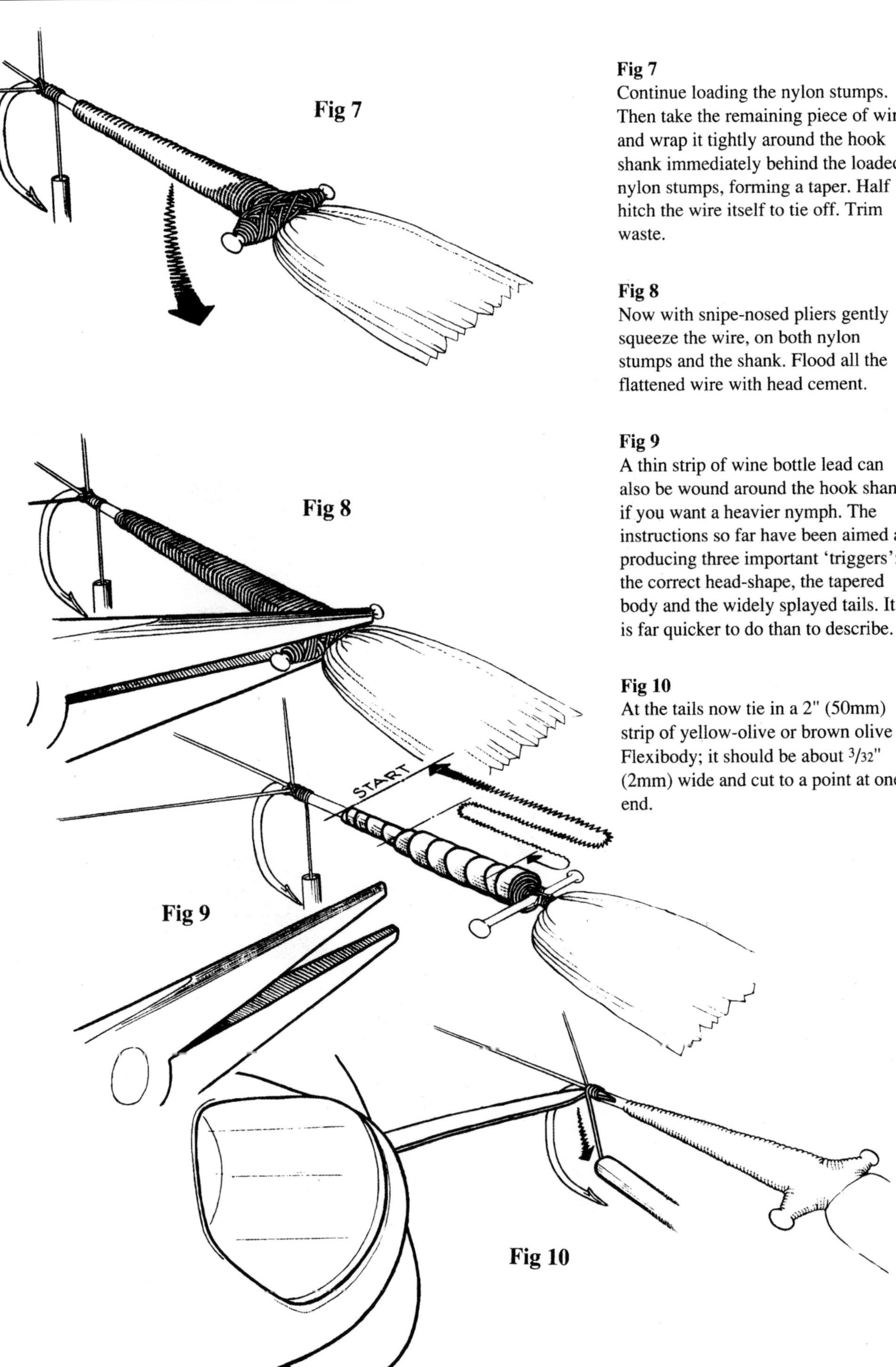

Fig 7
Continue loading the nylon stumps. Then take the remaining piece of wire and wrap it tightly around the hook shank immediately behind the loaded nylon stumps, forming a taper. Half hitch the wire itself to tie off. Trim waste.

Fig 8
Now with snipe-nosed pliers gently squeeze the wire, on both nylon stumps and the shank. Flood all the flattened wire with head cement.

Fig 9
A thin strip of wine bottle lead can also be wound around the hook shank if you want a heavier nymph. The instructions so far have been aimed at producing three important 'triggers': the correct head-shape, the tapered body and the widely splayed tails. It is far quicker to do than to describe.

Fig 10
At the tails now tie in a 2" (50mm) strip of yellow-olive or brown olive Flexibody; it should be about 3/32" (2mm) wide and cut to a point at one end.

Fig 11
Follow by tying in a length of yellow-olive ostrich herl which has been stripped of its flue all the way down one side. Advance the tying thread to mid shank position, let the bobbin holder hang.

Fig 12
Grip the end of the Flexibody in hackle pliers and wrap the herl around the Flexibody strip, advancing up the Flexibody in spiral fashion.

Fig 13
Now grip both herl and Flexibody in the hackle pliers and wrap them towards the centre of the shank. As you make each turn, ensure that you produce a slight overlap.

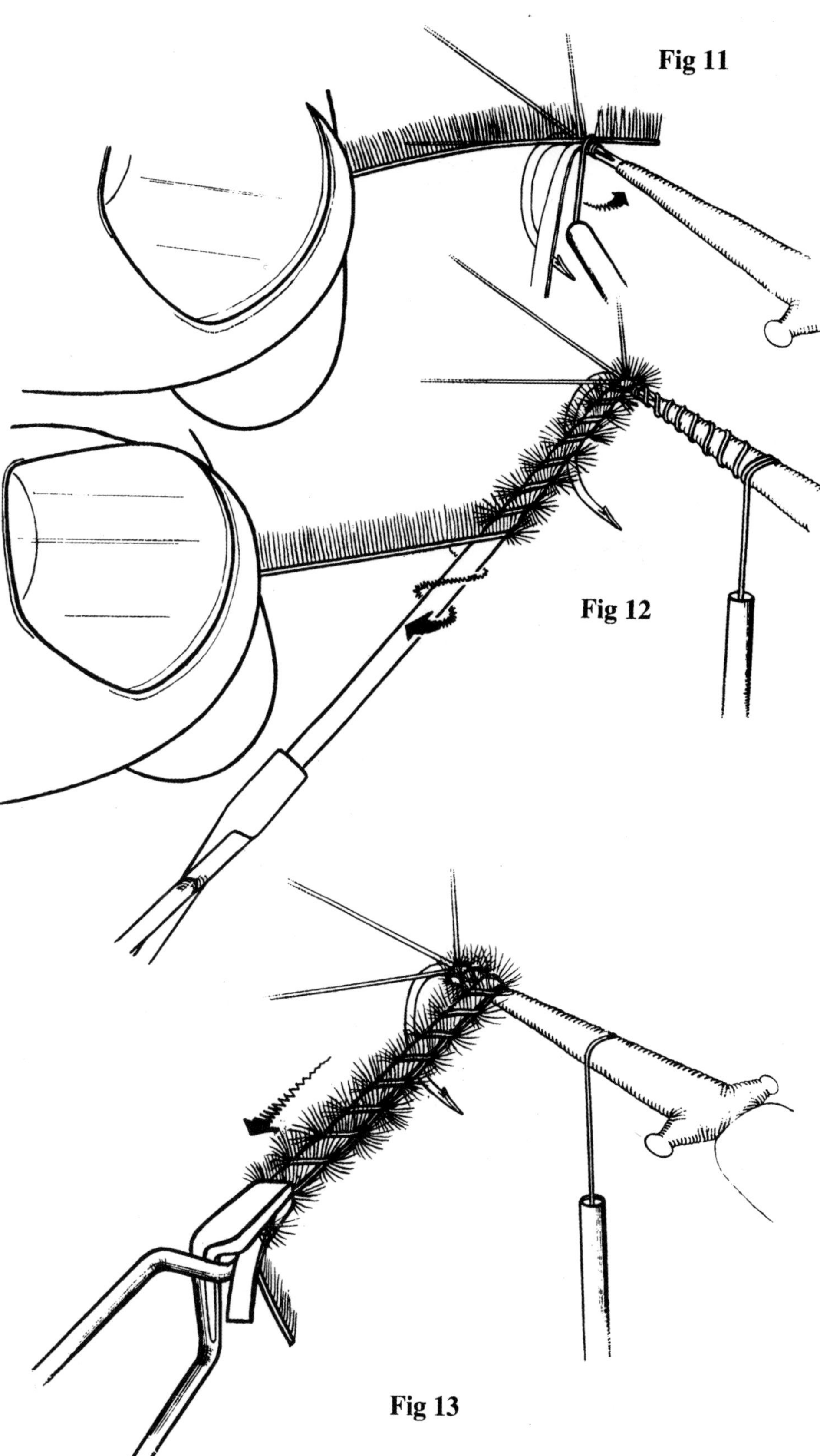

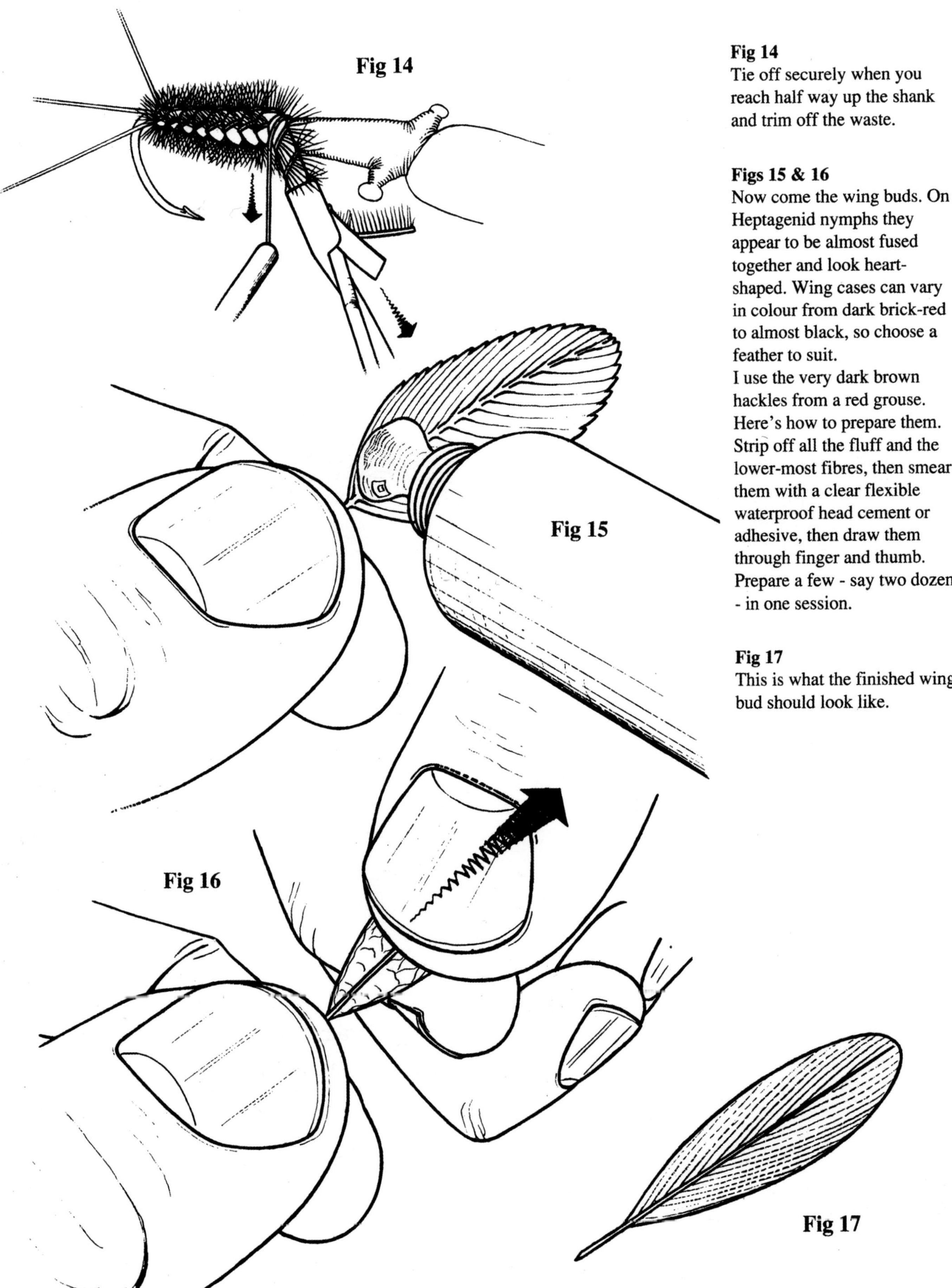

Fig 14
Tie off securely when you reach half way up the shank and trim off the waste.

Figs 15 & 16
Now come the wing buds. On Heptagenid nymphs they appear to be almost fused together and look heart-shaped. Wing cases can vary in colour from dark brick-red to almost black, so choose a feather to suit.
I use the very dark brown hackles from a red grouse. Here's how to prepare them. Strip off all the fluff and the lower-most fibres, then smear them with a clear flexible waterproof head cement or adhesive, then draw them through finger and thumb. Prepare a few - say two dozen - in one session.

Fig 17
This is what the finished wing bud should look like.

Fig 18
Tie in one of the prepared wing buds by the stalk end. Snip off the waste stalk.

Fig 19
Now come the legs. Choose a fairly large under covert from a guinea fowl wing. The ideal feather should have equal barb lengths on either side of the central quill and should be about 1 1/4" (32mm) wide by 3" (75mm) long. It will look ridiculously large for this nymph, but don't worry. Holding the feather by the tip, stroke the rest of the barbs backwards, so they separate. Tie the feather in by the tip with the concave side uppermost. The rest of the feather should be projecting backwards, over the bend. Trim off waste.

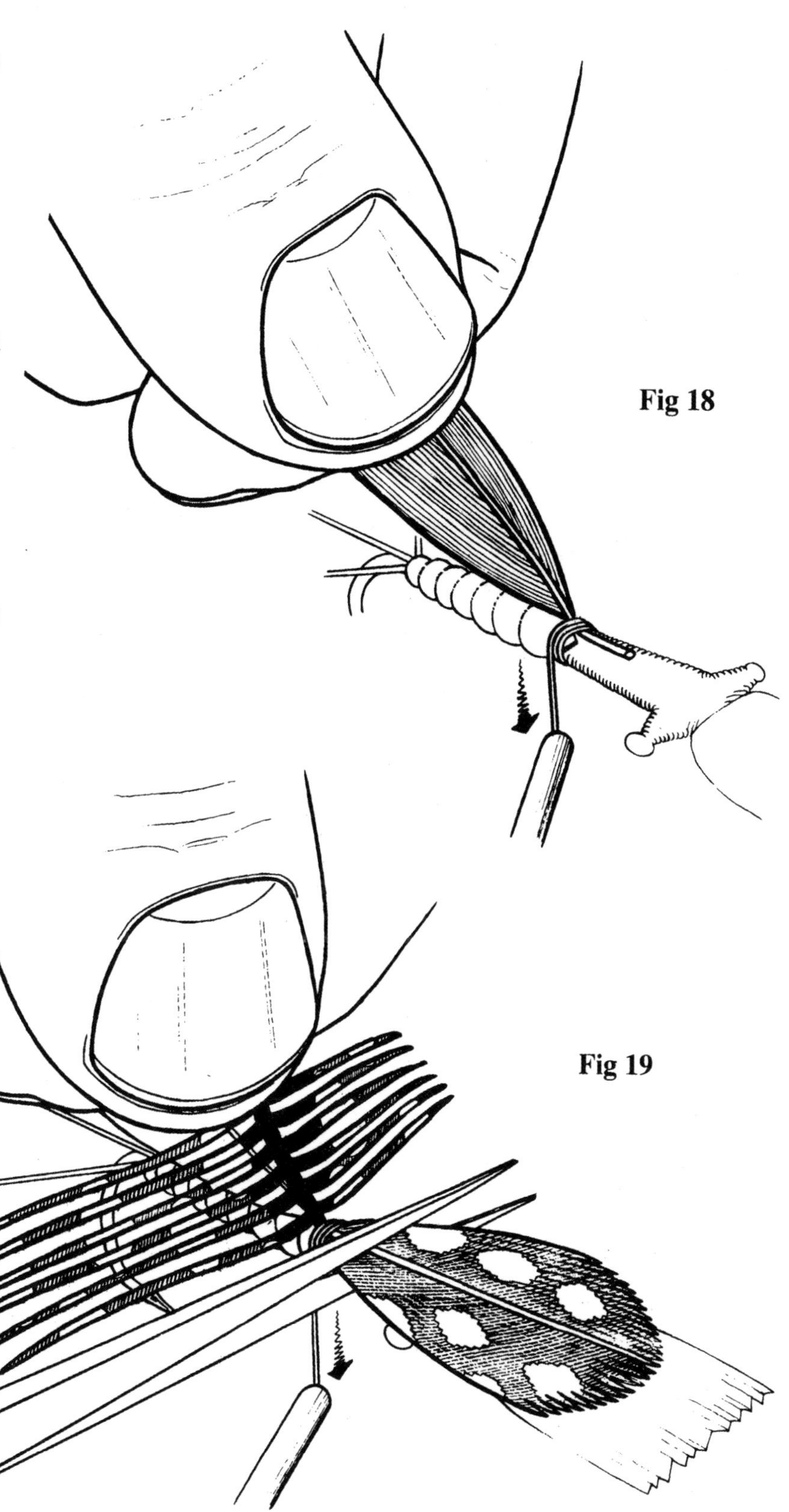

Fig 20
Next make a tight spindle of dubbing and wind forwards right up to the back of the head. Now spin on more of the same dubbing, making a very fine tight spindle, and anointing it with several drops of head cement as you tighten in the dubbing. Wind this dubbed spindle around the head foundation in much the same manner as you did when loading on the wire. Finish with the tying thread at the back of the head and let the bobbin holder hang. Give it another light pinch with the pliers, just to flatten the dubbing a little.

Fig 21
Pull over the guinea fowl hackle, tie down where the silk is hanging and snip of the waste. Let the bobbin holder hang.

Fig 22
Put a thin streak of head cement along the centre quill of the tied-down hackle.

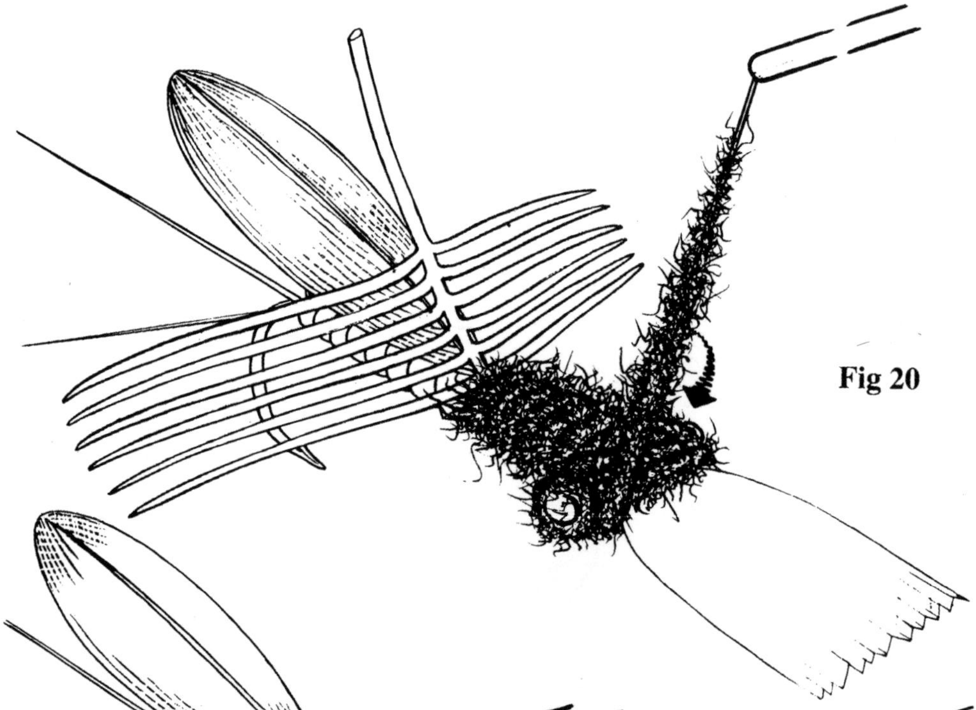

Fig 20

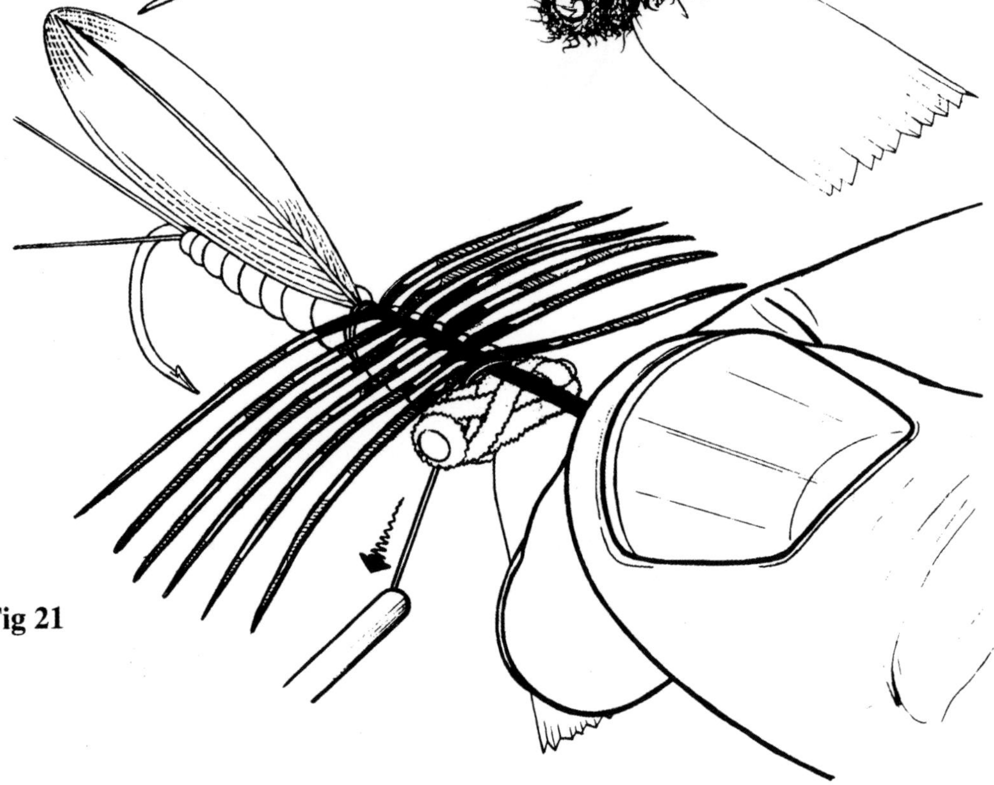

Fig 21

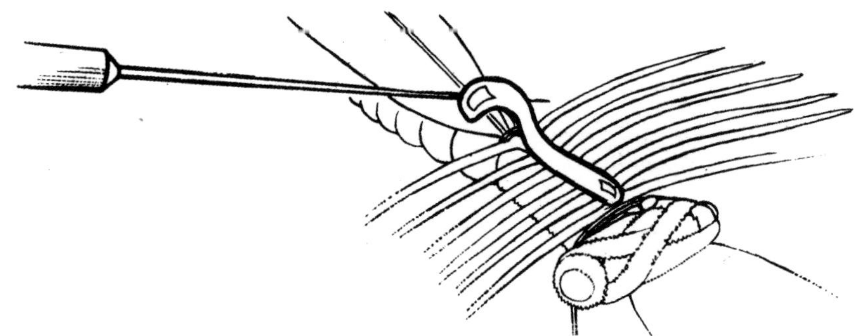

Fig 22

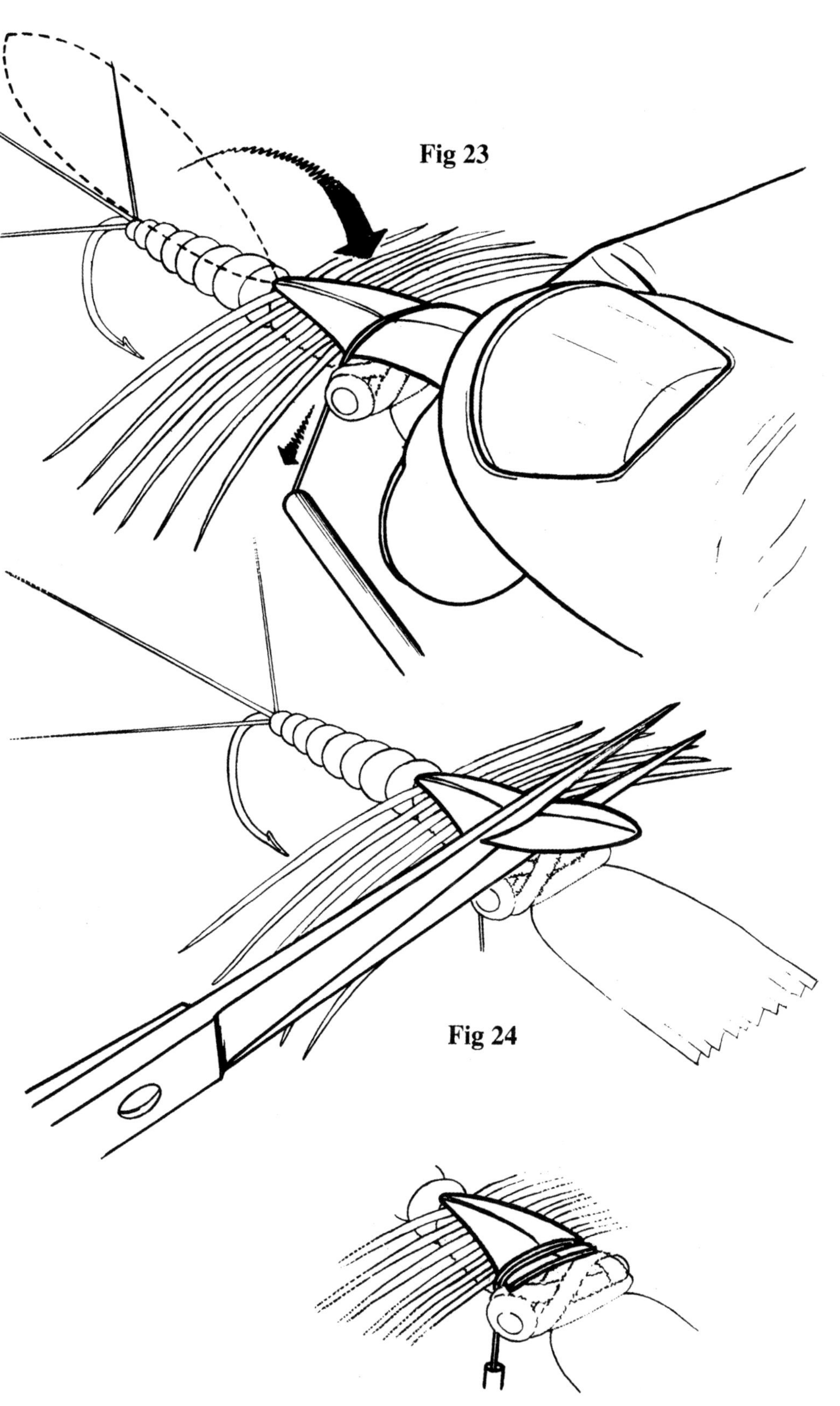

Fig 23
Follow now by pulling over the wing bud and tie down exactly where the guinea fowl hackle was secured

Fig 24
Trim off the waste wing bud feather.

Fig 25
Now cover the head with raffene to give it a nice smooth, rounded look. Moisten the Raffene.
Open it out to its full width and pull it over the head. Make sure that the edges of the Raffene wrap over the sides of the head, covering the heat-balled ends of the nylon monofil stumps.

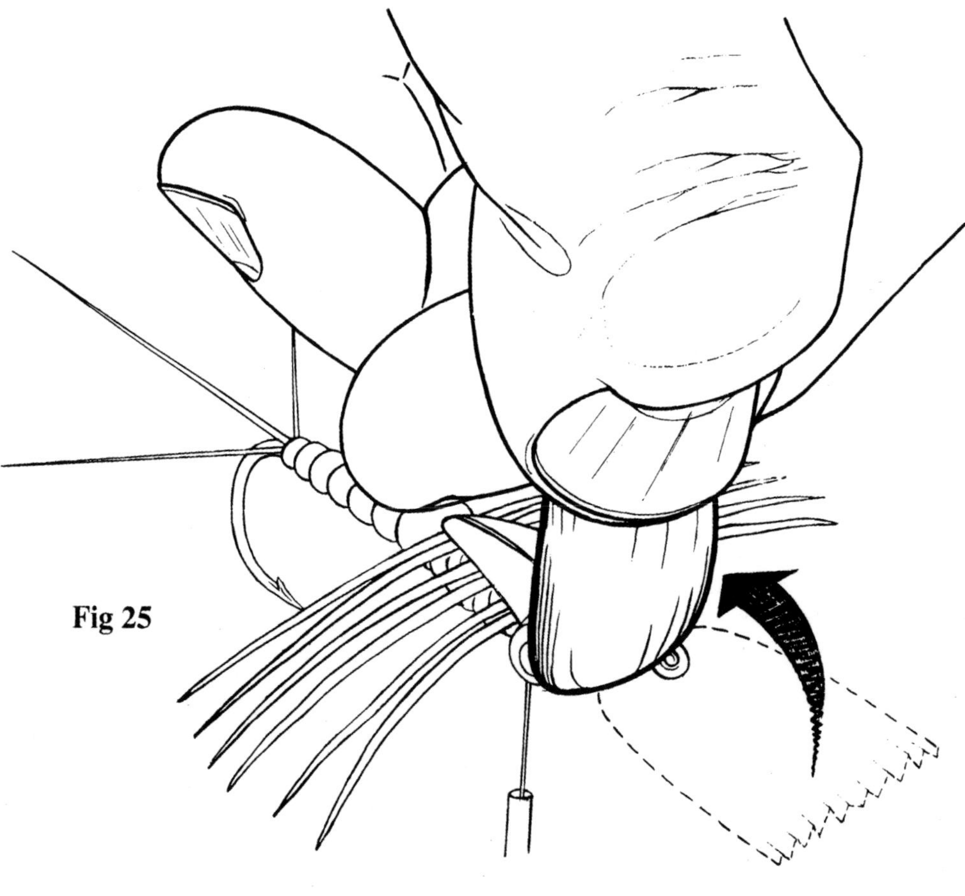

Fig 25

Fig 26
While holding the Raffene taut, with the tying thread at the back of the head, pull down quite tightly on the thread to produce a 'neck' at the back of the head. Follow this with another tight turn of tying thread.

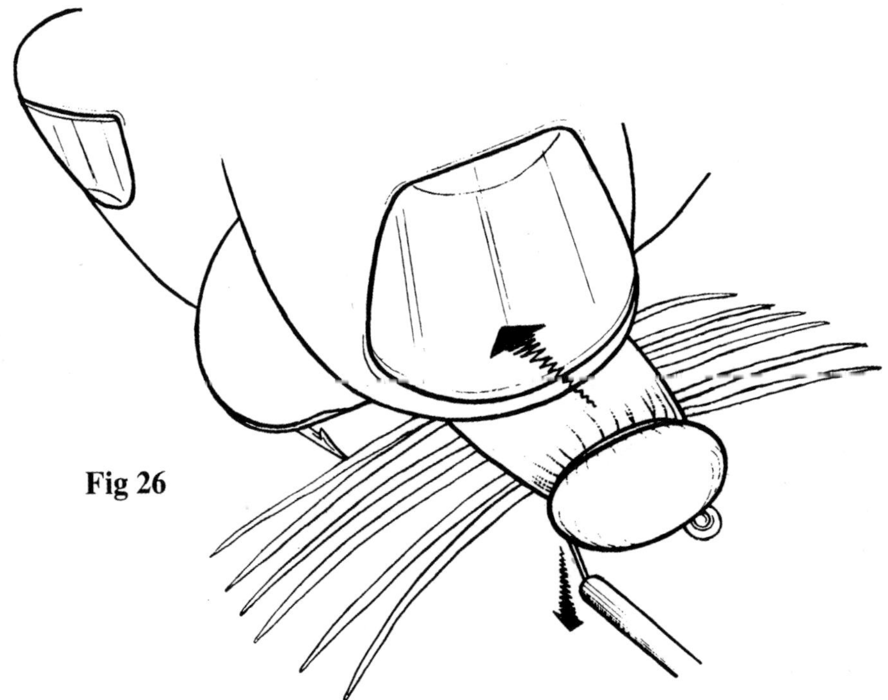

Fig 26

Fig 27
Trim off waste Raffene.
The first pair of stout legs of Heptagenid nymphs are set well forward. In fact they appear to spring from the back of the head, a characteristic feature of this family.

Fig 28
So, take hold of the first two hackle barbs on the far side of the nymph and pull them forward. While holding the barbs in this position, bring the tying thread hard behind them, pulling the barbs into the neck already made when tying down the Raffene. Repeat this procedure on the first pair of barbs on the near side. Now make a whip finish behind these front legs. Finally, trim off the tying thread.

Fig 29
Now shorten the nymph's legs, leaving them approximately three-quarters of the body length.

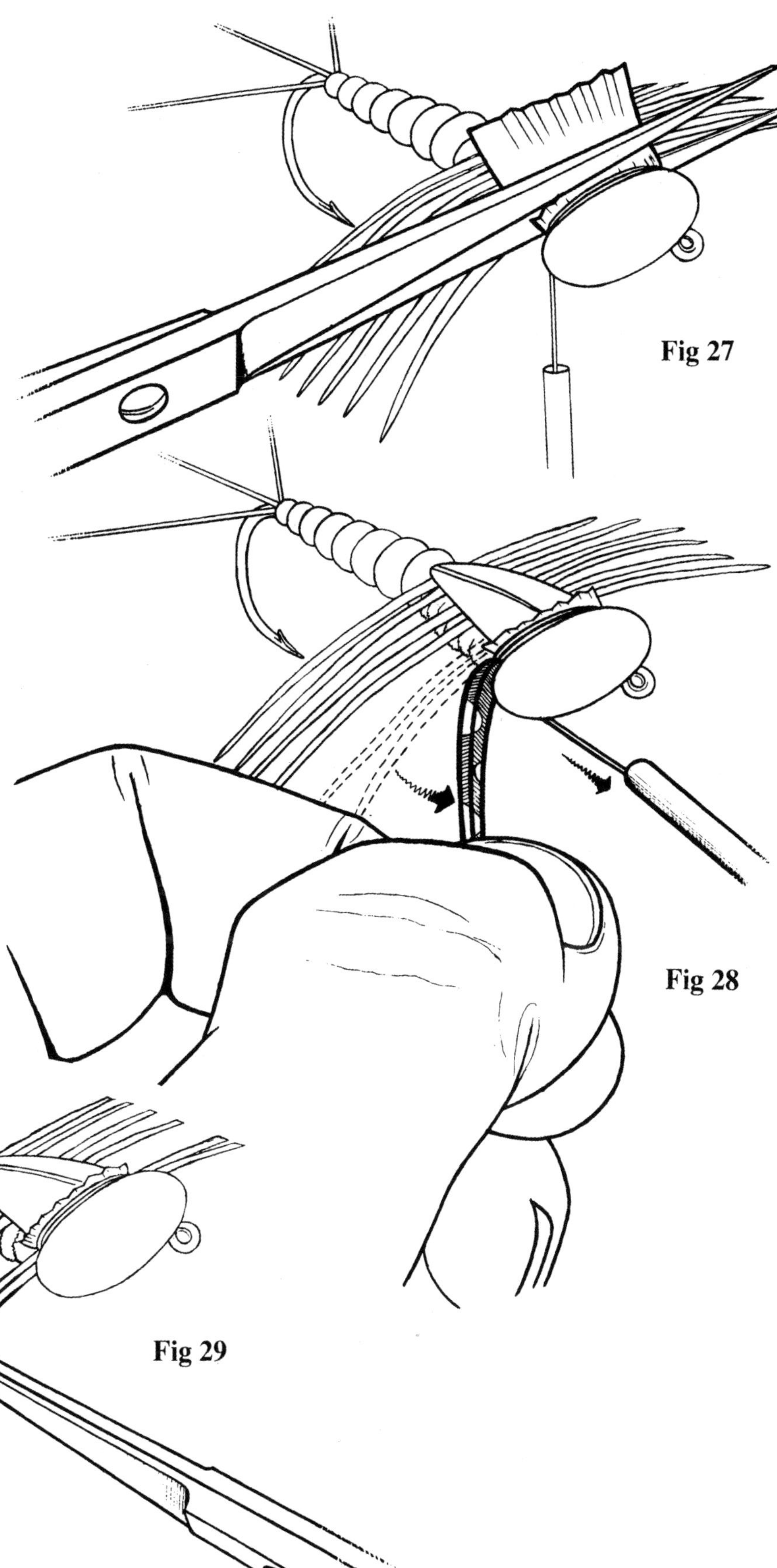

Fig 27

Fig 28

Fig 29

Fig 30
The final embellishment is kinking the legs. It is simple and takes only seconds. Hold the tips of fine-pointed tweezers over a lighter flame for a few seconds, then grasp each pair of legs half way along their length with the tweezers and twist forward at a very acute angle.

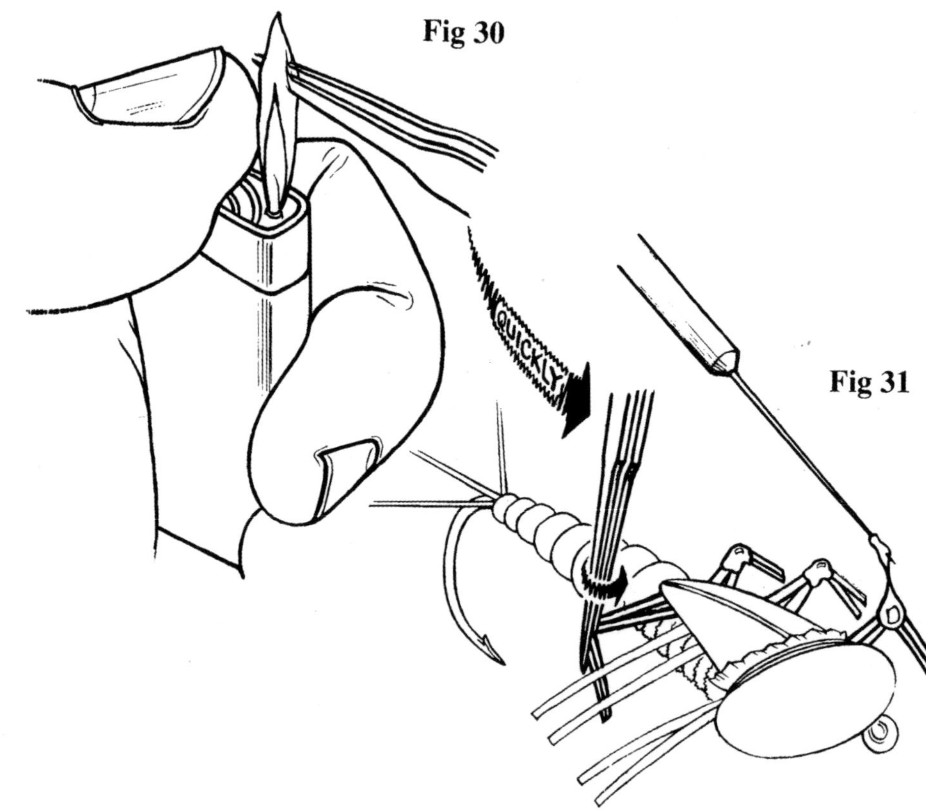

Fig 31
Hold in this position for a few seconds. For durability apply a drop of a waterproof flexible glue to each 'knee' joint.

Fig 32
The nymph is now completed.

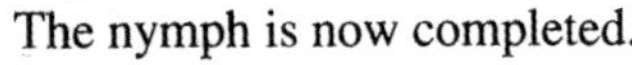

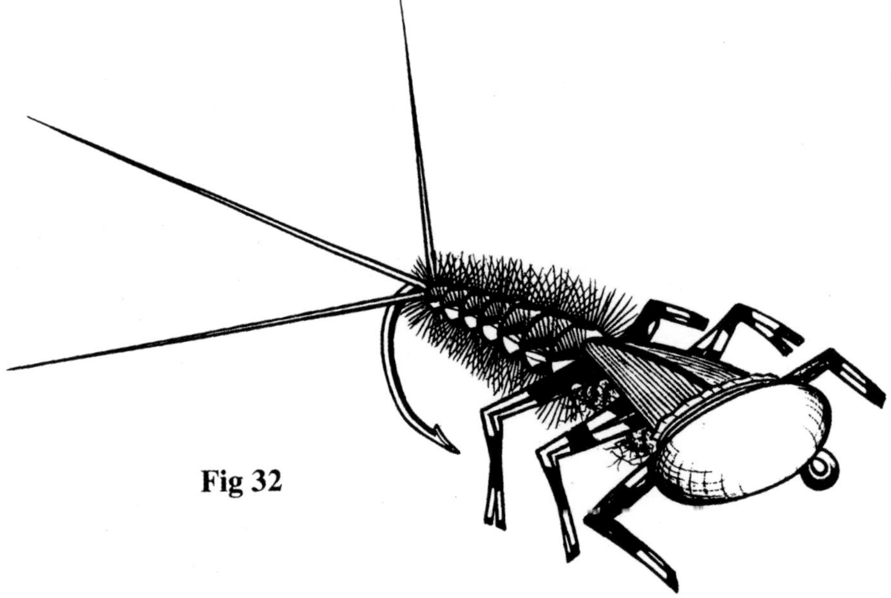

4. The Yellow May Emerger

The yellow may dun (*Heptagenia sulphurea*) is a most beautiful insect. Distribution is widespread throughout Britain and, from my own experience in Yorkshire, it is found in its greatest numbers as rivers flatten out in their middle to lower middle reaches. In other words, where the river is of good width and steady flow, interspersed with fast riffles. The species also has a preference for slightly calcareous water.

The yellow may is often quite wrongly called the 'yellow sally' - I suspect because it sounds a nice name and the insect is yellow! The yellow sally in fact belongs to an entirely different order of insects - it is a species of stonefly, a Plecopteran.

On the eastern side of the Pennines, we have good populations of the yellow may dun, for which we have to thank the North Craven Fault, that great upthrust of limestone which is so evident on the landscape as one travels up the river Aire to Malhamdale and again in Wharfedale in the Burnsall, Grassington and Kilnsey region.

The yellow may is also present on many of the southern chalkstreams as well as the Irish limestone loughs. The Irish yellow mays are particularly large specimens and are known as 'yellow hawks'.

My interest in the yellow may started many years ago. Yet my early readings told me that the fly was: 'of little or no interest to trout', 'rarely if ever taken', 'unpalatable'.

The Wharfe is heavily populated with the yellow may and since I have fished the middle and lower sections regularly for over twenty years, I have had plenty of opportunities to observe this lovely insect and the fishes' keen interest in it.

Emergence can start anytime from the last few days of April to as late as - in unfavourable weather - the first week of June. Usually though, by mid May, they are coming off regularly.

The yellow may is far from unpalatable and both trout and grayling and fast-water coarse fish take them. However the reaction of trout, in particular, to the yellow may dun is quite odd. Trout seem to be suddenly triggered into taking the duns and it seems that there is some other factor involved, other than pure numbers of duns riding down on the surface.

I don't pretend to have the answer as to what causes them to 'switch on' to the dun. Many times have I observed pods of trout knocking off every yellow may dun passing over them, yet on other occasions in seemingly identical conditions, the duns have floated away unmolested, eventually taking flight. I have witnessed similar trout reactions to other Ephemeropterans. Nevertheless, this stop-go reaction is most evident with the yellow may dun.

If there is one clue as to why on some days the dun is almost totally ignored, it could point to the emerger. The yellow may emerges from its nymphal form on the river bed, leaving the exuvia, the empty shuck, on a rock or stone.

As emergence time approaches the nymph becomes active, almost reckless, moving from its usual sheltered position on the underside of the rock or stone to the upper surface - exposed to current and predators! There it hooks its six single-clawed legs firmly into the rock and emergence takes place.

The creature which escapes the nymphal exuvia is neither nymph nor dun, it is in fact a true 'emerger'. Overall body length, excluding tails, varies between 5/16" and 3/8" (7-10mm), probably a gender difference. The abdomen tapers and occupies almost 2/3 of the overall length. The colour is pale primrose yellow and it is finely segmented. The thorax is short and stocky and has a pale orange tinge.

SOME NATURALS APPROPRIATE TO THIS PATTERN

BRITISH SPECIES:
Heptagenia sulphurea.
BRITISH FISHING NAMES:
Yellow May, Yellow May Dun,
Yellow Hawk (Ireland).

NORTH AMERICAN SPECIES:
Heptagenia minerva, Heptagenia hebe.
NORTH AMERICAN FISHING NAMES:
Little Evening Sulphur Dun,
Evening Yellow Dun.

The head of the emerger is wide (thorax width) but not as wide as the head capsule of the nymph. The two black eyes are very obvious against the pale creamy yellow head colour. The pale yellow legs are held in a particularly crumpled fashion; the middle pair probably propel the emerger towards the surface. There are two tails, grey-yellow, delicately ringed.

I have examined specimens whose embryo wings were quite short and stumpy, no more than 1/3 of the body's overall length, but also I have seen specimens with embryonic wings which had developed to more than 3/4 of the body length. I can only surmise that this difference of wing length demonstrates that they very rapidly expand as the emerger escapes its nymphal exuvia and heads for the surface. These uninflated wings are yellow with a light golden tinge and they are angled slightly downwards.

The emerger, on breaking through the surface film, must instantaneously pump its wings to their full size. They may in fact be at full expansion as the surface is reached! This act of breaking through the surface I have yet to observe at close quarters.

Wharfe trout love these pale emergers. I have caught trout in mid-June with a stomach-full. In fact over a five-year period of sampling I have rarely found a June fish which did not contain any of these emergers.

I have collected many samples, measured them and made notes regarding colour and form. This pattern is a fair copy of the natural, as far as size, colour and silhouette are concerned.

Note: At least one other Heptagenid escapes from its nymphal exuvia on the river bed. This is the dusky yellowstreak, sometimes known as the dark dun (*Heptagenia lateralis*).

NOTES ON MATERIALS AND TYING

'Swimming nymph' hooks are now commercially available. These are the types with an upward curve from mid-shank to the eye. You can, on the other hand, make your own by re-forming and this is the method I use. Bend the hook shank downward slightly then upward in a gentle sweeping curve, thus making a dip in the centre of the shank.

The lead foil is yet again from wine bottles, smoothed out, then cut into slivers. Lead wire is unsuitable as it invariably builds up too much bulk.

The introduction of a couple of turns of cul de canard is purely to give a little built-in movement and is not for its waterproof quality. Cul de canard feathers - plumes - can now be purchased in a wide variety of colours. If, when winding on the plume, you find that some of the individual barbs are a little too long then just nip them off between finger and thumb, do not snip them off. You should choose one of the smaller plumes.

For the legs, I use barbs from a wing quill of white hen (domestic). I dye these a pale yellow. Picric acid is not suitable. The colour you are looking for is a pale primrose. Any small white quill is worth experimenting with. However, do not be tempted to take your barbs from the leading

YELLOW MAY EMERGERS
Ventral and dorsal views, both in the long embryonic wing phase.

YELLOW MAY EMERGER DRESSING

Hook: Swimming nymph style or re-shaped curved nymph hook. Suggest Partridge 'Jardine Living Nymph Hook' Code GRS7MMB size 18 or 20 re-shaped.
Weight: Narrow strip of wine bottle lead foil.
Thread: Danville's 'Spider Web', untinted.
Cement: Dave's Flexament (USA) or Floo Gloo (UK), both thinned.
Tails: Stout, quick tapering, animal bristle, from a good quality shaving brush, dyed pale grey. Alternatives: moose mane, bleached elk or white deer, also dyed grey.
Abdomen: Clear polythene 0.008" (0.2mm) thick, or clear Flexibody. Under abdomen and head: Fine synthetic pale yellow dubbing, eg. Davy Wotton Finesse 'Masterclass' blend MC7.
Thorax: Fine synthetic dubbing pale orange-yellow eg. Davy Wotton Finesse 'Masterclass' blend 50/50 MC 7 and MC15.
Legs: Individual barbs from a white wing quill feather eg. domestic poultry, guinea fowl, duck, etc., dyed pale primrose yellow.
Hackle: Pale yellow cul-de-canard.
Embroyo wings: Pale yellow Raffene for long wing buds, golden yellow Raffene for short wing buds.
Head capsule cover: Pale yellow Raffene.

edge of a flight quill, these 'biot' barbs are too broad and hard.

If you have problems obtaining Flexibody, clear polythene is an acceptable substitute.

The eyes on this pattern are, of course, optional. However, the filament of black mono is used for constructing the broad head, so why not use it for the eyes too? It doesn't need heat-balling, the mono is simply snipped off to reveal its cross section.

Tying the Yellow May Emerger

Fig 1
Grip the hook firmly in the vice, then wrap on the lead foil ballast. It pays to touch the shank with superglue before wrapping on the lead, which should occupy the central section of the shank. Lightly cocoon over the lead with thread, say once or twice up and down the shank. Let the bobbin holder hang off the lead at the bend.

Fig 2
Now tie in two tails, one on either side of the shank. Hold in position and tie in with two or three 'pinch and loops'.

Fig 3
Adjust the tails so that the amount of overhang is about half the body length. When satisfied, bind them down tightly, making sure that they stay on either side. Angle the hook down slightly when doing this so that you can take the tail bindings a little way around the bend.

Fig 4
Tie the Flexibody strip in by its fine tip exactly at the last tail binding. Next, spin on to the thread a tight tapering spindle of dubbing, the fine end at the tail.

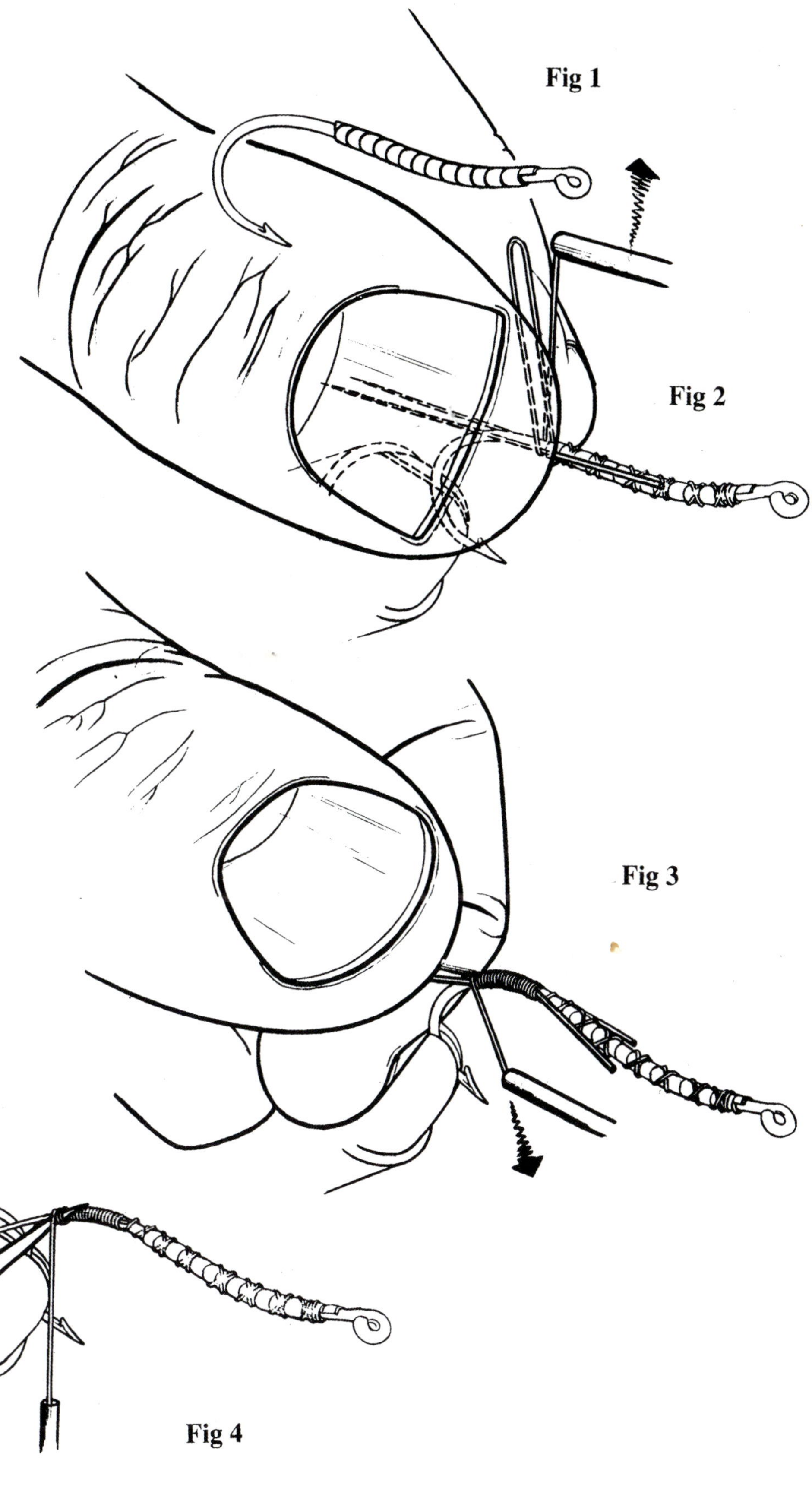

Fig 5
Wrap on this dubbing spindle in touching turns to cover about $^2/_3$ of the hook shank.

Fig 6
Follow this by overwrapping the Flexibody strip, ensuring that each new turn slightly overlaps the previous one, exactly as we did for the Baetis nymph (see page 9). Tie off the Flexibody at the end of the dubbed abdomen and trim off waste.

Fig 7
Strip off four stout feather barbs of about $^3/_4$" (20mm) in length. Align their tips and offer them up to the underside exactly where the Flexibody is tied off. Make two or three 'pinch and loops' to secure.

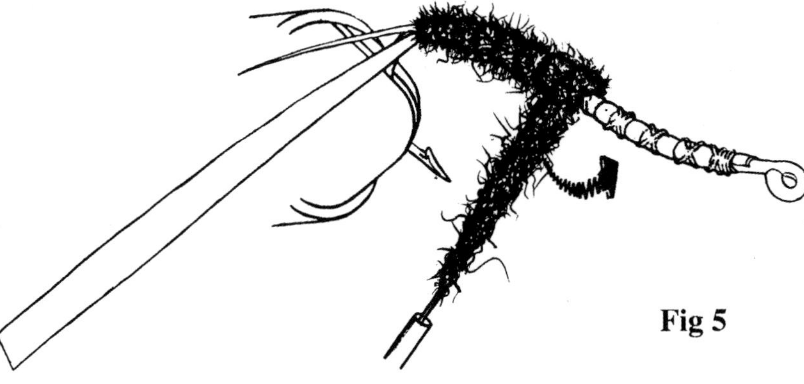

Fig 5

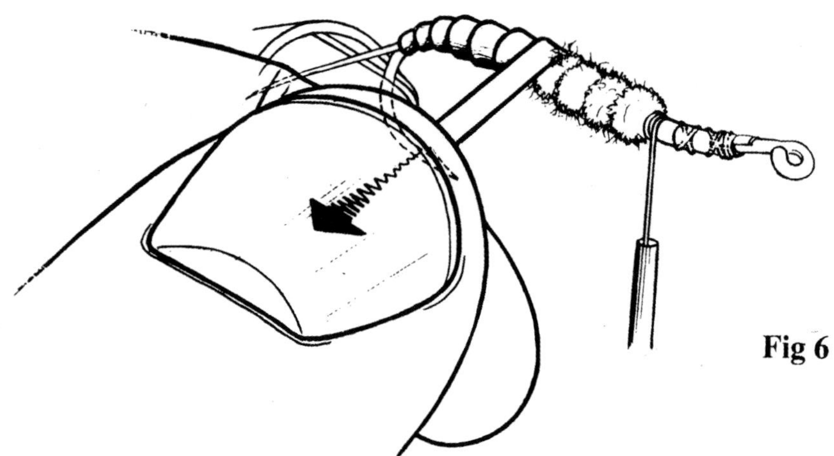

Fig 6

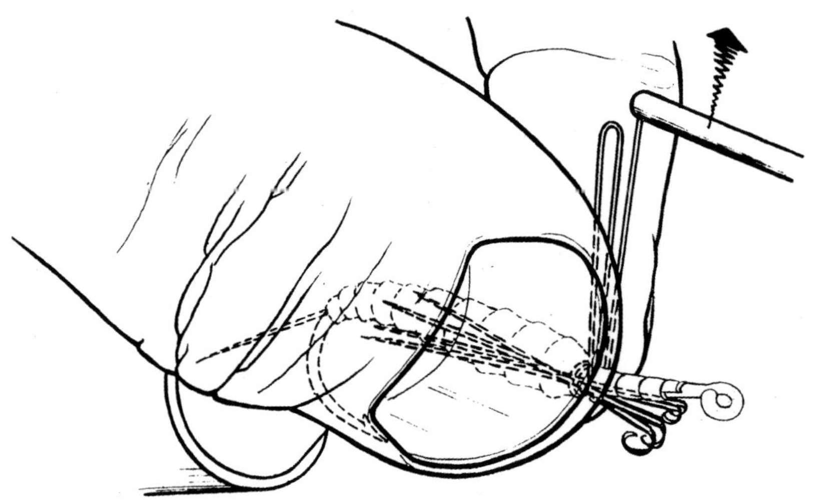

Fig 7

Figs 8 & 9
Now unclamp the hook, turn upside down and reclamp again. Then with thumb nail pressure, and a side to side rocking motion, separate the four legs into two pairs, spreading them quite widely. Secure with several tight turns of thread. Perfect symmetry is not necessary.

Fig 10
Raise the legs by taking a fine spindle of dubbing behind them - one turn should suffice.

Fig 11
Continue to wrap on the dubbing in front of the legs for one turn. Unclamp, return the hook to the vice the right way up and clamp again.

Fig 12
For the embryonic wings, I once again use Raffene, or Swiss Straw as it is known in the States. Take a 2" (50mm) length, open it out and cut off a strip 3/16" (4mm) wide. Fold it lengthwise, full length, creasing it tightly.

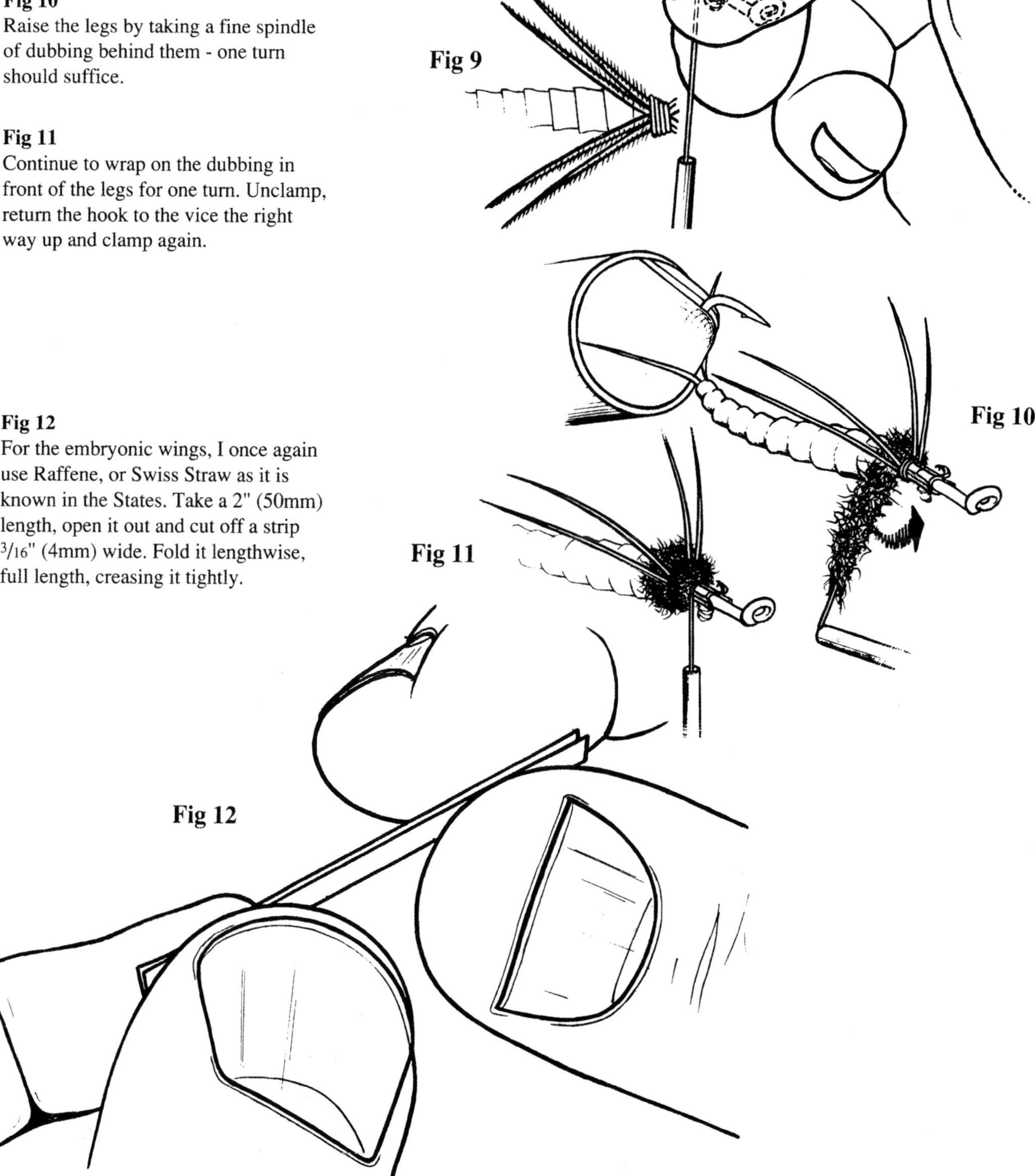

Fig 13
Then fold the strip equally, to make a pair of narrow wings. Offer these up to the top of the shank, lengthwise crease uppermost, and tie in where the dubbing ends.

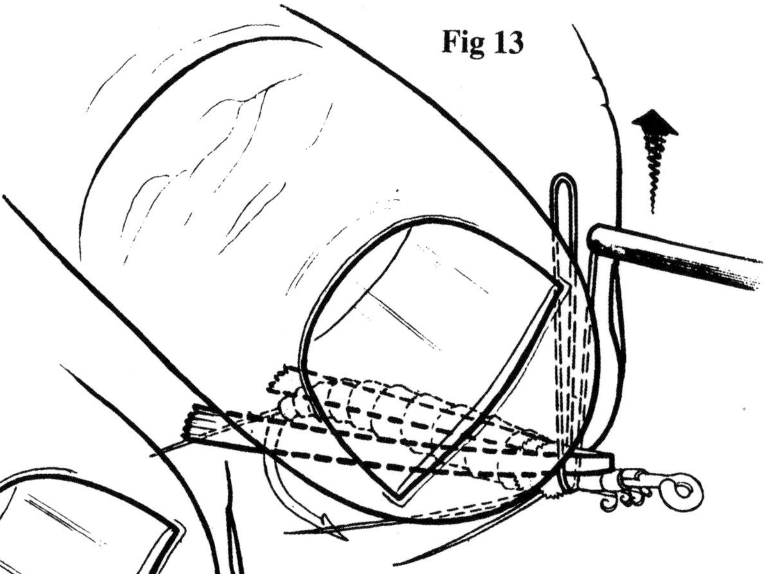

Fig 14
Angle them downwards slightly. 'Pinch and loop' two or three times followed by several more tight wraps of thread.

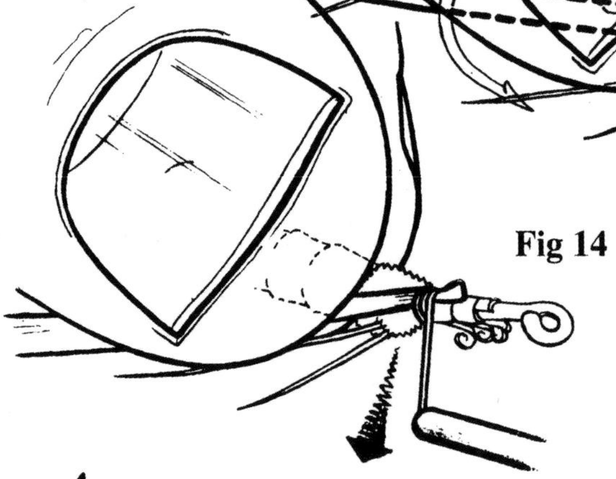

Fig 15
Next trim the ends of the Raffene so that both wings are about three quarters of the body length. Tie in a single cul de canard feather, by the tip end. Trap it on top with the tip of the index finger nail while a turn or two of thread is taken around.

Fig 16
Wrap on the cul de canard plume making no more than two full turns.

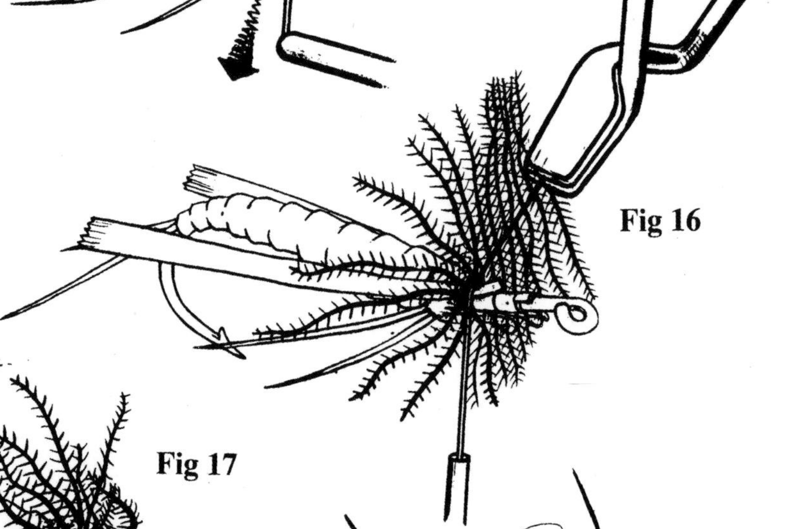

Fig 13

Fig 14

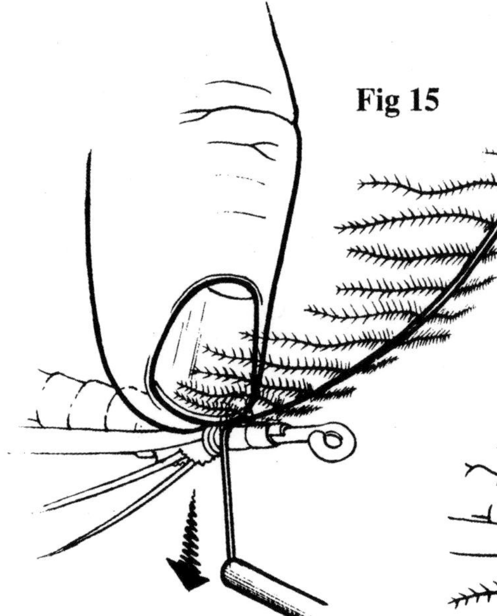

Fig 16

Fig 17

Fig 18

Fig 17
Secure it and trim off the waste end.

Fig 18
The wide head capsule is next. Take a 1" (25mm) length of Raffene, open it out and cut off a strip approximately 3/16" (4mm) wide. Gather in one end and tie it on top of the shank using the 'pinch and loop' method, the tying in point being tight up to the back of the hook eye.

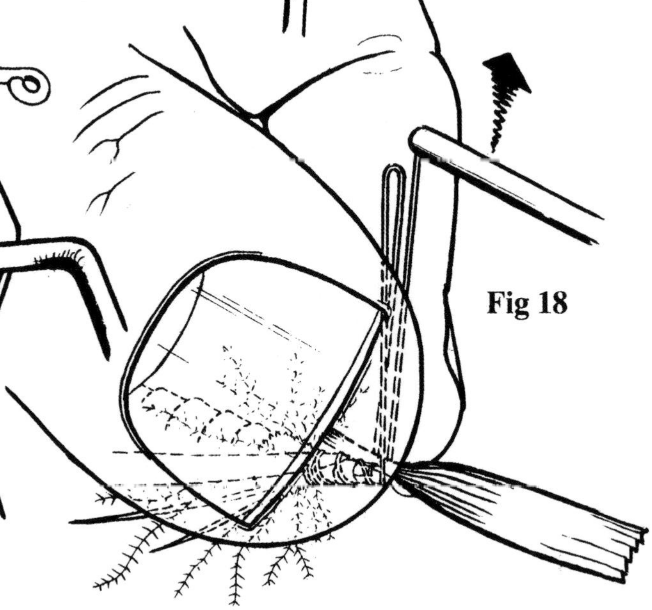

Fig 19
The head capsule is formed around a short length of black nylon monofilament of 10-15lbs BS. This mono is tied in figure-of-eight fashion on top of the shank, just a little way back from the hook eye.

Fig 20
Spin on another fine spindle of dubbing and work this around the nylon mono, figure-of-eighting it above and below the head.

Fig 21
When fully dubbed, flood with a flexible head cement.

Fig 22
While the cement is sticky, pull over the Raffene and tie it down tightly at the back of the head.

Fig 23
Continue binding down the Raffene working back to the base of the wings.

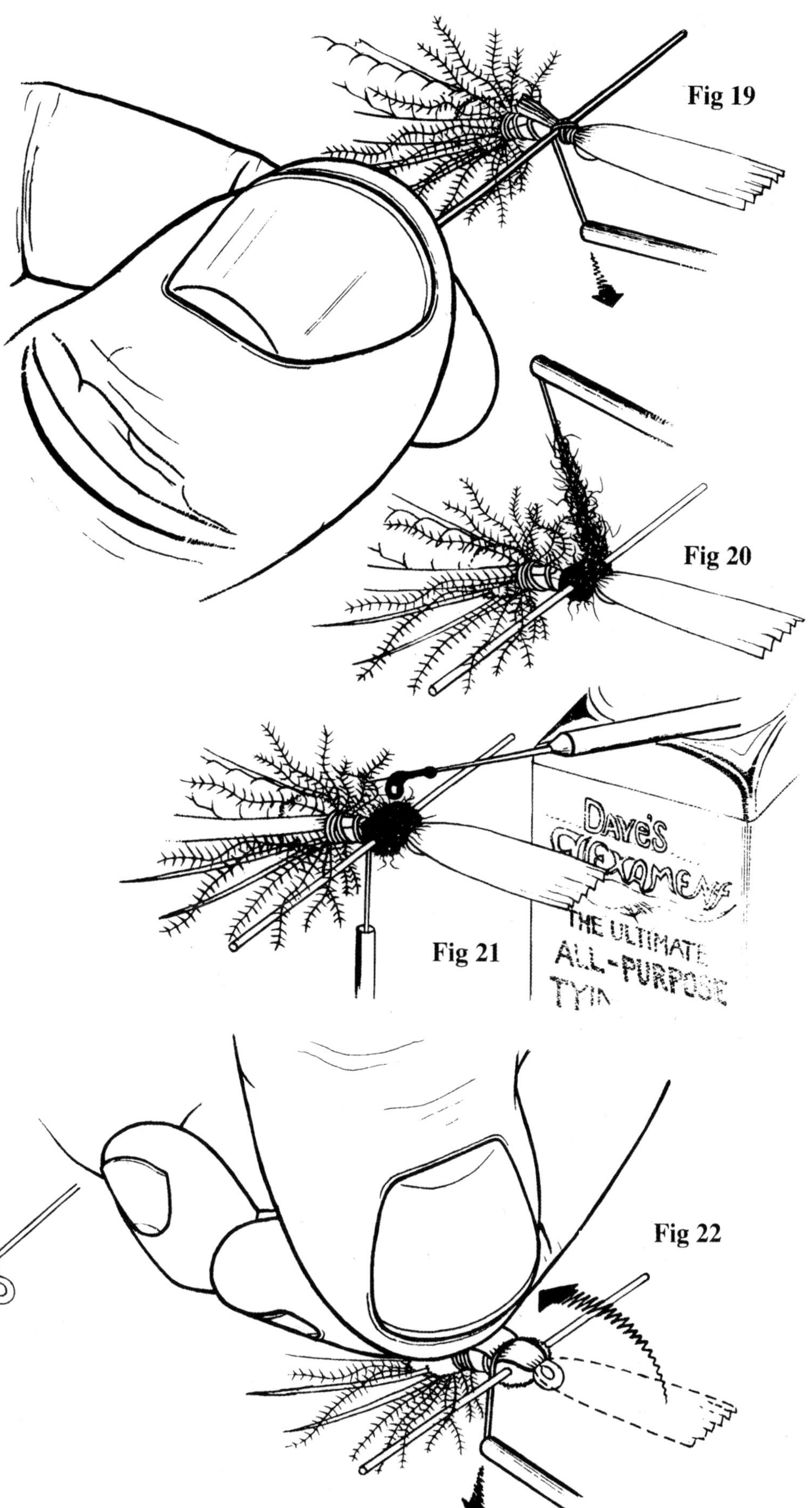

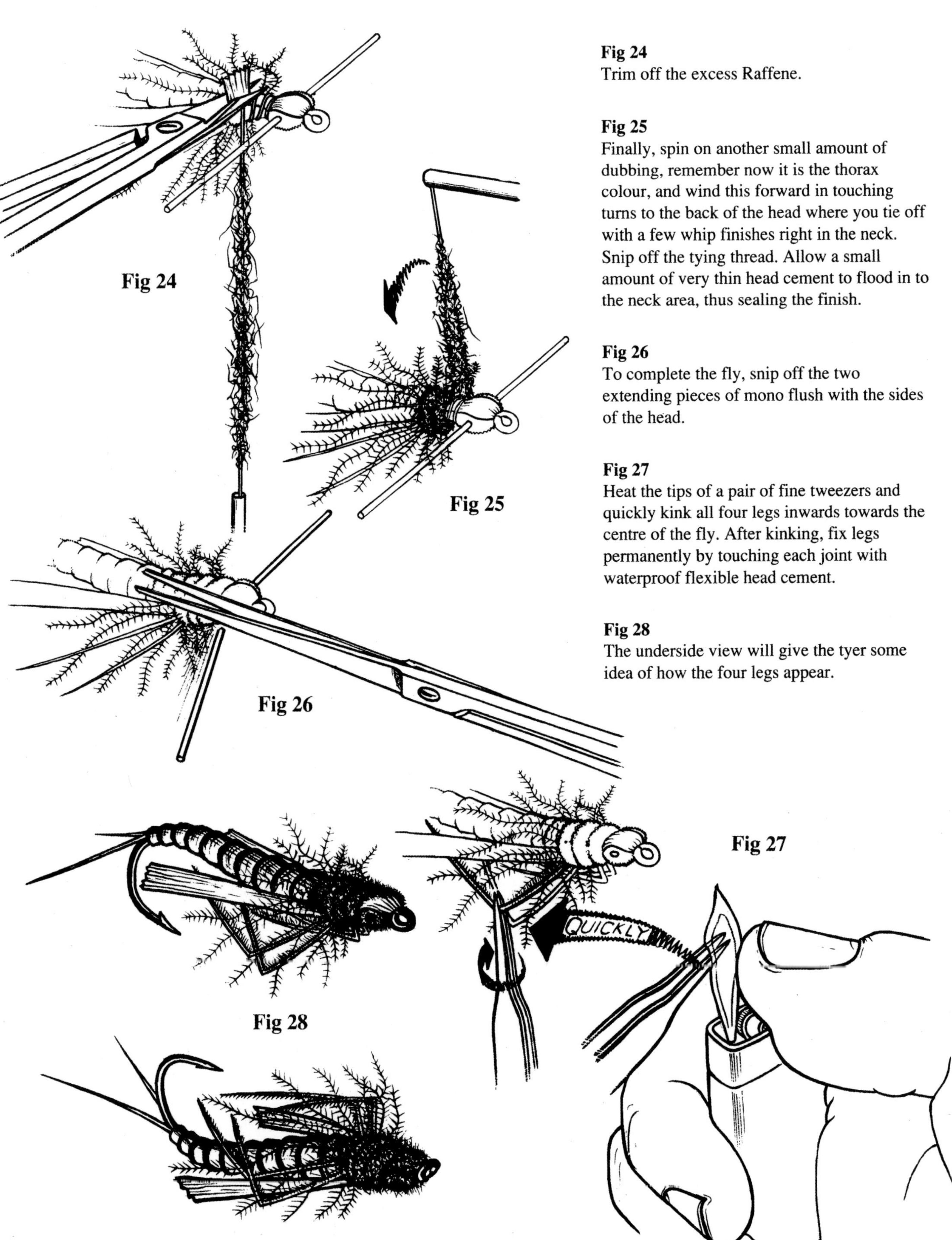

Fig 24

Fig 25

Fig 26

Fig 27

Fig 28

Fig 24
Trim off the excess Raffene.

Fig 25
Finally, spin on another small amount of dubbing, remember now it is the thorax colour, and wind this forward in touching turns to the back of the head where you tie off with a few whip finishes right in the neck. Snip off the tying thread. Allow a small amount of very thin head cement to flood in to the neck area, thus sealing the finish.

Fig 26
To complete the fly, snip off the two extending pieces of mono flush with the sides of the head.

Fig 27
Heat the tips of a pair of fine tweezers and quickly kink all four legs inwards towards the centre of the fly. After kinking, fix legs permanently by touching each joint with waterproof flexible head cement.

Fig 28
The underside view will give the tyer some idea of how the four legs appear.

5. The Emerging Dun

While much is known about the Ephemeroptera - the mayflies - one aspect still remains lightly studied. This is the act of emergence or eclosion. Here huge problems confront the field researcher. How can he observe an individual nymph of a riffle-dwelling species, following one to the surface, photographing, noting, recording its every movement until the creature eventually takes flight? A virtual impossibility in the wild.

A large pumped aquarium may seem the answer. But the observer would need to be blessed with cat-like reflexes to be ready with the shutter release the instant he suspected a nymph was about to head for the surface.

Maybe things could be made more ultra high-tech with automatic cameras, tripped by movement detectors: but at what cost, and funded by whom, and for whose benefit? Nymphs emerge into duns, all flyfishermen know that - so what!

Ten or twelve years ago, the word 'emerger' had hardly entered the parlance of the British flyfisher. However, during the past few years, we have been bombarded by it, and now 'emerger' is the buzz word on every flyfisher's lips. Today we have emerger mayflies, emerger stoneflies, emerger caddis, as well as emerger midges.

It has always puzzled me why the mayfly emerger patterns of North American origin as well as some from British tyers are usually tied as short-winged wets and fished sub-surface, as wets. I'm puzzled because, with few exceptions, the nymphs of the swimmer/darter and the swimmer/clinger groups swim or are buoyed all the way to the surface and during this journey they display no sign of metamorphosis. In other words, they are intact nymphs, albeit very ripe ones.

What happens at the surface, the act of emerging or eclosion, is one of nature's miracles. The ripe nymph takes on a semi horizontal position then pushes its thorax through the surface film - sometimes with great physical effort. Next, the skin of the mesothorax splits open on the centre line. The split goes through to the back of the head. The next stage of emergence can be very rapid - two blinks and you may miss it. First, the front part of the thorax and the head pull clear. Almost simultaneously, the rest of the thorax and the wings appear, as though being pushed smoothly upwards by hydraulic pressure. The wings are 'pumped' to full size almost instantly and the act is completed by a rapid withdrawal of the legs, abdomen and finally tails from the nymphal shuck.

The newly-emerged dun now scoots sideways a few millimetres off the empty nymphal shuck. Surface tension pulls it down a minute menisus incline or ramp which forms around the edge of the shuck. The new dun and empty shuck then drift with the current. The dun's wings under ideal conditions are drying and hardening rapidly. It may take to flight almost immediately. However, it often stays afloat for a few minutes and, in some weather conditions - cold, wind and rain - the dun may ride the current a long way unless, of course, it is eaten by a waiting trout.

Why then, do we ever fish emergers subsurface? And why do we adorn these emergers with stumpy, backward-sloping wings? It just does not make sense to me! Yes, of course such patterns will catch trout, but in my view these sunken 'emergers' are simply mistaken for nymphs by the trout.

So, do any of the nymphs of the Ephemeroptera cast their shucks underwater? According to field research in the UK we have one: the dusky yellowstreak (*Heptagenia lateralis*). However, my own observations suggest that at least one other Heptagenid slips its nymphal shuck underwater. This is the yellow may dun (*Heptagenia sulphurea*). I have observed this striking insect every summer and many times have watched how trout react to it. It was while examining stomach contents of fish that I discovered the yellow may emerger (see Chapter 4) and realised that our Wharfe trout feed heavily on them.

As far as I know, these two Heptagenia species are the only ones in the UK which shed their nymphal shuck on or near the stream bed. Once out of the shuck the emerger then heads for the surface. The nymph has metamorphosed. Now the abdomen is longer and narrower, the characteristic broad half-disc of the head has slimmed down considerably, and the distinctive colour of the dun is also present. However, one feature above all others puts it in the category of true emerger: the short slipper-shaped, backward-sloping embryonic wings. Gone are the dark wing buds of the nymph, replaced by these tiny uninflated wings.

Now and again, while fishing, a yellow may dun has popped up on the surface quite near me, once right by my waders, yet never have I found the empty shuck! They just break through the meniscus with their wings virtually full size.

The pattern under discussion here is in fact an emerging dun, a pattern to be fished *in* the surface film. The short cul-de-canard wing will hold an air bubble if you tug the fly under, which then pops back above the surface again when you release tension on the leader. The two bands of expanded foam also lend a hand in supporting the fly. However, the main role of this foam is to simulate the glistening rim formed around the splitting thorax of the nymph as the dun emerges. This phenomenon was first publicised by the American flyfisherman/entomologist Gary Lafontaine, who aptly named it the 'halo effect'.

This pattern, tied in the appropriate colour and to the correct size, will cover the whole gamut of those mayflies which rise to the surface as a nymph, then while *in* the surface film complete metamorphosis into the dun, be they European or American.

NOTES ON MATERIALS AND DRESSING

This pattern is suitable for all European and North American small to medium sized surface-emerging Ephemeroptera.

I have formed the abdomen by using the tightly-twisted yarn technique. Basically it's a question of matching the yarn colour - when wet, remember - to the abdomen colour of the natural.

Remember too you are striving for lightness, so leave out wire ribbing. A fine wire rib can amount to about 20% of the weight of a size 18 wire hook.

As with many of my patterns, I have used hair for the tails rather than feather barbs. Good, stout, finely-tapering hair, such as moose body, provides

EMERGING DUN DRESSING

Hook: Medium wire 2x to 3x longshank or curved shank. Suggest Partridge 'Capt. Hamilton Nymph' Code H1A size 16 or 18 or Partridge 'Oliver Edwards Nymph/Emerger' Code K14ST size 16,18,20.
Thread: Danville's 'Spider Web'.
Cement: Dave's Flexament (USA) or Floo Gloo (UK), both thinned.
Tails: Dark moose body hairs (left grey or dyed olive), or dark speckled barbs from a partridge tail quill feather for the Blue Winged Olive (European).
Abdomen: 4-ply knitting yarn, 100% synthetic or synthetic and natural blend, preferably with the addition of Antron or similar reflective sparkle fibres. Colour to suit natural you wish to copy.
Thorax: As abdomen.
Splitting thorax membrane: Shiny, clear, closed-cell foam (packaging material).
Emerging wing: Natural grey or dun cul-de-canard.
Legs: Natural grey or dun cul-de-canard. A few fibres from the emerging wing.

strong, well-defined tails. Such hair holds the 'splay', one of the essential triggers, much better than feather barbs.

Wings of cul-de-canard will not support much hook weight, but it is a marvellous wing material to use on *small* mayfly, caddis and midge patterns. These insects, particularly the mayflies and midges, have wings usually light to dark grey (slate grey being probably the most common). So cul-de-canard feathers taken from the wild bird are perfect, since those from wild duck are predominantly in the grey to dun brown range.

On small patterns, say sizes 18 to 22, I find it necessary to use two whole feathers. On sizes 14 and 16, three are better. When you pull the two or three feathers through the tying thread, you gather and bundle the outer barbs towards the centre. The finished short wing is composed of many of these outer barbs plus the very tip of each feather.

Each barb on these extraordinary feathers is 'clothed' with tiny hair-like barbules, giving each barb a herl-like appearance. At the base of each barbule, some experts say there is a microscopic amount of the duck's preen gland excretion. However, current thinking is that it is the total number of free-standing barbules in any given wing clump which provides the feather with its flotation quality.

Tying the Emerging Dun

Fig 1
Grip the hook in the vice with the shank very slightly tilted. Attach the tying thread at approximately mid-shank position and run it in open turns to the start of the bend. Let the bobbin holder hang. Now snip out three moose body hairs, align the tips, then offer the three hairs up to the top of the shank as a bundle. They should project about half the shank length.

Fig 2
Change hands and tie the hairs in using the 'pinch and loop' method. Now securely lash them down and return the thread to the base of the tails. Snip off the waste.

Fig 3
Next, force the outer tails to splay by pushing in to their base with the tip of your thumbnail.

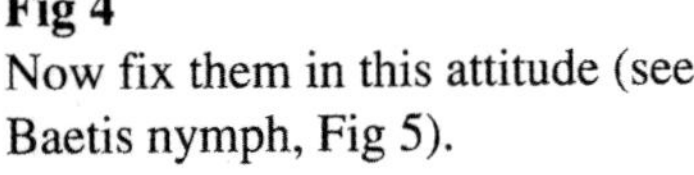

Fig 4
Now fix them in this attitude (see Baetis nymph, Fig 5).

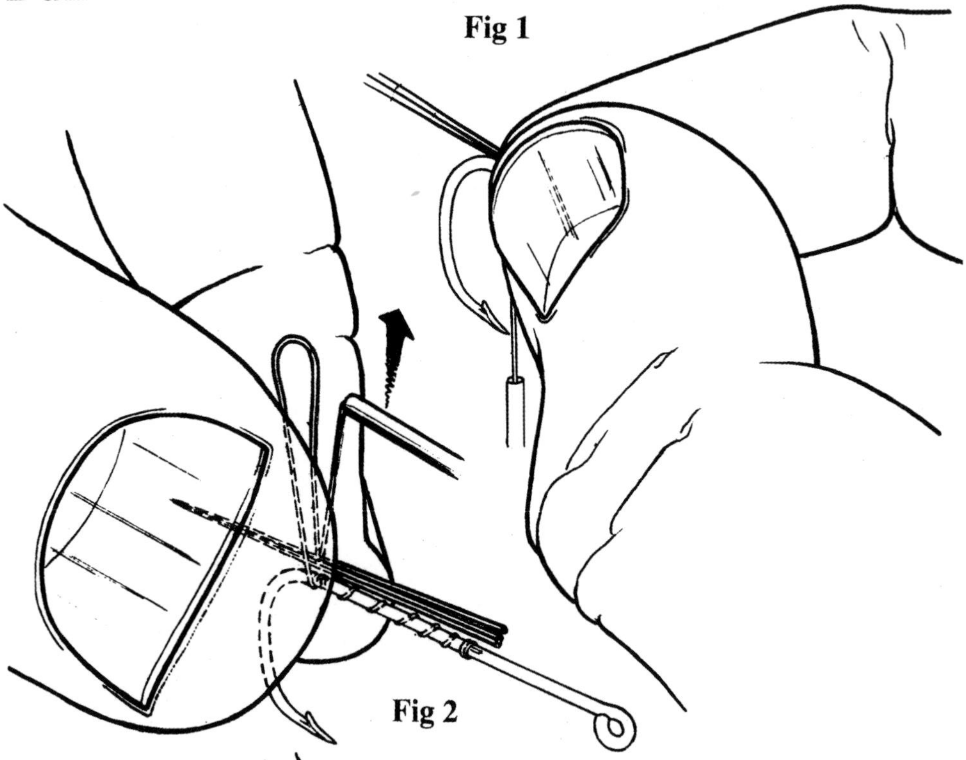

Fig 1

Fig 2

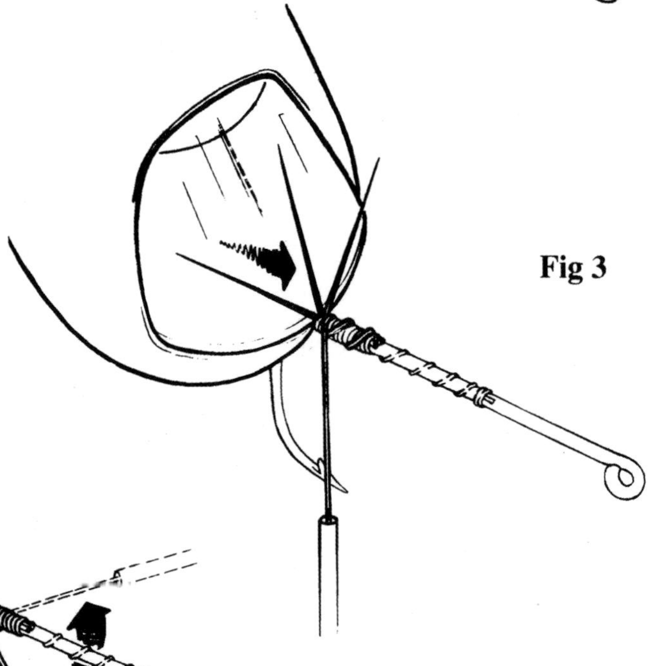

Fig 3

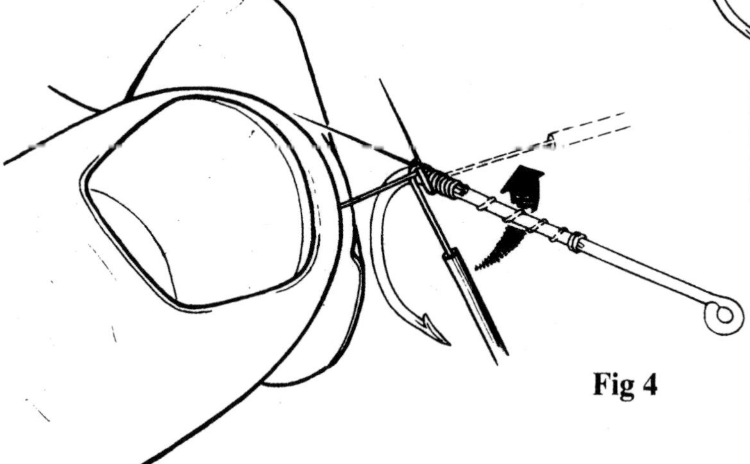

Fig 4

EMERGING DUNS

(Top to bottom) Blue-Winged Olive - Pale Watery/Spurwing - Large Dark Olive

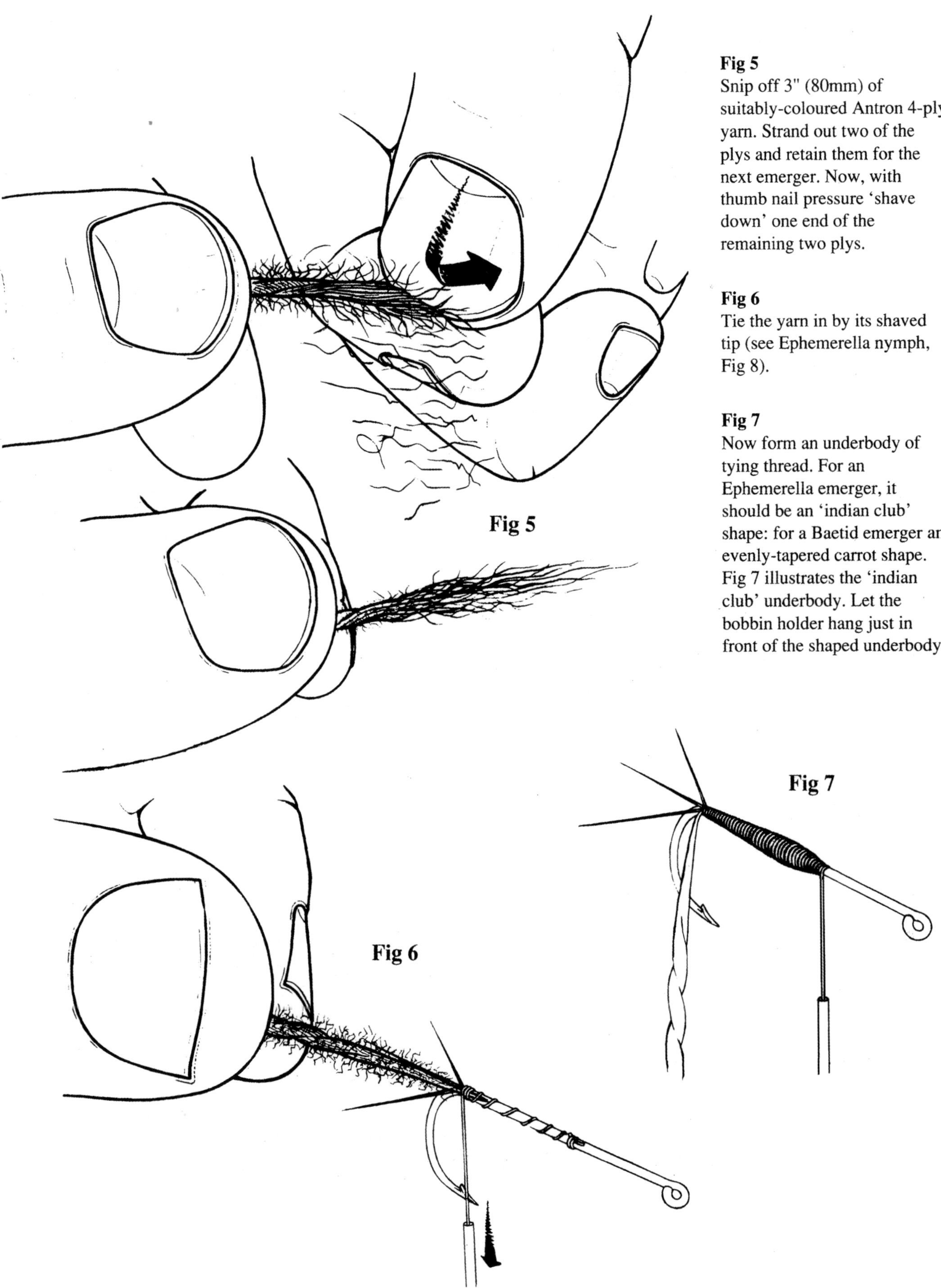

Fig 5
Snip off 3" (80mm) of suitably-coloured Antron 4-ply yarn. Strand out two of the plys and retain them for the next emerger. Now, with thumb nail pressure 'shave down' one end of the remaining two plys.

Fig 6
Tie the yarn in by its shaved tip (see Ephemerella nymph, Fig 8).

Fig 7
Now form an underbody of tying thread. For an Ephemerella emerger, it should be an 'indian club' shape: for a Baetid emerger an evenly-tapered carrot shape. Fig 7 illustrates the 'indian club' underbody. Let the bobbin holder hang just in front of the shaped underbody.

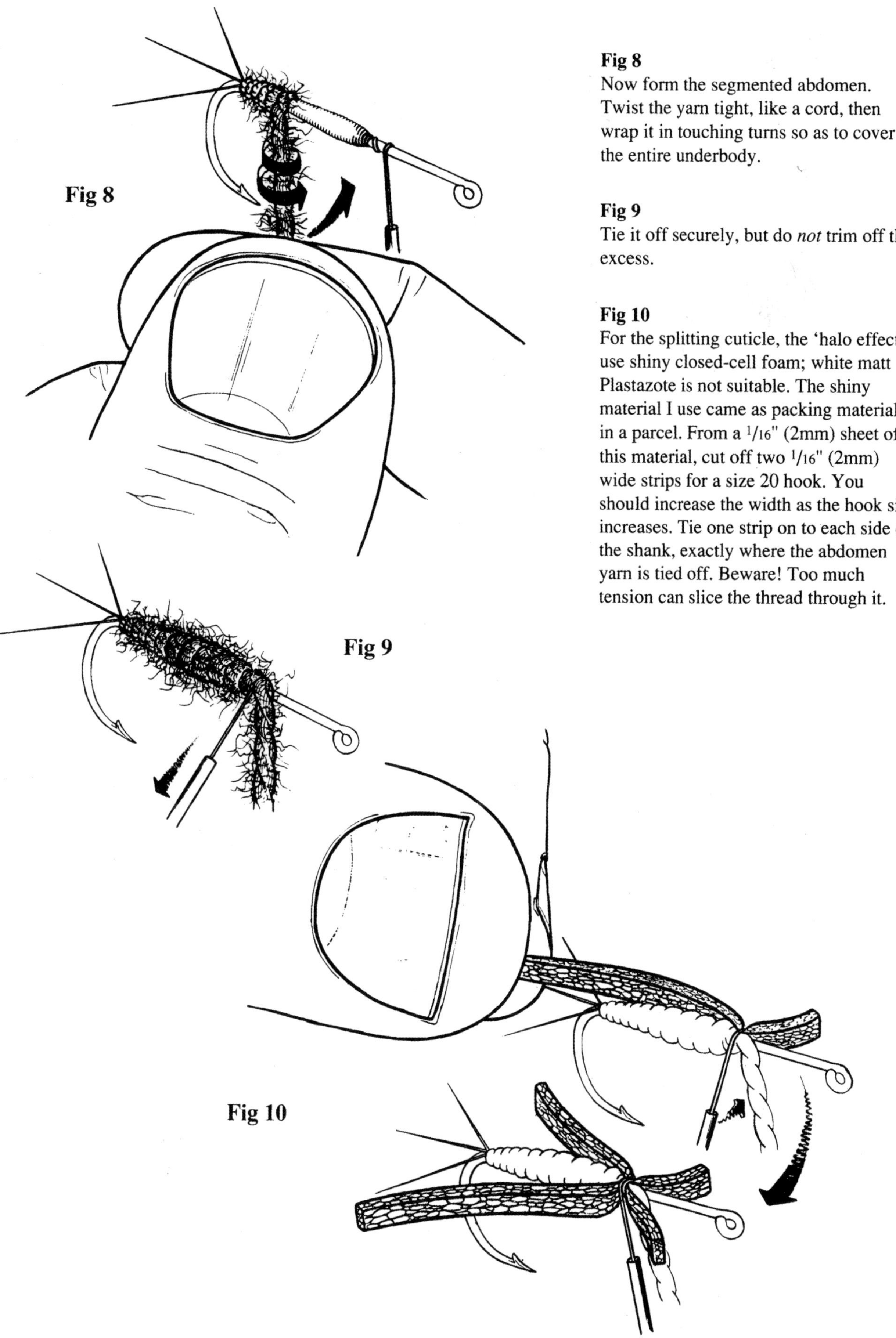

Fig 8
Now form the segmented abdomen. Twist the yarn tight, like a cord, then wrap it in touching turns so as to cover the entire underbody.

Fig 9
Tie it off securely, but do *not* trim off the excess.

Fig 10
For the splitting cuticle, the 'halo effect', use shiny closed-cell foam; white matt Plastazote is not suitable. The shiny material I use came as packing material in a parcel. From a 1/16" (2mm) sheet of this material, cut off two 1/16" (2mm) wide strips for a size 20 hook. You should increase the width as the hook size increases. Tie one strip on to each side of the shank, exactly where the abdomen yarn is tied off. Beware! Too much tension can slice the thread through it.

Fig 11
Trim off waste ends.

Fig 12
Run the tying thread forwards a few turns. Twist the yarn tight again.

Fig 13
Make two further turns of the yarn. Tie off the yarn, but don't trim off the excess. Let the bobbin holder hang.

Figs 14 & 15
Now for the cul-de-canard. Take two or three whole feathers, lay one on top of the other, aligned. Offer them up on top of the shank, exactly where the last thread wraps are, with the quill butts towards the hook eye. Take two fairly tight turns of thread around the quills.

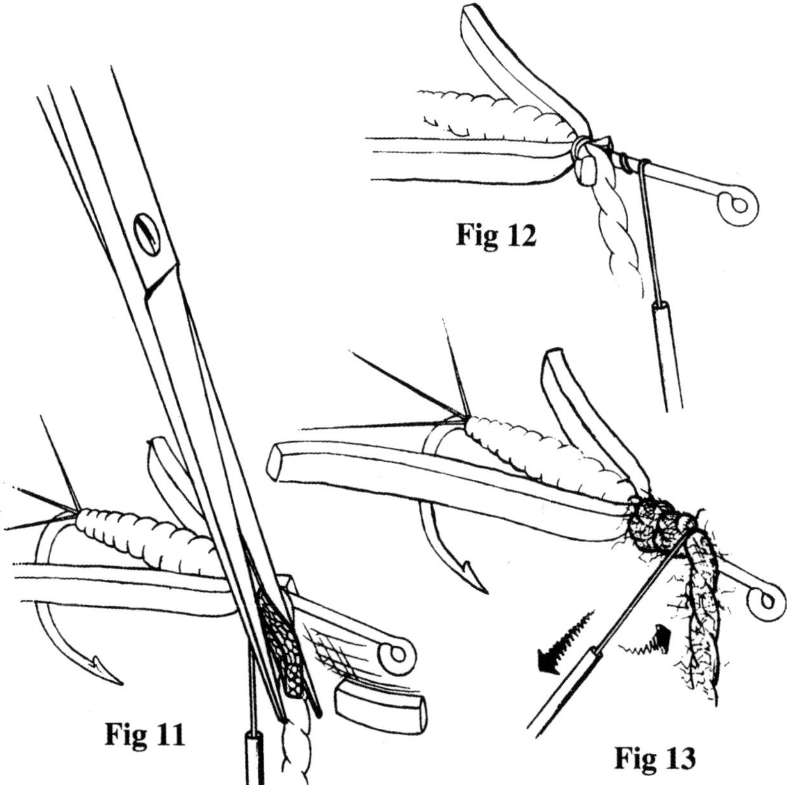

Fig 12

Fig 11

Fig 13

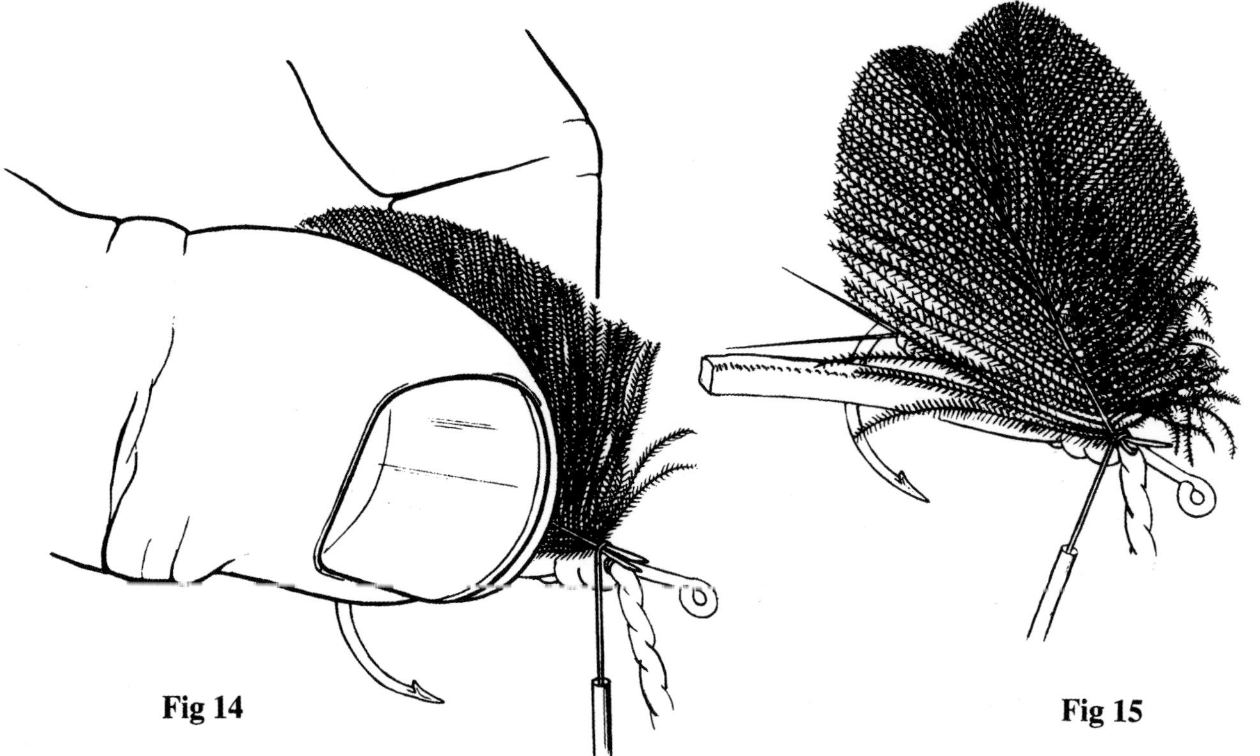

Fig 14

Fig 15

Fig 16
Then, grasp all the quill butts and pull the feathers through the thread smoothly. Stop when you have a wing which is about 3/4 the shank length. Tie them off securely. Don't trim off the waste quill butts yet.

Fig 17
Advance the tying thread a few more turns, followed by two more turns of the twisted yarn. Both the tying thread and the twisted yarn now wrap over the quill butts of cul-de-canard. Tie off the twisted yarn and trim off the waste, but still do not trim off the cul-de-canard butts.

Fig 18
Bring forward the foam strips, keep them at the side, avoid stretching them and tie each one off exactly where the yarn has just been tied off.

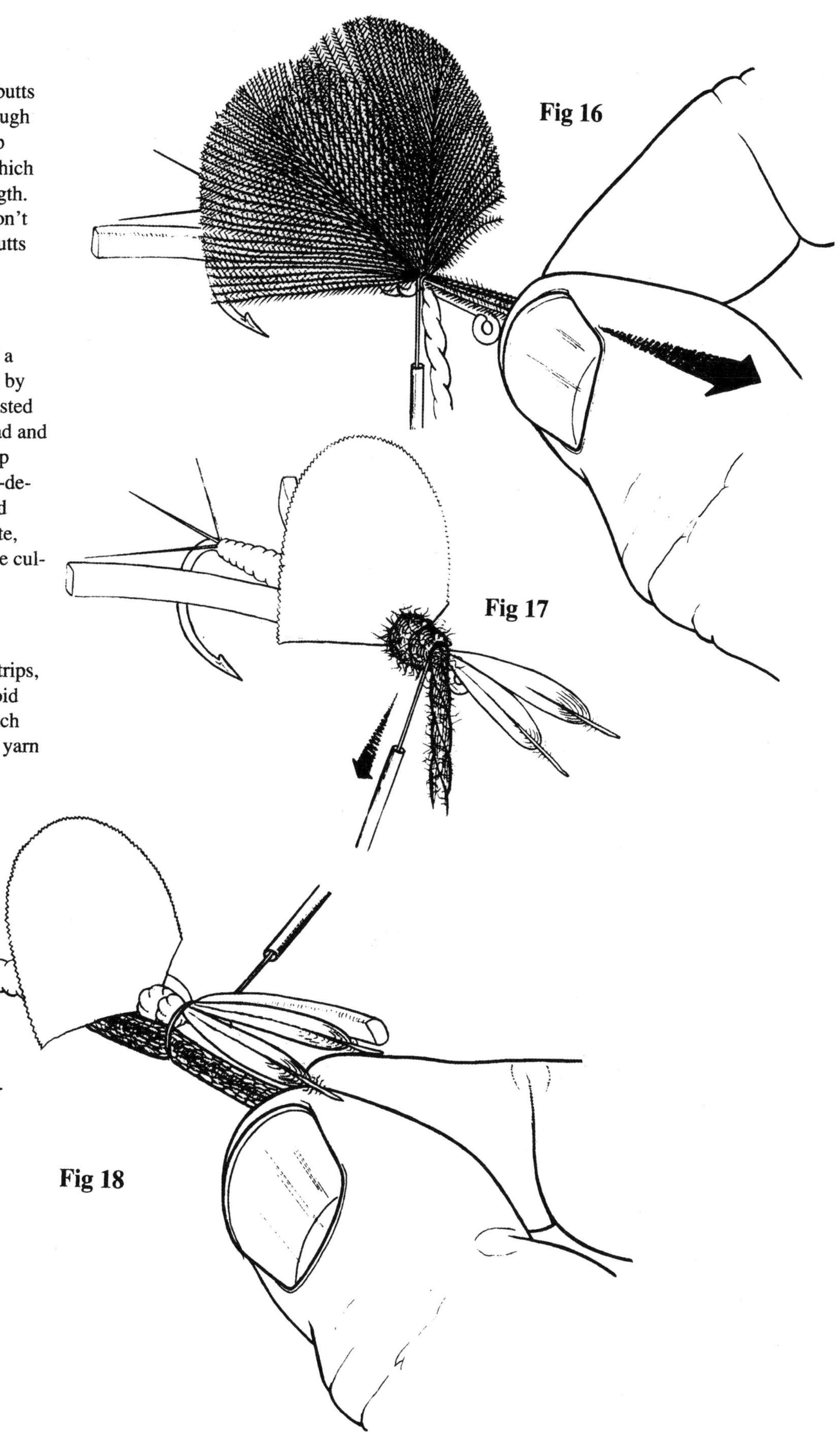

Fig 19
Trim waste ends of foam. You should now have two shiny crescents on each side of the thorax.

Fig 20
Finally, snip through the centre quill of the cul-de-canard feathers, cutting through just in front of the thread wraps. You should also cut through most of the remaining barbs, but leave four or five barbs on each side uncut.

Fig 21
These you sever where they attach to the centre quill so that you have four or five short barbs projecting forward on either side of the hook eye.

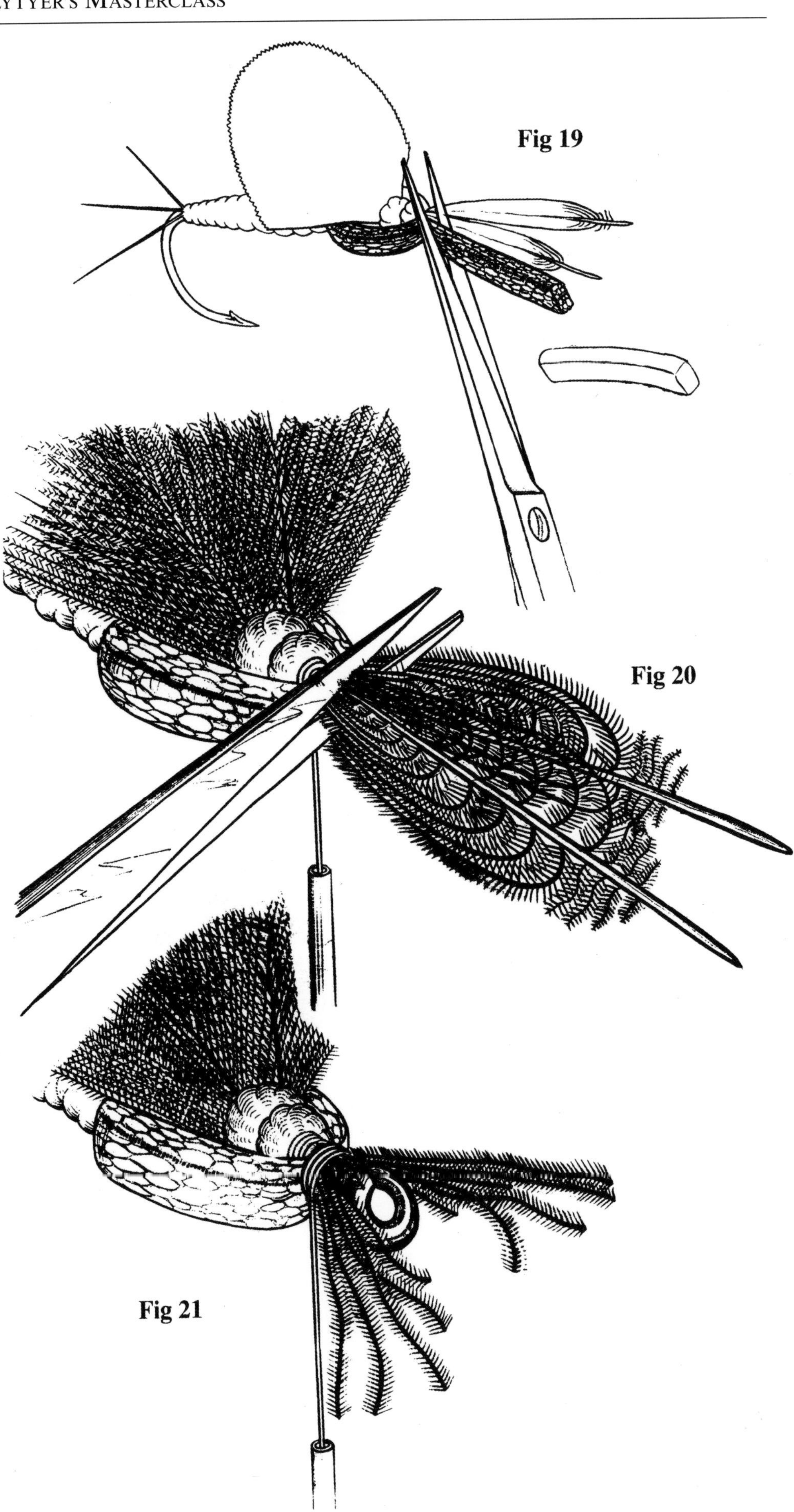
Fig 19
Fig 20
Fig 21

Figs 22 & 23
Then, with finger and thumb, simply push these backwards at an angle, and fix them in this position with a few turns of thread.

Fig 24
Form a small neat head, whip finish, trim off the thread and apply cement.

Note! Never, ever, grease or treat cul-de-canard feathers with a floatant. When, eventually, your fly becomes waterlogged, blowing on it or rapid false casting will snap the water out in nine cases out of ten. If this fails, simply tie on a fresh fly.

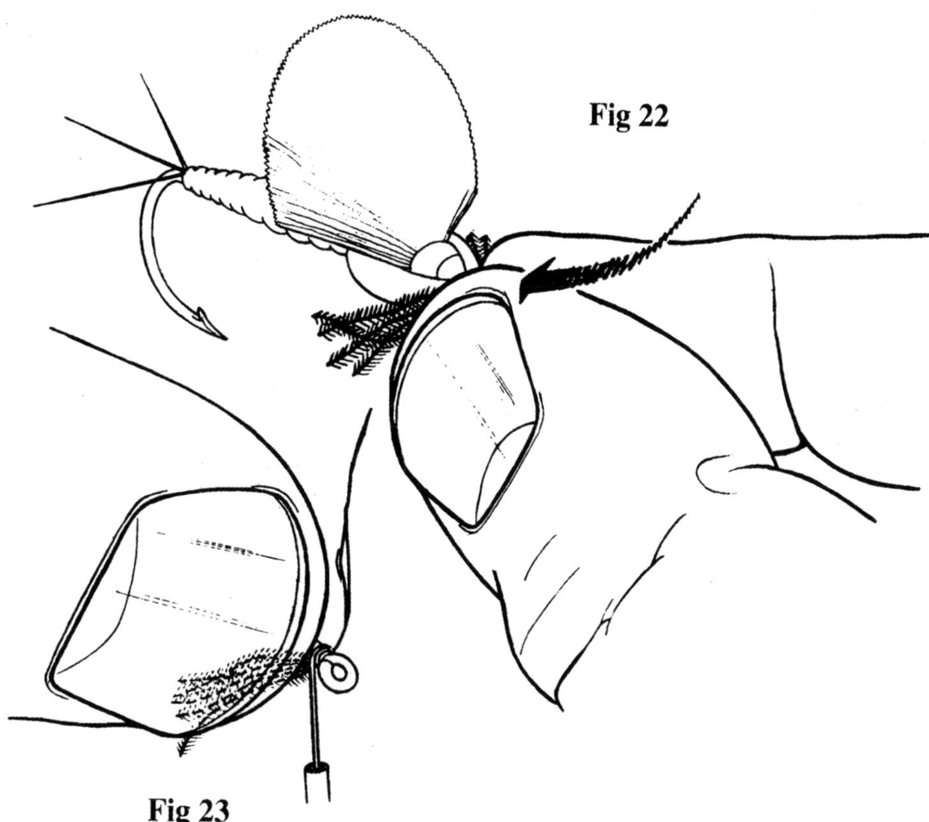

Fig 22

Fig 23

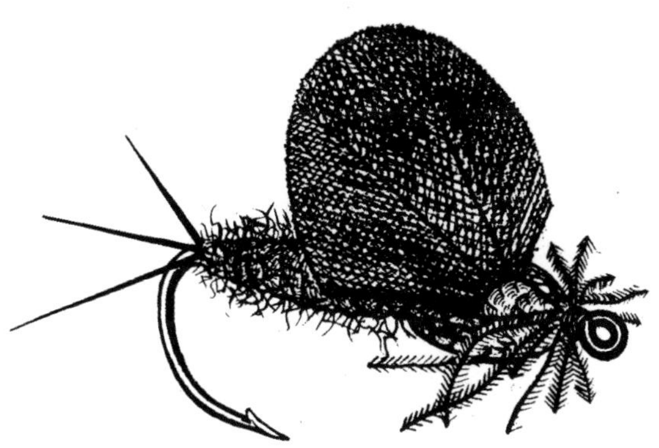

Fig 24

CUT WING DUNS

(Top left) March Brown - showing unique body and tails construction.
(Top right) Large Dark Olive *(Bottom)* Large Spurwing/Pale Watery

6. The Cut-Wing Dun

I first saw this dry fly in 1977 when I bought a copy of Poul Jorgensen's *Modern Fly Dressings for the Practical Angler*. I was most taken by the well-shaped, upright wings and the cunning way the extended body was constructed.

The wings, shaped from whole feathers, I had seen before but the reverse-feather barb *body* extension was new to me. I knew of reversing feather barbs for making wings - the method has been used by British flydressers for quite some time. In the States, however, reverse feather barb bodies, complete with self tails, have been around since the late 1950s and are attributed to that famous American flydresser Harry Darbee of Livingstone Manor, New York. Somehow, they had eluded me for twenty years or so.

As a winged pattern this style has one major advantage over dry flies tied with conventional feather slip wings. Such wings - either cut to shape or produced by the wing-burner method - are far more robust and hold their shape much better, even after the maulings of several fish. When they finally become bedraggled, they can still be primped back to a reasonable shape - after drying, of course. The old feather slip wings popularised by Halford, on the other hand, become quite useless once they have been really chomped. They lose their shape hopelessly and can rarely be coaxed back.

My early trials with this new 'discovery' were very frustrating though, for rarely could I avoid that perennial problem - propellering - causing dramatic leader twist.

One of the contributary factors to the leader twist problem is line speed. The faster the delivery the more exaggerated the twist, and dry fly casting is often high-speed. When I used a leisurely delivery, akin to the more open loop of a wetfly cast, I could often get away with it. However, if a downstream breeze got up, forcing me to speed up my casting a little, back came leader twist.

There are two design problems with wings of this style. The first is the outward curve of the wings when finally tied in position. Obviously the less divergent the wings, the less the twisting problem. The second problem is the stiffness of the wings. The two wing feathers have rigid masts, the centre quills, and these exacerbate the propeller effect. Shortening and trimming also tends to increase the stiffness.

However if, like me, you are a believer in the importance of having wings on your artificial duns, you will not lightly give up on such an obviously attractive pattern.

I kept having little doodles at the vice, trying to get those wings more vertical, less diverging. Then on one occasion it hit me! Why bother trying to make two wings anyway. Why not just one wing? The single-winged dry fly never seems to have been fully accepted. So, the solution was simple, even with curved feathers. I would use the two feathers as before but now tie them face to face, with their tips coming together. If, as you tighten the turns of hackle around their bases, the two feathers still divide, then at least they curve inwards. The fish won't mind in the least that your fly has only one wing and, believe me, now your fly will not spin.

The parachute hackle also still causes concern among some dry fly pundits who claim, correctly, that this style of hackle is the least effective for imitating the 'footprint' of a dun. They argue that newly-emerged duns make contact with the water's surface in only six places - their feet - with the abdomen also just touching. So, these six tiny feet produce, to the fish, a highly recognisable footprint in the meniscus. These indentations in the surface, although small, become greatly magnified as the meniscus is depressed by each foot. On the mirror-smooth surface of pool tails and glides, they are clearly visible when viewed from the fish's perspective.

The many flat radiating barbs of a parachute hackle, on the other hand, produce an entirely different surface pattern. One might imagine that any fish - let alone a wary one - would be alerted immediately. However experience has shown this not to be so. Parachute drys are currently very much in vogue in the flyfishing world.

Nevertheless I have taken many fish on this pattern during hatches of small and medium sized mayflies. My Pale Watery version seems to be particularly deadly during a hatch of these delicate little duns and many times it has fooled fish which have been selectively 'keyed on' to this species.

There does in fact seem to be something rather special about this style of dry fly. It looks right in the vice and it looks right on the surface.

CUT-WING DUN DRESSING

Hook: Fine or medium wire up-eyed dry fly hook. Suggest Partridge 'Capt. Hamilton' dry fly hook Code L3B size 10-18.
Thread: Danville's 'Spider Web' (tinted to match dubbing with a felt pen, or untinted if natural is very pale).
Cement: Dave's Flexament (USA) or Floo Gloo (UK), both thinned.
Abdomen: Detached or extended style complete with self tails. Pre-formed from cock neck hackles, colour to suit underside of abdomens of naturals you wish to copy, eg. pale straw, various olives, various browns etc.
Under abdomen: Fine synthetic dubbing, colour to match pre-formed abdomen colour. Pre-form fixative: Loctite Clear Glue or Bostic All Purpose Clear Adhesive.
Thorax: Fine synthetic dubbing, colour same as under abdomen or slightly darker shade.
Wings: Soft 'webby' hen hackle, neck or saddle.
Colours: grey, from almost white (silver grey) through slate to dark 'iron blue' grey, or mottled brown for the March Brown.
Hackle: Top quality dry fly neck hackle. Pale ginger, sandy, blue dun, white, cream, dyed and undyed grizzle, etc. Basically, you should choose a colour that tones in with the rest of the fly.

NOTES ON MATERIALS AND TYING

Make the extended bodies first. Forsake the vice for a while and make, say, ten or a dozen. In fact, it is even better to make enough to see you through a season. I make them in olive-brown, pale tan, brown and cream. I advise making a good number simply because, whatever product you use as a fixative, you can be sure that your fingers and thumbs will become gunged-up, so one good session is quite enough! I make all mine while watching TV!

For the fixative, or glueing medium, Poul Jorgensen recommends a clear silicone rubber gel - the type used around bath and sink surrounds. While this gel does make satisfactory extensions, the film smeared on to the feather can be too thick, making the finished extension a little heavy. So, I have taken to using a clear adhesive: Bostick All Purpose clear adhesive. So far I cannot fault it and, in a simple test of 12 hours continuous total immersion in water, the body extension looked just 'as made'.

The hackles I use for these extended bodies are all from my old poor-quality capes. (See, there's always a use for your junk so don't throw anything away!) Incidently, if you want to do some colour matching to a particular natural by using an instant marker pen, remember to do the tinting before applying the adhesive, and give it plenty of time to dry.

For the wings, look for rounded, soft feathers from poultry hens or game birds. Neck feathers, back feathers and outer wing coverts from hens are suitable. Duck, goose and turkey body feathers also make nice wings if you can get hold of them. Generally they will all be curved to some degree along their length but now that we are going to mount the two feathers face to face, their curvature will be cancelled out against one another. Look for greys mostly, but speckled browns are useful for the large brown duns.

I would encourage you to use Danville's Spider Web thread, as even your regular 8/0 midge thread will produce too much bulk when tying off the smallest sizes.

Since this pattern sports a body extension, the hook size has to be reduced and I drop it by one size (even numbers). So, on a standard dry fly requiring a size 16 hook, on this pattern I would use a size 18.

A short shank is also desirable because otherwise the overall fly length can become excessive. An up-eyed hook can also be a help when tying this pattern.

Tying the Cut-Wing Dun

This is a straightforward fly to tie, with few components and very amenable materials. The fact that the body is pre-constructed, and is complete with self-tails, speeds things up considerably.

First make the extended body
If your artificial is to represent one of the smaller Baetids, for instance something you would normally dress on a size 16 hook, then as a general guide you will require the extended body to be about 3/16" (4mm) long with tail barbs somewhat longer, say 1/4" (6mm).

Fig 1
Tweak out one of the smaller hackles from your chosen cape, hold it firmly by the tip, with the best side uppermost. Now, with the other hand, ease back the barbs on both sides of the centre quill, just below where you are gripping it. Once you have the barbs separated out at right angles at this division, you can make a judgement as to the barb length you require for the tails of your fly. If they are too long, then simply move your grip position further towards the tip of the hackle and re-separate out the barbs again in this new position. If you still do not have short enough barbs, then clearly you have chosen too large a hackle in the first place. It doesn't take long to master this and, within a short while, you will be finding the correct-size hackle first time.

Fig 2
Now you have your hackle held by its tip and the barbs stroked back on both sides of the centre quill. Take your tube of clear adhesive and apply a dab to the hackle.

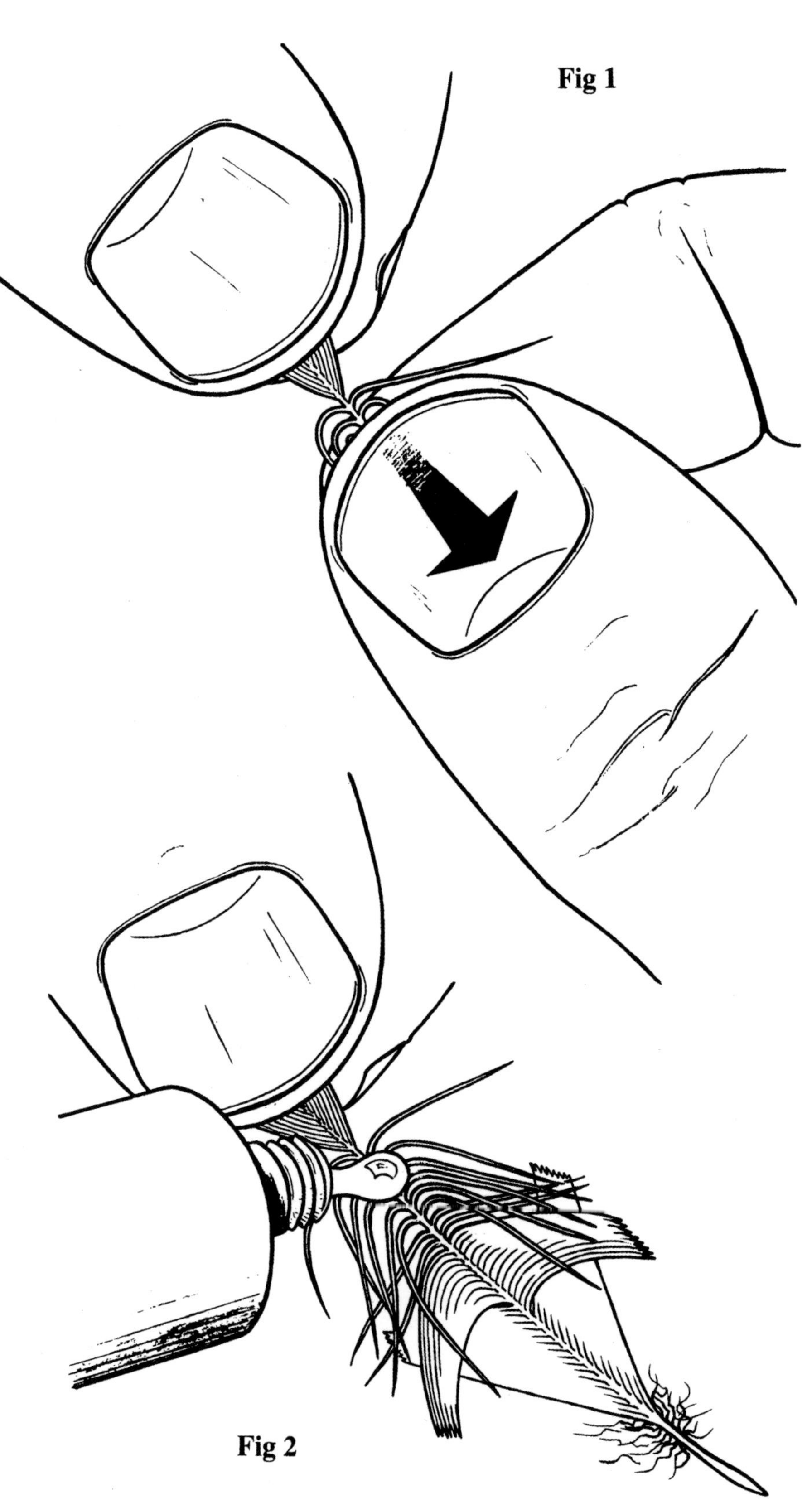

Fig 1

Fig 2

Fig 3
Now quickly trap the hackle between index finger and thumb of your other hand, coming down quite firmly with your thumb right on top of the adhesive. Then, in one continuous smooth action, stroke all the hackle barbs backwards, maintaining quite a firm pressure between index finger and thumb. You will find three or four forming strokes are necessary. The last stroke has to be drawn out quite slowly as by now the adhesive will be just at the tacky stage. It is important that you draw all the fibres back tightly as this makes the abdomen thin and tapers it in the correct direction. Within a few seconds you can handle the extension.

Fig 4
If you examine it closely, you will notice that the outer edges are slightly higher than the centre quill. In other words, a section across it is a shallow vee. I now squeeze the sides gently towards the centre - increasing the vee - starting at the very end and working down the hackle for about 1/2" (12mm).
And that's it, simple to do, a little more lengthy to describe. It takes me about a minute to make one and at least 60% of that time is spent actually finding and making the initial division of the hackle barbs.

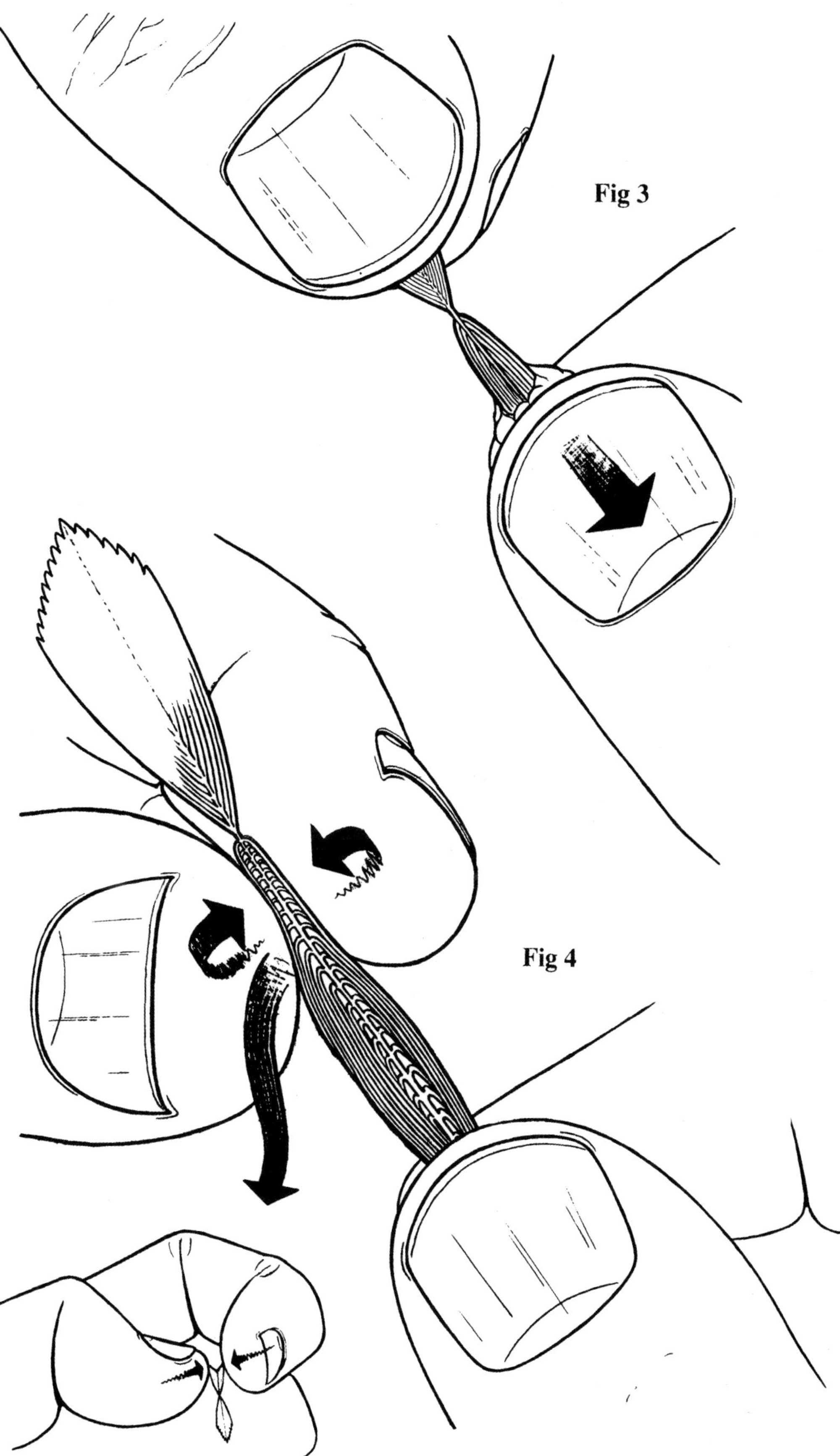

Now for the fly itself

Grip the hook firmly in the vice with the shank horizontal. Catch on the tying thread about a third of the way along the shank and run the thread in open turns to the bend. Next spin on a tiny amount of fine dubbing. Spin it on fairly tightly then wind it on the shank to one third from the eye. Let the bobbin holder hang.

Fig 5

Now take your prepared abdomen extension, snip off the waste stalk end so that it is about 3/4" (20mm) long. Position it on top of the shank with the vee groove straddling the dubbed shank. Adjust the extension so that it protrudes by about a shank length, or slightly less. When satisfied that it is correctly positioned, bind it securely to the top of the shank about half way along the dubbing. Advance the thread, and when you reach a position one third from the eye with the thread, stop and let the bobbin holder hang. Trim off the waste end of the body extension.

Fig 6

Now select two rounded body feathers for the wings. Find two which are symmetrical about the centre quill. Strip off the basal fluff and a few of the lower barbs, ensuring that both feathers are virtually identical. Next, lay one feather on top of the other with their natural curvatures pressing together. Ensure that their base fibres are aligned. This is important. Pick both feathers up together and poke their stripped quill ends through the eye of the hook This little trick automatically holds the quills side by side on top of the hook shank. Now position the two feathers on top of the shank so that the bases of the wings are in line with the hanging tying thread.

Fig 7

Securely bind them to the shank initially with 'pinch and loops' then make several touching turns of thread, working towards the eye. Make sure that the web of the feather is directly in line with the hook shank. I recommend you have at least 2mm of quill bound down. Return the thread to the front of the wings, let the bobbin holder hang and snip off both waste quill ends.

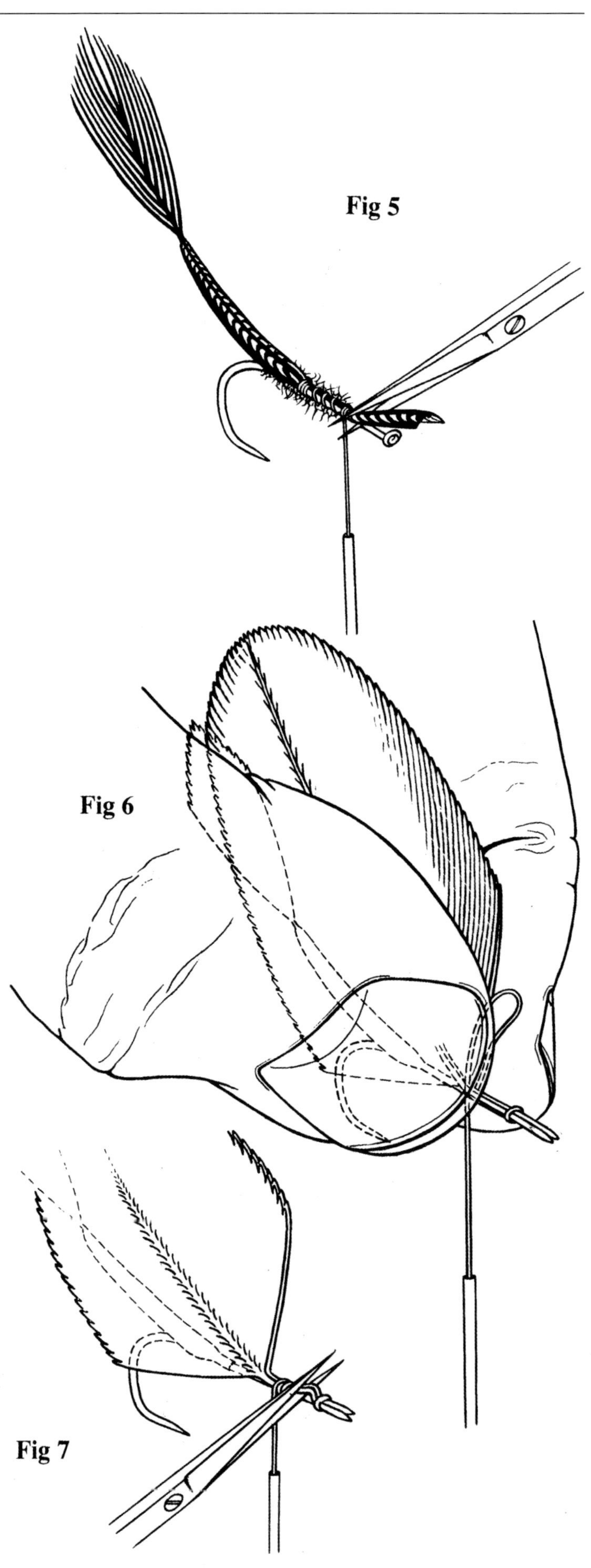

Fig 8
Soak these bindings with head cement. Now raise both wings together to the vertical by kinking the quills forward - the front of your thumb nail is the ideal tool for this.

Fig 9
The hackle goes in next. For all 'parachute' flies, it is acceptable to use a hackle which is slightly longer in barb length than you would use on a conventional dry fly. Strip off the lower barbs for a fair distance up the hackle, particularly if it has a thick centre quill. Offer up the hackle to the top of the hook shank on the far side of the wings. The stripped quill end should be pointing towards the bend, the start of the hackle barbs should be at the base of the wings and the hackle should be lying flat - horizontal - with the 'best' side on top. Bind it to the top of the shank in this position, the binding at the rear of the wings. Ensure that the hackle is very secure, about 2mm of close binding should be enough. Let the bobbin holder hang and snip off the waste end of hackle stalk.

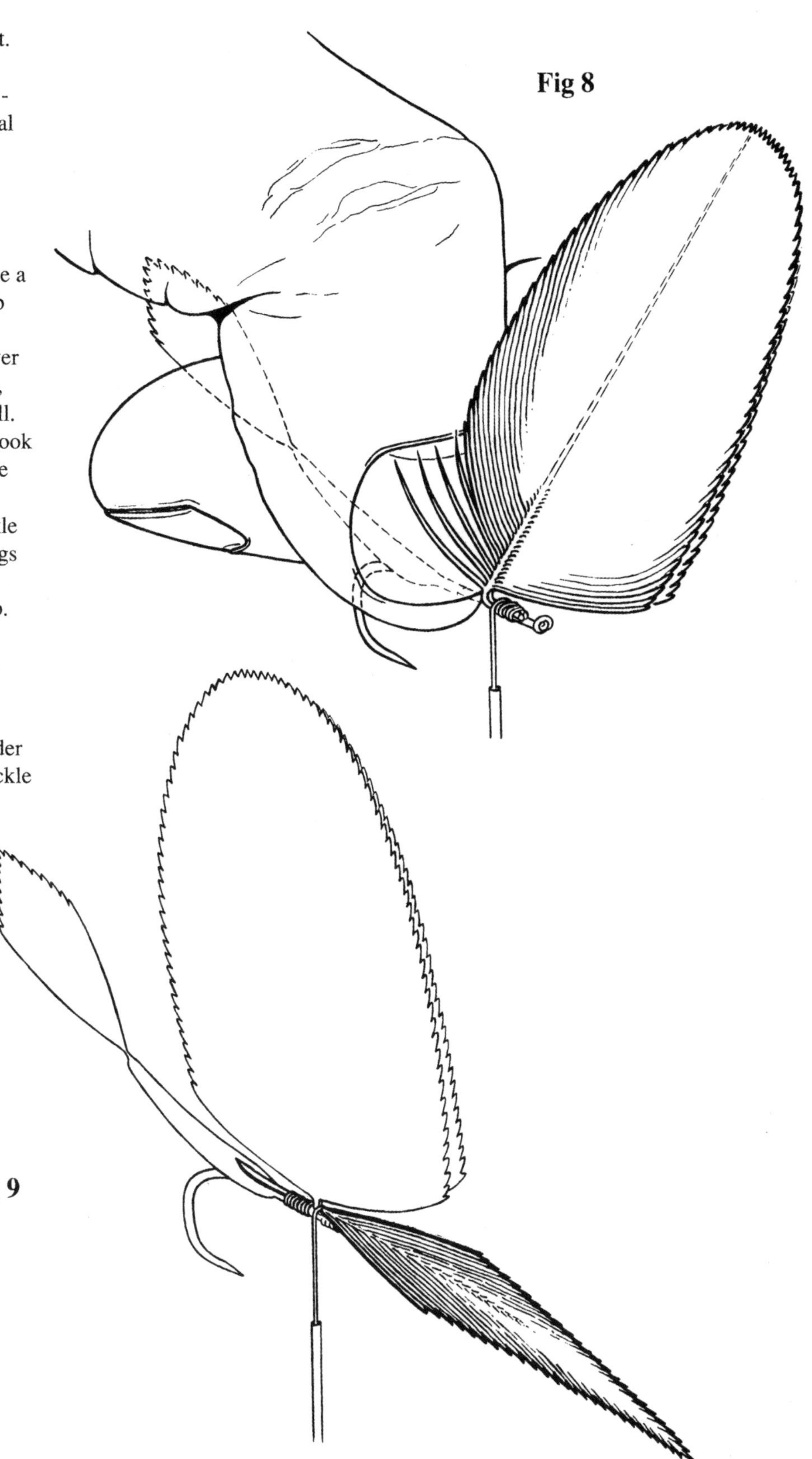
Fig 8

Fig 9

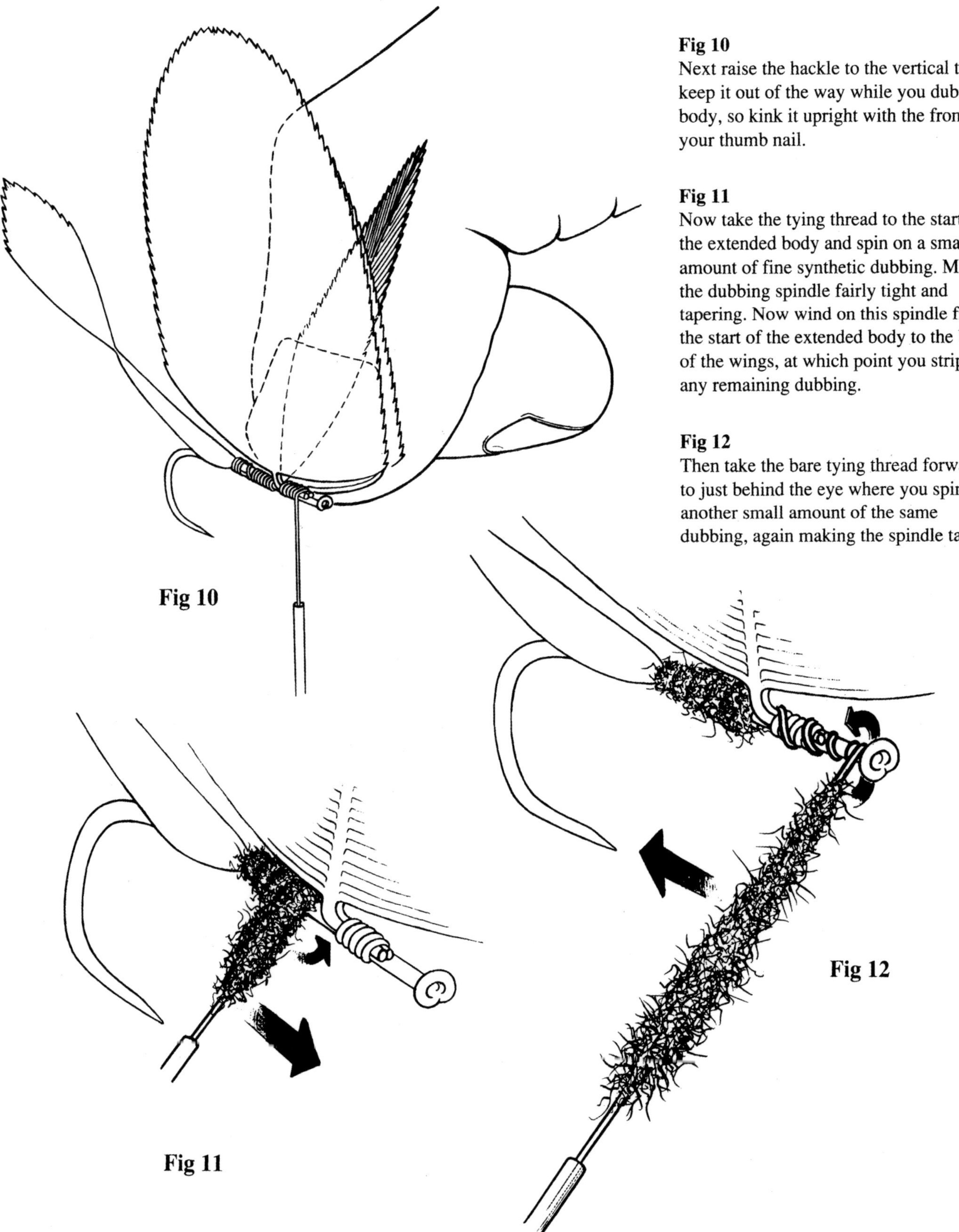

Fig 10

Fig 11

Fig 12

Fig 10
Next raise the hackle to the vertical to keep it out of the way while you dub the body, so kink it upright with the front of your thumb nail.

Fig 11
Now take the tying thread to the start of the extended body and spin on a small amount of fine synthetic dubbing. Make the dubbing spindle fairly tight and tapering. Now wind on this spindle from the start of the extended body to the back of the wings, at which point you strip off any remaining dubbing.

Fig 12
Then take the bare tying thread forward to just behind the eye where you spin on another small amount of the same dubbing, again making the spindle taper.

Fig 13
Wind on this dubbing working backwards towards the front of the wings. Strip off any surplus dubbing. Let the bobbin holder hang.

Fig 14
Now for the parachute hackle. Press the hackle down to lie flat again, clip on the hackle pliers and wind it horizontally around the base of the wings, ensuring that each turn of hackle goes below the previous one - three turns are sufficient.

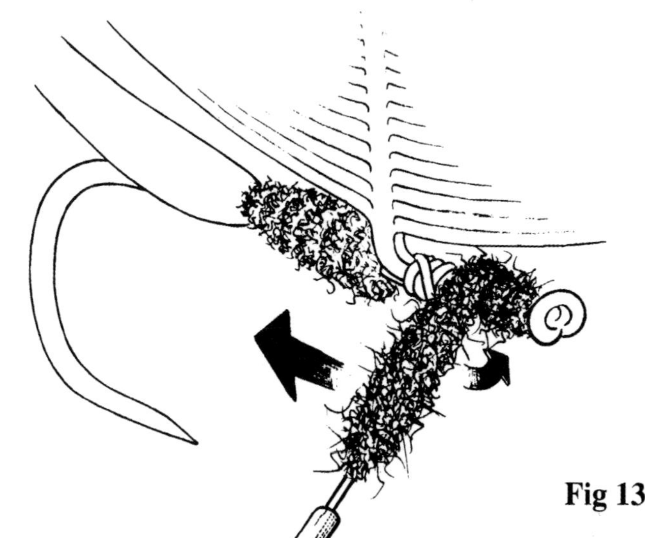

Fig 13

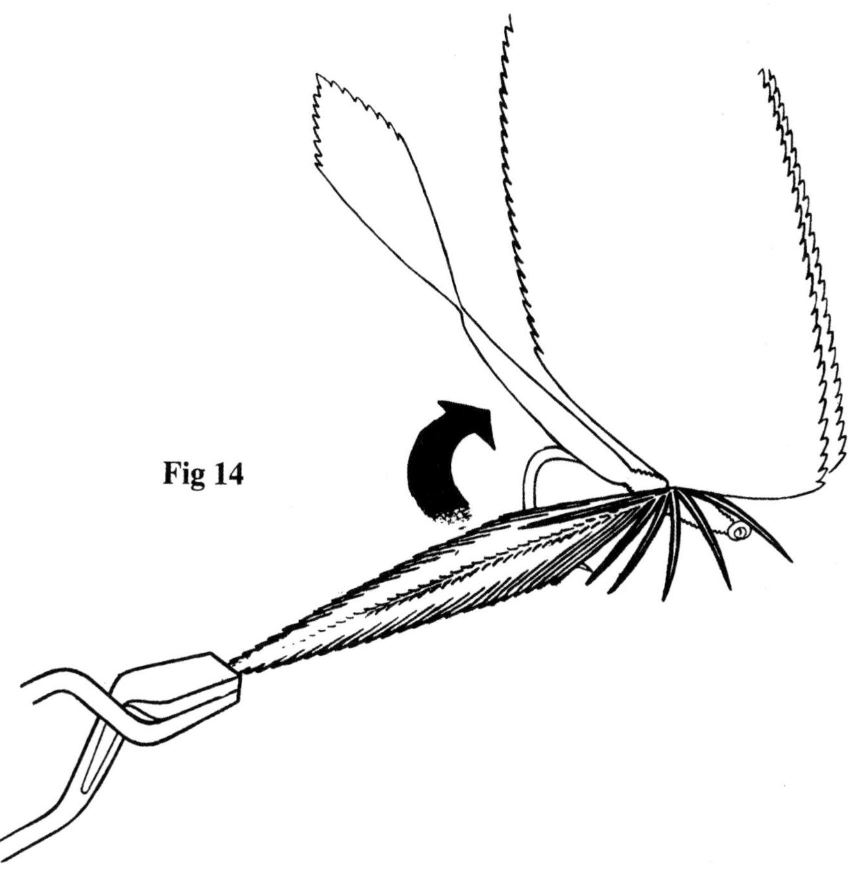

Fig 14

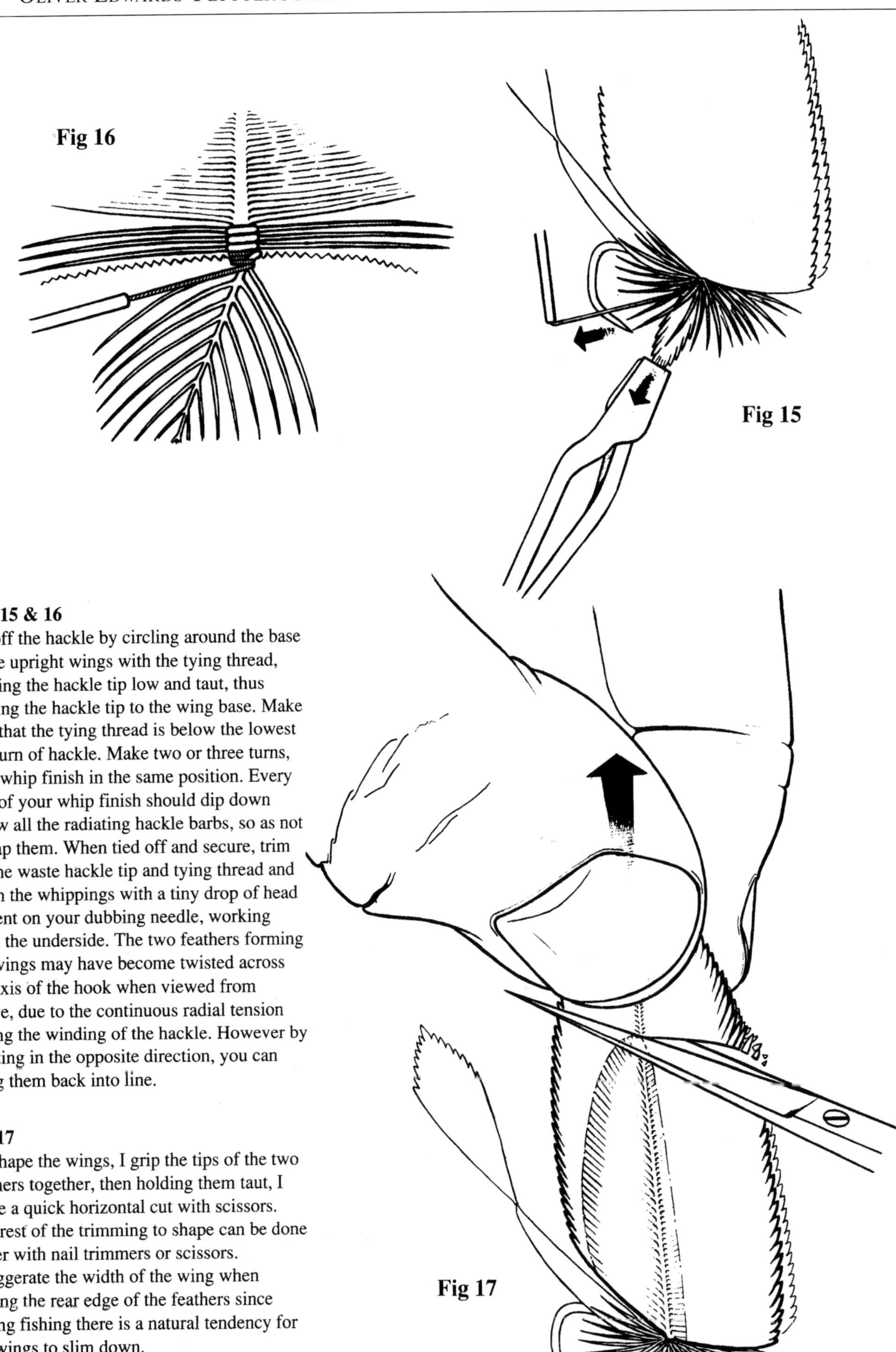

Figs 15 & 16
Tie off the hackle by circling around the base of the upright wings with the tying thread, keeping the hackle tip low and taut, thus binding the hackle tip to the wing base. Make sure that the tying thread is below the lowest full turn of hackle. Make two or three turns, then whip finish in the same position. Every turn of your whip finish should dip down below all the radiating hackle barbs, so as not to trap them. When tied off and secure, trim off the waste hackle tip and tying thread and touch the whippings with a tiny drop of head cement on your dubbing needle, working from the underside. The two feathers forming the wings may have become twisted across the axis of the hook when viewed from above, due to the continuous radial tension during the winding of the hackle. However by twisting in the opposite direction, you can bring them back into line.

Fig 17
To shape the wings, I grip the tips of the two feathers together, then holding them taut, I make a quick horizontal cut with scissors. The rest of the trimming to shape can be done either with nail trimmers or scissors. Exaggerate the width of the wing when cutting the rear edge of the feathers since during fishing there is a natural tendency for the wings to slim down.

Fig 18
Finally to form the tails, simply separate out the extreme edge barbs on each side of the extended body tip. Keep them forced wide apart while you carefully cut out the remaining central barbs. Don't cut too close though, follow Poul Jorgensen's advice by leaving a short stump between the tails.

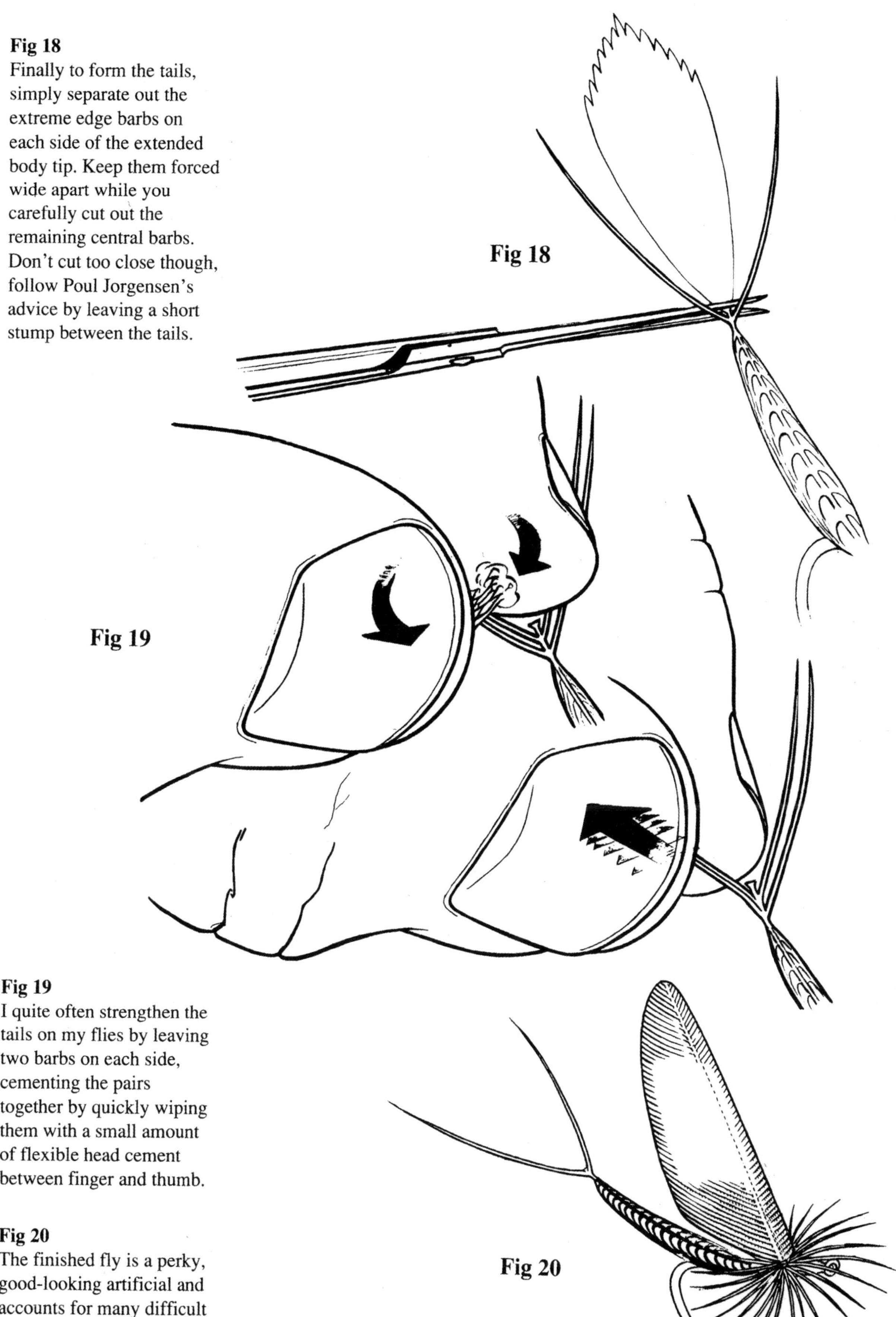

Fig 19
I quite often strengthen the tails on my flies by leaving two barbs on each side, cementing the pairs together by quickly wiping them with a small amount of flexible head cement between finger and thumb.

Fig 20
The finished fly is a perky, good-looking artificial and accounts for many difficult fish each year.

JOINTED EPHEMERA NYMPHS
(Top) Tied on a straight shank hook.
(Bottom) Tied on a curved shank hook.

7. The Jointed Ephemera Nymph

We flyfishers of the British Isles have to thank our angling ancestors for christening the largest British Ephemeropteran 'mayfly'. We instantly know it to be the huge dun with the 1" long cream-coloured body and 1" high drab olive, dark-veined wings and three 1" long tails. However, UK flyfishers visiting North America (and vice versa) may be most confused, as in the USA, the word 'mayfly' does not imply a particular species, nor even a genus, but every single species of that supremely important order Ephemeroptera. Over the years this misnomer has generated a fair amount of confusion. I personally prefer the American system, so I have decided here to call our 'mayfly' by its generic name, Ephemera.

Although in the UK we officially have three species of the genus Ephemera, one, *Ephemera lineata*, is so rare as to be of no importance in flyfishing. In fact it may already be heading for extinction in these islands.

Of the remaining two species, *Ephemera danica* and *Ephemera vulgata*, it is *danica* which is of the greatest importance to the British flyfisher. This is the fly which fills the valleys of the famous rivers of Hampshire, Wiltshire and Dorset for a few precious weeks in late May and early June, and I am sure that there is no serious flyfisher in the world who has not heard of the rivers Test and Itchen and maybe even the Kennet, Avon and Wylye. The Frome in Dorset is the only one unlikely to be well-known internationally. When the mayfly is 'on', foreign ambassadors, retired admirals and top legal and medical men, cancel appointments, doff wigs, dust off their trusty Hardy, and head in haste to Hampshire.

This is the fly of the so-called 'Duffers Fortnight' when, hopefully, the really big fish of these streams show a more than usual interest in taking a surface fly and theoretically become less difficult to deceive - although landing them is another matter!

Ephemera danica seems to have a definite preference for alkali water, hence its stronghold in the southernmost, chalk-rich counties of England. Once away from these counties, *Ephemera danica* is present with reasonable reliability wherever geological chalk and limestone occurs in sufficient mass. Some of the notable streams of the Cotswolds, for instance the Coln, a small tributary of the upper Thames, has good populations. It also emerges in good numbers on some of the Thames' larger tributaries, the Kennet being the prime example, rising from Marlborough Down.

Over to the east of the country, there used to be some noteworthy 'mayfly' hatches, not far from the town of Bedford: here the rivers Ivel, Hiz and Chess spring to mind. I am reliably informed that the insect still emerges on the river Lea. Unfortunately many such small streams in the east and south-east have been decimated by the effects of deep borehole pumping for domestic supply.

Further north, Derbyshire is probably in second place only to the three southern chalkstream counties as 'mayfly territory'. The Peak District of Derbyshire has massive deposits of limestone and some beautiful streams: the Dove, Wye, Derwent and Manifold, all of which have excellent and sustaining populations of *E. danica* - a real stronghold!

In my own county of Yorkshire, Ephemera danica seems to be much more common today than it was in my youth. I recall that many years ago, the only Dales river where you could rely on seeing this huge impressive fly was the river Nidd. Today, I'm pleased to report that both the rivers Ure and Wharfe are showing good signs of re-population.

The best and most reliable hatches of *E. danica* in Yorkshire occur in the north-east of the county. The five or six small rivers and streams which drain the North York Moors all hold varying populations of *E. danica*. Paradoxically, only one of these streams, the river Costa, is a true chalkstream. Two of the streams, the rivers Rye and Dove, have excellent hatches and, on the delightful river Rye, I have witnessed and fished through some tremendous hatches, the air filled with escaping duns. I strongly suspect that the Rye's canopy of overhanging trees is a major factor for its year-after-year reliability by providing quick cover for newly emerged duns, and good assembly or reference points for mating swarms.

Further down the eastern side of Yorkshire there flows a stream with a great trout fishing reputation - Driffield Beck. It is a true chalkstream, on a par, in terms of water quality, aquatic flora and trout, with any chalkstream in the south. Unfortunately, this glorious stream lost its entire population of *E. danica* nearly 50 years ago and, despite attempts at re-introduction in the 70s and 80s, it is still mayflyless!

The further north you travel, the less likely you are to encounter *E. danica*, but there are still odd populations scattered about. It is a fairly rare insect in Scotland, but strangely there are a few lochs right up at the very northern edge of Scotland with good populations. Loch St John's in Caithness, for instance, has a good reputation for producing a hatch most years.

In Ireland, it is the large loughs rather than their rivers which are the prime 'mayfly' fisheries. Loughs such as Corrib, Arrow, Sheelin, Mask and Derg, are just a small sample of the more famous ones, and again, most of these are situated in areas of geological limestone.

The nymph of *Ephemera danica* prefers a clean substrate of very fine sand and other fine particle sediment such as marl. The substrate must not be too hard packed and the nymph seems to need this material at least 2" (50mm) deep in which to make its burrow. It avoids areas which are subject to repeated deposits of decomposing vegetation such as slacks, bays and backwaters where deposits of dead leaves ultimately give rise to black gaseous mud. This is a creature of the main flow. It loves smooth glides and pool necks rather than popply stickles and is particularly fond of those banks of clean pale silt which build up on the downstream side of emergent shoots of ranunculus.

These nymphs are classed as burrowers and their anatomy is very efficiently modified for such purposes. Their legs are fairly short but stoutly proportioned, the front pair particularly so, the femur and tibia looking quite disproportionately wide and spade-like. Indeed digging is just what they are designed for, since each leg is tipped with a well developed curved claw for scything through the substrate. These front legs are also held in a most unusual inward-facing attitude. You will get some idea of what I mean if you picture in your mind the front legs of a mole.

They also have a pair of unusual appendages protruding forward from their small heads. These appendages are like a pair of miniature elephant tusks, converging at their tips and they may be of secondary importance as burrowing tools.

They are herbivorous creatures, classified entomologically as collector-filterers, feeding on fine particles of vegetable detritus and algae, which pass through the nymph's tunnel on a current produced by its own body undulations, and by the rhythmic beating of its feathery gills.

The other Ephemera of importance to flyfishers is the species *vulgata*. Despite its name, it is not at all common, except in small pockets. It is reputed to favour large slow rivers but my own observations of this insect lead me to believe it is more likely to be encountered on stillwaters. It will tolerate less alkali-rich water quite happily, and the nymph has a preference for a muddy substrate.

Some flyfishers have difficulty in separating

the duns and nymphs of the two species. Side by side and in the hand, there need never be any confusion. *Ephemera vulgata* is much the darker of the two - both dun and nymph. In the dun, the wings of *Ephemera vulgata* appear to be more heavily veined, the dorsal side of its abdomen is also more heavily marked with dark paired lateral splashes on all segments. On *Ephemera danica*, these paired dorsal markings are to be found on the last three (tail end) segments. The other segments are a clear creamy colour with only the very faintest of paired markings. The nymphs of the two species can be separated by using the same dorsal abdominal marking system.

Both species are said to have a two-year life cycle. However, once again, entomologists can't agree since one and three year cycles have been recorded.

There have been several attempts down the years at copying the nymphs of the Ephemera, both here and in the USA, and some have been very successful. If I have an argument with any of these patterns today it is that they are often dressed far too fat. The nymphs of the Ephemera are long and quite thin (particularly the British species). Simply look at the dun and imagine it without wings. When dressed fat and zipped back at breakneck speed through a 'put and take' stillwater fishery, it becomes quite simply a small fry imitation and I know that some are used for just that purpose.

Another quite unnecessary feature which most flytyers now insist upon are the two or three distinct dark brown bands encircling the rear of the abdomen. There are dark abdominal markings on both *E. danica* and *E. vulgata*, but they are on the upper (dorsal) side of the nymph, the underside being a plain dirty cream. Now, since in most instances, the real nymph will be intercepted as it is rising to the surface, the attack will come from below. The trout does not see dark ventral markings on the natural, so why include them on the artificial? If you insist on having these markings, then put them on the dorsal surface where they belong - a quick stroke with a Pantone pen. Similarly, it is almost mandatory these days to use a good clump of dark ruddy cock pheasant tail barbs to simulate legs. Why? The legs on the real thing are virtually the same colour as the whitish abdomen. In any case, the real nymph tucks its legs underneath its thorax when swimming. So adding a fan of ruddy brown legs is not only unnecessary, it may even be a detraction. I have included legs on my pattern, but they are not primarily intended as close copy appendages. I purposely chose the softness and mobility of ostrich herl, to give an illusion of movement. They are not essential.

'Wiggle nymph' is the term usually given to nymphs of this construction. I first came across this unique style when I bought *Selective Trout* by Doug Swisher and Carl Richards in the 70s. Unfortunately, I simply cannot get them to wiggle, no matter how loose I make the nylon monofil joint! Move, yes, but not wiggle! I think that I (and probably others) have been naive in imagining that the abdomen portion will thrash about like some demented damsel nymph. It simply doesn't.

I like to see this jointed design on Ephemera and other large nymphs for totally different reasons. There is far less leverage exerted by the angler - and fish - on a short or normal shanked hook than there is on a 3x or 4x long shank which is the more usual type of hook used for 'mayfly'

SOME NATURALS APPROPRIATE TO THIS PATTERN

BRITISH SPECIES: *Ephemera vulgata, E. danica, E. lineata.*
BRITISH FISHING NAMES: Mayfly, Greendrake, Spent Gnat (Ireland - spent females), Grey Drake.

NORTH AMERICAN SPECIES: *Ephemera guttulata, E. simulans, E. varia, E. blanda, E. compar.*
NORTH AMERICAN FISHING NAMES: American Greendrake, Brown Drake, Yellow or Pale Yellow Drake, Pale Sulphur Drake, Western March Brown.

nymphs. The other thing I like about large jointed nymphs is that there will be a certain amount of collapse when the trout crunches. Instead of the fish grabbing a long hard stick, which it may quickly spit out, it hits something which, if not exactly as soft as the real thing, will at least move. I accept that this is mere supposition - there's an awful lot of it in flyfishing and the development of fly patterns. No-one has yet had a conversation with a trout!

It could be argued also that this style, with a hook well towards the front, will produce 'false knocks' if pursued by a 'tail nipper'. From my own experience over several seasons, this doesn't appear to be the case.

One final point: because you are limited as to how much lead you can load on to this pattern, there will be times when it won't sink as quickly or as deeply as you would wish. In such situations two options are available. The first is to use this nymph in conjunction with one of the fast sinking front end loaded leaders such as the excellent 'bottom bouncing' types devised by Roman Moser. The other option is quite straightforward. Simply crimp on 'non-tox' split shot, say 8-10" from the nymph. This latter method can be highly effective, if somewhat lacking in finesse. Amongst UK flyfishers it may be seen as anathema, but it hardly raises an eyebrow in the USA.

NOTES ON MATERIALS AND TYING

I've probably made too many sketches, but don't let it put you off. Sit down and follow the sequence through until you have the route fixed in you mind. It does take a little longer to tie than many other patterns - jointed types always do. You are effectively tying two flies, don't forget!

Ensure that the rear half of the pattern is very free to articulate. It is easy to make the monofil loop too short and tight!

Antron yarn, as it comes off the spool, is a marvellous material to use and can be brushed up with a velcro scrubber to give a very airy, translucent look. It can also be shaved down to make a taper of any angle, then twisted tight to give regular segmentations. For the tails, you will need a whole plume of ostrich herl. Follow the quill all the way to its tip - there you will find some mini herls. Make sure their fine tips are present.

The marabou plume I've used for the gills is quite a small one, about 2" (50mm) wide, and I cut out a 3/4" (20mm) piece. If the central quill is a little thick, which it often is, I slice it down lengthwise with a scalpel and then scrape out the pith. The resulting semicircular section of quill nicely wraps around the hook shank.

When you loop each clump of marabou back to make the gills, try to trap them down as near

JOINTED EPHEMERA NYMPH DRESSING

Rear hook: Medium wire 3x longshank straight eye. Suggest Partridge Straight Eye Streamer Hook Code D3ST size 12 and 14. Rear hook could have a slightly curved shank such as Partridge Code K12ST.
Front hook: Medium wire standard length shank. Suggest Partridge 'Capt. Hamilton Dry Fly Hook' Code L3A size 10 and 12.
Weight (front hook only): Narrow strip of wine bottle lead foil.
Thread: Regular 6/0 or midge 8/0, Danville's, Unithread, etc. Colour: cream.
Cement: Dave's Flexament (USA) or Floo Gloo (UK), both thinned.
Tails: 3 ostrich herl tips, natural grey, off white or dyed pale tan.
Abdomen (rear hook): 4-ply knitting yarn, 100% synthetic fibre, or synthetic and natural fibre blend, preferably with the addition of Antron or other highly reflective sparkle fibres. Colour: white, off white or cream.
Abdomen gill: Section of whole small turkey marabou plume, natural grey or off white.
Thorax (front hook): As abdomen.
Legs (optional): Ostrich herl tips, natural grey or dyed pale tan.
Wing buds: Well marked tail quill feather section from a golden pheasant.
Head: Tying thread.
Front tusks (optional): 2 natural cream or pale grey goose biots.
Abdomen marking (optional): Fine black or dark brown waterproof felt tip pen.

their tips as possible. Moisten the marabou when ready to make the gills: this simple act makes all those wispy ends completely manageable.

When loading the front hook, keep the wraps of lead very tight and strive to produce a torpedo shape. To prevent the lead rotating, give the first turn a dab of superglue on the hook shank.

The two golden pheasant sections are taken from the largest tail quills. When you snip out the sections, aim to get equal amounts of light and dark banding on both.

I've also shown the legs added one at a time but, with a bit of practice, you will find pairs easy to tie in. Note that they sweep backwards and out to the side. I sometimes tie in the first pair pointing well forward to produce more movement. However, if you find the legs a fiddle then just omit them.

I've put in the two biots at the head simply because the natural has a long, tapering front. It's a small, possibly unnecessary, point, but it takes less than a minute.

Tying the Jointed Ephemera Nymph

Start by tying the rear or abdomen portion. Grip the long shank very firmly in the vice. You will be doing a fair amount of pulling about so make sure the hook is very securely held.

Fig 1
Catch on the tying thread near the eye and run it down to just short of the bend in open turns. At this point, tie in the three mini ostrich herls. Their tips should extend by approximately 3/8" (8mm). Make sure they are situated on top of the shank.

Fig 2
Bind them down all the way to the bend.

Fig 3
Now splay the two outer tails by taking several turns of the tying thread between the two outer tails and the inner one, pulling each turn of thread in the general direction of the hook eye. Ease each of the two outer tails out at right angles to the shank when performing this operation.

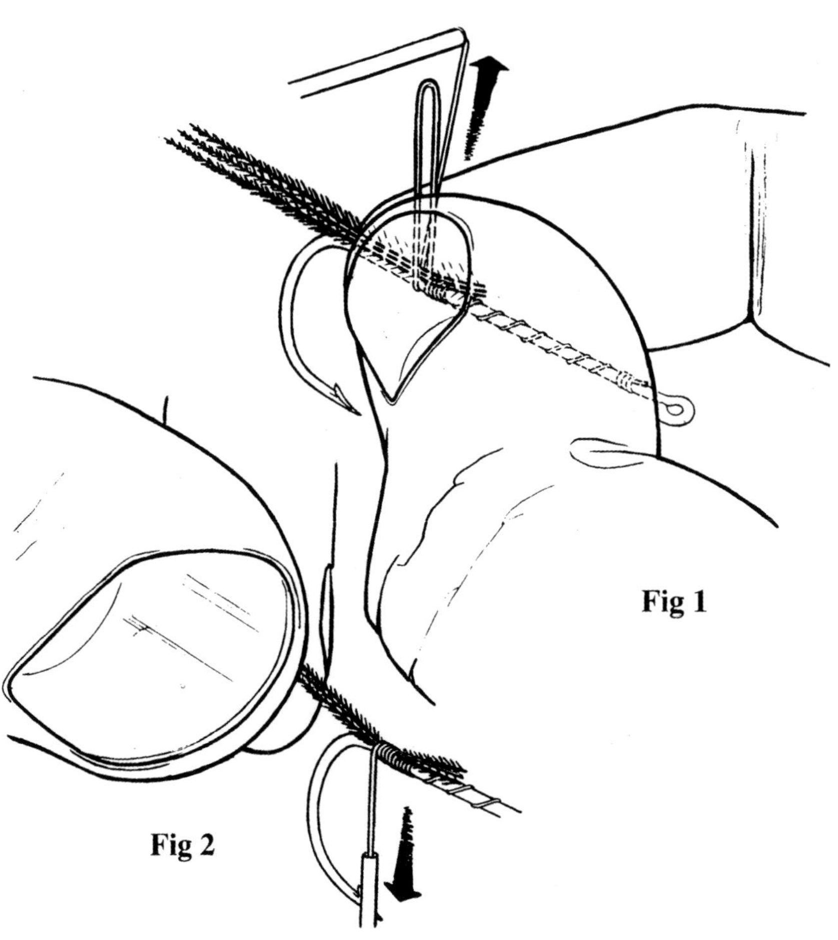

Fig 1

Fig 2

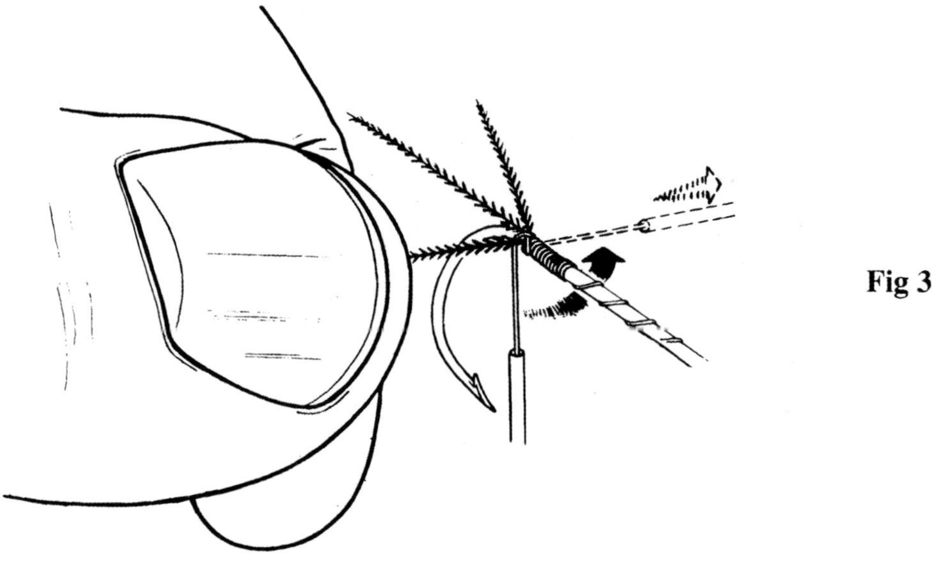

Fig 3

Fig 4
Take next a 4" (100mm) length of 4-ply Antron yarn and remove one of the plys, then with your thumb nail, 'shave down' one end to form a fairly long taper.

Fig 5
Tie the yarn in by this fine tip directly on top of the tail tyings.

Fig 6
Now take the tying thread back up the shank to just past the half way point where you securely tie in a 3/4" (20mm) section of marabou. Tie it in by its centre quill.

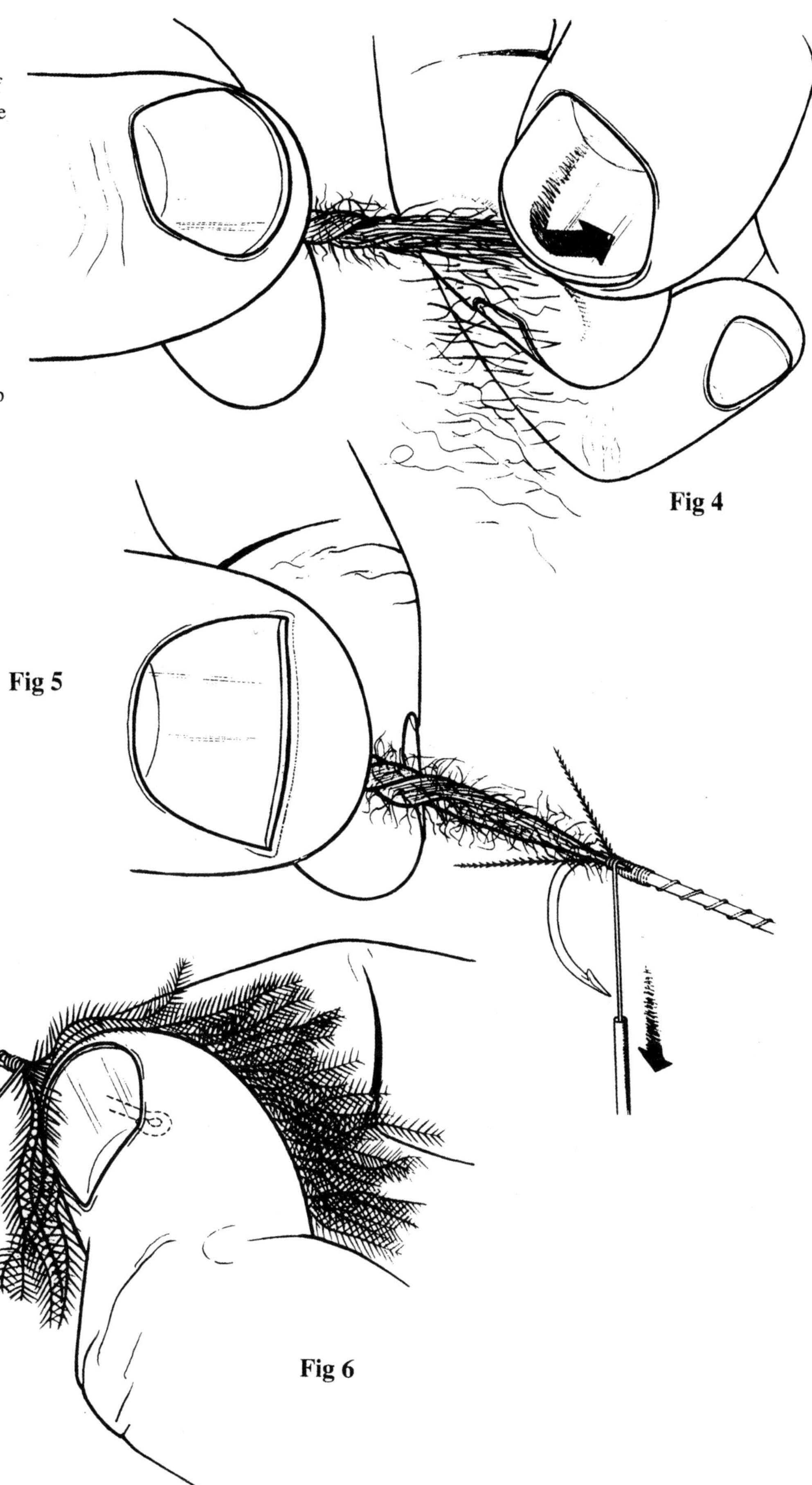

Fig 4

Fig 5

Fig 6

Fig 7
When secure, lift up the marabou and run the tying thread up to the eye.

Fig 8
Twist the yarn to produce a tight cord. Make sure that the direction of twist will not unravel as you wrap it on the shank.

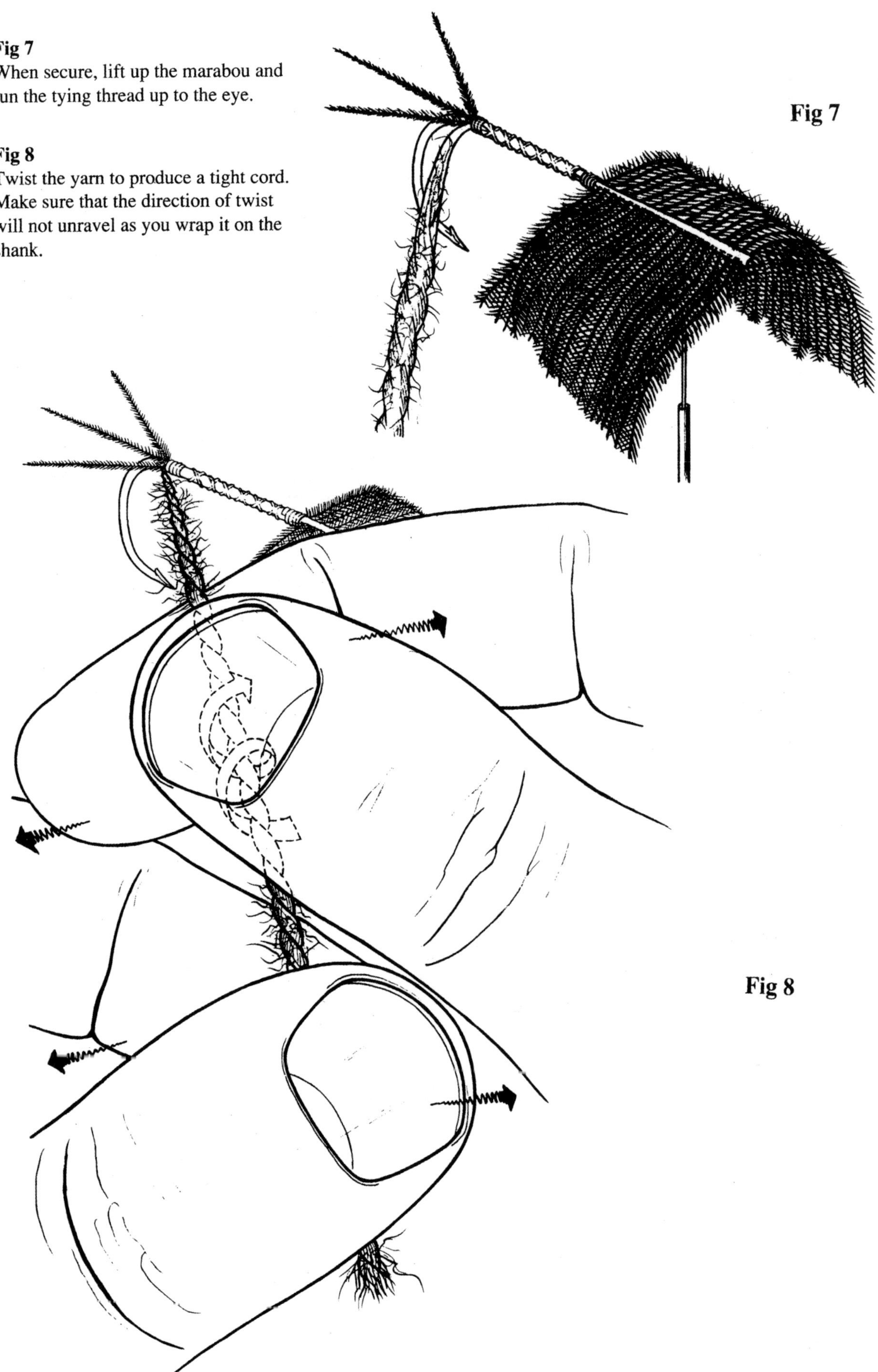

Fig 7

Fig 8

Fig 9
Wrap it along the shank in touching turns as far as the marabou. Loop a small clump of marabou backwards and trap it underneath the twisted yarn. The trapped tips should be upright, on top, and at a slight angle (see Fig 11). Remember to moisten the marabou.

Fig 10
Next trap down a similar amount of marabou from the opposite side, looping the clump back in the same way.

Fig 11
The tips again should be on top and angled, so that the two clumps make a slight vee.

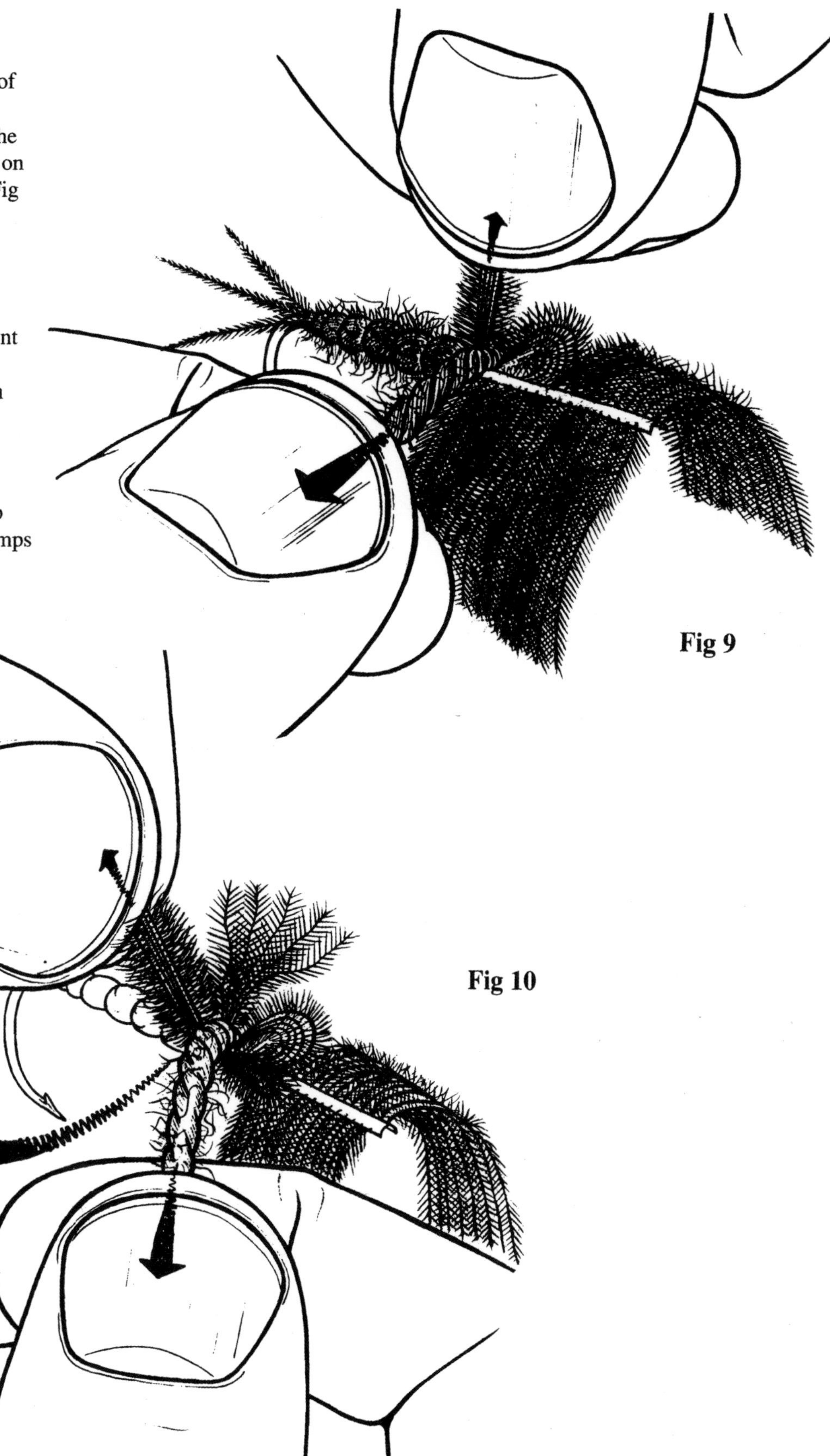

Fig 9

Fig 10

Fig 11

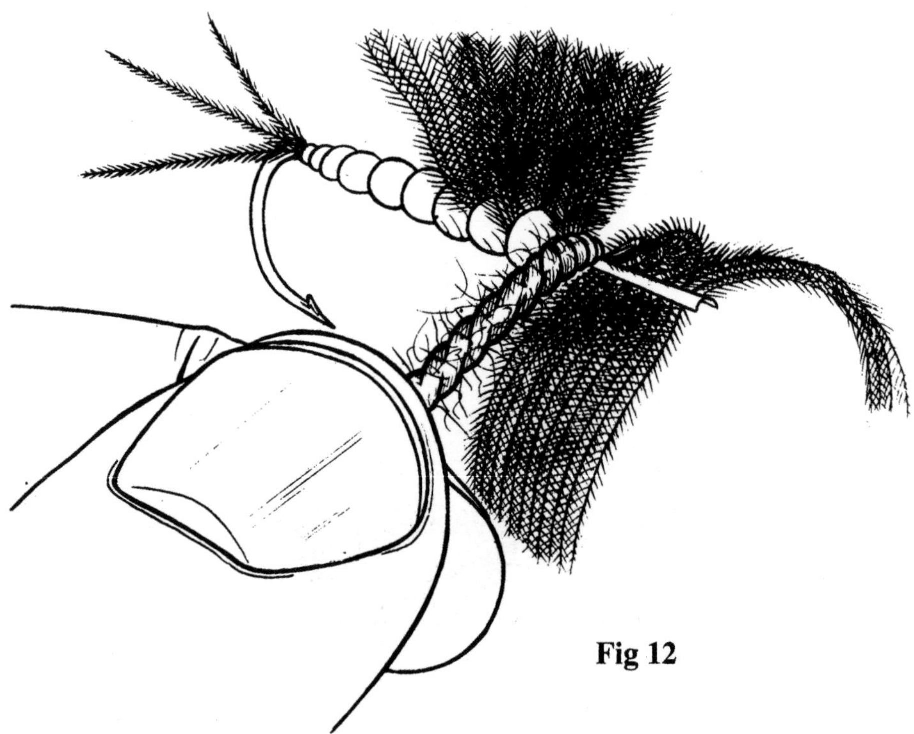

Fig 12

Fig 12
Continue wrapping on the tightly twisted yarn and, with each wrap, trap down more clumps of marabou exactly as previously described.

Fig 13
When you have completed four or five sets of tufts, you should be just behind the eye with the twisted yarn, at which point you tie off the yarn very securely and whip finish. Trim off the waste yarn, any remaining marabou centre quill, and the tying thread. Touch the thread wraps with head cement and remove from the vice.
The abdomen portion is now finished except for some further final trimming.

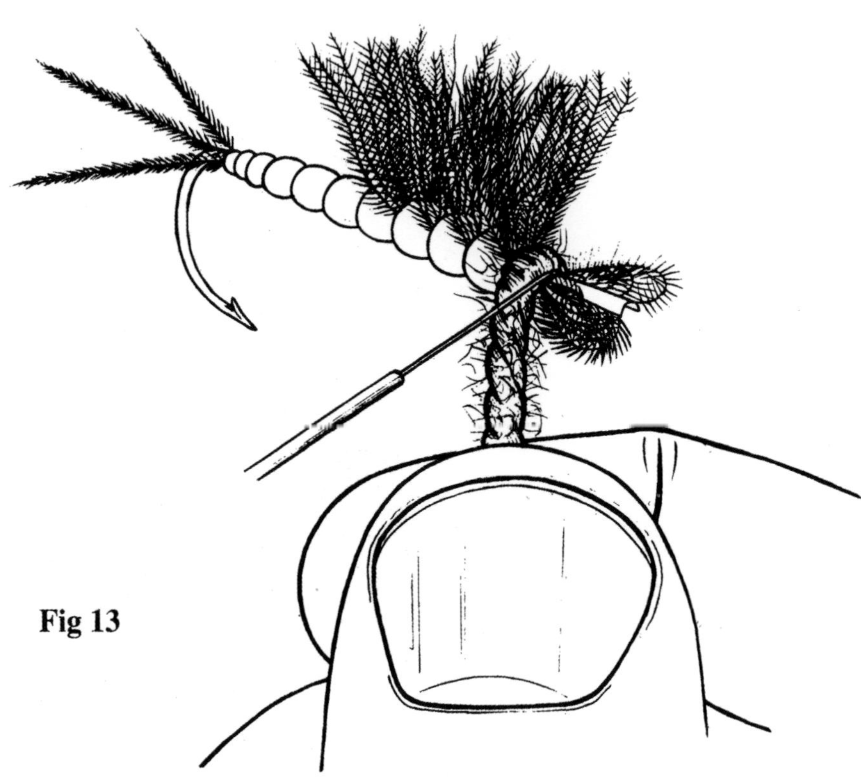

Fig 13

Fig 14

Now firmly grip the front hook in the vice, catch on the tying thread near the bend and securely bind down a 2" (50mm) length of 4-6lb BS nylon mono. Thread the nylon monofil through the eye of the newly-completed abdomen. Pull the mono back, make a loop and bind it down. Try to keep both bound-down ends of the monofil directly on top of each other. I sometimes flatten the bound-down portion of mono with pliers to facilitate this. Make sure when binding down the loop of nylon mono that the abdomen portion of the nymph can move very freely.

Fig 15

At this stage, I trim the 4 or 5 pairs of tufts made earlier on the abdomen portion. The amount left protruding should be about 1/8" (3mm) to 3/16" (4mm).

Fig 16

I then crop off the entire hook bend close to the tails using pliers or wire cutters. Seal this cut end with a drop of head cement applied to the base of the tails.

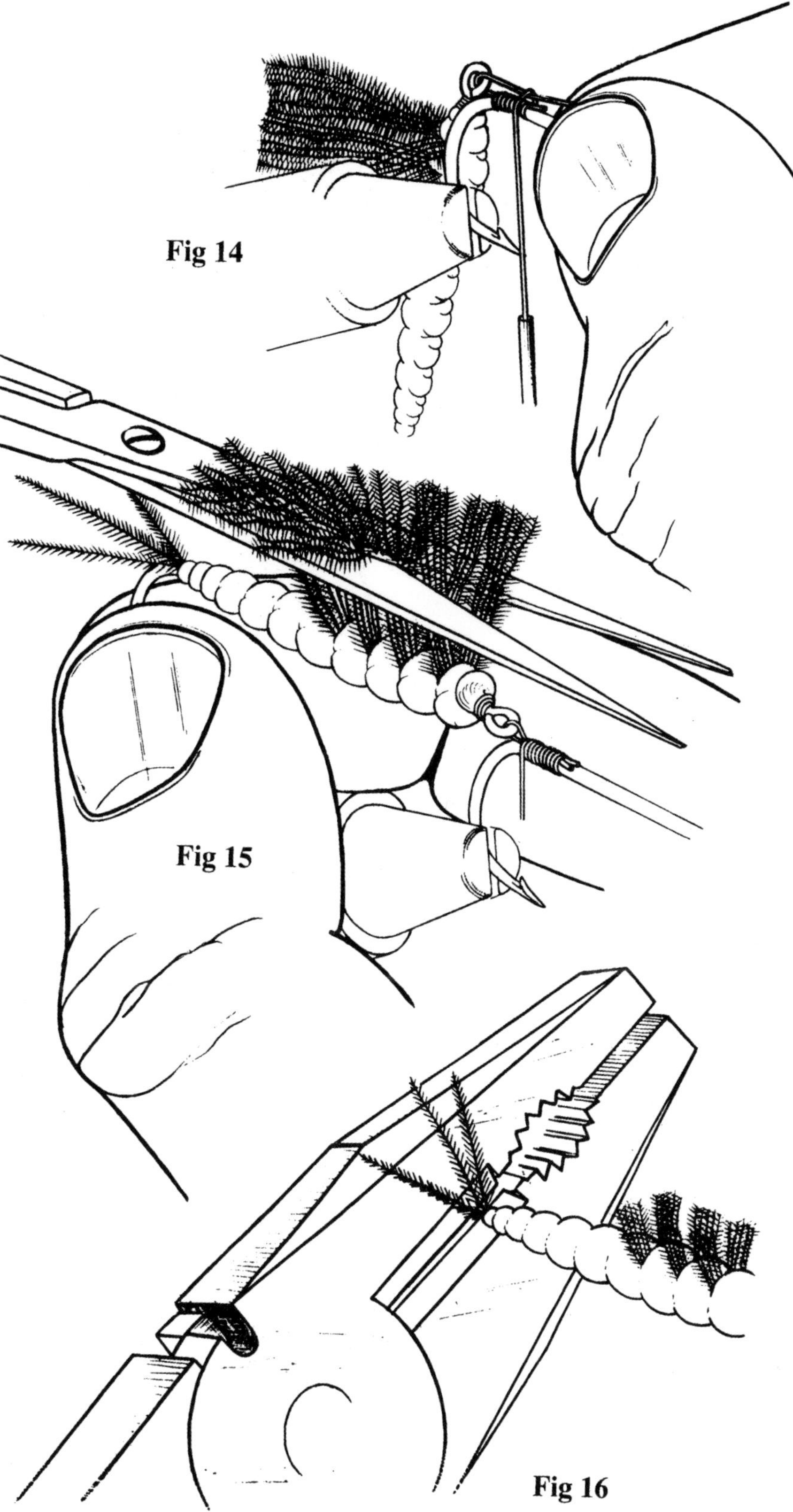
Fig 14

Fig 15

Fig 16

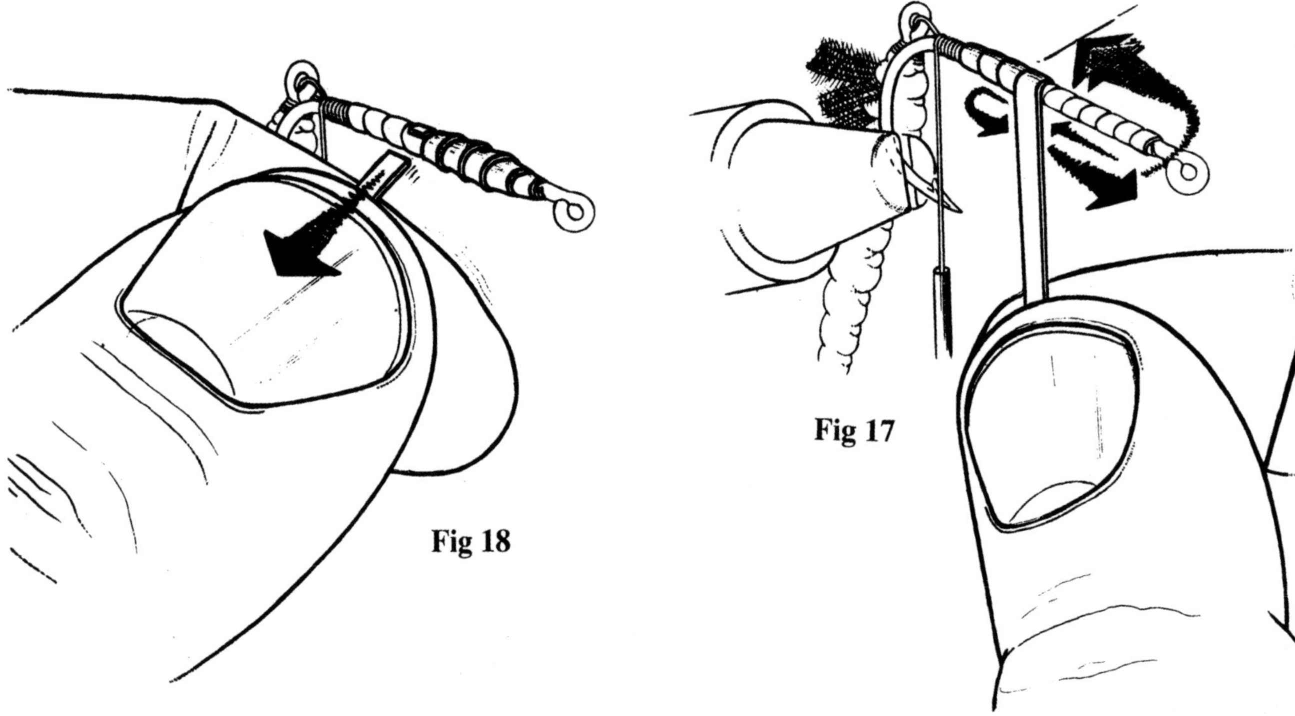

Figs 17 & 18

The next operation is to ballast the front hook. I use a 1/16" (2mm) wide strip of wine bottle lead foil. The amount you wrap on will be governed by the type of river you fish and how deep you want your nymph to sink. I usually wrap on 2½ layers and aim for a tapering torpedo shape by overlapping on the last layer. Break off the waste.

Fig 19

Next tie in a 3" length of the same 4-ply Antron yarn that was used for the abdomen. Again with one of the plys removed, 'shave' down a fine point as before and tie it in very securely at the bend by this very fine tip.

Fig 20

Advance the thread about a third up the shank and let the bobbin holder hang.

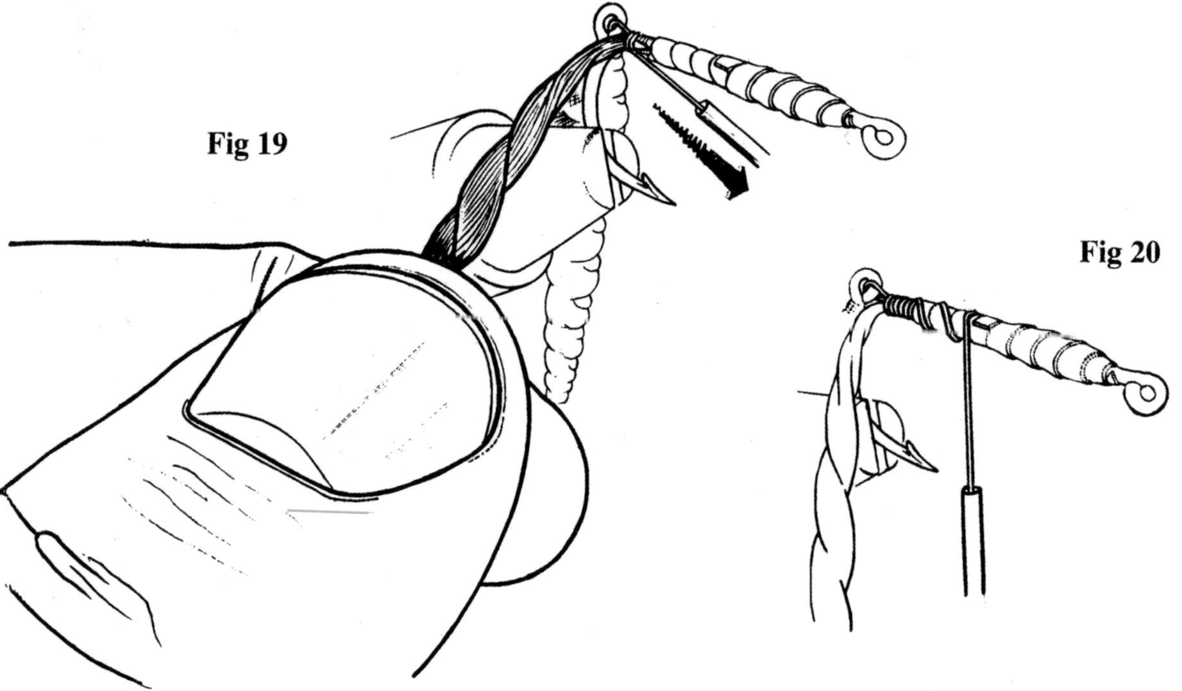

Fig 21
Then, as before, twist the yarn tightly and wrap it on the shank as far as the hanging thread, where you tie it down securely.

Fig 22
Next tie in the two sections of golden pheasant tail for the wing buds. They should both be equal, say 1/8" (3mm) wide. Tie them in, one on either side with their best sides facing one another. The tying-in point is exactly over the bindings which secure the twisted yarn.

Figs 23 & 24
Follow the golden pheasant sections by tying in the rear pair of legs, one on either side, projecting slightly backwards and splayed out sideways in a vee.

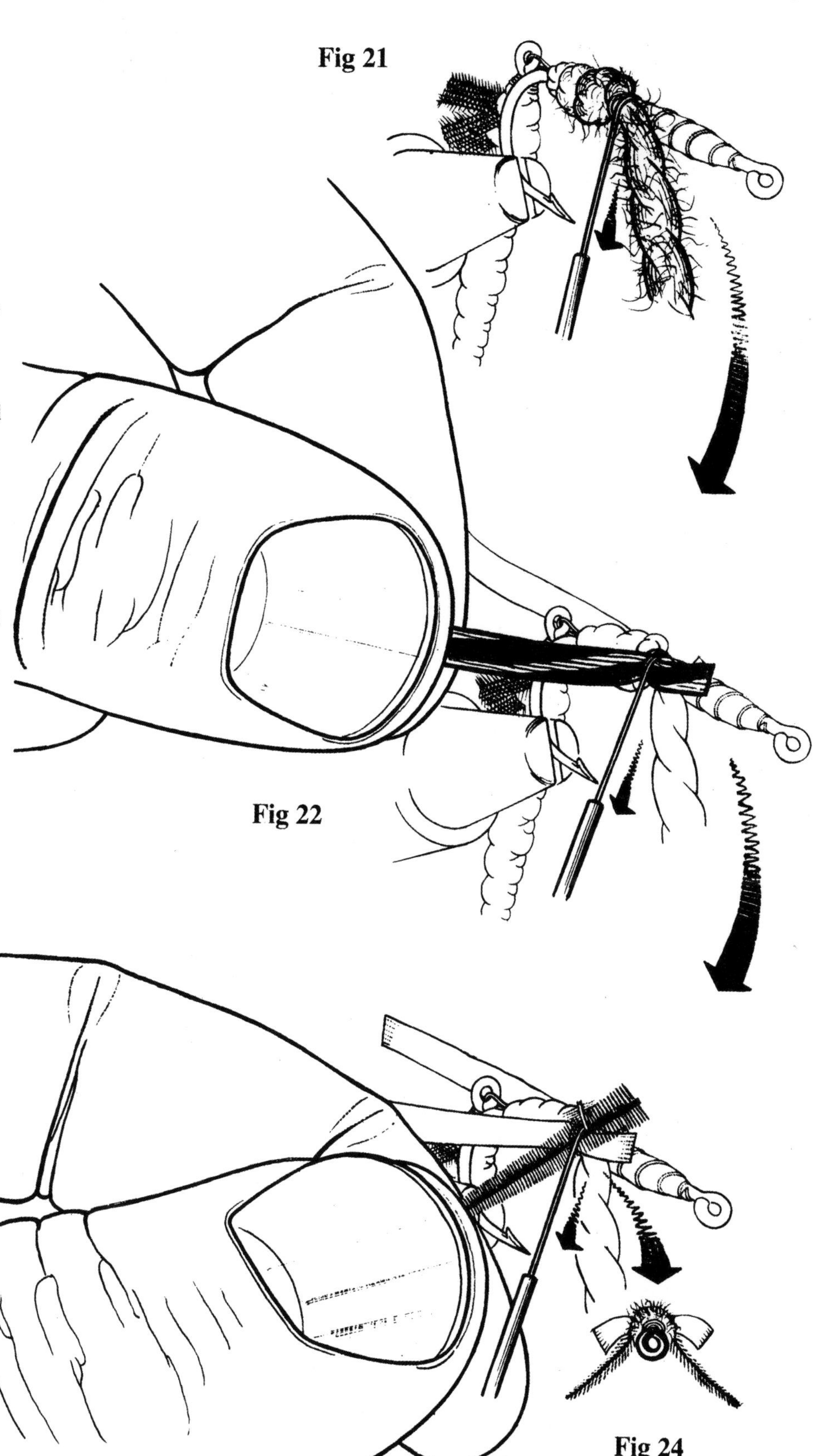
Fig 21

Fig 22

Fig 23

Fig 24

Fig 25
When these legs are securely tied down, advance the thread again, let the bobbin holder hang, and make two more full turns of the twisted yarn. The first turn will wrap over and hide the bindings which tied down the golden pheasant and the ostrich herl legs. Securely tie down the yarn.

Fig 26
Offer up and tie in the centre pair of legs - again they should slope backwards and sideways, as before.

Fig 27
Advance the thread once more, let the bobbin holder hang, twist the yarn tight, make two more wraps and tie down again.

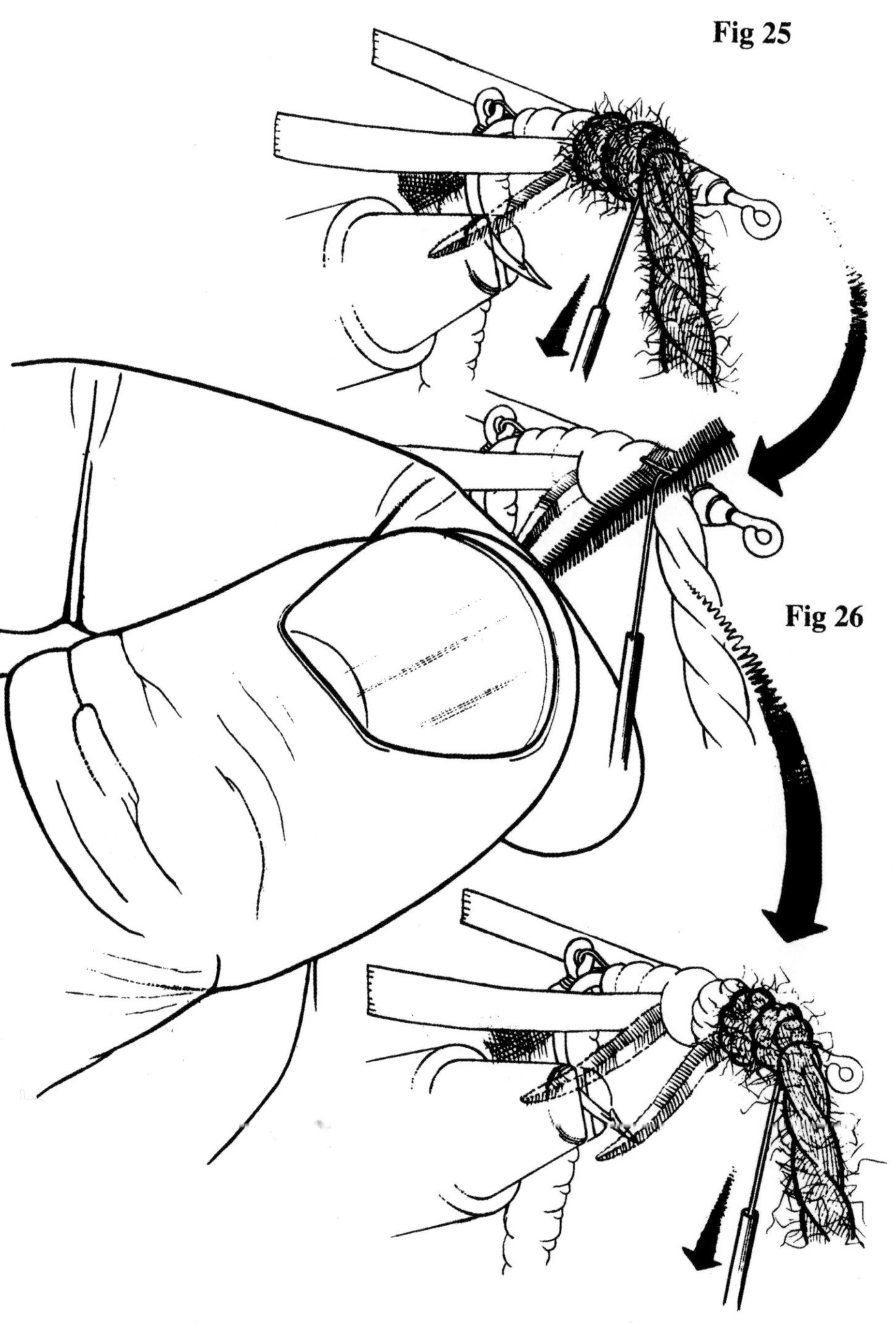

Fig 25

Fig 26

Fig 27

Fig 28
Tie in the front pair of legs exactly as before. I sometimes make these shorter than the others, or even facing forward.

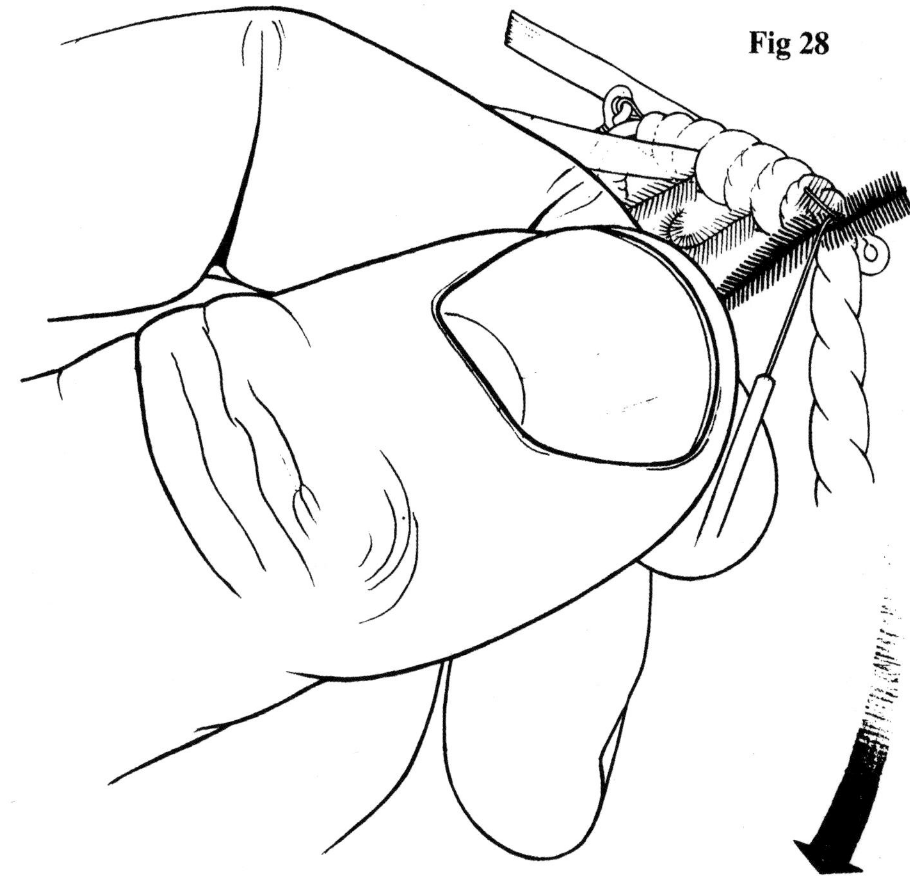
Fig 28

Fig 29
This done, advance the thread to behind the eye and make further turns of the yarn until you arrive just short of the eye, where you tie it off very securely. Trim off the waste yarn.
Now, if you wish, add the two goose biots representing the weird tusk-like projections on the natural.

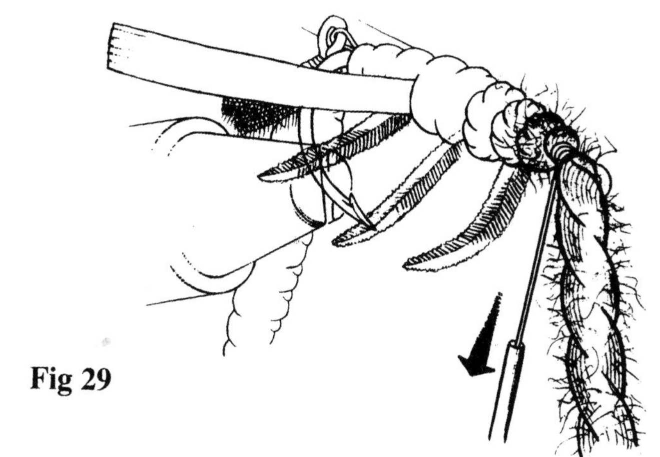
Fig 29

Fig 30
Position one each side of the eye and slightly to the underside.

Fig 31
The tips should project about 1/8" (3mm). Tie down securely.

Figs 32 & 33
Trim off the waste thick butt ends of the biots, when securely tied in.

Fig 30

Fig 31

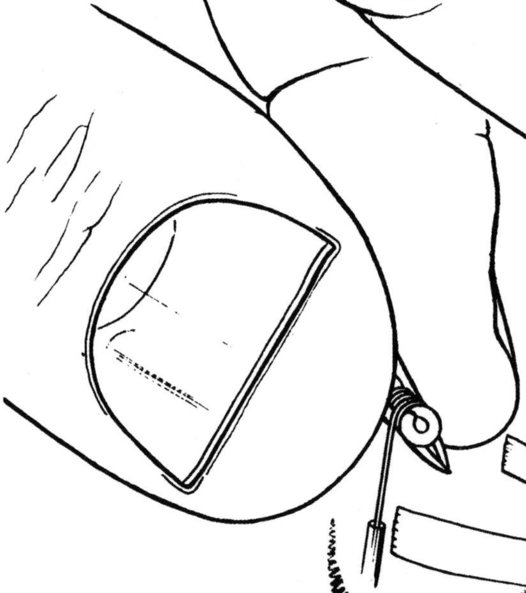

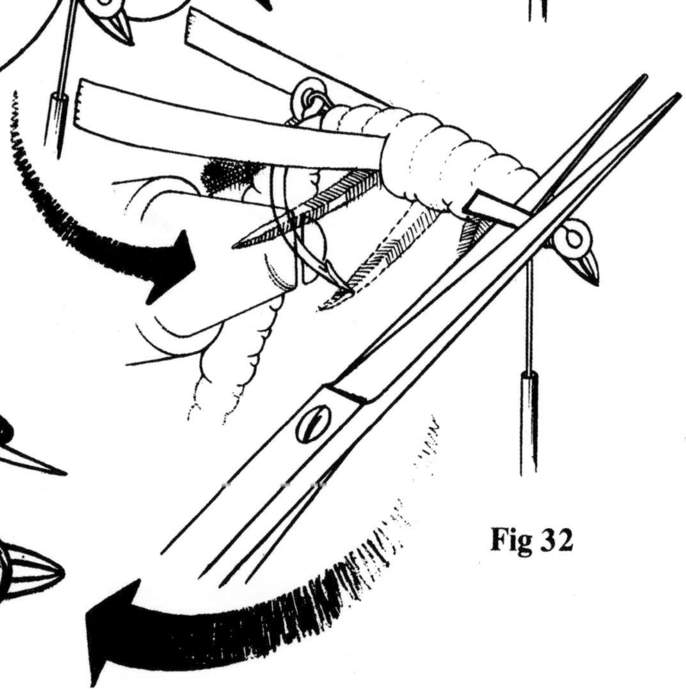

Fig 32

Fig 33

Fig 34
Finally make the wing buds. Pull over the near side golden pheasant quill section, pull it fairly tight, crossing it to just beyond the centre and securely bind it down.

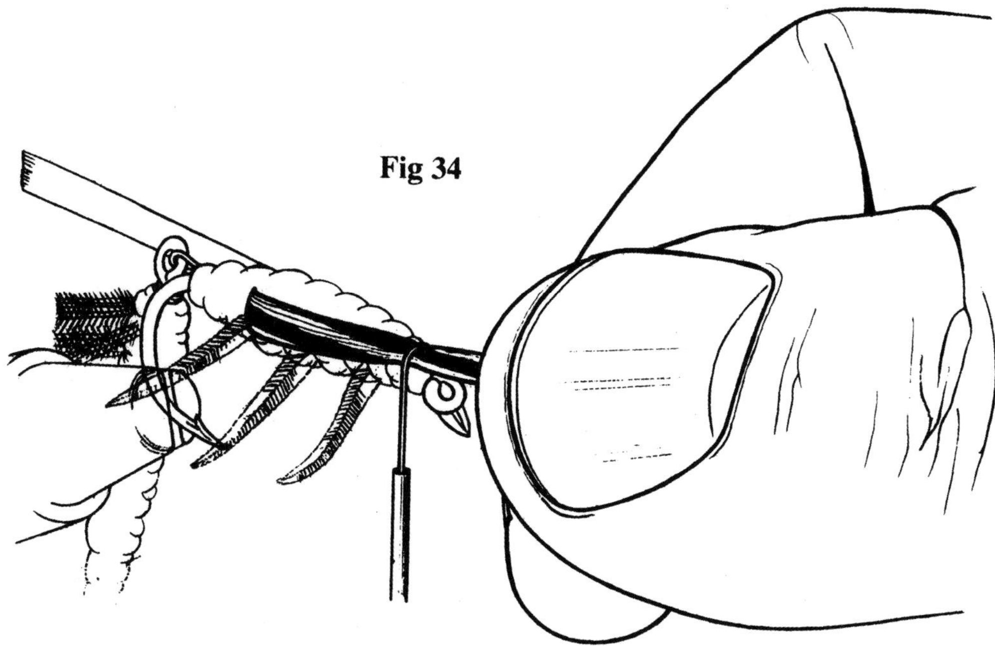
Fig 34

Fig 35
Do likewise with the far side wing bud, crossing it over the first one. Trim off the waste quill sections.
Form a neat tapering whip finish and snip off the thread.

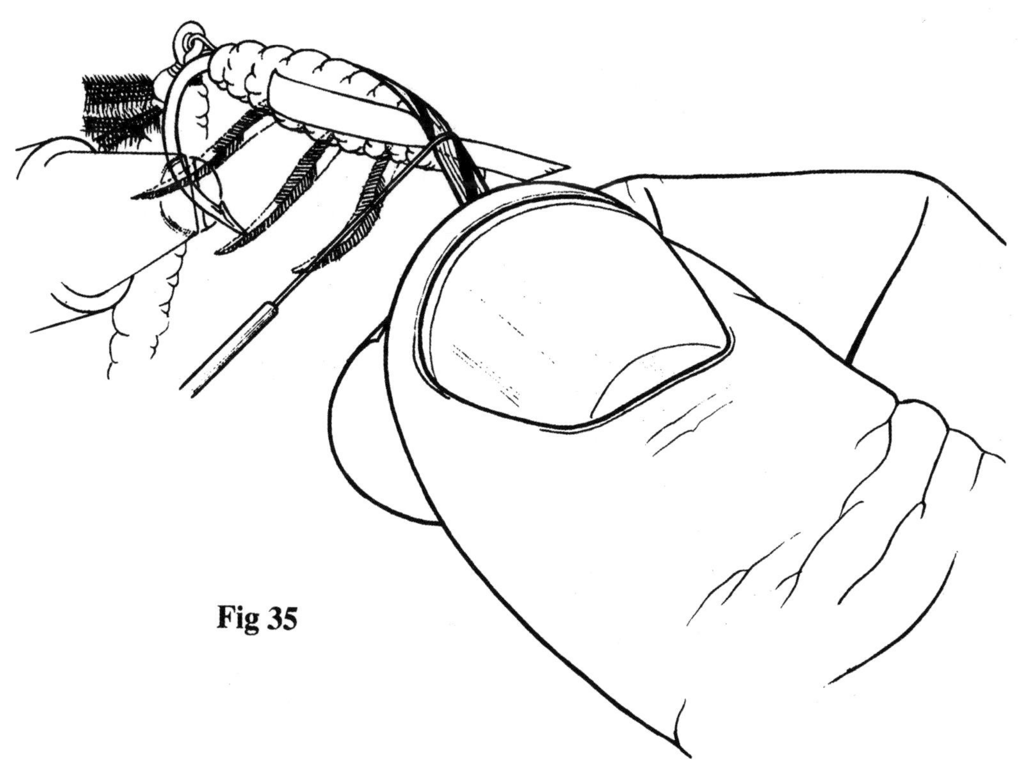
Fig 35

Fig 36
Now complete the nymph by brushing out some of the Antron fibres along the sides of both rear and front sections of the nymph. Support the abdomen (rear) portion in the crook of the index finger and, using your velcro scrubber, brush out the fibres all along the sides and underneath. Pay particular attention to that part of the front portion next to the junction, teasing out plenty of fibres to hide the junction. Finally, apply cement to the head whippings.

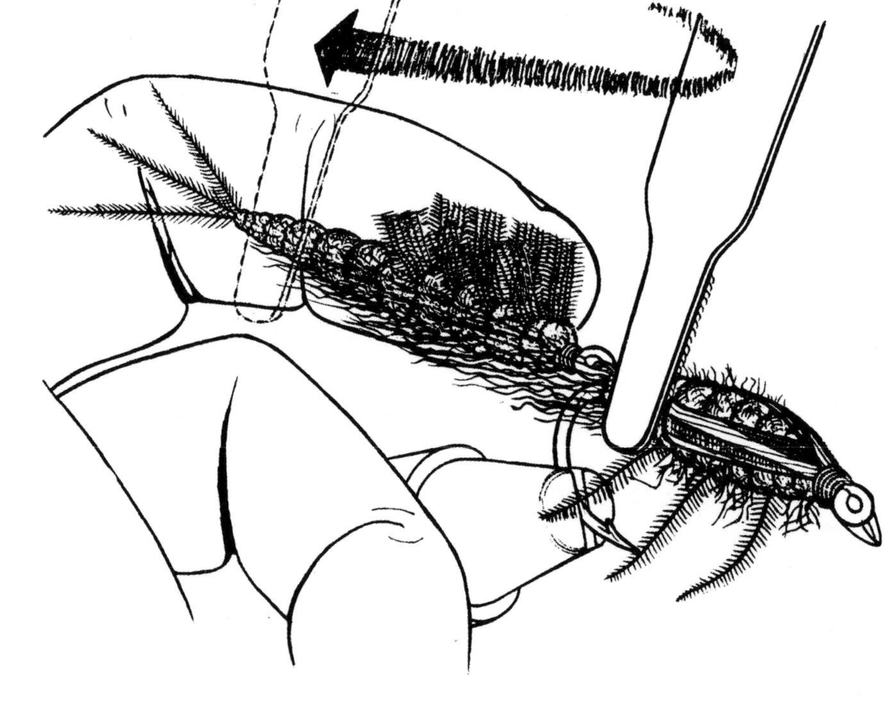

Fig 36

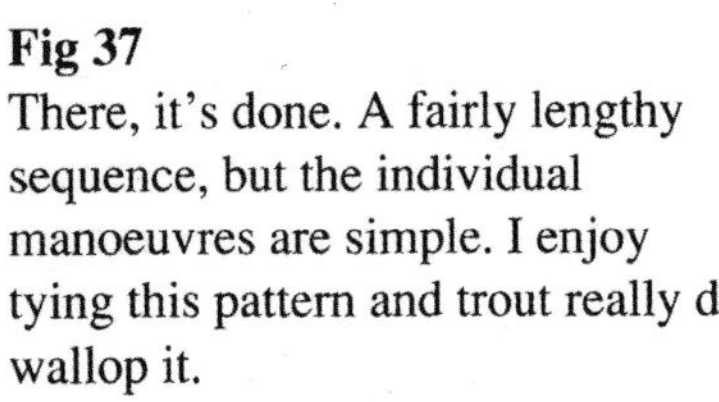

Fig 37
There, it's done. A fairly lengthy sequence, but the individual manoeuvres are simple. I enjoy tying this pattern and trout really do wallop it.

Fig 37

8. The Mohican Mayfly

Many times have I watched flyfishermen drift their 'standard' mayfly patterns over fish which were taking the duns confidently, only to be refused. These fish were gulping down naturals within seconds of the angler's artificial passing overhead.

It happened to me too on a memorable occasion when I was using a simple hackled thing I'd knocked up. Trout are not fussy when on the 'mayfly', I said to myself.

I was on my favourite little river, the Rye. There was a grand hatch on this late spring day; it was warm, sunny and still, with the valley smothered in its new coat of green. I thought I was in heaven. I had released several fish, taken on this hackled fly, when I realized that the hatch was slowing, with just the occasional heavy slurps occurring on the edges of the little bays between the alders.

However, try as I might, I couldn't interest one of those fish. They were difficult, and, despite getting some very good drifts over them, I was refused time and again. It became obvious that further flogging would be useless. Time to put on the old thinking cap! Had they now switched to taking the emerging nymph as sometimes happens?

I took my own advice - for once - and sat down to observe. In less than half a minute, a couple of duns came floating down, about three feet apart. Six feet to go to the nearest fish. 'Don't fly off!' I muttered. The dun played the game and stayed put. There was a sudden lighting swirl and it was gone. The second dun was ignored by the first fish but was intercepted about two yards further down. Nevertheless, it must have passed over at least six fish before it was finally nabbed. I watched at least 25 of these large duns float by. Of those, only about a third were taken, the rest passed over this pod of fish unmolested.

However, the rises were certainly to the duns. I could discount my hatching nymph theory. These fish were clearly choosy. The 'bun fight' had ended. The mad scramble, when the duns were coming down thick and fast, when it was everyone for himself, was over. In these times of plenty a kind of feeding frenzy can build up, even among wild fish. The trout pellet syndrome, they excite one another and it becomes infectious.

Those fish I was observing had passed that stage, they had settled down to irregular feeding. Such fish are the ultimate challenge at mayfly time and I wanted an artificial which would pass their scrutiny. It was quite clear when I dropped my hackled pattern on the surface that it hadn't a hope in hell of seducing these fish.

My fly lacked the smooth lines of the natural, it also lacked another significant feature - a pair of very large upright wings, held together like a single unit. I hadn't a winged pattern in my box, so that was that.

The following year, I was fully prepared, wings and all! This was the start of an obsession: my quest, to create a Mayfly that would outwit the choosiest of fish.

The pattern I took to the Rye that year was, on reflection, no great shakes. More or less the same as the previous year's pattern, but with the addition of a good upright wing of dyed mallard breast feather barbs, nothing fancy. It worked after a fashion. But my pattern had a technical problem. The wing made it top heavy and it had a tendency to roll on its hackle points and topple over. It would also, fairly often, land on its side.

The following year, I cured the rolling by simply converting the fly to a paradun, winding an olive-green hackle around the base of the same clump of wing. This pattern worked very well and I felt I was at last getting there.

The next spring at Chatsworth Angling Fair, I found myself sharing the tying bench with the late Jim Nice. When Jim tied a fly, everyone stood and gaped: his dry flies were perfection.

After the show, over a mug of tea, Jim let me in on a few of his wrinkles. I popped the question of mayflies: did he have a favourite pattern? 'Mayflies! Oh yes,' he replied, 'a natural blue dun cock hackle and a grizzle cock hackle dyed in Picric, both wound together. She's lethal!'

I had some aqueous picric acid in the garden shed and my one and only Metz was a grizzle too. Ah well, c'est la vie, Jim says so, so it must be sacrificed. At about the same time, I was flirting with the idea of turning the hook upside down on some of my dries. I had the crazy idea that trout were upset by the hook bend clawing through the surface. Also, the Partridge Swedish Dry Fly hook (code K3A) was now available and purpose-made for this application. So the next mayfly version was born, and it featured Jim's double hackle, a good big wing of lemon wood duck and the relatively new upside down hook.

I was so pleased with its performance that I included it in a series of articles I was doing in *Trout & Salmon* magazine. It still is a very effective fish fooler, but unfortunately it does have an achilles heel. When soaked, say after playing a fish, it requires a major drying off job before re-dunking in the floatant.

Finally, I turned to closed-cell foam for the body and the Mohican mayfly was born. This pattern floats like a cork, always alights the right way up, doesn't roll or blow over, and the entire fly is durable and easy to tie. It is made from readily-available materials.

Furthermore, that bane of all dry flies, weight, can be reduced on this pattern. Since it is a detached body type, the hook doesn't have to be long shank. Despite the fact that the hook is half way up the body, it is a good hooker and holder and, most important of all, the trout love it.

The inspiration for this large fly came from the detached elk hair bodied Paradrakes used by the flyfishers of Michigan. The double-layer abdomen and circumferential ribs I first saw in Darrel Martin's masterpiece, *Fly Tying Methods*. It's basically a simple fly to tie, only the double-layer abdomen slowing you down.

NOTES ON MATERIALS AND TYING

The hook should be short in the shank with a good big bite - the gape and the throat. The one I use has a black japanned finish. I'd prefer it to be nickel finish, but the trout don't seem to mind.

The foam for the body is the Plastazote lining material for fly boxes. Unfortunately, it is really too white, the colour I would love to find for this pattern is the colour of old ivory piano keys. However, again the trout don't seem to mind. Failing Plastazote, experiment with any fine closed-cell foam. One important point here: try not to crush the foam too much between finger and thumb or you'll be destroying its tiny air pockets. Don't use adhesive backed foam.

When you're manoeuvring the thread along the inner core, travelling towards the tail, compressing the two strips down to make a small diameter, it can be a fiddle, since you have to support the tail end with one hand while you perform 'drop bobbin passes' with the other. Some people insert a very fine beading needle in the centre to support the abdomen at this stage, to make tying easier. Beware, however, the needle may not pull out afterwards.

The inner core should taper towards the tails by increasing thread wraps and tension. Crush it down severely with the thread so as to produce a fine inner core. If you don't like making the true circumferential segments, as I've described and illustrated, there's nothing to stop you simply spiralling the tying thread all the way along as in conventional ribbing. However, you should be aware that such a rib could completely unravel,

MOHICAN MAYFLIES
One illustrated facing to show the narrow "Mohican" wing.

one end to the other, were it to be ragged by a toothy trout! The way I've illustrated it means that unravelling is arrested, since the thread, after forming each true segment, dives 'underground' to wrap around the inner core, out of harm's way.

There's nothing special about the other materials. The wings are from good quality Texas Whitetail Deer, dyed drab olive. When you're selecting your tails from the moose patch, look for the longest and stoutest ones, but check that they have fine tips.

If you insist on using picric acid for dyeing your grizzle hackle, you will definitely have problems finding a supplier. In its dry state, it is highly explosive and illegal to possess I am told. So don't, I repeat don't, accept picric acid crystals or powder from anyone. It must be an aqueous solution. As such, it is quite safe but it dyes skin instantly so don't go dabbling your fingers in the stuff. When dyeing feather or fur in picric, wash it first in warm soap suds then rinse in cold water. Now you simply dunk your chosen material in the jar of picric, swish it about and keep checking for colour set. Then rinse and dry. Always keep your picric solution in a screw-top glass container, clearly labelled and safely stored. If you can't get hold of any picric, don't panic, an ordinary yellow dye is quite acceptable.

THE MOHICAN MAYFLY

Hook: Wide gape medium wire standard shank or short shank hook. Suggest Partridge 'Capt. Hamilton' International Middleweight Hook Code CS7MW, sizes 10 or 12.
Thread: Fine Kevlar type or Kevlar blend, any brand, pale yellow, pale olive or pale grey (if white, tint with a felt pen).
Cement: Dave's Flexament (USA) or Floo Gloo (UK).
Tails: Dark moose mane or moose body hair.
Abdomen: Fine closed-cell foam, white (or cream if obtainable).
Thorax and head: As abdomen.
Wing: Texas whitetail deer hair dyed yellow-olive or bleached and dyed yellow-olive.
Hackle: One grizzle dry-fly-quality dyed pale yellow and one blue dun dry-fly-quality (natural or dyed).

Tying the Mohican Mayfly

Fig 1
Grip hook firmly in vice with shank horizontal. Catch on tying thread at mid-shank position and make four or five butting thread wraps. From your moose patch, tweak out three or four (fourth for insurance) identical, long, tapering hairs. Align all four fine tips and offer them up to the top of the shank and temporarily tie them in using a few 'pinch and loops'. Their tips should extend out beyond the bend by one body length plus one tail length. Don't skimp or you'll curse later!

Fig 2
When happy with position and length, bind them down securely, working towards the bend ensuring that they stay on top of the shank.

Fig 3
Trim off the waste butts. Return the tying thread to nearer the eye. Let bobbin hang. The wings now go in. Snip out, as near the pelt as possible, a clump of the dyed deer hair.

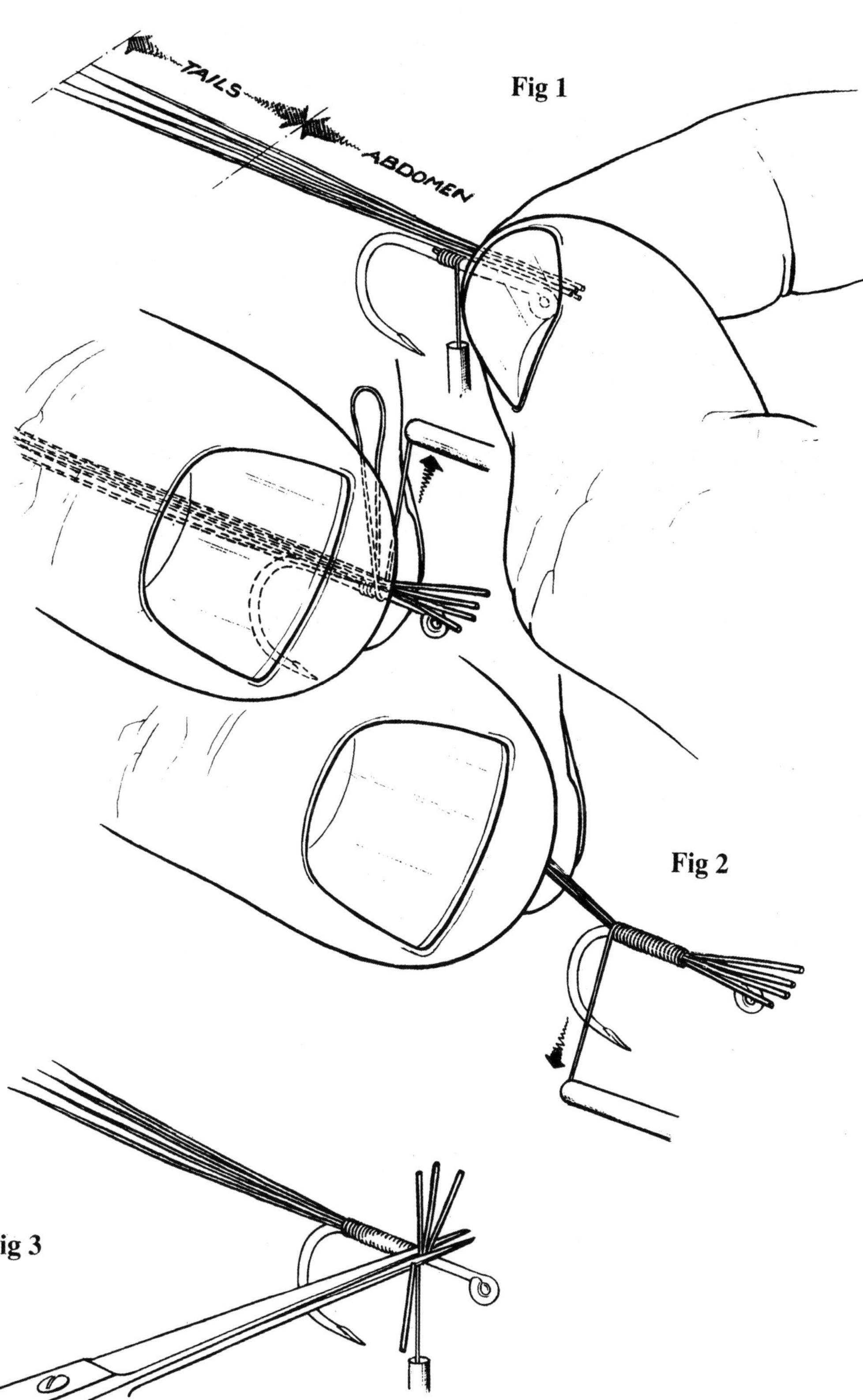

Figs 4 & 5
Comb or strip out the fine basal underfur then drop the clump into a stacker, tips down and tamp even. Slide the base from the stacker, grip the tips and pull the clump from the stacker.

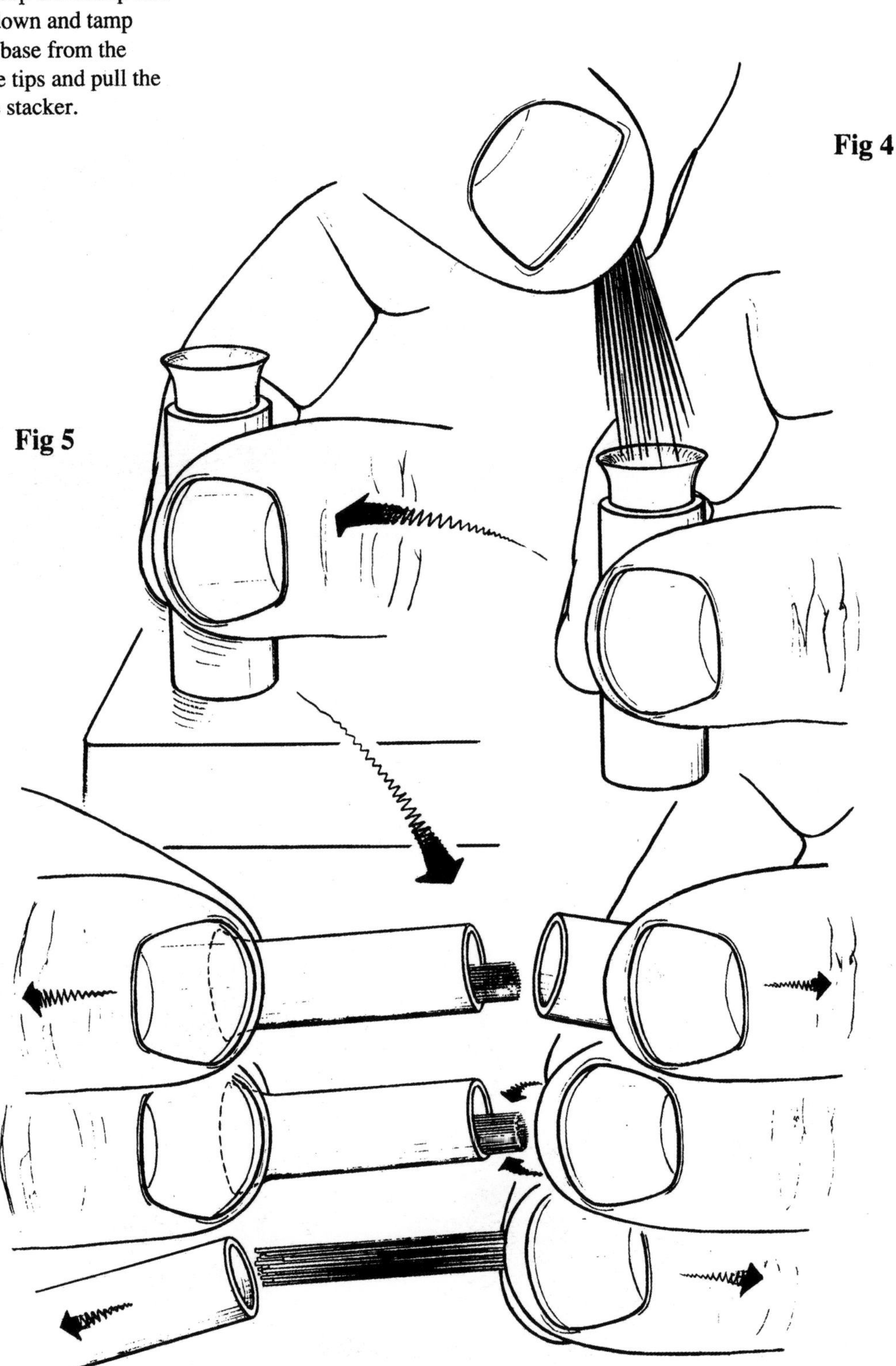

Fig 6
Now take this clump and offer it up to the top of the shank, the tips projecting out by 3/4" (19mm) beyond where the thread is hanging.

Fig 7
Grip the hair butts tight then circle around with the tying thread and make an initial 'pinch and loop' binding of moderate tension, the tips will flare.

Fig 8
Follow this with another 'pinch and loop' with more tension, creating much more flare. Repeat until firmly bound down.

Fig 9
Now release your grip and trim the waste butts on the slope.

Fig 10
Touch the butts with head cement and securely bind them down.

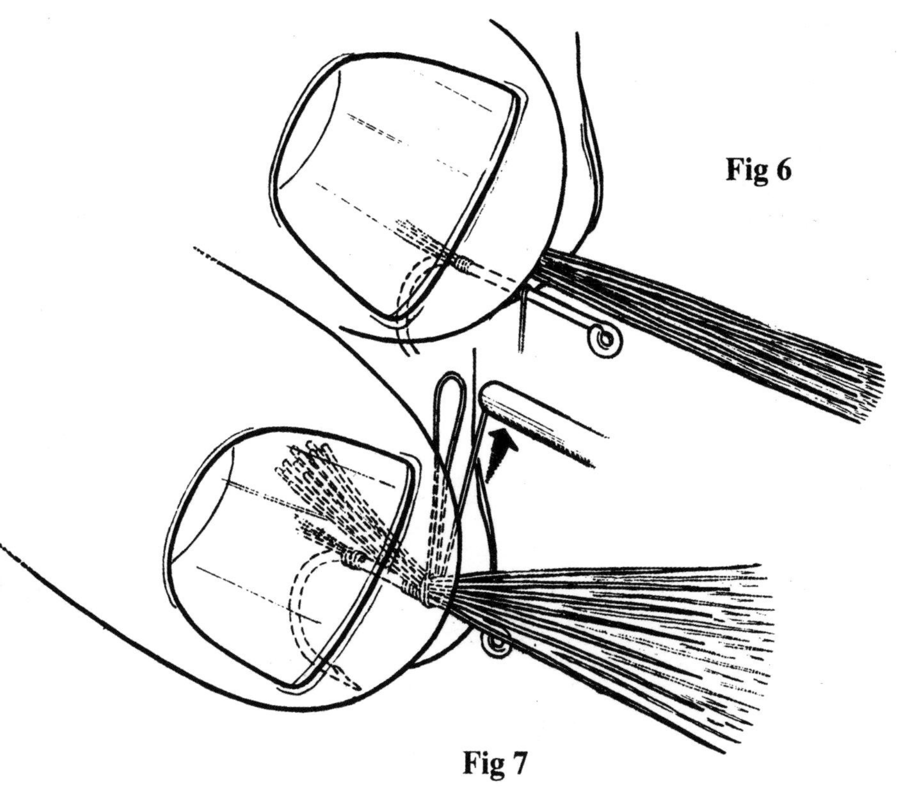

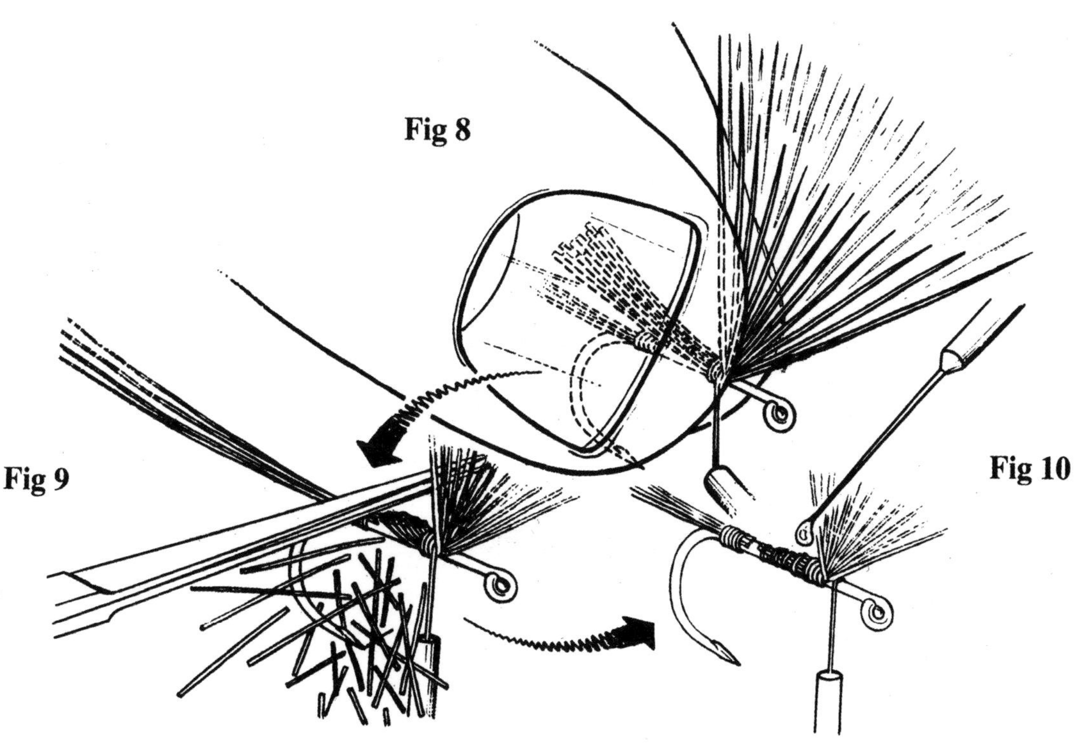

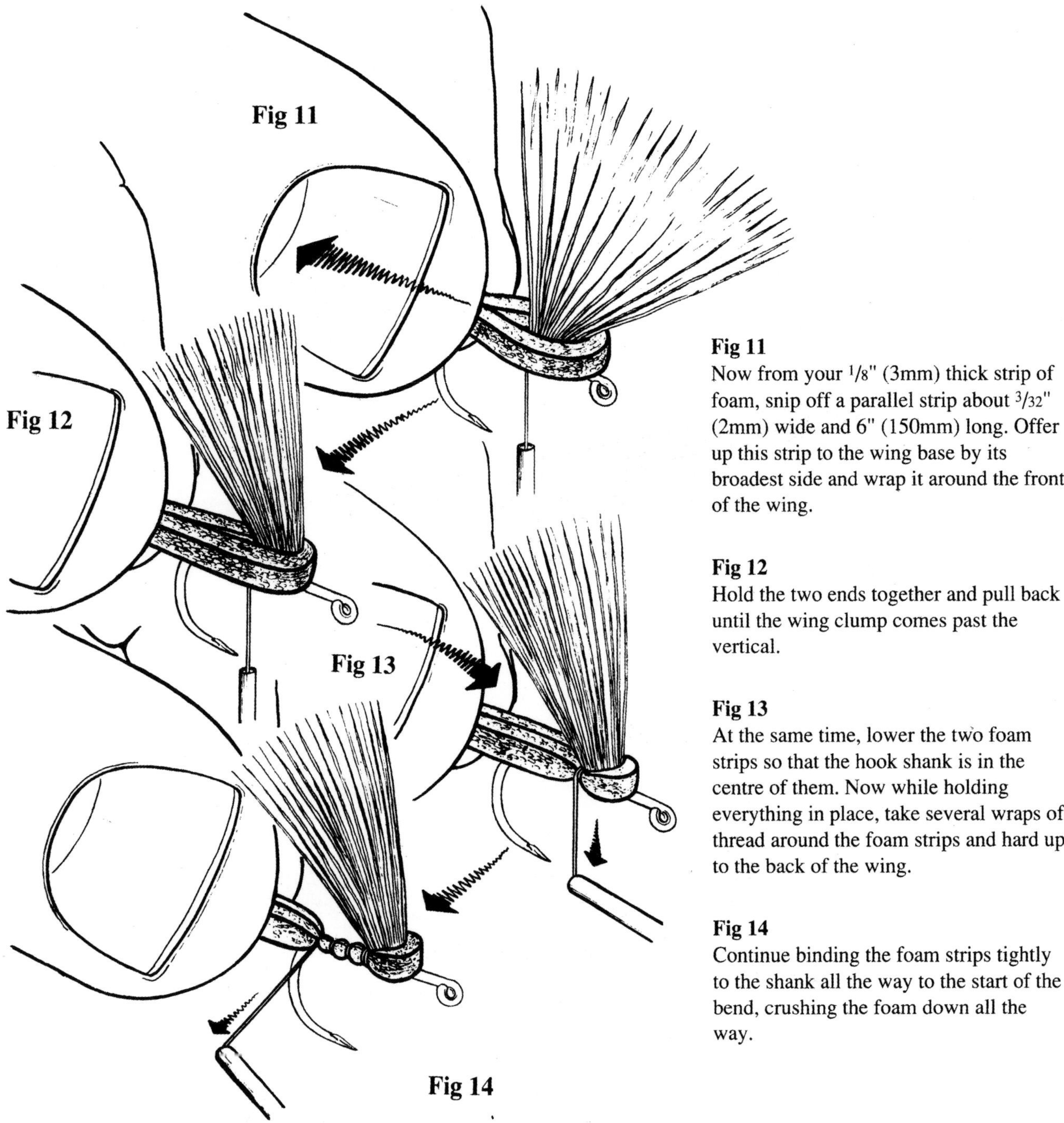

Fig 11
Now from your 1/8" (3mm) thick strip of foam, snip off a parallel strip about 3/32" (2mm) wide and 6" (150mm) long. Offer up this strip to the wing base by its broadest side and wrap it around the front of the wing.

Fig 12
Hold the two ends together and pull back until the wing clump comes past the vertical.

Fig 13
At the same time, lower the two foam strips so that the hook shank is in the centre of them. Now while holding everything in place, take several wraps of thread around the foam strips and hard up to the back of the wing.

Fig 14
Continue binding the foam strips tightly to the shank all the way to the start of the bend, crushing the foam down all the way.

Fig 15

Now you have to unclamp the hook, turn it around and reclamp, dangling bobbin and all. Now you have to bind the two foam strips to the four tails, ensuring that the tails stay central between the strips. Grip the two foam strips to the tails and continue binding tightly using the 'drop bobbin' method.

Fig 16

As you progress along with the thread, produce a taper by both increasing tension and reducing the distance between thread wraps. In fact the thread wraps should virtually touch each other. When you've completed the binding for a distance of approximately 3/4" (19mm) beyond the bend, stop and make about 3 or 4 thread wraps on the spot.

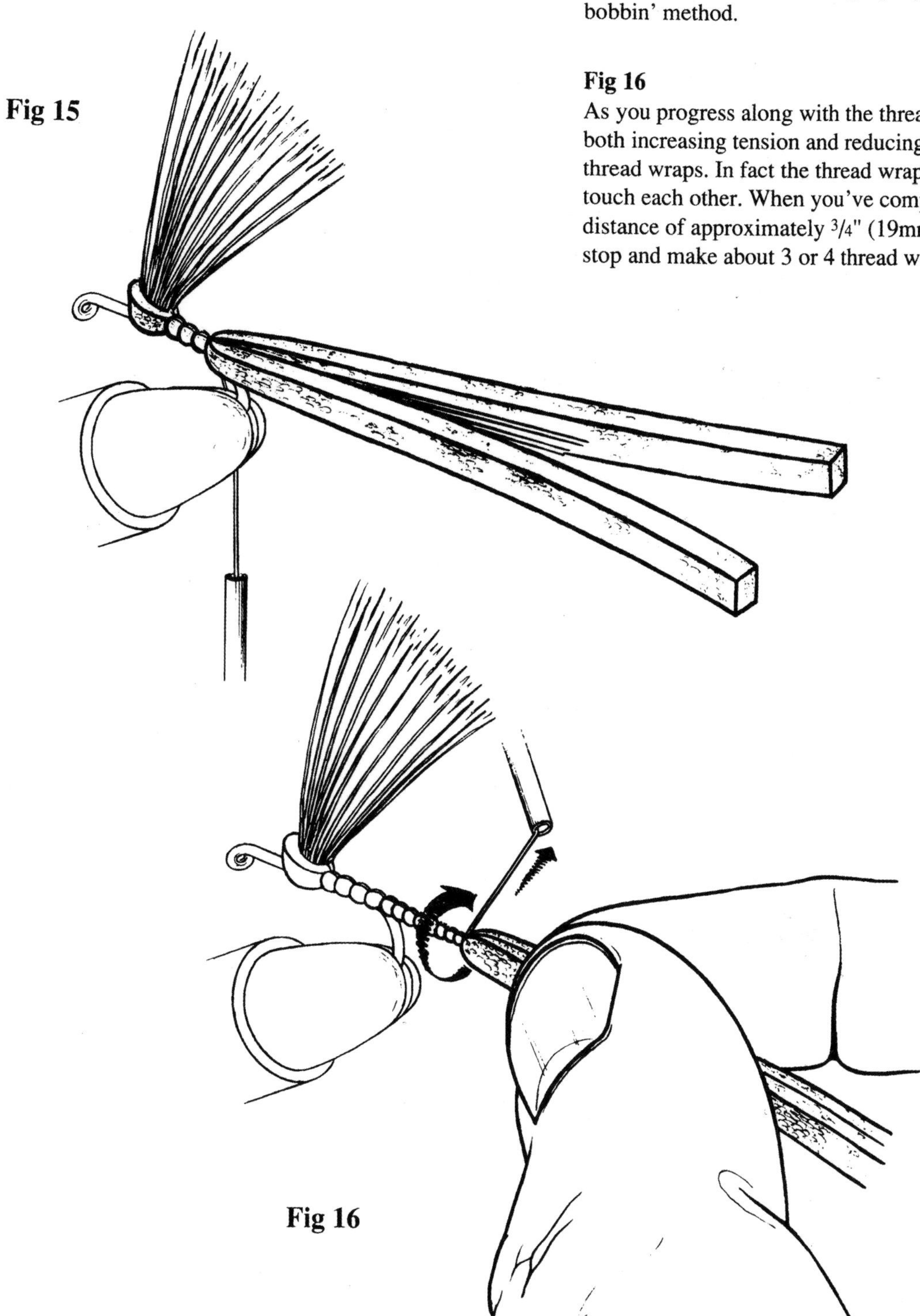

Fig 15

Fig 16

Figs 17 & 18
Now pull back the two foam strips and make about three thread wraps on the spot just back from the end of the abdomen, thus completing the first segment. Then separate the two foam strips and take the thread to the inner core.

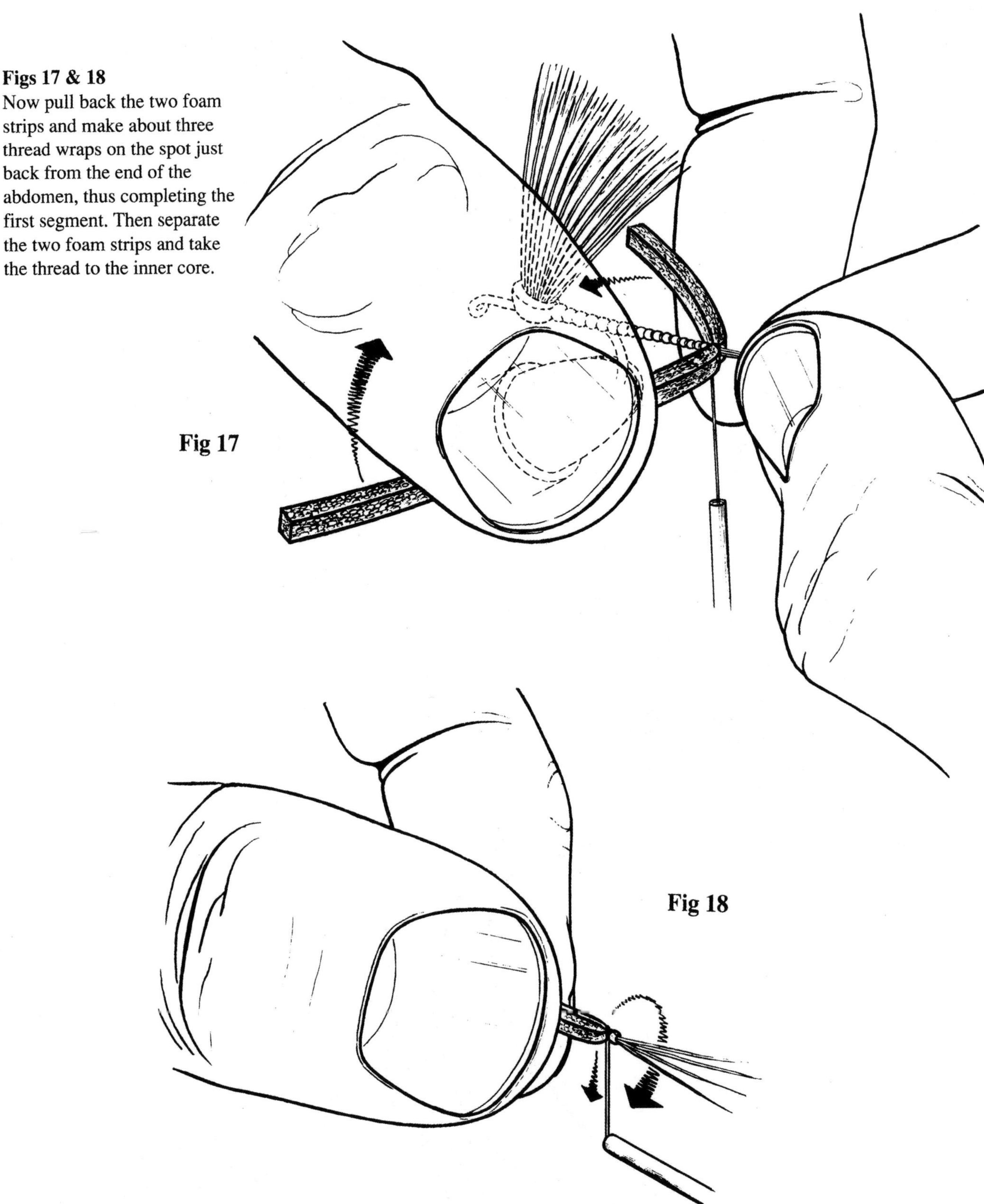

Fig 17

Fig 18

Fig 19
Once on the inner core, work back towards the hook bend with the thread one segment width.

Fig 20
Bring the two foam strips together again, circle around with the tying thread three or four times on the spot to make the second segment.

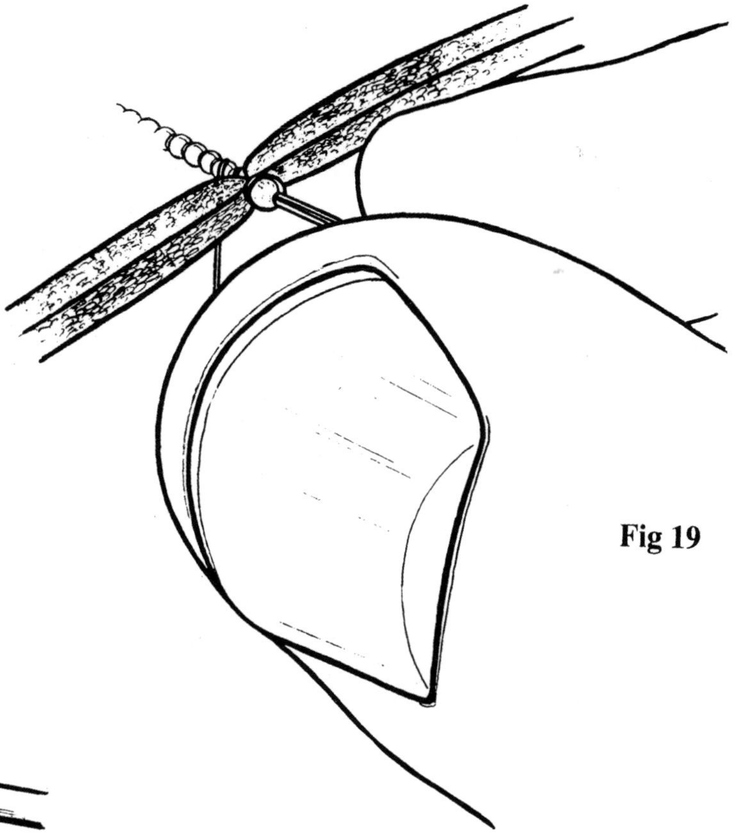

Fig 19

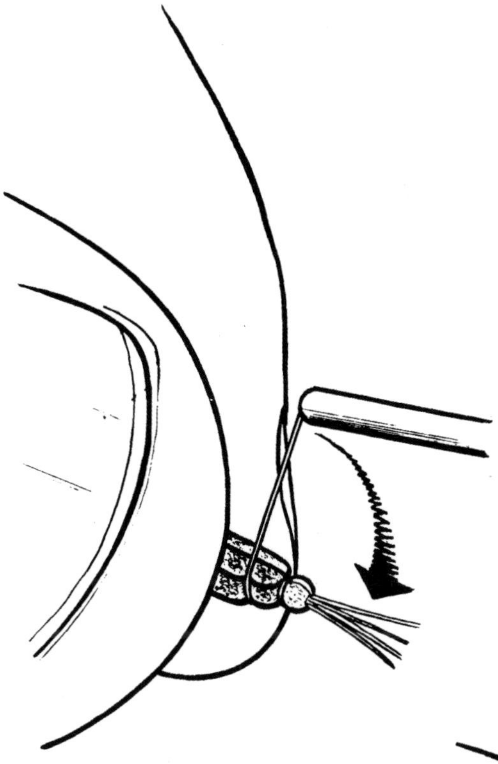

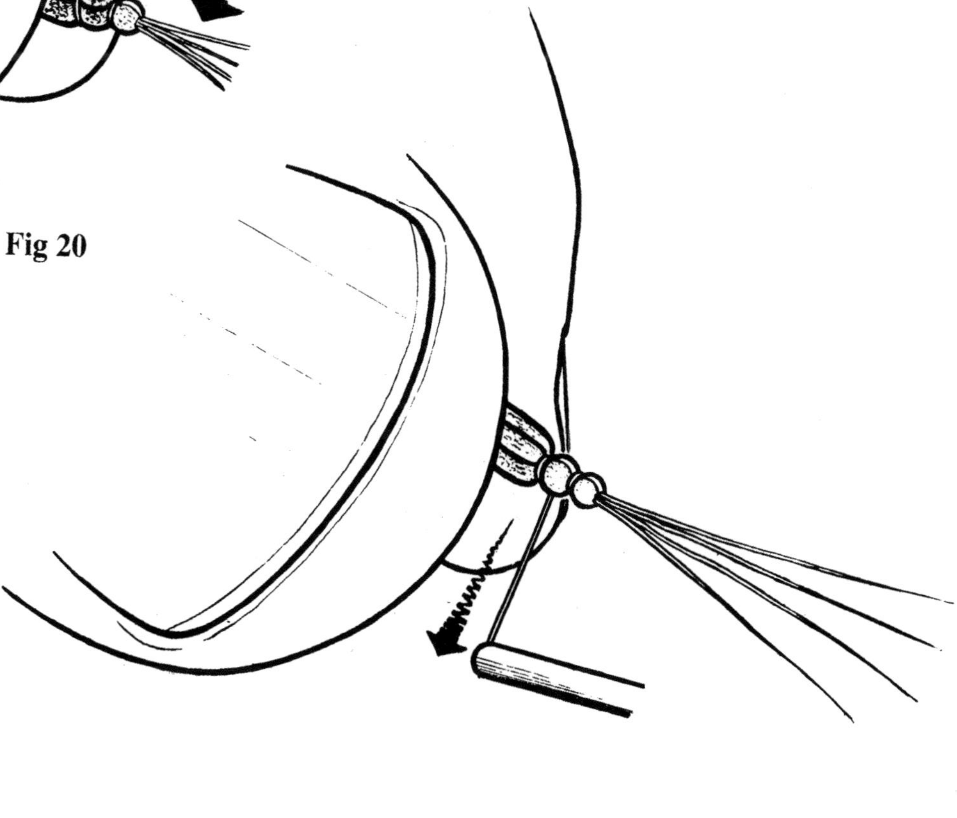

Fig 20

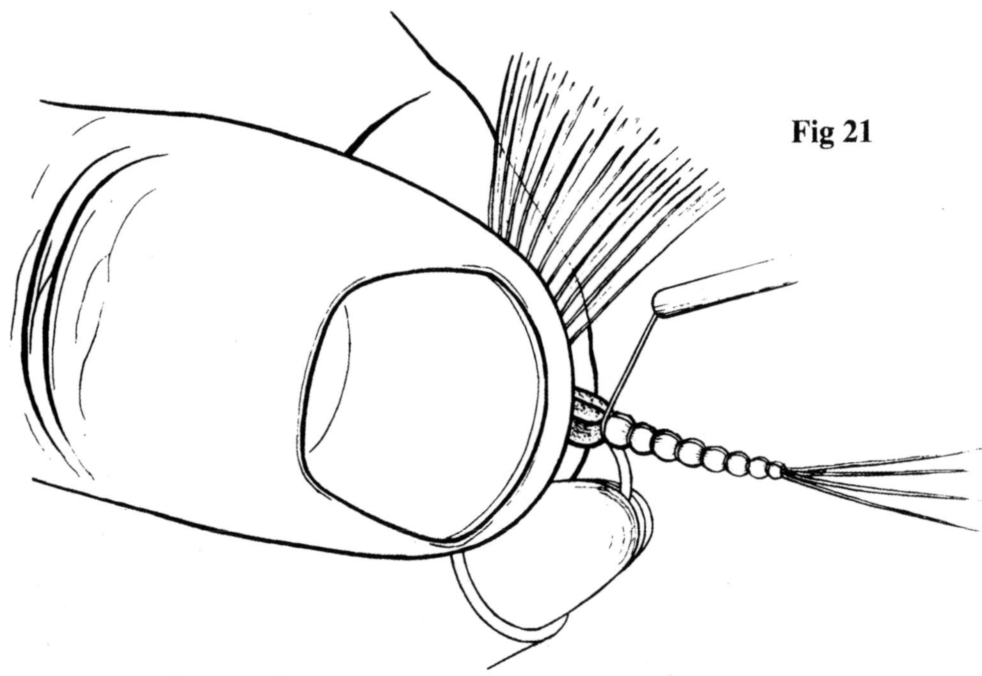
Fig 21

Fig 21
Continue with this process, making seven or eight full circumferential segments until you arrive back at the hook bend.

Fig 22
Let the bobbin hang. Unclamp again and return the hook the usual way around. Reclamp, and continue to make another two or three full circumferential segments now around the hook shank. At this stage you will have arrived at the back of the wing.

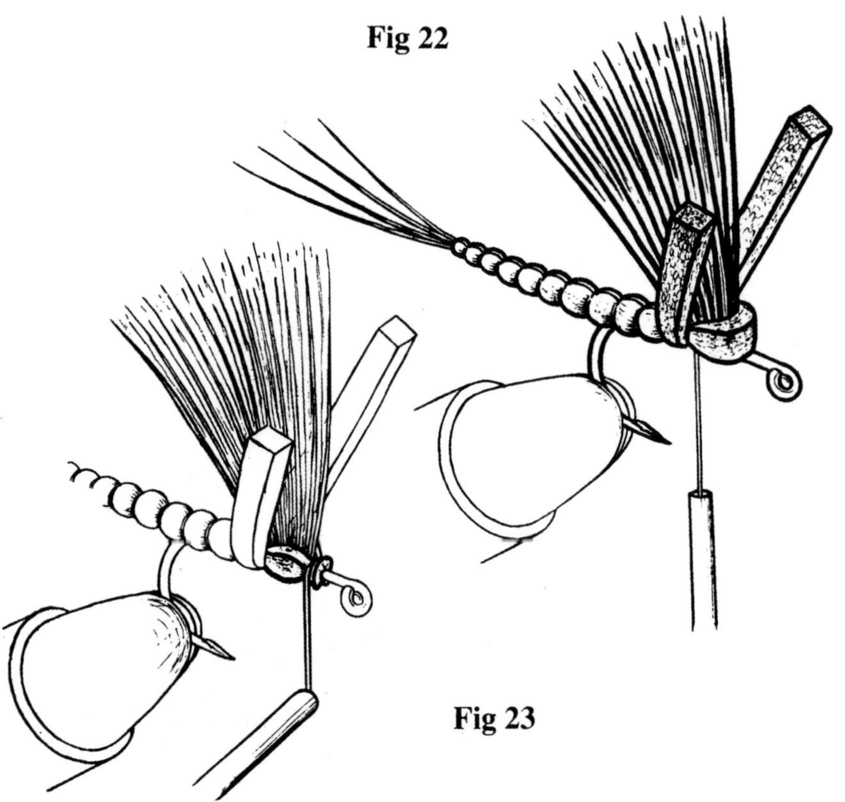
Fig 22

Fig 23

Fig 23
The two foam tags now project upwards and outwards. If they don't project upwards, give them a little gentle persuasion to make them do so. Now bring the tying thread to the front of the wing and compress down the front fold of foam with the tying thread.

Fig 24
The next items to be tied in are the two hackles. Strip off the lower fluff and the inferior barbs and bind the pair to the shank, one sited above the other. Strive to keep the barbs in the horizontal plane. Make sure also that they are on the correct side for winding on parachute fashion without folding back on themselves. When very secure, snip off the waste quill butts.

Fig 25
Now grip both hackles together in your hackle pliers and circle them around the base of the wing and the two upstanding tags of foam. Make two or three wraps, producing a parachute hackle.

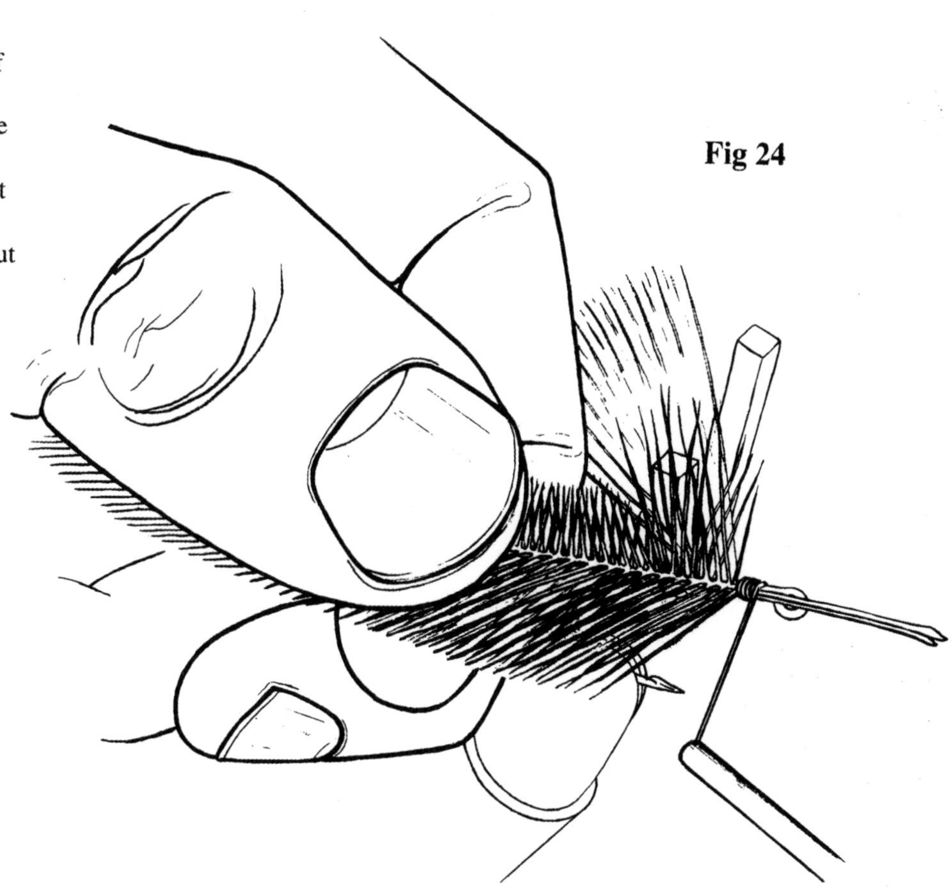

Fig 24

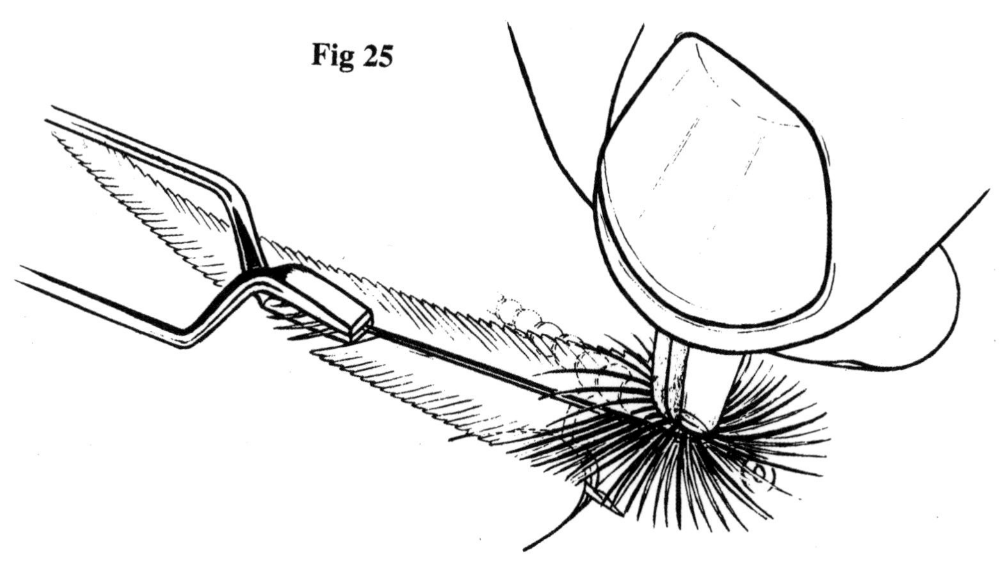

Fig 25

Fig 26

Finally, bring the hackle tips to the bare hook shank in front of the wing where you bind them down securely. In so doing, you will most likely also trap down several of the hackle barbs. Don't worry, forward facing barbs aren't really necessary anyway so I simply snip them off close to the centre quill.

Having securely tied down the two hackles, snip off their waste tips, but not too close to the bindings. Let the bobbin hang.

Fig 27

Bring over the two upstanding tags of foam. Bring them over as a pair, as I've illustrated. They pass over the radiating hackle barbs, each one snugging tightly into the hair wing making distinct thoracic humps. They also make excellent buoyancy tanks! This manoeuvre has the effect of spreading the hair, making the wing longer at its base and quite thin - a mohican tuft.

Fig 28

Bind the two tags of foam down, forward of the front of the wing.

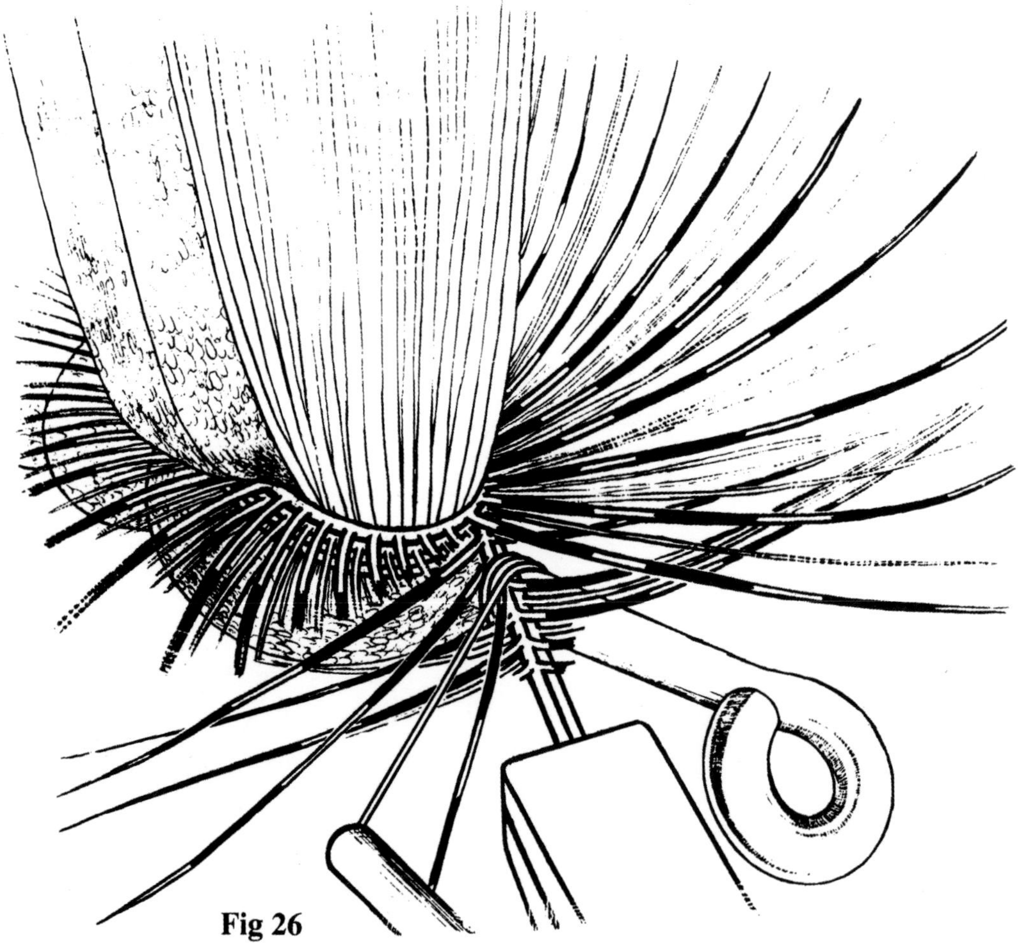

Fig 26

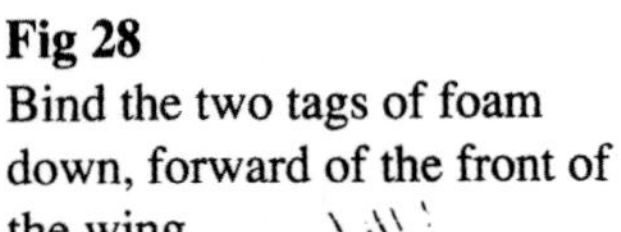

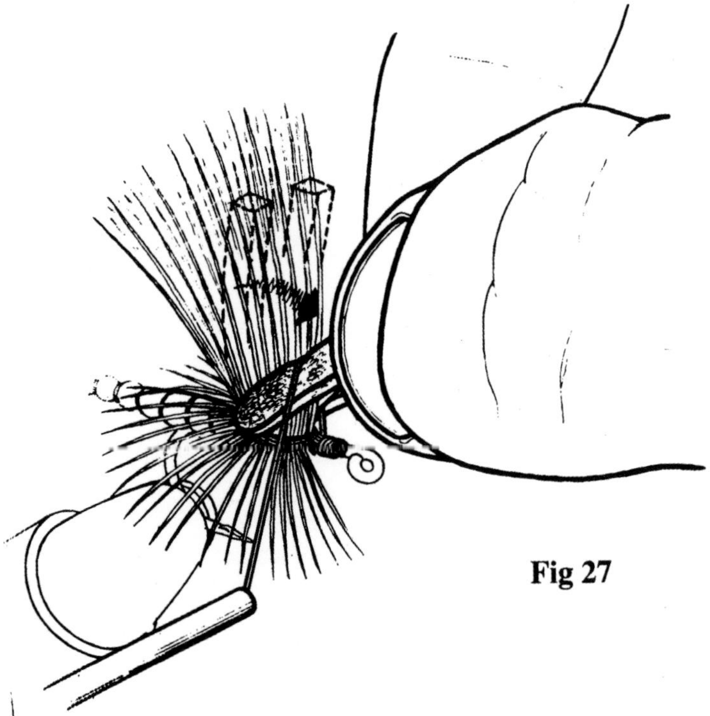

Fig 28

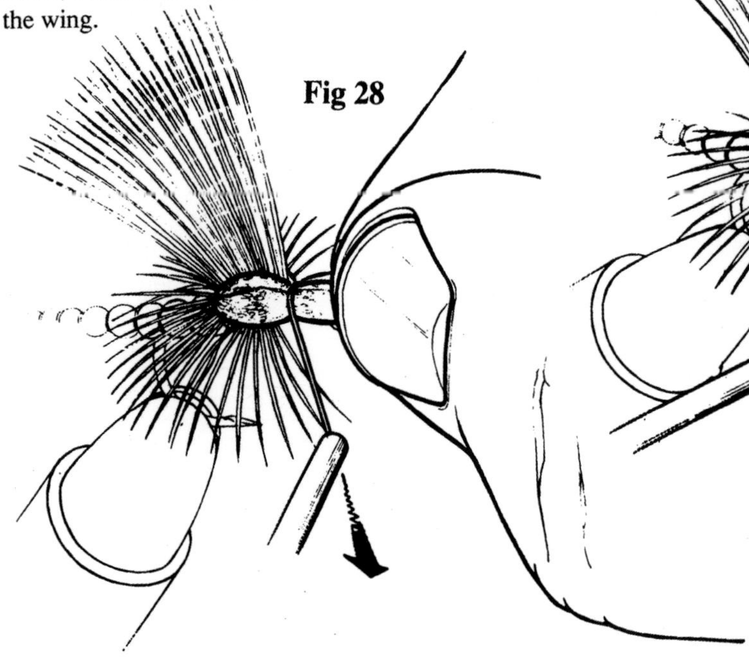

Fig 27

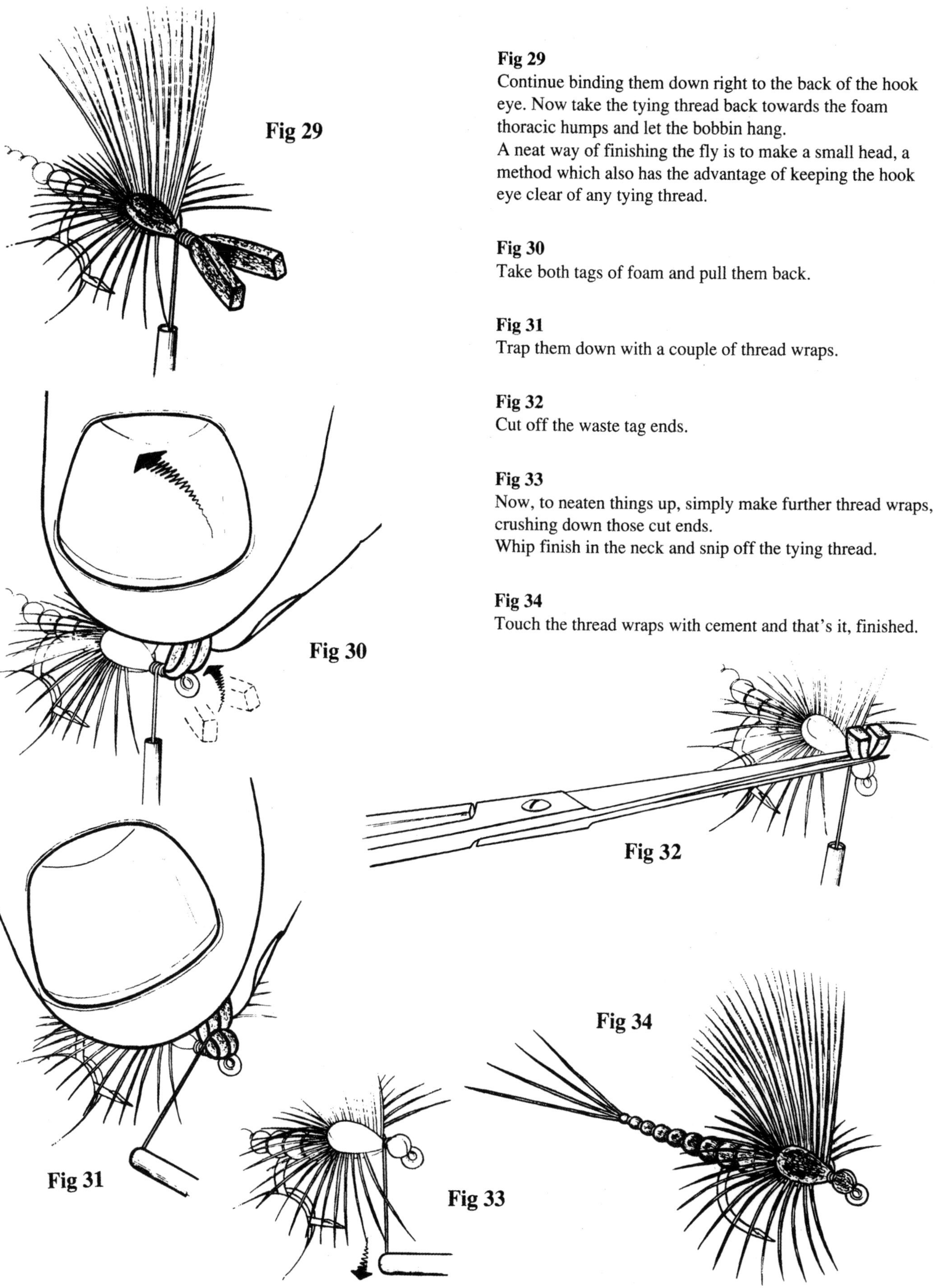

Fig 29
Continue binding them down right to the back of the hook eye. Now take the tying thread back towards the foam thoracic humps and let the bobbin hang.
A neat way of finishing the fly is to make a small head, a method which also has the advantage of keeping the hook eye clear of any tying thread.

Fig 30
Take both tags of foam and pull them back.

Fig 31
Trap them down with a couple of thread wraps.

Fig 32
Cut off the waste tag ends.

Fig 33
Now, to neaten things up, simply make further thread wraps, crushing down those cut ends.
Whip finish in the neck and snip off the tying thread.

Fig 34
Touch the thread wraps with cement and that's it, finished.

9. The Rhyacophila Larva

This is a very important genus of caddisfly for river fishermen, particularly for those fortunate enough to have access to the faster streams with plenty of broken water, typified by the rocky-bottomed, rainfed rivers found in most of the 'natural' game fishing regions of Britain.

All fish take Rhyacophila caddisfly at all stages in its life cycle. However, the larval and pupal stages are unsurpassed as fish food. From the third week in May right through to August, the ascending and emerging pupae of the Rhyacophila caddisflies constitute up to 80%, by weight, of a trout's daily food intake. This figure is based on my own observations from many autopsies on trout taken from Yorkshire rivers during May, June and July over a period of several years.

The fully-formed adult, on the other hand, is not often found in stomach contents. The reason for this is readily appreciated once one witnesses how fast they emerge and rocket off the surface to safety. Adults which I have found in trouts' stomachs - rarely more than three among scores of pupae - have, I suspect, been females, taken while drifting away after egg laying, since the females of this genus dive to the stream bed to egg lay.

The caddisfly, or sedge, is one of the most familiar and certainly the easiest of all water-born flies to recognise. To a great many flyfishermen the name 'caddis' means only one thing - the adult winged form. Most (but by no means all) of the adults are a buff-brown shade and have the same outline and this outline has resulted in a 'broad spectrum' approach by the flytyer over the years. This approach, it has to be said, has worked very well and there are many of these 'general' patterns - both old and new - which have accounted for tremendous catches of trout and grayling.

The pupal stage of this insect on the other hand has only become really popular with flyfishers in Britain over the last two decades. The establishment of many large reservoirs, like Grafham in 1965, put an emphasis on pupa imitations for stillwaters. Meanwhile pupal patterns for *river* fishing remained largely unconsidered and undeveloped.

My own interest in river caddisflies was aroused some 20 years ago when I fished a club stretch of the river Wharfe. At that time heavy sedge hatches were guaranteed throughout the months of May, June and July (tailing off a little in August), particularly if the weather was warm and settled. I used to be driven crazy by fish swirling at what I thought were adult caddisflies in the failing evening light.

It took me a while to realise that these great swirls were not at the *adult* sedge. What really confused me was that often I would see the adult insect only inches above the swirl, heading towards the trees at great speed. Eventually, however, by sheer persistence plus a helping of luck, one of these 'big swirlers' did in fact fall to my dry sedge.

I needed that fish badly, so I was relieved that it was large enough to be culled. Its stomach content was a revelation. That trout made me think long and hard about all my past river trouting, for its stomach was full of bright green-bodied pupae - 43 in total - and only 6 winged adults.

I've since fished a stretch upstream of my happy hunting ground of 20 years ago, and it's a pleasure to be able to say that little has changed. The caddis are still there, possibly in even greater numbers. But now I'm more experienced, and armed not only with a good ascending pupa pattern, but also an excellent larva pattern which I use through the winter months for grayling.

The caddisfly under discussion here is known in America as the 'green caddis'. I much prefer this descriptive term to the old British name of 'sand fly' which was given to it, or at least popularised by, Alfred Ronalds in the nineteenth century. There are four species of green caddisfly in Britain, all belonging to the family Rhyacophilidae. Of these four green caddis, the most common and widespread is *Rhyacophila dorsalis*. The other three species look similar enough to be copied by the artificials under discussion.

The preferred habitat of the green caddis is the swifter parts of the river, even right into the rapids. However, the current doesn't have to be broken and turbulent for there to be populations of these larvae. They can also be encountered in fast glassy glides, as long as there are stones or rocks on the stream bed. Food availability is another factor determining population. But the deciding factor is current speed, and it is in fast current speeds of 2-3 feet per second that they will most commonly be found. It is recorded that a tearing current speed of 6.5 feet per second is required to dislodge these larvae!

The larvae of this genus are the only true free-living, free-roaming types found in the UK. They make neither net, nor trap, nor tunnel and find their prey by, I can only imagine, literally stumbling upon it. The larvae are mainly carnivorous, feeding on the early instar nymphs of the Ephemeroptera and Diptera - in fact any small invertebrate is likely to be devoured.

The full-grown larva of *Rhyacophila dorsalis* is a striking creature, with an underbelly which is a semi-translucent, bright-green with a tinge of blue in it. The dorsal surface is darker, making the larva look olive when viewed from above. However the single most characteristic feature of this larva - and the one which is important to the flytyer since it could well be the trigger for fish - are the deep segmentations which run the full length of the creature. The general impression is of a short string of beads tapering in size at both ends. These segmentations, I have to stress, are very clear, make a definite silhouette and are worth imitating.

The larva moves in a primitive, concertina fashion. The tip of the larva's abdomen is equipped with a pair of efficient anal claws and when the larva moves, these claws hook into the substrate, whilst simultaneously the three pairs of legs walk forward, stretching out the larva. At this point, there is a brief pause, while the larva unhooks its anal claws then concertinas its entire abdomen towards the three pairs of legs at the head end. In simple terms, it is probably best described as stretch-pull, stretch-pull.

SOME NATURALS APPROPRIATE TO THIS PATTERN

GENUS: Rhyacophila.
BRITISH FISHING NAMES:
Sand Fly, Ronalds Sand Fly.
BRITISH SPECIES:*Rhyacophila dorsalis, R. munda, R. obliterata, R. septentrionis.*

NORTH AMERICAN FISHING NAMES:
Green Caddis, Green Sedge.
NORTH AMERICAN SPECIES:
Over 100 species, including *Rhyacophila fuscula, R. carolina, R. angelita, R. vaccua, R. verula, R. coloradensis, R. bifula.*

When dislodged and at the mercy of the current, the larva contracts quite dramatically, making itself about three-quarters of its normal outstretched length, whilst also taking on a slightly curved appearance. It is this form which my artificial represents - the drifting larva.

There are nine abdominal segments all more or less the same size except the last three or four which taper fairly quickly. Eight of these segments are equipped with a pair of fine tuft-like gills. These gills are barely visible to the naked eye. The three thoracic segments are slightly longer than the longest of the abdominal segments and the first

RHYACOPHILA LARVAE

Note the darkened dorsal surface and the darker thoracic segments - also the green rib lining the segmentation grooves.

one (after the head) has a dark patch on its dorsal surface. The six legs - one pair to each thoracic segment - are short and pointing forward, pale yellow with dark markings at their joints.

When fully-grown and outstretched, a *Rhyacophila dorsalis* larva measures 3/4"-1" (20-25mm) in length and they are eagerly taken by trout and grayling whenever they make the mistake of presenting themselves in the open.

The larvae can be found at all times of the year but the greatest concentration of large specimens appears during the autumn and winter months and so it is during this time that I most often fish this pattern.

In the USA, the genus Rhyacophila has over 100 species, ranging right across the continent, wherever there are streams of clean, rushing water and beds of rock and stone. The larva, pupa and adult echo closely the British species.

My advice to any flyfisher - European or American - who has access to a rocky fast-flowing river is as follows: establish first that the river has good populations of Rhyacophila caddisflies by examining the underside of rocks and stones. If you find plenty of their pebble shelters, then fish this larva or pupa pattern. Fish them with confidence. I am sure you will be rewarded.

NOTES ON MATERIALS AND TYING

The single most challenging problem I had with this pattern was how to construct those well-defined, deep segmentations. What now appears so simple, eluded me to the point of almost giving up on the pattern. I tried folding back dyed deer hair over a dyed foam underbody, with a strong nylon rib. The results were reasonable but untidy and shape control was difficult and time-consuming.

Then I tried coloured foam on its own, and thick layers of poly dubbing, all with a deeply-sunk rib. All were scrapped when I finally stumbled upon the method and material which I now use, which is simply to twist a short length of Antron yarn into a tight rope, then wrap it on the hook shank.

The result at the riverside was quite dramatic. On my first autumn and winter season with the Antron version, I averaged 16 fish per trip with one real field day of 21 in late November - all grayling. But the biggest thrill for me was that more than 70% fell for my new larva.

The ribbing medium needs to be strong. For a while, I used the fine clear Swannundaze. Unfortunately it is not strong enough for the job and has the annoying habit of breaking when you are half way down the larva. My favourite material now for the rib is clear mono 6-8lb BS. However, latterly I have been experimenting with a single strand of pale green Flashabou. This is a flat, coloured mylar which is about 1/32" (0.5mm) wide. It makes a most attractive rib. Unfortunately it is not as strong as the monofil.

For the short legs, I don't think you can beat a light speckled partridge hackle, dyed very pale yellow or natural. I mark the dorsal surface of the first and second thoracic segments with a black waterproof Pantone. Latterly, I have been experimenting by marking the dorsal surface olive (again, using Pantone pens) and I have a feeling that it does improve the fish-appeal.

RHYACOPHILA LARVA DRESSING

Hook: Medium to heavy wire curved shank hook. Suggest Partridge 'John Veniard' grub/shrimp hook Code K4A, size 10 or 12.
Weight: Narrow strip of wine bottle lead foil.
Cement: Dave's Flexament (USA) or Floo Gloo (UK).
Thread: Fine and very strong. Colour: yellow.
Abdomen and thorax: 4-ply knitting yarn, 100% synthetic fibre, or synthetic and natural fibre blend. Preferably with the addition of Antron, or other 'sparkle' fibres. Colour: bright mid-green.
Upper abdomen tint: Medium olive waterproof felt pen. First three segments dotted with a black waterproof pen.
Rib: 3-5lb BS clear or dyed green nylon mono, or single strand of pale green Flashabou, or doubled strand of Datam Glo-Brite Fluorescent floss, yellow shade 10.
Legs: Partridge grey hackle barbs dyed yellow-olive.
Head: Yellow tying thread or tint yellow if using white thread.

Tying the Rhyacophila Larva

Fig 1

Grip the curved grub hook firmly in the vice with the straight portion near the eye, inclined downwards about 30°. Catch on the tying thread just behind the eye and run it in open turns to well round the bend. Let the bobbin holder hang. Now cut off a 1/10" (2mm) wide strip of wine bottle lead (flat lead is much more suitable for this pattern than lead wire), tapering one end to a point. Now catch this tapered end of lead onto the shank at about the start of the bend and wrap it forward in touching turns, stopping well short of the eye. If you require more weight for your particular river then simply double back with the lead strip, but if you do this, stop short of the original starting point. Break off the excess lead and coat with head cement. Now while the cement is still wet, criss-cross the lead with the tying thread so as to roughly cocoon it.

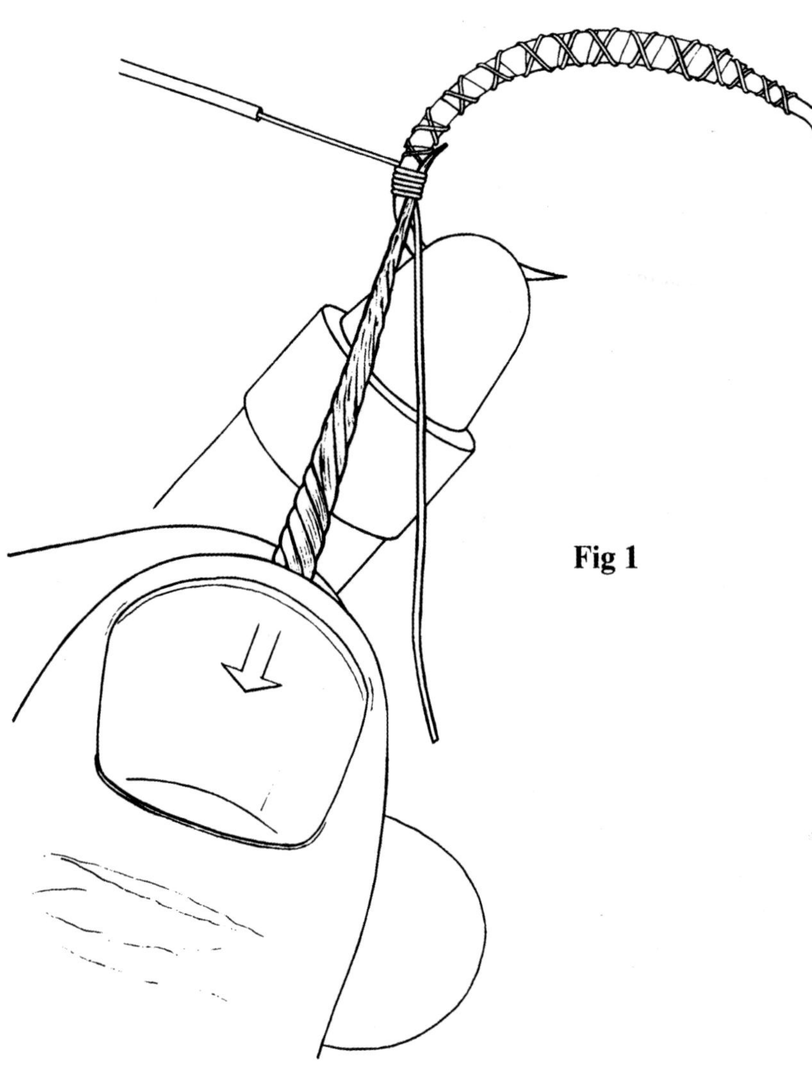

Fig 1

Next tie in a 4" (100 mm) length of clear nylon monofil - 6-8lb BS - for the rib. Do make sure that your turns of thread at the tying off point are very tight. Now return the thread to the centre of the lead ballast.

The next stage is important if a correctly tapered abdomen is to be achieved. So, cut off a 3" (75mm) length of bright mid-green 4-ply Antron yarn, and untwist and remove one of the plys (3-ply is ideal for a 10 or 12 hook, but for a size 14 you must reduce it to 2-ply). Now vigorously shave down one end of the Antron yarn by stripping out fibres between the ball of your index finger and the front edge of your thumbnail. In fact we give the yarn exactly the same treatment we did for the Ephemerella nymph (see page 21) but for this pattern you should aim to shave down about 3/4" (20mm), tapering almost to a point. Tie in the Antron by the tapered end using the wrap-and-pull method, exactly as described on page 22. Bind down the tapered end of the Antron where the nylon monofil is tied off, a little to one side. Make sure that these tying thread bindings are tight.

Now take the tying thread up the shank to a position 1/8" (3mm) back from the eye. Let the bobbin holder hang.

For the legs of this larva, I aim to produce three short clumps of hackle barbs which will become spread out leg-like on the underside of the larva when the 'rope' of Antron is wrapped on the shank. Overleaf is the method I use.

Fig 2

Take three dyed partridge hackles and with the point of your scissors, snip out the top third of each hackle by cutting through the centre quill only. Offer up the first hackle at a position about 1/8" (3mm) back from the eye - where the bobbin holder is hanging. The hackle should be on the side of the shank, and slightly to the underside which will bring the barbs to the underside when the Antron rope bites into them. With the hackle held in position thus, circle it twice with the tying thread, applying moderate tension. Now take hold of the hackle by the stalk and pull it slowly and evenly through the turns of thread until you have about 1/4" (6mm) of hackle tips protruding. Apply two more turns of tying thread, this time with full tension, and trim off the waste hackle butt.

Figs 3 & 4

Repeat for the other two hackles each about 1/8" (3mm) behind the other.

Fig 5

The next job is to raise each clump, starting with the last one to be tied in. This is done by forcing your thumbnail in hard at the tying-in point. Bring the tying thread in front of the barbs making two tight abutting turns, beading the tying thread hard up against them. Repeat this on the other two clumps. Your tying thread should finish just behind the eye but don't just let the bobbin holder hang. It is important at this stage to half-hitch the tying thread. If you don't, you will experience a drastic slip of the thread over the hook eye during the next manoeuvre.

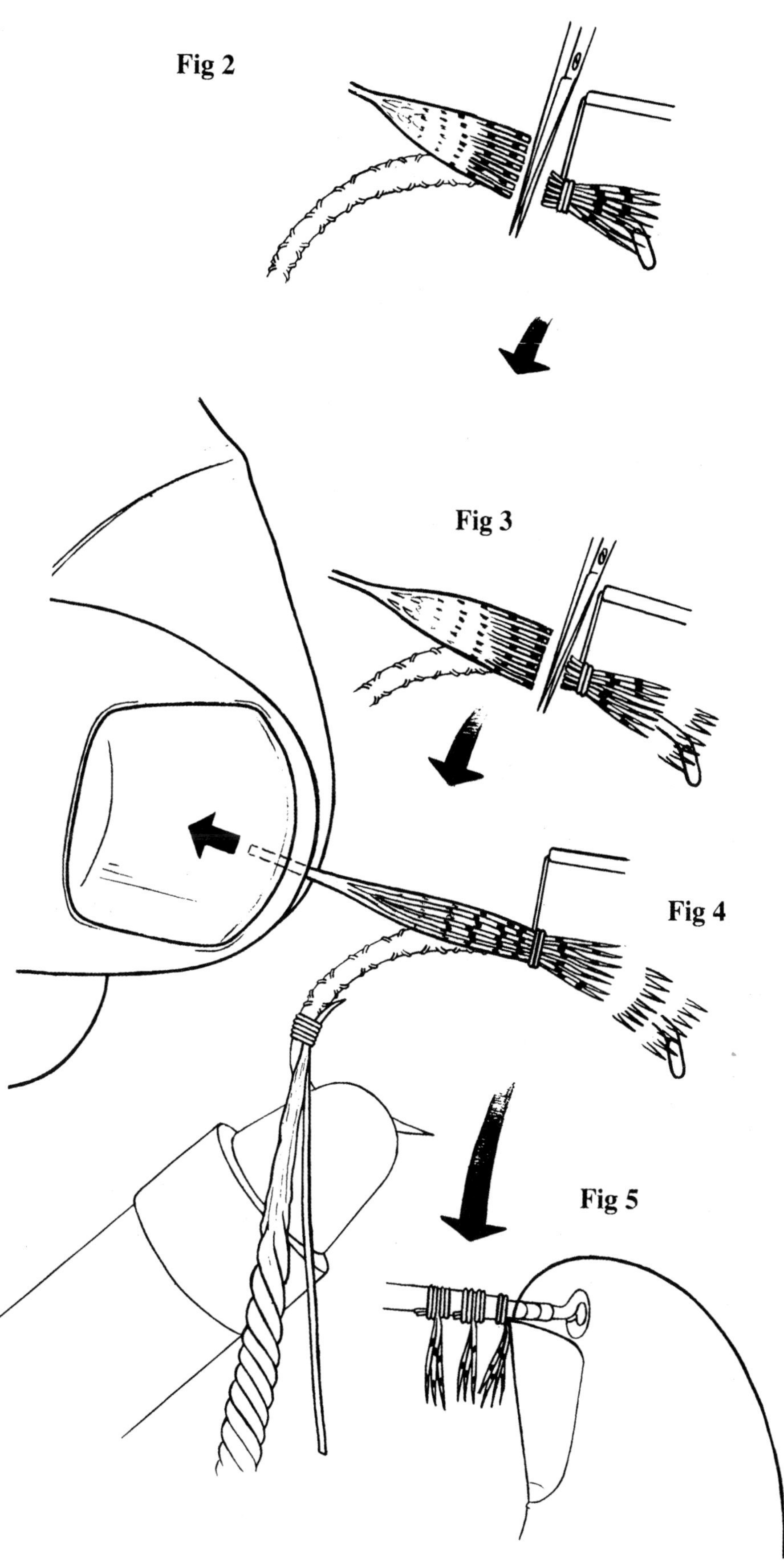

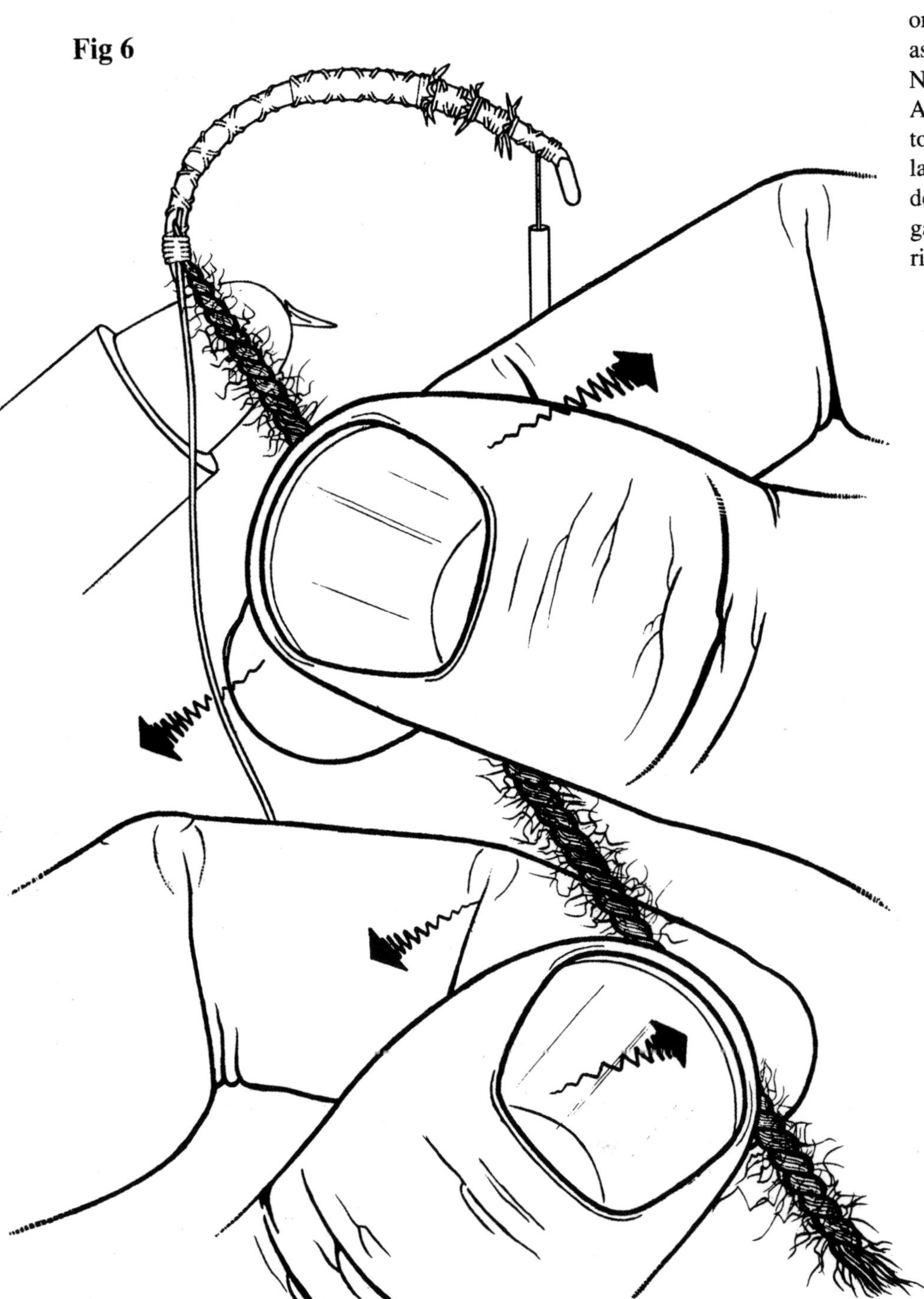

Fig 6
Holding the free end of the Antron yarn, twist it to make a very tight 'rope'. Check your twist direction on the yarn. It must tighten as you wrap it on the hook. Now wrap on this rope of Antron progressing towards the centre of the larva. Make sure the wraps do not touch. Leave a small gap the thickness of your ribbing material.

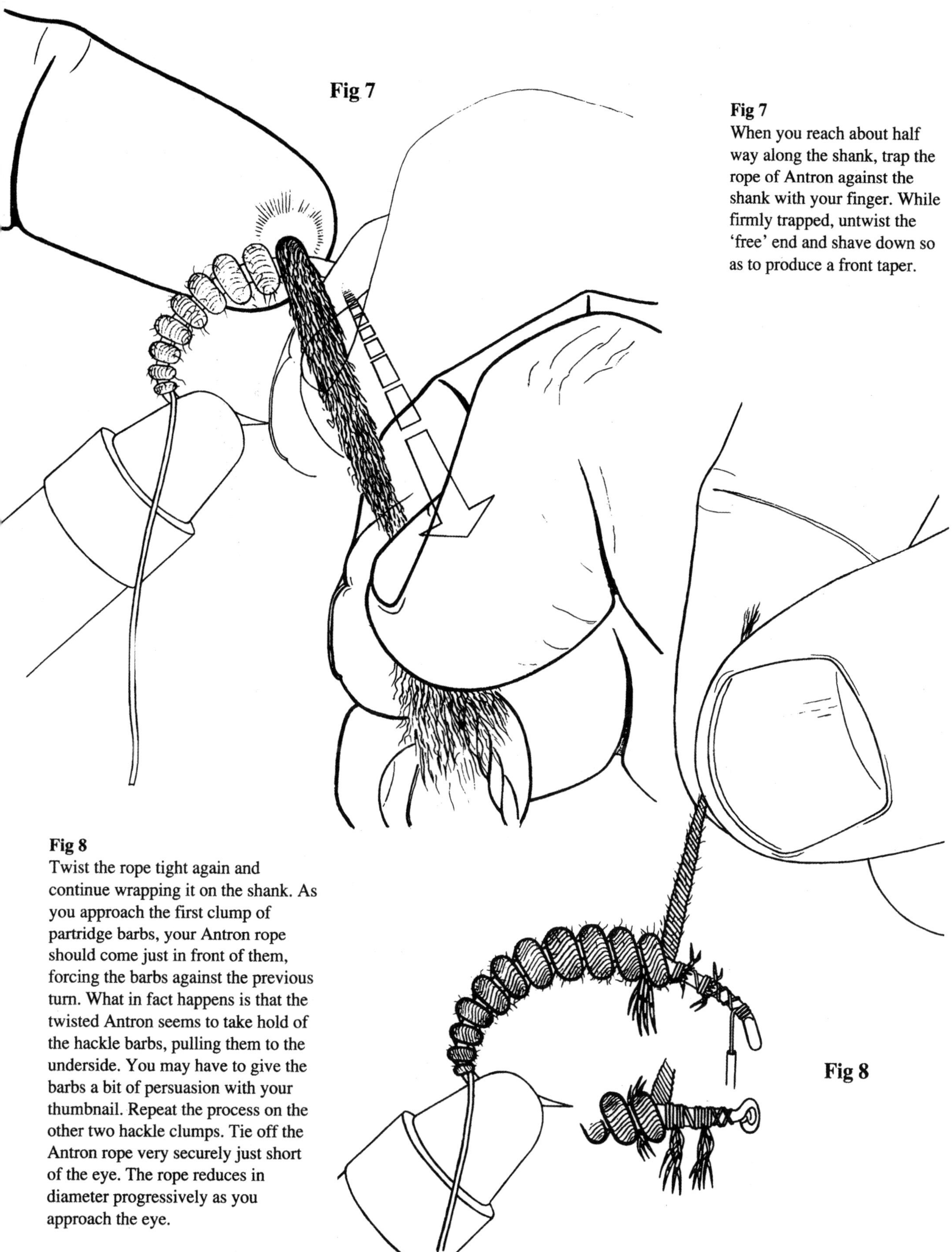

Fig 7
When you reach about half way along the shank, trap the rope of Antron against the shank with your finger. While firmly trapped, untwist the 'free' end and shave down so as to produce a front taper.

Fig 8
Twist the rope tight again and continue wrapping it on the shank. As you approach the first clump of partridge barbs, your Antron rope should come just in front of them, forcing the barbs against the previous turn. What in fact happens is that the twisted Antron seems to take hold of the hackle barbs, pulling them to the underside. You may have to give the barbs a bit of persuasion with your thumbnail. Repeat the process on the other two hackle clumps. Tie off the Antron rope very securely just short of the eye. The rope reduces in diameter progressively as you approach the eye.

Fig 9

Finally run the ribbing material all the way up the larva, following the 'valleys' of the segments. If you are using nylon monofil you can pile on the pressure. If, however, you use a weaker ribbing medium (like the pale green Flashabou) you must be more gentle. I have a trick which works quite well when I use the Flashabou rib. I first of all go up the abdomen with a separate piece of thick mono. This shuffles the segments about as I pull the monofil into each 'valley'. Unwrap and remove the thick mono, and you are left with gaps between each segment just about wide enough for the flat Flashabou rib to nicely drop into. Tie off the ribbing material and form a long, neat head - don't make it bulky!

Fig 10

To finish, tint the head whipping dull yellow (I'm using Burgess Multistrand Super Ex Fine thread which is 'translucent' white). Then tint the entire dorsal surface olive and the dorsal surfaces of the first two segments - behind the head - using a black waterproof felt pen. Be careful, though, when doing this, since the Antron has a habit of soaking up more colour than you want. Finally apply head cement or clear nail varnish to the head.

Fig 11

You have now tied a lethal caddis larva.

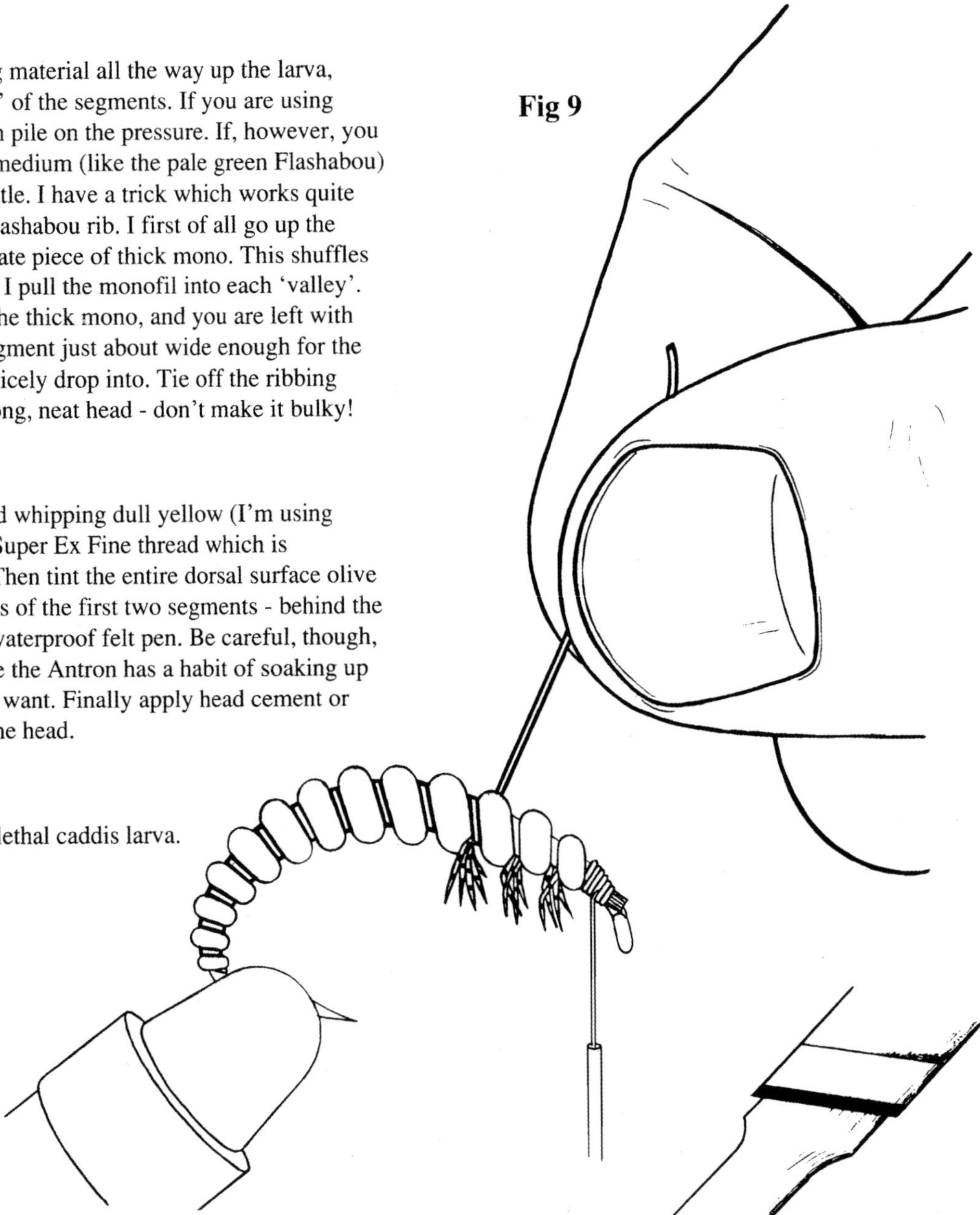

Fig 9

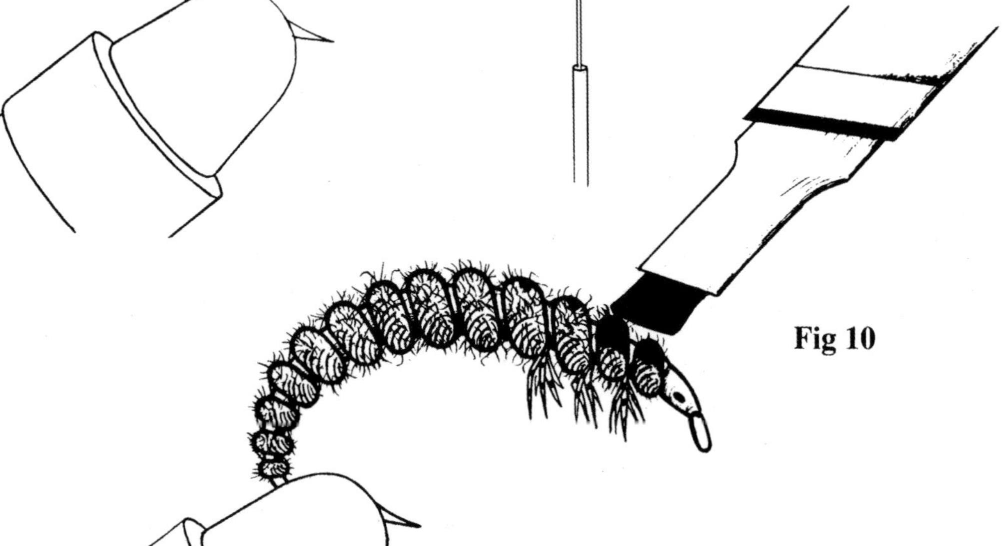

Fig 10

Fig 11

10. The Rhyacophila Pupa

At pupation time Rhyacophila larvae construct irregular hummocks of small stones and pebbles, cemented together with the larva's own secretions. The completed pebble shelter is attached by the same secretion to the underside or edges of sizeable rocks and stones, always in areas of high current speed.

Inside these shelters, the larva envelops itself in a cigar-shaped silken cocoon which is reddish brown in colour and about 11/16"(15-18mm) long with rounded ends. The outer casing is roughly oval, measuring about 1 2/5" x 1" (35mm x 25mm). Often it is possible to find several larvae that appear to have 'set up home' together, all crowding on to one particular area of rock to pupate, giving the appearance of one large pupal shelter when in fact it is five or six all stuck together.

It is the prevalence of these pupal encrustments which will give you some idea of just how many green caddis inhabit your own trout stream. Remember though that to disturb the stream bed is to disturb a micro-habitat, so please do so as carefully as possible, returning the rock or stone slowly and the correct way up. On one stretch I fish, the green caddis is present in quite incredible numbers and it is easy to find from 10 to 15 pupal shelters on the underside of a rock the size of this page.

At emergence time the pupa tears open the end of its cocoon, then somehow escapes out of the pebble shelter. How it achieves this last Houdini act, I'm not sure. I've poked around under stones and many times have found their shelters with empty cocoons inside but I've never been able to locate the escape hole in the actual shelter.

Once out, the pupa 'rows' rapidly towards the light, beating rhythmically, with its centre pair of legs which have special adaptations for this purpose, being wider than the other legs and having also a dense fringe of hair. The pupa has further assistance getting to the surface in the form of body gas trapped underneath the shuck. Emergence at the surface is rapid and *Rhyacophila dorsalis* must easily be the record holder amongst British caddisflies. So rapid is its emergence and departure off the surface, that at one time I suspected that it casts off its pupal shuck subsurface in the same way as some of the mayflies. However I am assured by a friend, who corresponded with the American expert, Gary Lafontaine, that emergence is in fact performed entirely on the surface. Amazing as it may sound, the total time from bursting through the meniscus to flying away is only about two seconds.

In Britain, the genus Rhyacophila is reputed by many authorities to be a daytime emerger. However, on the rivers of Yorkshire which I fish, the emergence of *R. dorsalis* is crepuscular.

I often fish this pattern. It always occupies point position on my cast either singly or with my Popa pattern (see page 179) on a dropper about 3 foot (1 metre) away. I fish the tails of pools, riffles and pocket water casting slightly upstream, allowing the current to swing them. As they're starting to swing I either twitch with the rod tip, or I occasionally do a few figure-of-eight retrieves. I never allow them to swing far, mostly I fish short drifts then pick off and re-cast. Working upstream is usually the best.

NOTES ON MATERIALS AND TYING

I developed this pattern more than ten years ago and have altered it little since the original tying. One of the key features of all ascending caddis pupae are their dark wing buds, which are held in a distinctive drooping attitude, occupying about half the pupa's length. I believe these are a major trigger to the trout. The droop of the wing buds is particularly accentuated when the pupa is about to emerge. My early trials to get these wing buds looking correct involved goose and duck quill sections and trimmed hackle tips. The quill sections split up making it necessary to coat them with a flexible cement, which then made them too stiff! The trimmed hackle tip idea was also scrapped as it never looked distinct enough. My final choice of folded Raffene has proved very effective and easy to tie. Its two major advantages are that it always looks well-defined on the artificial and it becomes beautifully soft when wet.

RHYACOPHILA PUPA DRESSING

Hook: Medium or heavy wire curved shank hook. Suggest Partridge 'John Veniard' grub/shrimp hook Code K4A size 12 or 14.
Weight: Narrow strip of wine bottle lead foil.
Cement: Dave's Flexament (USA) or Floo Gloo (UK), both thinned.
Thread: Danville's 'Spider Web' tinted light brown with waterproof felt pen or Midge 8/0 light brown.
Abdomen: Fine synthetic dubbing, bright mid-green, eg. Davy Wotton Finesse Masterclass Blend MC10.
Abdomen/thorax dorsal side: Quill feather slip dyed olive.
Thorax: Hare's mask fur with guard hairs.
Rib: Fine gold wire.
Wing buds: Raffene (Swiss Straw, USA). Colour: black.
Legs: Sandy-coloured barbs from the tip of a golden pheasant tail.
Head (optional): Cock pheasant (ringneck, USA) centre tail barbs.
Antennae: Any long, finely tapering, animal hair (eg. moose body) or animal face whiskers (eg. rabbit, hare).

The legs of the ascending pupa are surprisingly long. It is, however, only the middle pair of legs which are really visible on the pupa as it make its way towards the surface; the other two pairs are tucked up to its underside. Nevertheless it is advantageous, I find, to exaggerate the number of legs on the artificial to give the illusion of movement.

My love for partridge hackle barbs as legs did not prove to be the answer on this particular pattern. For the length of leg I wanted, the barbs were too weak, and the distinctive speckling, for once, was all wrong. The golden pheasant provides sandy brown barbs which are perfect for imitating the legs of most caddis pupae. This sandy brown area is to be found at the tips of the longest tail feathers. I tie in five or six barbs but four can also give the artificial a nice balanced look. The thing you must never do, though, is simply tie them in and leave it at that, as they will look much too straight, and lifeless. I have tried and used three different methods for achieving realistic legs:

1. Tying the barbs in as a clump, spreading them fanwise, then quite brutally crumpling them up to the point of making a tight ball. The individual legs are then separated out with the point of the dubbing needle. The resulting effect is one of thrashing legs with lots of 'ankles and knees'. The flies can then be strengthened and set by wiping along each one with flexible head cement using a dubbing needle.

2. Heat kinking. It looks very attractive but, to keep the effect, touch each joint with a drop of flexible head cement.

3. The method on the fly illustrated here: knotting each barb. Yes, I know it is a real pain having to put a knot in something about an inch long, and I realise that it depends on the temperament of the individual flytyer. However, I must confess that it is by far the most reliable. The legs look especially life-like and, more importantly, they stay that way.

I always include two long, wispy antennae on my pupal patterns. Lemon wood duck barbs look perfect, but unfortunately they don't last long. So I now use any finely-tapering animal guard hair. My current favourite is moose mane - the finer hairs. Rabbit and hare whiskers also work well.

RHYACOPHILA PUPAE
One showing the golden pheasant tail barb legs on the underside - note also the 'set' of the dark wing buds.

Tying the Rhyacophila Pupa

Fig 1

Grip the hook firmly in the vice with the straight portion near the eye inclined downwards. Catch in the tying thread just back from the eye and run it in open turns up to a position well around the bend. Let the bobbin holder hang. Now cut off a 1/16" (2mm) wide strip of wine bottle lead, tapering one end to a point. Catch this tapered end on to the shank where the tying thread is hanging and wrap it forward in touching turns, stopping half way along the hook shank. Break off the excess lead and coat all the lead wraps with head cement.

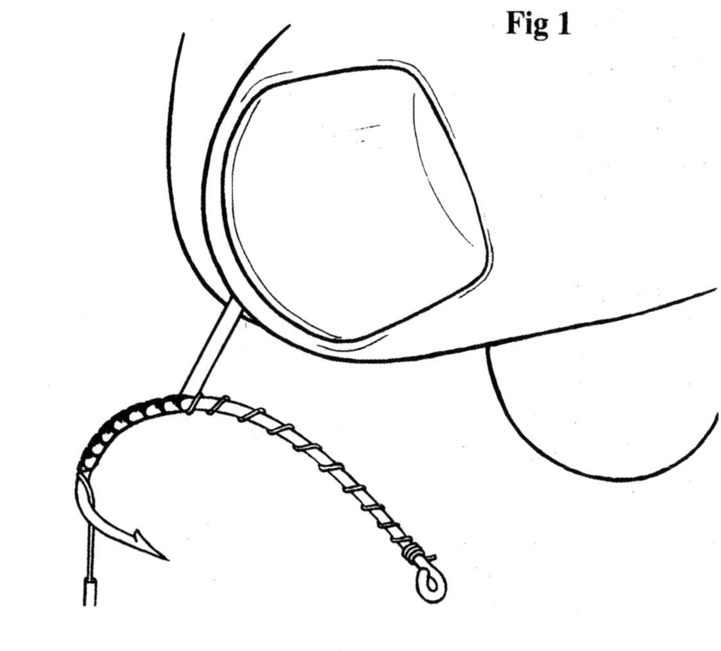
Fig 1

Fig 2

Criss-cross the tying thread over the lead wraps. Return the tying thread to the start of the lead wraps. Next, tie in 2" (50mm) of fine gold wire for the rib. Follow this by tying in a narrow section from medium olive dyed goose quill - this section of goose quill should be tied in by the tip end with the 'dull' side underneath. It should be on top of the hook shank, projecting out beyond the bend. (The term 'dull' here refers to that side of the feather which you actually see on the bird. The other side, the shiny side, is that nearest the bird's skin).

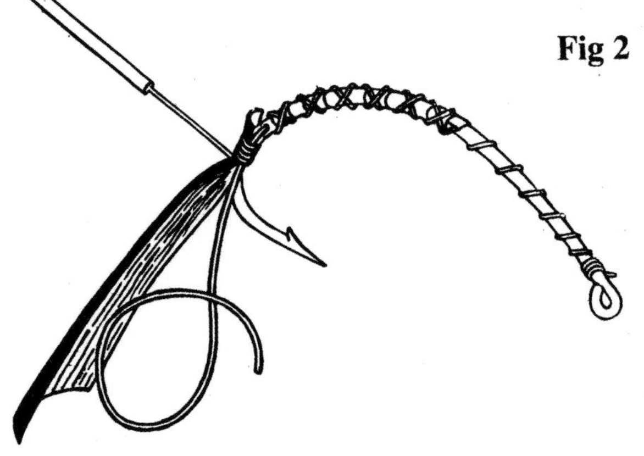
Fig 2

Fig 3

Now spin on to the thread some fine synthetic dubbing, adjust the distribution of the dubbing so that the spindle will have a slight taper at each end. Make this spindle tight. Wrap it on in touching turns, entirely covering the lead, finishing about 2/3rds up the shank (where the thorax will start). Let the bobbin holder hang.

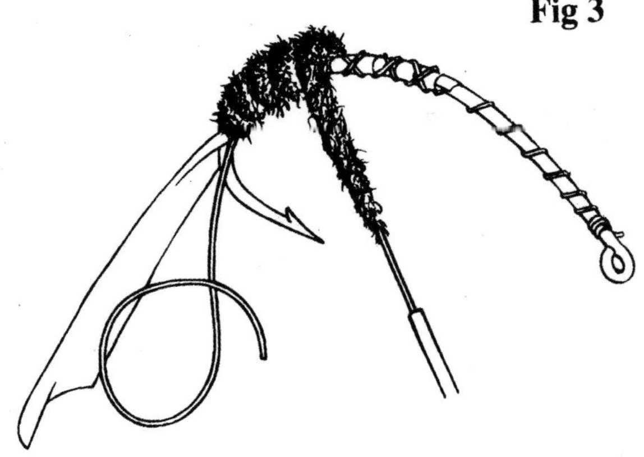
Fig 3

Fig 4
Grip the goose quill section and pull it over the top of the abdomen. Then, while holding it taut, spiral the gold wire all the way up the abdomen making seven or eight evenly-spaced ribs binding the quill section to the top of the abdomen. Make sure when you are applying these ribs that the goose feather doesn't become pulled more to the side. It should be wide enough to have a slight wrap around effect and should occupy the upper third of the abdomen along its full length. Pull each turn of rib hard enough to produce a slightly segmented effect. Secure the wire and twist off the waste. Don't yet trim off the remaining goose section - I use this as the dorsal covering for the thorax so just flip it backwards and take a couple of turns over to hold it back.

Fig 5
Now reposition the hook in the vice so that the straight portion near the eye is horizontal. The all-important wing bud material is to be tied in next. From a hank of very dark brown or black Raffene cut off a 2" (50mm) piece. Open it out to its full width and cut a strip about 1/4" (6mm) wide, then fold it lengthwise making it now approximately 1/8" (3mm) wide. Next fold it over the tying thread.

Fig 6
Then, trapping the two ends together between finger and thumb, slide the Raffene up the tying thread to the underside of the thorax and secure it in that position with, say, two tight turns of thread.

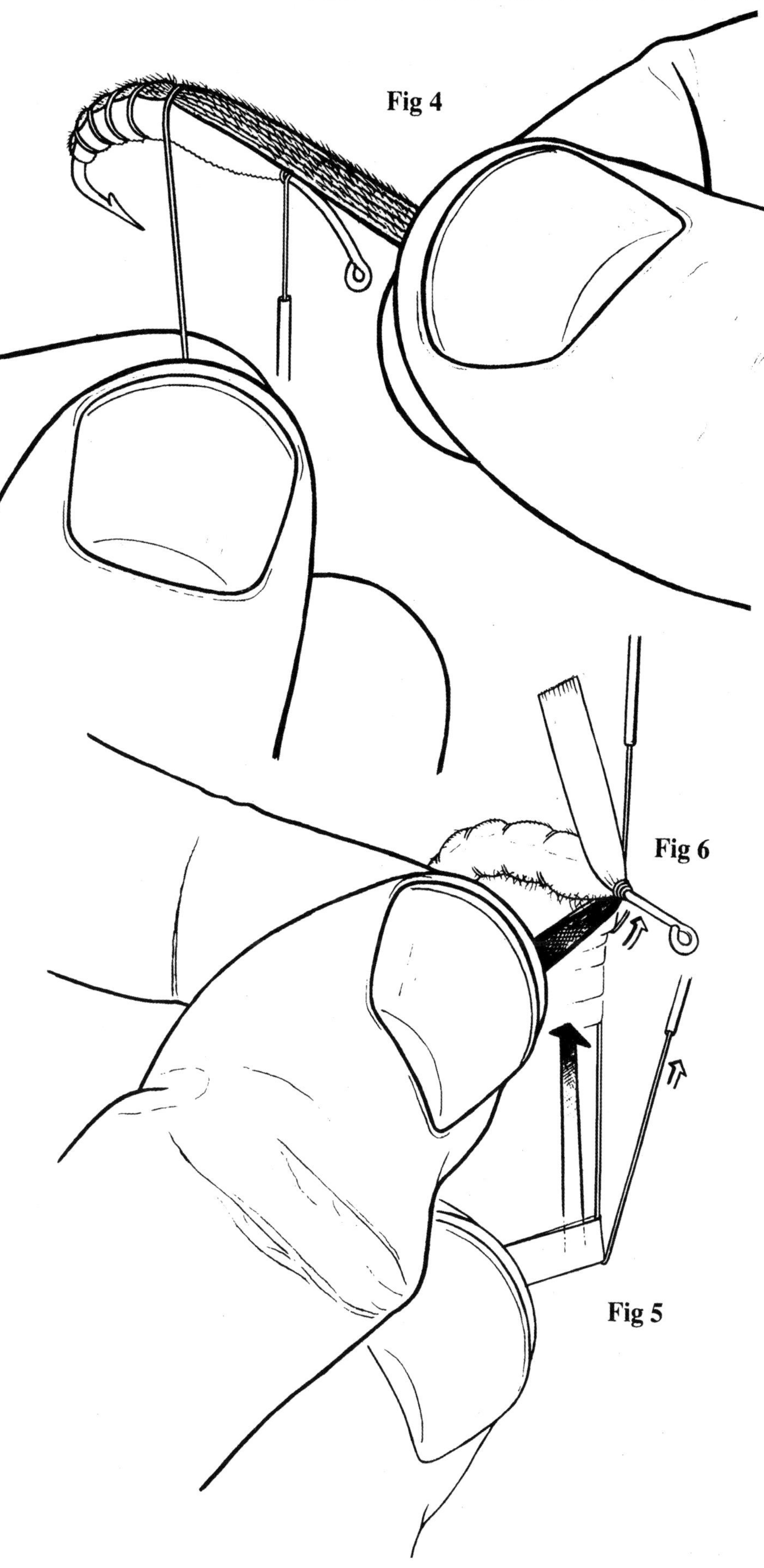

Fig 7
The ends of the Raffene should be projecting out beyond the bend. Take hold of the two ends of Raffene and place one on either side of the abdomen. Gripping both ends between finger and thumb, pull the Raffene taut, backwards and slightly downwards, securing it in this position with several tight turns of thread.

Fig 8
The final turns of thread must start to climb up on to the beginning of the abdomen. The two Raffene strands should now meet on the underside in a vee configuration.

Fig 9
Now spin a tight spindle of hare's mask fur on to the thread, making sure you get some of the spiky guard hairs. Wind on this spindle of dubbing, ensuring that the thread binding the Raffene in place is well covered. Stop about 1/16" (2mm) short of the eye. Let the bobbin holder hang.

Fig 10
Pull forward and hold tight the remaining piece of goose quill section, tying it down securely where the bobbin holder is hanging. Trim off waste.

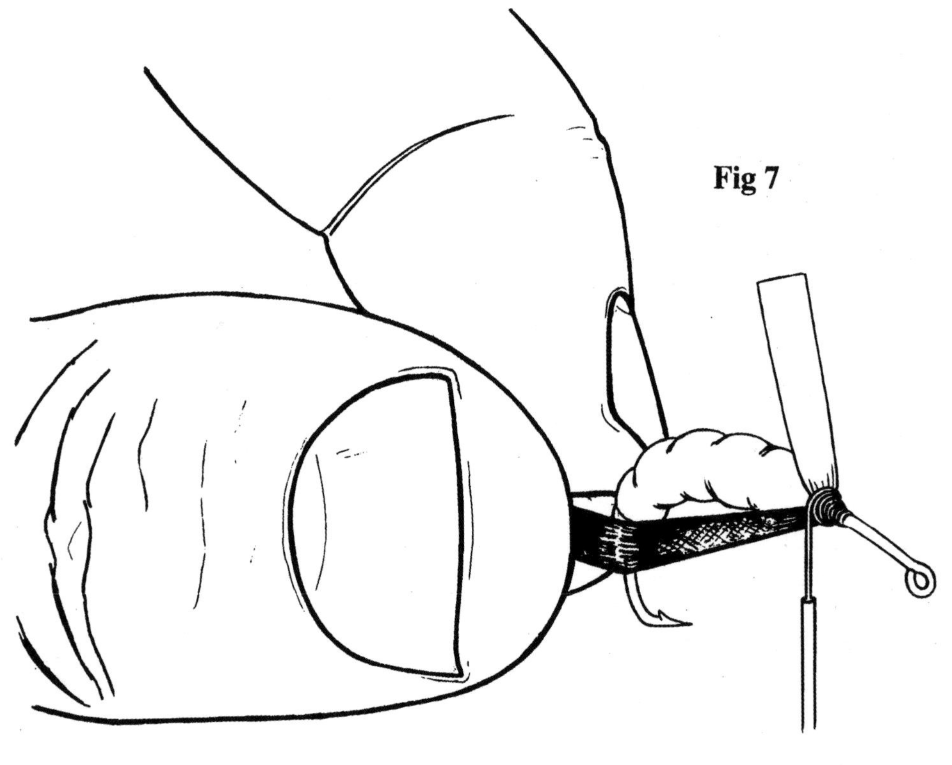

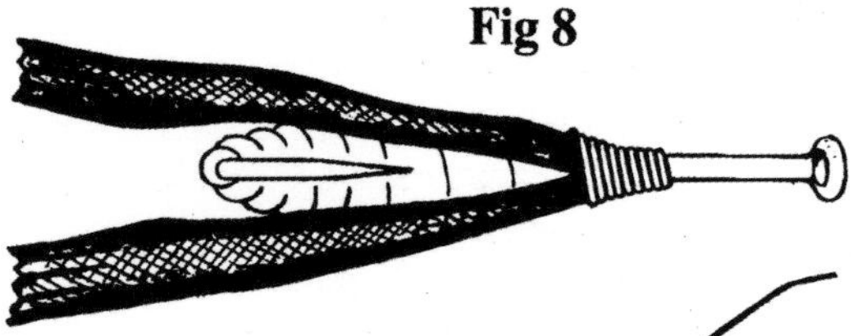

Fig 8

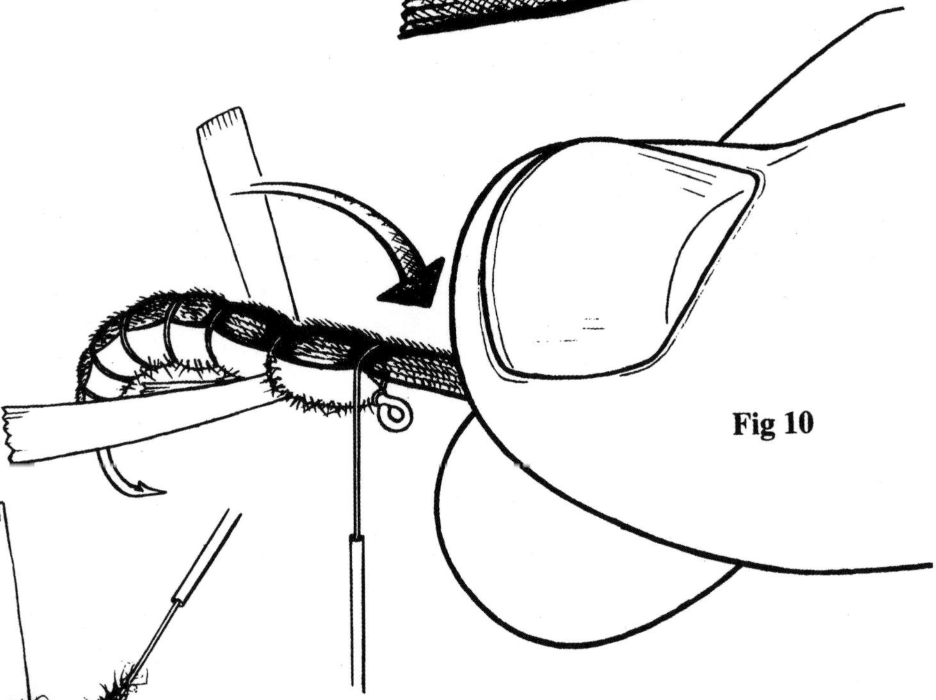

Fig 10

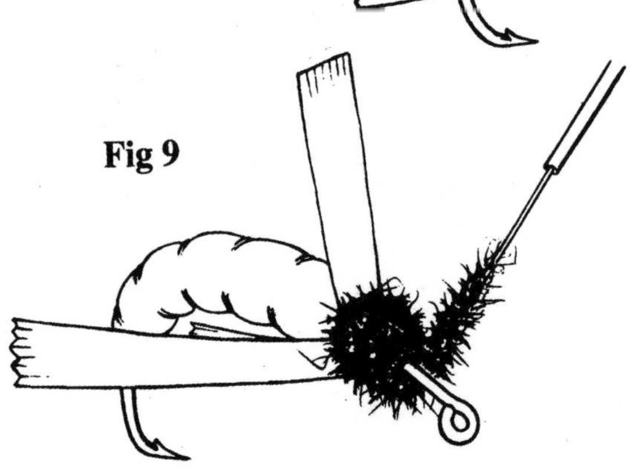

Fig 9

Fig 11

The next operation is to form the wing buds. Give the two Raffene ends a very light wetting. Place your dubbing needle over one of the Raffene strands holding the needle against the abdomen. Fold the free end over the needle, taking it back up to the front end of the thorax, keeping the dubbing needle firmly held. Then, while slipping the needle out of the fold, press the Raffene against the thorax, trapping it. Bind it twice to the hook shank. When you have made the second wrap of thread and, just before you make it tight, pull upwards on the waste end of Raffene. This has the effect of compressing the strand, making it quite narrow at the tying down point. Don't snip off the waste end of Raffene yet.

The whole procedure is now repeated on the other side of the pupa. There is one thing to watch out for, though, when tying in this second wing bud. Do make sure that the fold-over point is a mirror image of the first one. If it is too short, simply slip the needle back into the fold and pull back, thus feeding more Raffene through the bindings. If, it is too long, then pull on the waste end, again with the needle in the fold, offering resistance.

Fig 12

Finally, when you are satisfied that you have them both looking correct, add a couple more tight turns of thread, and trim off the waste ends of Raffene.

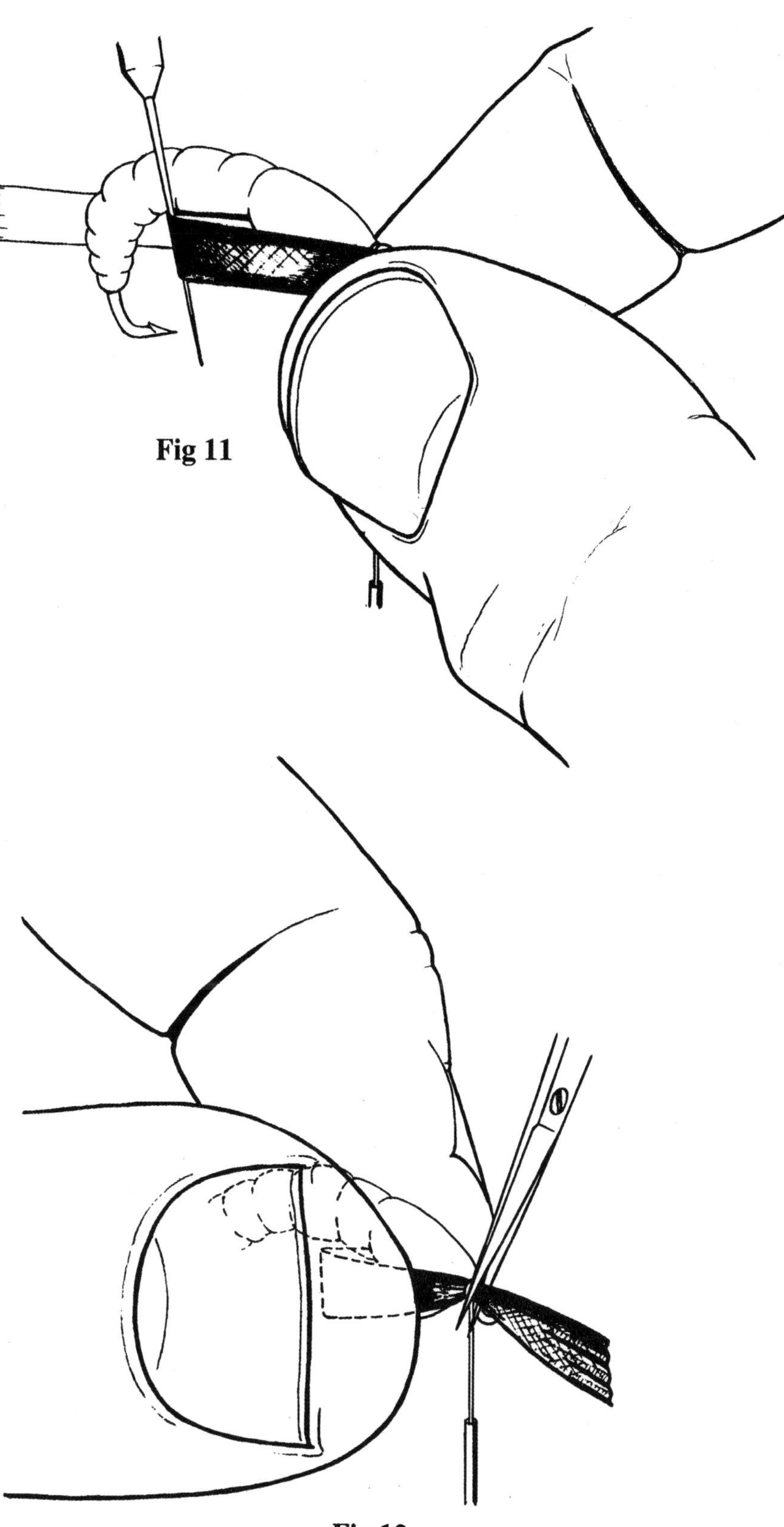

Fig 11

Fig 12

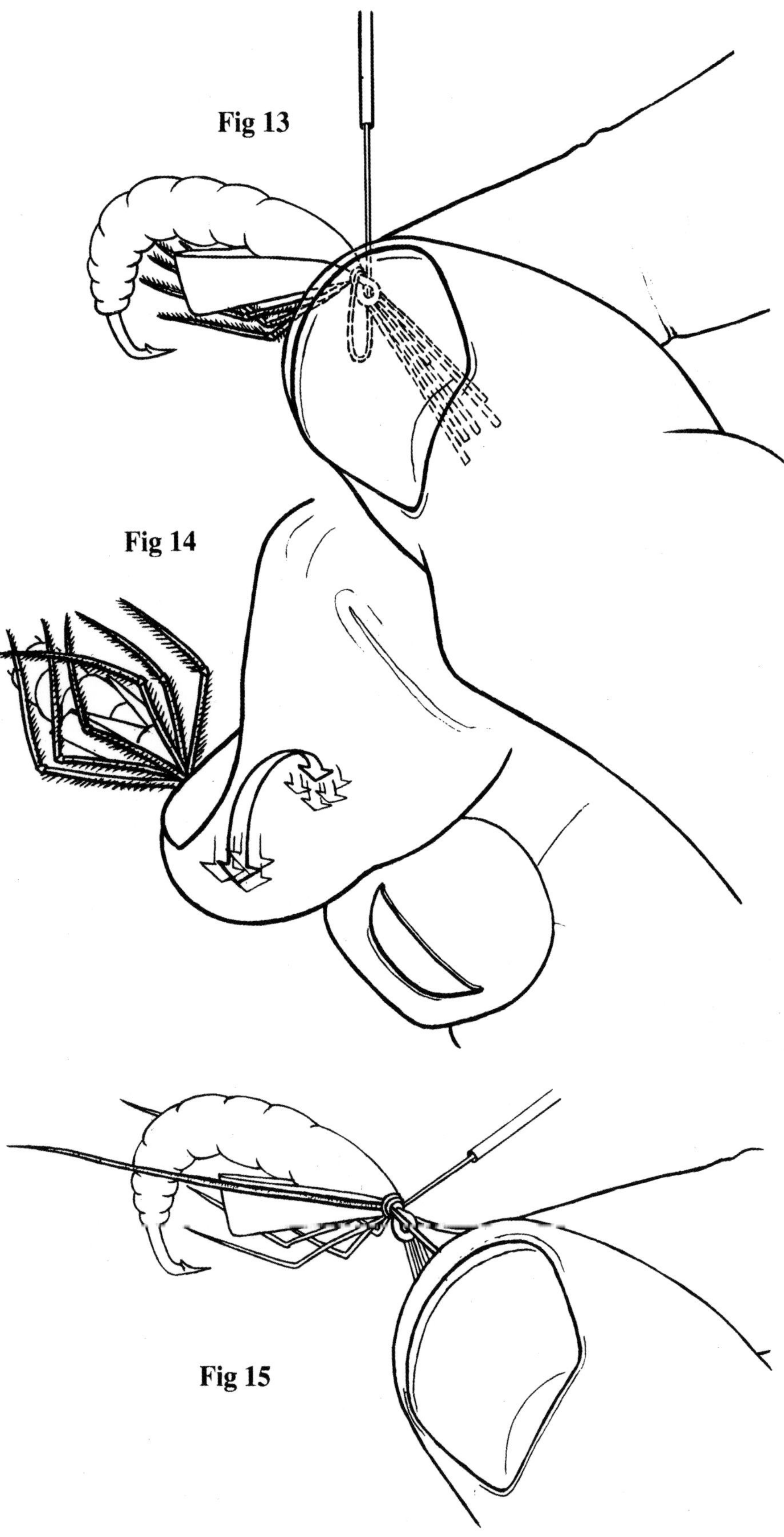

Fig 13
Next to be tied in are the six legs. Take the six feather barbs and offer them all up together to the underside of the shank. Make a loop of tying thread around them, an inverted pinch-and-loop, drawing the bundle of fibres up to the underside of the shank. That done, take another turn of thread around the barbs. Now adjust them for length by pulling through on either the butt ends or the tips. Remember that caddis legs are long and, at this stage, the pupa is virtually an adult. So, the tips of the barbs should reach the end of the abdomen. I sometimes pull just two barbs even further through to make them longer still.

Fig 14
It makes for a more realistic overall effect if the bundle of barbs is spread around the underside of the pupa. Press into the bundle with the front edge of your thumbnail and rock it from side to side. You may need to turn the hook upside down to do this. When you are finally happy with the leg positions, apply two tight turns of thread.

Fig 15
The last items to be tied in are the two long antennae. Offer these up, one on either side of the leg bindings. Make a couple of turns of thread, ensuring that both hairs mirror one another. Adjust them for length. They should extend about 1/4" (6mm) to 3/8" (10mm) beyond the end of the abdomen. Add two more tight turns of thread when the 'set' is correct. Trim off waste ends.

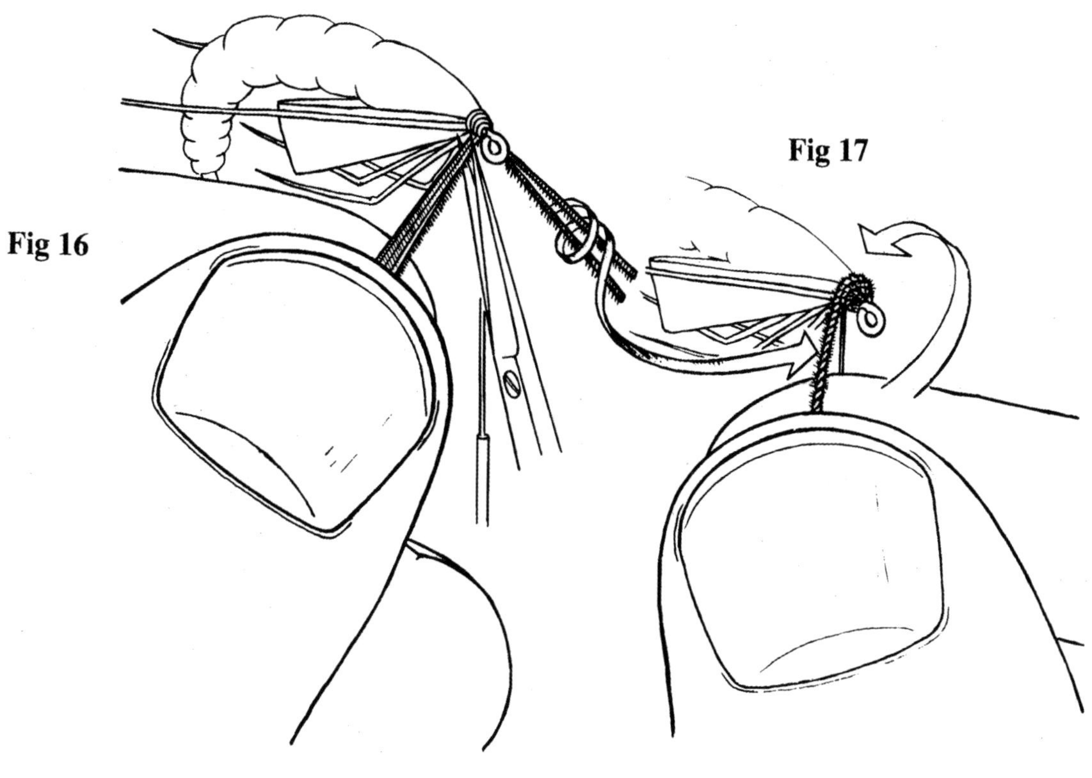

Fig 16

Fig 17

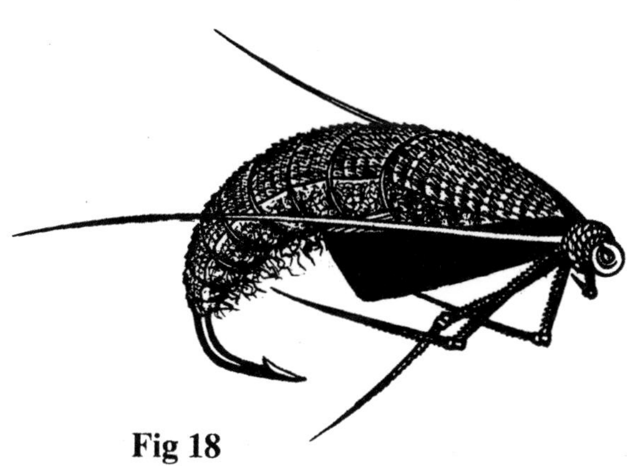

Fig 18

Figs 16 & 17

Finally trim off all but two of the waste butts of the legs. Smear those two remaining leg butts with flexible head cement, twist them together to form a 'rope' and wind on to the shank immediately behind the hook eye to form a small rounded head.

Fig 18

Tie them off at the back of the head, in the neck, using about three turns of a whip finish which, when drawn tight, should disappear behind the head. Snip off the tying thread and apply carefully a fine streak of cement to the head whipping. This is an excellent pattern, one of my all-time favourites. It is my first choice as a point fly in summer as dusk approaches and accounts for many fish every year.

HYDROPSYCHE LARVAE

Note the characteristic forked 'tail' and the distinct abdominal gills.

11. The Hydropsyche Larva

The Hydropsyche is another very important caddisfly encountered by the flyfisher of fast, well-oxygenated rivers and streams. These caddisflies are extremely widespread and abundant - good news for the flyfishers of Britain, Continental Europe and North America. North America is particularly well blessed, with a great many individual species of Hydropsyche.

Like the Rhyacophila, these larvae are devoured with great relish whenever they are encountered by trout and grayling. No fish misses a chance of taking these fat juicy grubs. Strangely, there has never been a specific pattern to imitate this larva in the UK.

For those flyfishers like myself who fish for winter grayling when the water temperature is down to 35/36°F, this artificial is a must.

Hydropsyche larvae are one of several non-casemaking caddis larvae and, as such, are classed as 'free living'. However, whereas the Rhyacophila larva is a true 'roaming' larva, the Hydropsychids tend to be more sedentary and construct fixed dwellings or retreats.

These are simple shelters of small stones, pebbles or odd bits of vegetable matter, cemented together with the larva's own secretion. At the front of the shelter, the larva spins a fine funnel-shaped silken web or net. The configuration of the shelter and web vary from species to species. Certain types of vegetation are also favoured by the Hydropsyche and heavily moss-felted rocks often harbour teeming colonies.

You might expect a creature which lurks at the end of a funnel-shaped web to be a carnivore. However, this larva is an omnivore. Very early instar nymphs and other tiny invertebrates are devoured quite regularly and they are even recorded to be cannibalistic. In fact, anything which is carried along by the current and lodges in the net is likely to be pounced upon. If it is inedible or too large, it is simply ejected; if edible and of suitable size, it is rapidly grasped by the prothoracic legs (first pair) and immediately set about with its mandibles.

There is, also, much evidence to suggest that Hydropsyche larvae consume much vegetable matter, as algae and other plant fragments are regularly found in their gut, and some authorities believe that they consume more vegetable than animal matter.

Of all the caddis larvae, this particular one appears to have been designed for imitating with the modern curved-shank caddis hook. It seems that they spend much of their lives in a quite pronounced dorso-ventral curve, particularly so when lying in wait in their lairs.

Over the years, I have found many Hydropsyche larvae in fish autopsies and they too have always been well curved. On odd occasions, I have actually come across a live specimen from stomach contents which has become very lively when placed in a dish of river water. Yet these live specimens have still maintained the characteristic body curvature and have seemed almost incapable of straightening out.

Clearly this is a feature on which the modern flydresser can capitalise. They *can* straighten out, of course, and I strongly suspect that this curled up attitude is adopted if they are dislodged from their shelter or if they voluntarily decide to move 'home' by releasing their grip of the substrate and drifting away with the current.

Besides the pronounced body curvature, the Hydropsyche larva has two further very distinct physiological features. The first of these is the pronounced plume-like feathery gills on abdomen segments 1 to 6 on the ventral side of the larva. When viewed under a good hand lens, say x10, you will notice that they are arranged in pairs arising from the centre of the abdominal segments. There are also more of these plume-like gills near the base of the hind and centre legs.

The second feature is unique to the genus and makes identification positive. This is an obvious hairy tuft at the end of the abdomen which can be seen with the naked eye. When viewed under a lens you will see in fact two tufts, each one at the end of a pair of long rod-like appendages. All caddis larvae have these claspers and they are always arranged in pairs. Besides the very distinct hairy tuft, each appendage is tipped with a well hooked, sharp claw. All caddis larvae have these claws. Many other species of caddis larvae have tufts of hair near the claws, but none are as densely and as obviously tufted as on the Hydropsychids. So, with these hairy tufts, the obvious plume-like gills and general curved appearance, there can hardly be any confusion with the identification.

SOME NATURALS APPROPRIATE TO THIS PATTERN

BRITISH SPECIES:
Hydropsyche siltalai, H. contubernalis, H. augustipennis, H. pellucidula, H. fulvipens, H. instabilis.
BRITISH FISHING NAMES:
Grey Flag, Marbled Sedge, Small Brown Sedge.

NORTH AMERICAN SPECIES:
too many to list but includes *H. simulans, H. recurvata, H. vexa, H. oslari, H. morosa, H. betteni, H. californica, H. occidentalis, H. alternans.*
NORTH AMERICAN FISHING NAME:
Spotted Sedge.

Their general ventral colour can vary from a dirty dull yellow to yellow-brown, to a dark grey. The dorsal surface - the back of the larva - is generally a shade or two darker and sometimes with a hint of brown. Towards the front of the larva, there are three very distinct black thoracic segments. The six legs are also black, or very dark brown. They are sturdy and forward facing. A final instar (mature) larva will measure from 5/8" (15mm) to 7/8" (20mm) in length, they are quite tubby in appearance, obviously segmented, but nowhere near as deeply segmented as the Rhyacophilids.

My first Hydropsyche pattern was tied in 1987 and, looking back now, I'm amazed it took me so long to realize the potential of this caddis larva. After all, I had been catching fish on my green Rhyacophila larva for several years. Furthermore, I had many times come across Hydropsyche larvae in autopsies.

The first few I tied were not particularly successful. I think I tied them too slim and they were also much too pale - almost cream. I hit the jackpot though with my fourth attempt at the vice. It was one of those occasions when you know you've cracked it: the size, the shape, the colour - everything. All I had to do now was to let it trundle and roll about on the river bed. I was sure it would take fish.

I used it in real earnest during the winter of 1989. Results were encouraging despite bouts of high and coloured water. My first 'red letter' day was 30 December. The venue was the river Dove in Derbyshire and the occasion was an organised live grayling removal by the Grayling Society for purposes of restocking a nearby small stream. Individual rods had knotless keepnets for retaining their catch for collection at the end of the day by tanker. I fished below the apron of a very interesting weir, casting into water of 3 or 4 feet deep. I had my 'new' Hydropsyche larva on the point with a lighter leaded Shrimp on a single dropper. I took a small grayling almost immediately, on the Hydropsyche, and was soon into a rhythm, using short casts into the turbulence at the bottom of the weir sill, then allowing the artificial larva to bump and tap along the stream bed. I started picking up good grayling at regular intervals and the takes were unmissable. My final tally was 19, not a tremendous catch by some standards, but the quality was outstanding for there was hardly a single fish under the pound, and one lovely fish of 1¾ lbs. Of my 19 fish, 17 took the Hydropsyche larva.

Consequently, throughout the winter of 1990/91 I used this pattern almost exclusively. On many of my visits, the river was running quite high and strong. However, I only blanked once, and even then I did hook and play a good grayling for a short while, and this was on a day of a big water which was still rising and with a water temperature of only 37°F.

For these winter grayling forays, I find it is absolutely essential to use one of the modern fast-sinking leaders. The type I prefer are braided and have a heavily weighted front portion to which I attach a short length (3ft) of nylon mono of 3 to 4lbs BS.

Although they may not be the most pleasant thing in the world to cast, they nevertheless do their job very efficiently and get your artificial right down to where it matters - on the bottom. When the artificial doesn't get hung up on the bottom ten or twelve times during a few hours fishing then it's not fishing correctly. If I don't start snagging on the bottom, I know I should change to a heavier leader. The leaders which I prefer are designed by Roman Moser and are available in the UK.

I try wherever possible to make my initial delivery slightly up-stream, with a mend or reach cast. The idea is to allow the larva to get down quickly, then trundle along the bottom. The reach cast with an exaggerated downstream lean is very useful for this method. Takes can come anywhere, but the very end of a drift, as the larva lifts off the stream bed, is often a deadly spot. Takes with this leader arrangement on a fast, swollen river, nearly always register very positively, with the loop of fly line lifting smartly. They're usually unmissable.

NOTES ON MATERIALS AND TYING

The hook for this pattern plays a vital dual role. Not only has it to be a good hooker and holder, it must also be the correctly shaped spine for producing the important semi-curled appearance. I tie virtually all my caddis larvae on the Partridge code K4A Veniard Grub/Shrimp hook and it is the hook which I thoroughly recommend for this pattern. The two sizes I use are 10 and 12.

I again use wine bottle lead foil for the ballast. However, on some, I keep the weighting to a minimum and I reserve these for use in conjunction with my fast sinking leaders. The combination of a fast sinking leader and a really heavily weighted larva often spells disaster.

For the abdomen, I use the same brand of 4-ply Antron sparkle yarn that I use for tying the Rhyacophila larva and I also prepare the tying-in point by shredding or 'shaving' it down with the thumb nail.

On this particular pattern though, I don't twist the yarn into such a tight rope when I wind it on, since this larva hasn't the deep well-defined segments that the Rhyacophila larva has. The colour I prefer is a light fawn brown with the merest hint of yellow. It darkens very slightly when wet and it copies the natural's colour quite accurately.

For the back of the larva, I use a section from a brown mottled turkey quill feather. You may think this a waste of an expensive and fairly rare feather, so any mottled brown quill feather is worth experimenting with, such as a mottled hen quill. However, do make sure that the quill you use is not a reddish brown shade. The correct shade is a donkey or mousey brown.

Whatever feather you decide to use, it must first be prepared by applying a very thin even coating of flexible head cement to the shiny side of the quill. I find that it is quite essential to apply this flexible cement as it nicely holds all the barbs of the quill section together as you rib the larva.

The obvious choice for simulating the plumose gills of the larva is ostrich herl dyed a fawny beige or light mousey brown - again beware of reddish brown! Initially, I simply wound on the

HYDROPSYCHE LARVA DRESSING

Hook: Medium or heavy wire curved shank hook. Suggest Partridge Grub/Shrimp Hook Code K4A sizes 8, 10, 12.
Weight: Narrow strip of wine bottle lead foil.
Thread: Fine and very strong. Any of the Kevlar blends. Colour: light brown or grey.
Cement: Dave's Flexament (USA) or Floo Gloo (UK).
Tail: Filoplume or aftershaft feather from a partridge body hackle.
Abdomen and thorax: 4-ply knitting yarn, 100% synthetic or synthetic and natural fibre blend, preferably with the addition of Antron some reflective sparkle fibres. Colour: fawn, dirty yellow, drab grey-yellow or grey-olive.
Back: Speckled quill feather section, mousy brown (not red-brown), undyed or dyed light grey. Speckled turkey is ideal.
Rib 1: Fine gold wire.
Rib 2: 3lb BS mono. Colour: clear or neutral.
Abdomen gills: Ostrich herl, dyed to match abdomen yarn colour.
Legs: Partridge hackle dyed black.
Thorax tint: Black waterproof pen.
Head: Tint black with waterproof felt pen.

herl 'palmer' hackle fashion, but this obscured the belly colour of the larva which I want the fish to see. Also it produced dark transverse bars (the quill of the herl) across the belly.

The method I finally adopted, of pulling the two herls lengthwise along the underside of the larva and binding them to the abdomen with a ribbing, proved to work very well. However, this method does mean that you require two ribs.

The first is fine gold wire which binds down and ribs the quill section. The second is what I call the invisible rib, of 3lb BS transparent or pale nylon mono. This rib follows the gold wire and binds down the two ostrich herls. The result looks good and nicely copies the natural.

I also tie in a little tuft at the very end of the larva to represent this very obvious feature on the natural. My favourite material for this is a couple of those wispy downlike feathers you find adhering to most body hackles - the filoplumes or aftershaft feathers.

This pattern is basically an easy tie but it has a distinct route which I find cannot be changed much. It's also a good pattern for teaching you how to handle several materials which are all tied in at one position. This means you will need to watch how many turns of thread you use!

There is also a kind of unwritten rule when you have many materials tied in, in one spot, which then have to be used in a certain order. This rule is: first in - last out!

Tying the Hydropsyche Larva

Grip the hook firmly in the vice with the straight portion near the eye inclined downwards by about 30°. Cut off a narrow strip of lead foil and wrap it on the shank in touching turns all along the curved part of the shank. Two layers are usually sufficient. Apply head cement to the lead. Then, attach the tying thread and immediately criss-cross it, thus cocooning it.

Fig 1
Now at a position well around the bend, where you decide the end of the larva will be, tie in two filoplume feathers taken from partridge hackles. (These are the soft plumose down-like feathers attached to body hackles).

Fig 2
When tied in, trim these filoplume feathers so as to make a short but distinct tuft of approximately 3/16" (3mm).

Fig 3
Tie in a 4" (100mm) length of 3lbs BS nylon mono.

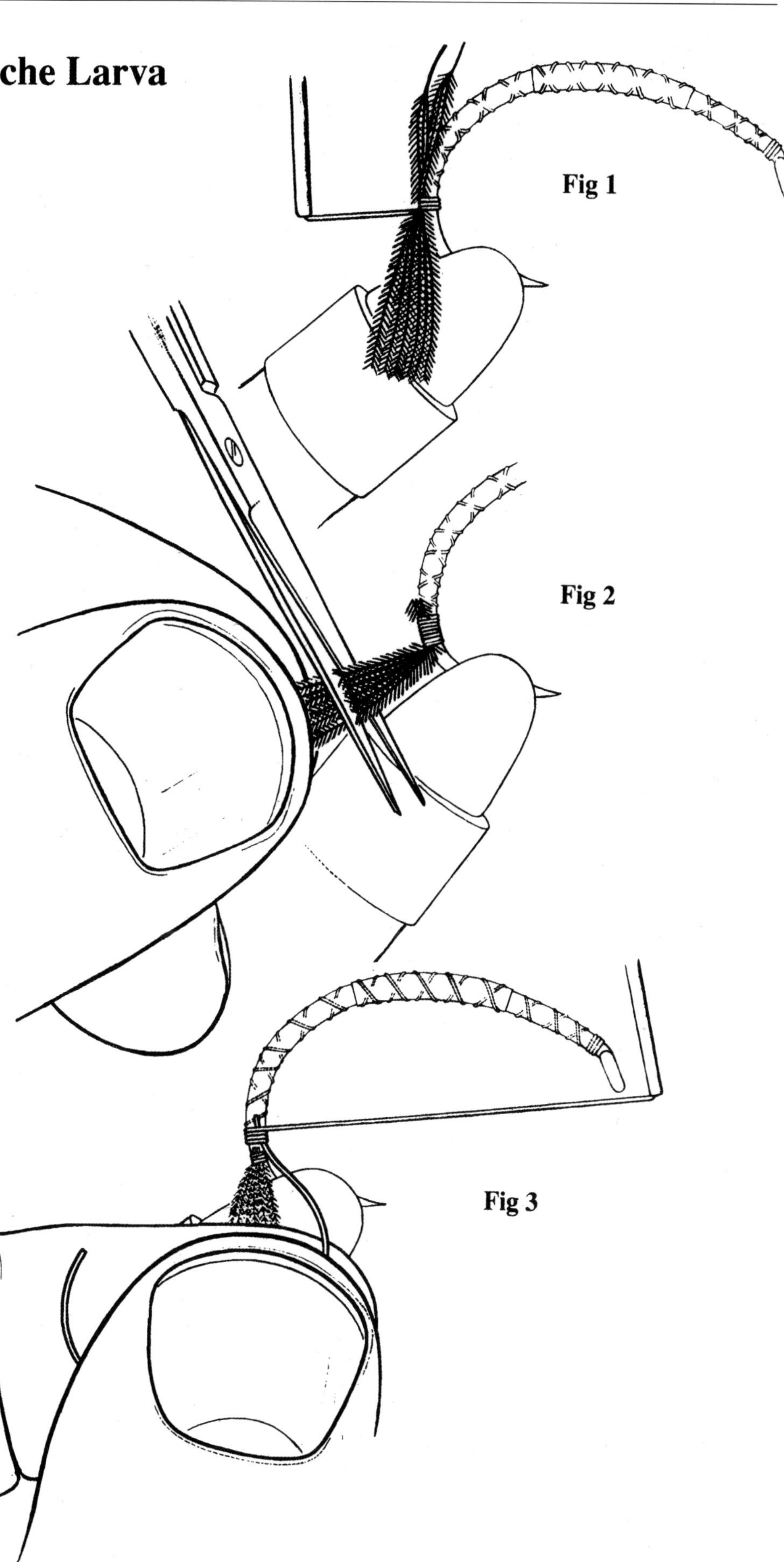

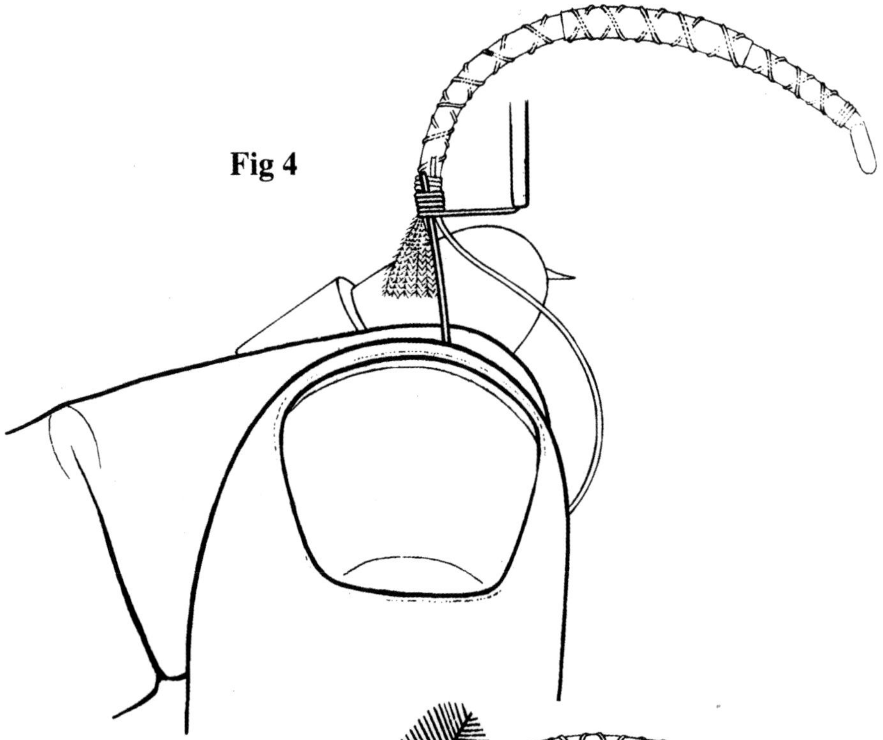

Fig 4

Fig 4
Then tie in a similar length of very fine gold wire.

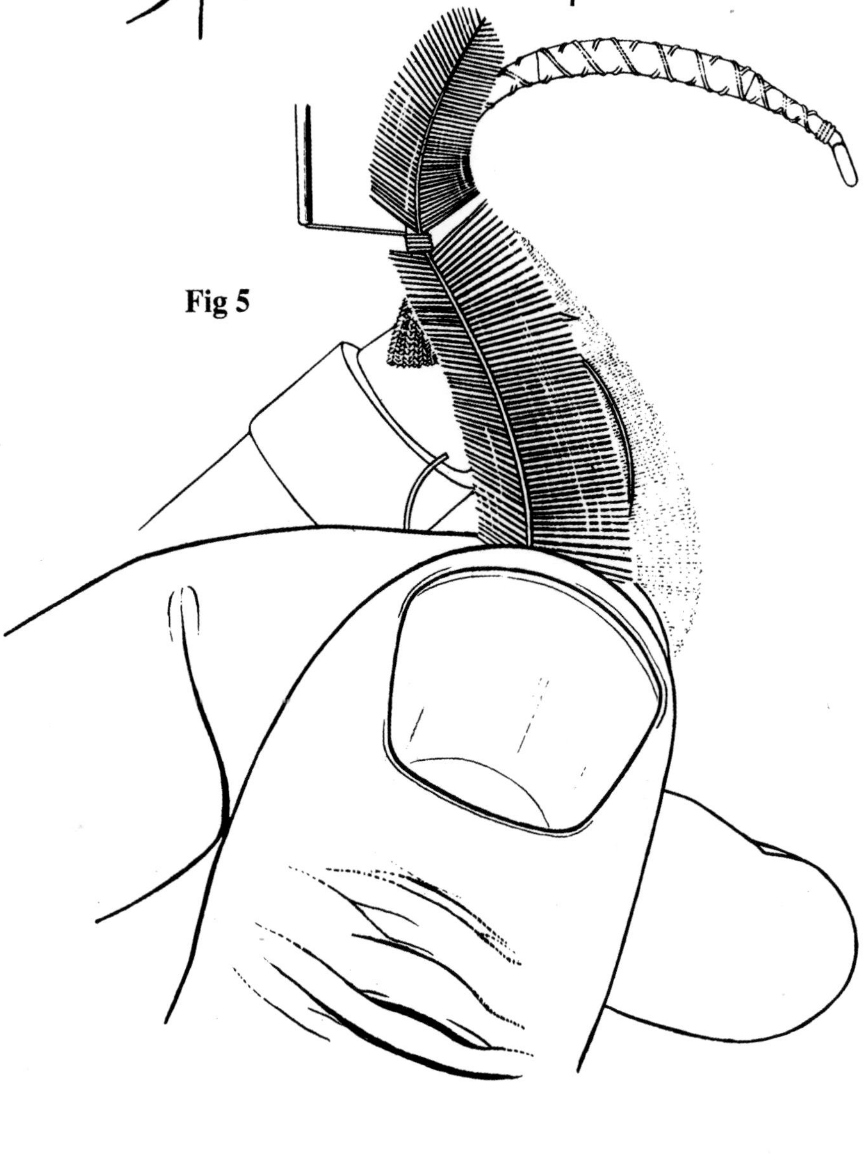

Fig 5

Fig 5
Follow this by tying in, in the same spot, two strands of dyed ostrich herl - these herls should be positioned one on either side erring more towards the underside.

Fig 6

The next component to be tied in is the upper abdomen covering, the 1/8" to 3/16" wide (3-4 mm) section of brown mottled quill feather. It should be tied in with its shiny side uppermost on the shank.

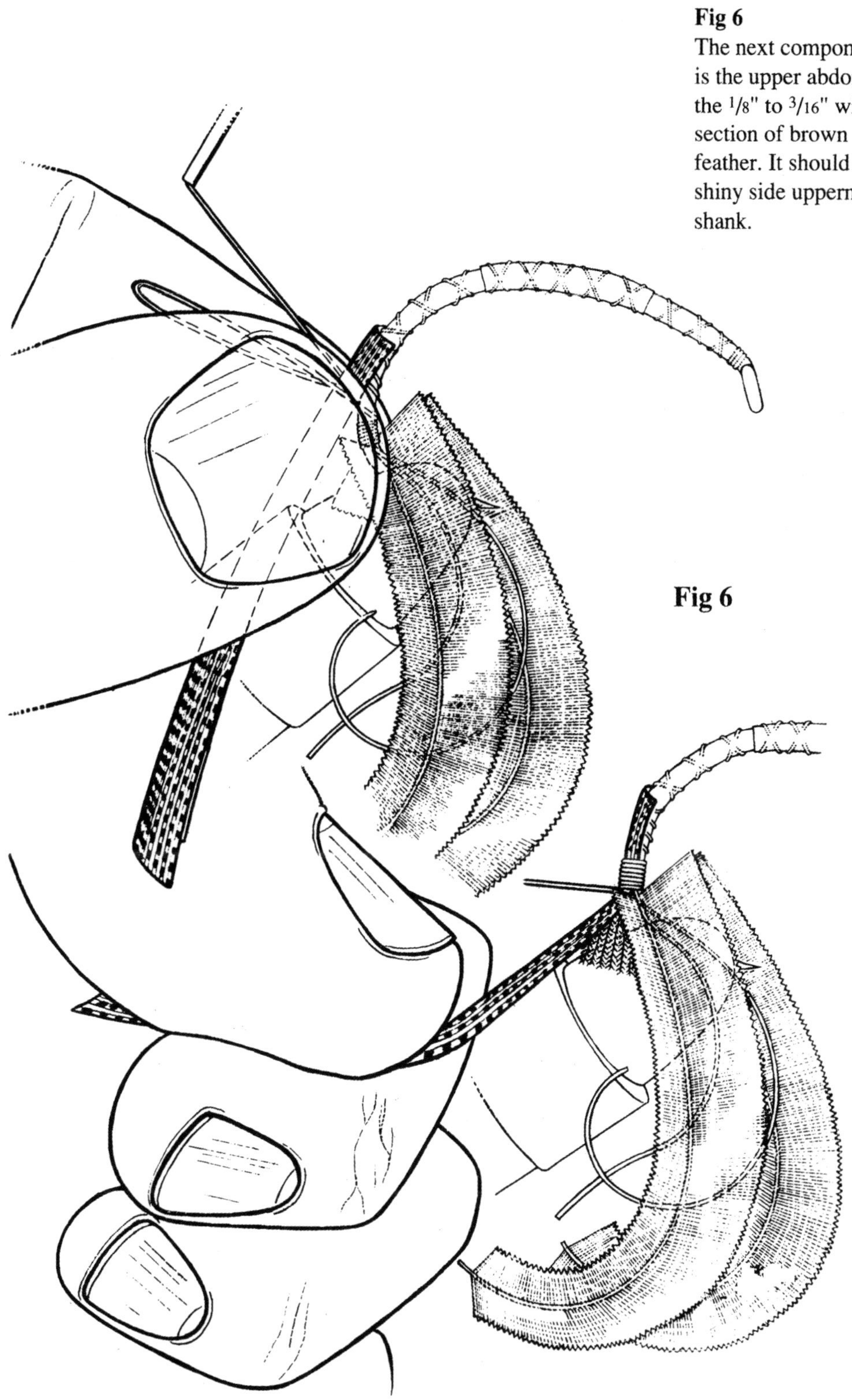

Fig 6

The last item now to be tied in is a 3" length of the 4-ply Antron yarn. Shave the end of the yarn down first so as to produce a nice taper just as we did for the Rhyacophila larva and tie it in by this fine tapered tip - do make sure that it is tied in very securely. Figure9 on this page illustrates the position of the yarn.

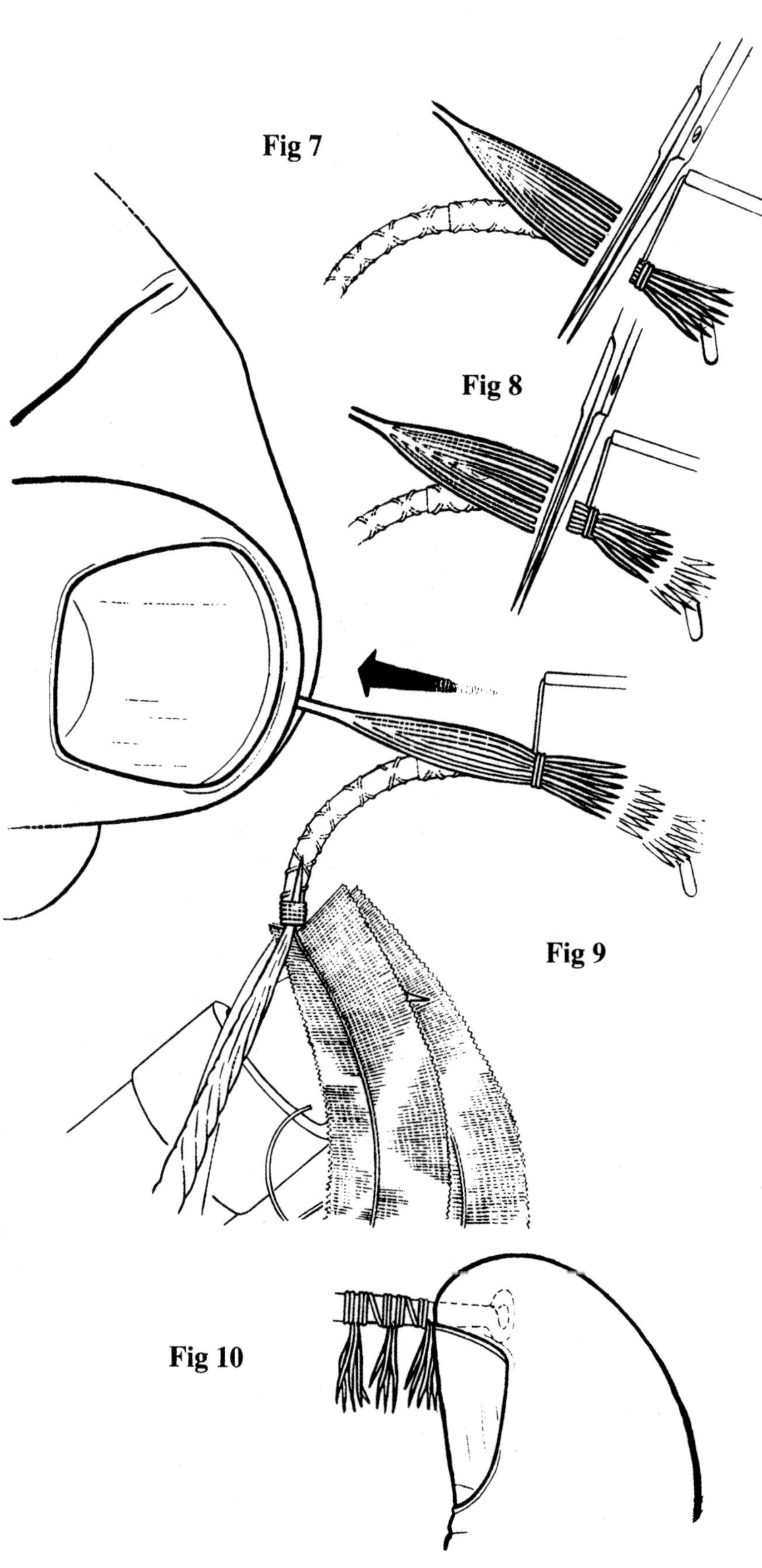

Fig 7
Now take the tying thread up the shank to a position 1/8" to 3/16" (3-4 mm) back from the eye and let the bobbin holder hang. For the legs, select three dyed partridge hackles and with the point of your scissors snip out the top third of each hackle, severing through the centre quill only. Now offer up the first hackle right where the thread is hanging. The hackle should be placed against the side of the shank with the tips out beyond the eye. Take a couple of turns of thread around this clump of hackle barbs - apply moderate tension. Now slowly pull back the hackle until you have about 1/4" (6mm) of hackle tip beyond this bind-down point. Follow this by applying another couple of turns of thread at full tension. Trim off the waste butt end of hackle.

Figs 8 & 9
You now tie in the other two hackles again by their tips, in exactly the same manner, each clump about 1/8" (3mm) behind the other.

Fig 10
Raise each of the three clumps by forcing your thumb nail or edge of dubbing needle hard in at their tying-in points. Bead up against the front of each clump with the tying thread - coming forward with the thread towards the eye as you perform with each clump - then throw on a couple of half hitches behind the hook eye.

Fig 11
Twist the Antron yarn to make it a fairly tight cord, but not too tight, you don't want this larva to be as distinctly segmented as the Rhyacophila larva.

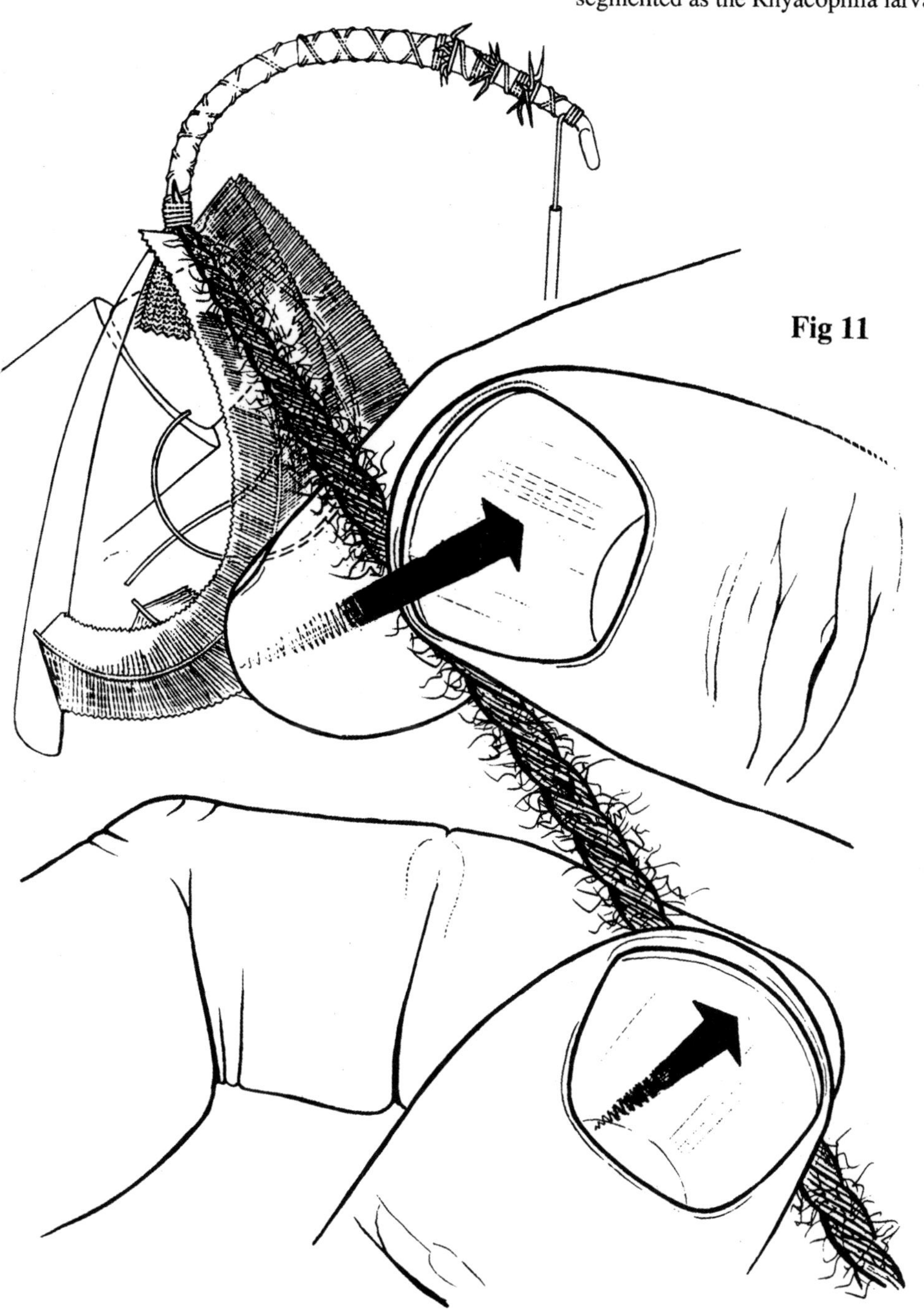

Fig 11

Fig 12

Wind on the yarn in touching turns and when you arrive at about the centre body position trap the yarn against the shank with the tip of your index finger. With the free hand, you should 'shave' down the rest of the yarn so as to produce a gentle front taper, again as we did for the Rhyacophila larva (see page 119). This done, twist up the shaved yarn and continue winding it on towards the eye.

Fig 13

At the first clump of partridge barbs, manoeuvre the yarn so that it grips the barbs and pulls them around to the underside of the larva. Continue with the wrapping, pulling around the other two clumps of hackle barbs in exactly the same way as for the Rhyacophila larva. Don't go right up to the eye with the twisted Antron, stop about 1/16" (2mm) from it, where you tie off the Antron very securely and trim off the waste. Now pull the quill section over the back of the larva and hold it exactly central along its full length.

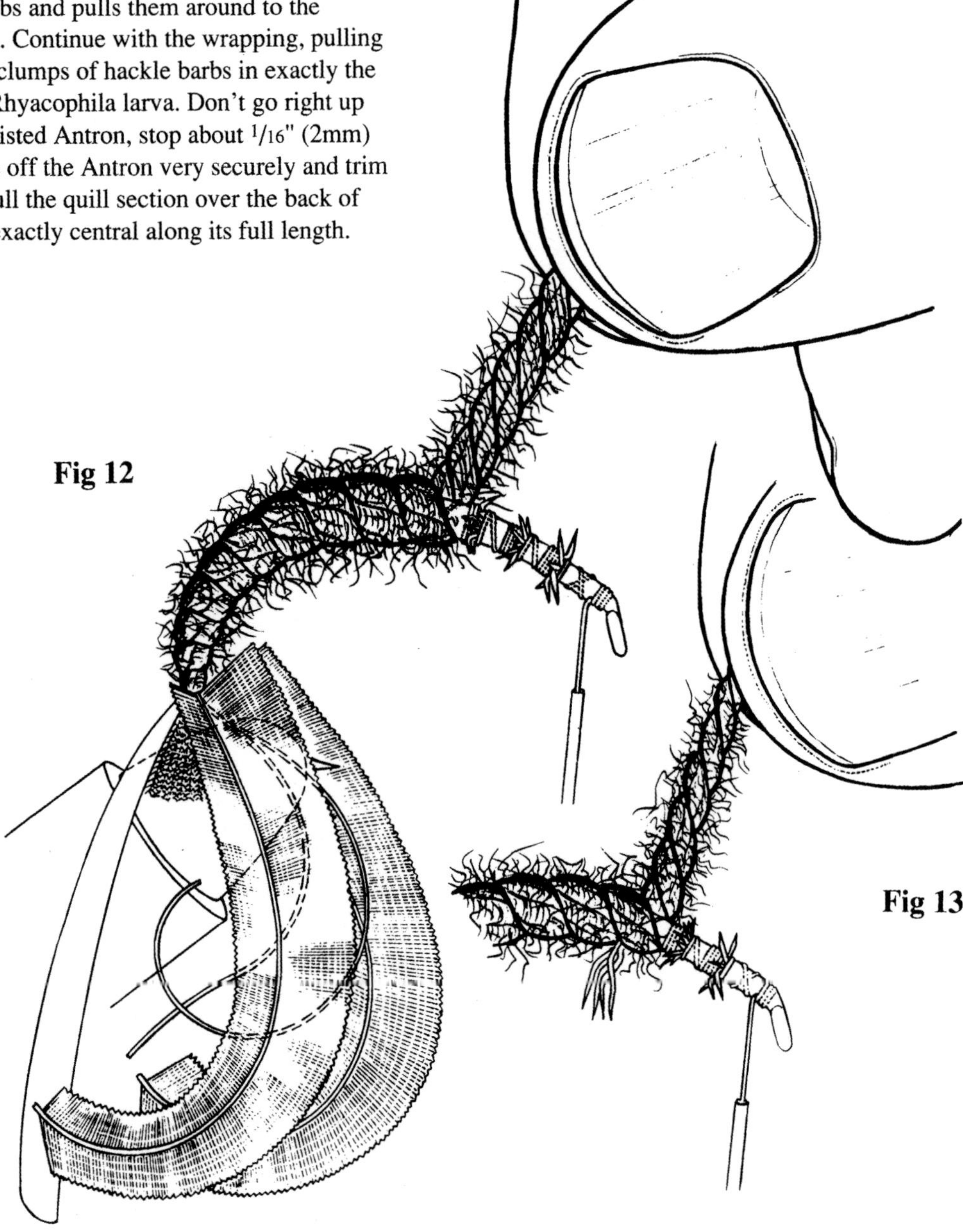

Fig 12

Fig 13

Fig 14
While holding it thus, take the fine gold rib around it, pulling the wire moderately hard into the quill section to produce a slight segment. Continue spiralling the wire all along the larva. Tie off the gold wire securely at the hook eye.

Fig 15
Next, gently pull the two ostrich herls underneath the belly of the larva, one on each side, and position them so that they lie just underneath the bottom edge of the quill section. When in this position, bind them down by spiralling the 3lb BS mono up along the larva, following the gold wire rib exactly. (Note: it produces a fuller effect if you press the two sides of each herl together like a double hackle). Tie off the nylon mono rib at the head very securely. Finally form a neat, long head and trim off the waste. Tint the head yellow or yellow-brown if your thread is one of the white Kevlar types.

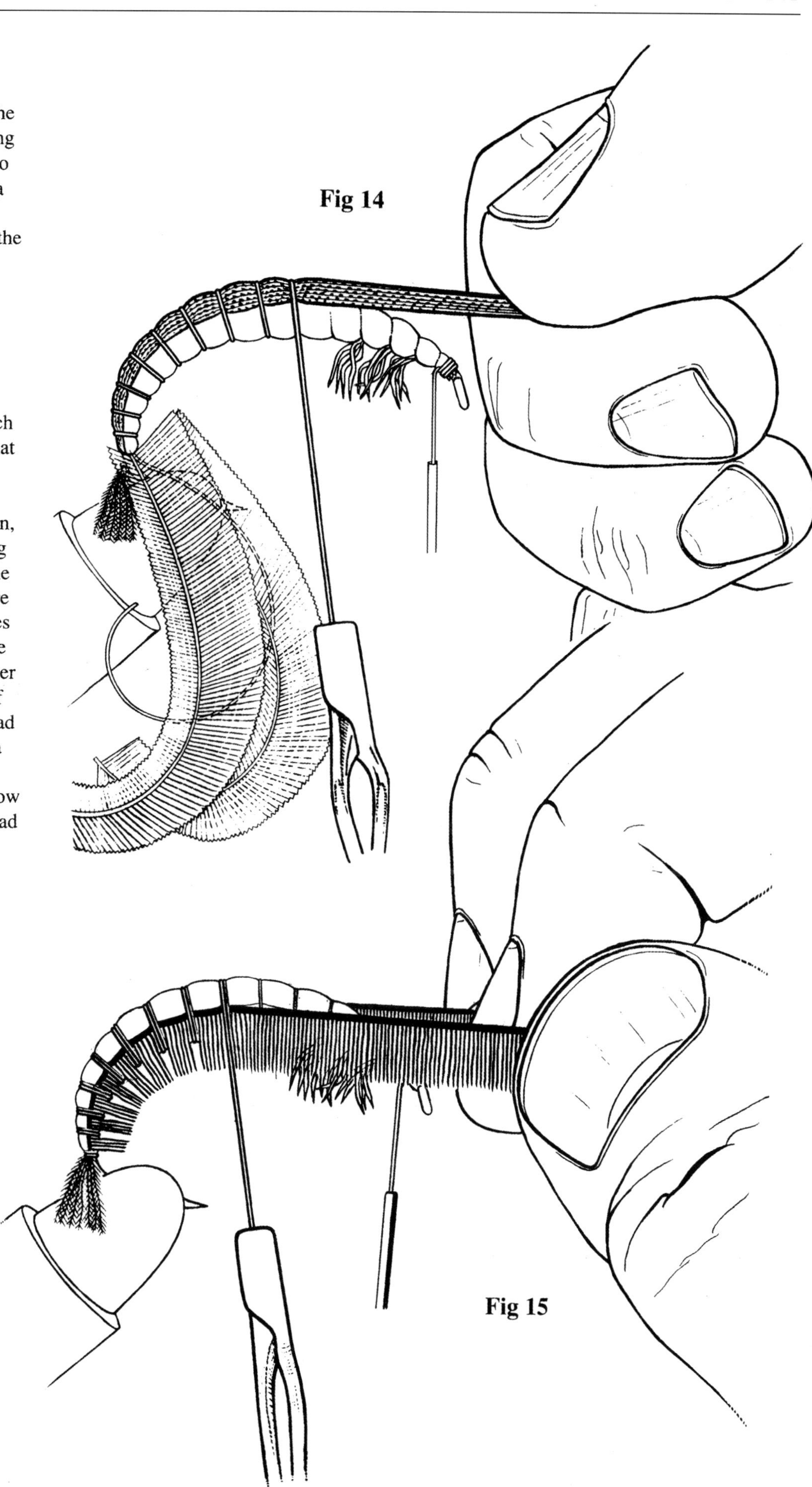

Fig 16
I also darken the top of the first three segments next to the head, using a black or dark brown Pantone pen to produce the three very dark thoracic segments of the Hydropsychids. Give the head two coats of cement.

Fig 17
This is a very deadly pattern and it is worth learning the steps as three or four of these in your fly box can produce the goods during winter grayling forays. Hydropsyche can also be very useful in the summer months for trout during coloured spate conditions.

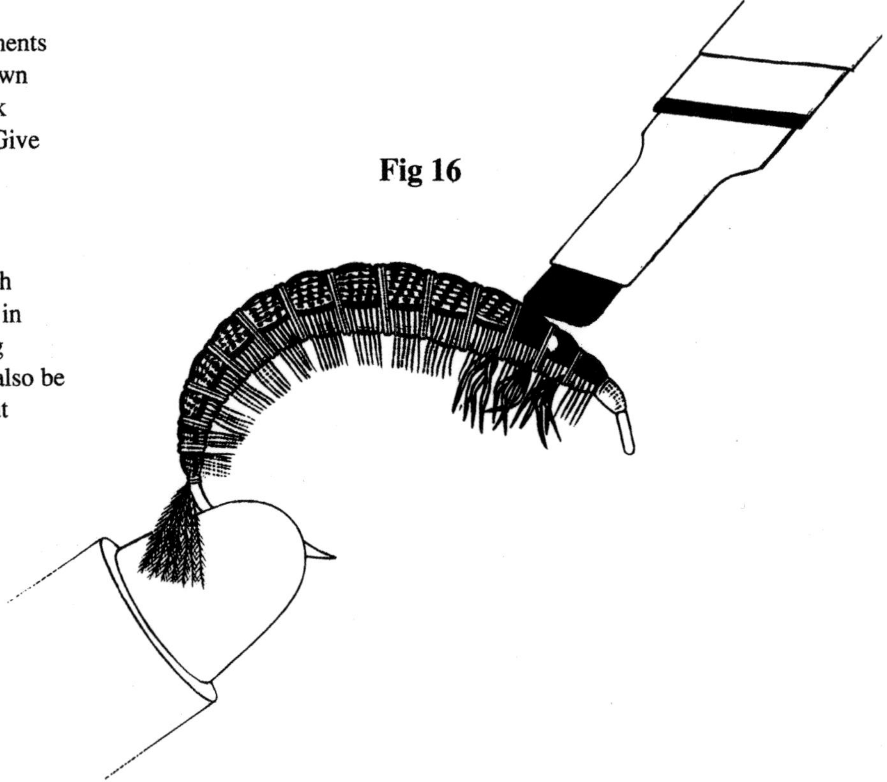

Fig 16

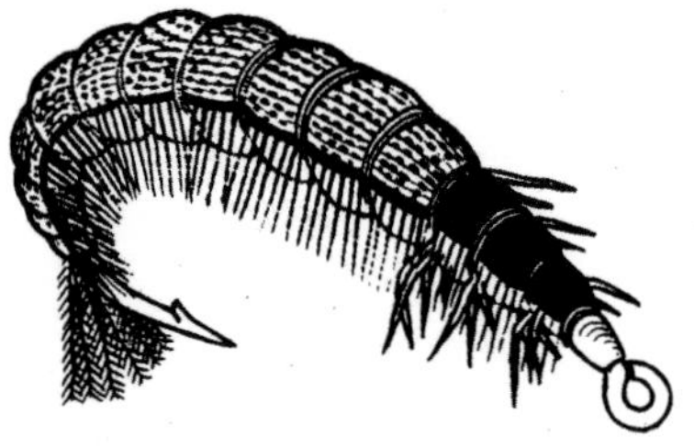

Fig 17

12. The Peeping Caddis
and the Hans van Klinken Leadhead

Entomologists divide caddis larvae into two distinct groups: Campodeiforms, the free-living types (roamers, tunnellers and net spinners) and the Eruciforms, the case-makers. It is the latter which concerns us here.

The case-making group are to be found in just about every aquatic habitat imaginable from cascading alpine torrents to stagnant ditches. There is even one British caddis larva which makes its home on dry land, amongst the leaf litter of a specific species of tree.

The two patterns featured in this chapter imitate those caddisflies whose larvae make their cases from mineral matter: sand grains, tiny pebbles, grit, etc.

Those species which construct their cases from cut pieces of green plant material have been omitted from the listing later in this chapter. Hence the omission of the very important family Phryganeidae.

The family Limnephilidae is included because some species are known to use both mineral and plant matter for their cases. The cinnamon sedge (*L. lunatus*), for instance, is a good example.

To assist the flydresser, it may be helpful at this juncture to give some idea of the size of their tubular cases plus any odd feature which may be significant.

THE CINNAMON SEDGE (*Limnephilus lunatus*) constructs a case which is more or less straight and can be as long as 1" (25mm) by about 3/16" (4mm) wide. It is often made of pieces of plant leaves but it can also be constructed from sand particles and tiny pebbles.

THE LARGE CINNAMON SEDGE (*Potamophylax latipennis*) has, strangely enough, a smaller case, about 7/8" long (22mm) by 3/16" (4mm) wide. It is slightly curved and is usually made from larger pieces of mineral matter than the previous species.

THE CAPERER (*Halesus radiatus*) makes one of the largest cases of all British caddisflies, up to 1 3/8" (36mm) long by 1/4" (6mm) wide. It is an unusual case in many ways, since the larva seems unable to decide on which type of material to use: pieces of waterlogged bark, smooth pieces of stone with infills of sand grains are all used. Often it decorates the outside of the case with long pieces of straight stick or twig, the twigs usually quite neatly arranged, longitudinally.

THE BROWN SEDGE (*Anabolia nervosa*) is another Limnephilid which likes to decorate its case with a stick or two. However, in this species, there always seems to be one stick which is abnormally long, often twice as long as the actual case! The case itself, being approximately 1 1/8" (28mm) long by 1/4" (6mm) wide, is constructed from sand particles.

WELSHMAN'S BUTTON (*Sericostoma personatum*). The larva of this oddly-named caddis tapers markedly towards the end of the abdomen. Therefore, as you would expect, its case is also tapered, the tip being about half the diameter of the front opening. It is slightly curved and quite smooth. The case is constructed from sand particles and it measures about 1/2" to 5/8" (12-16mm) long.

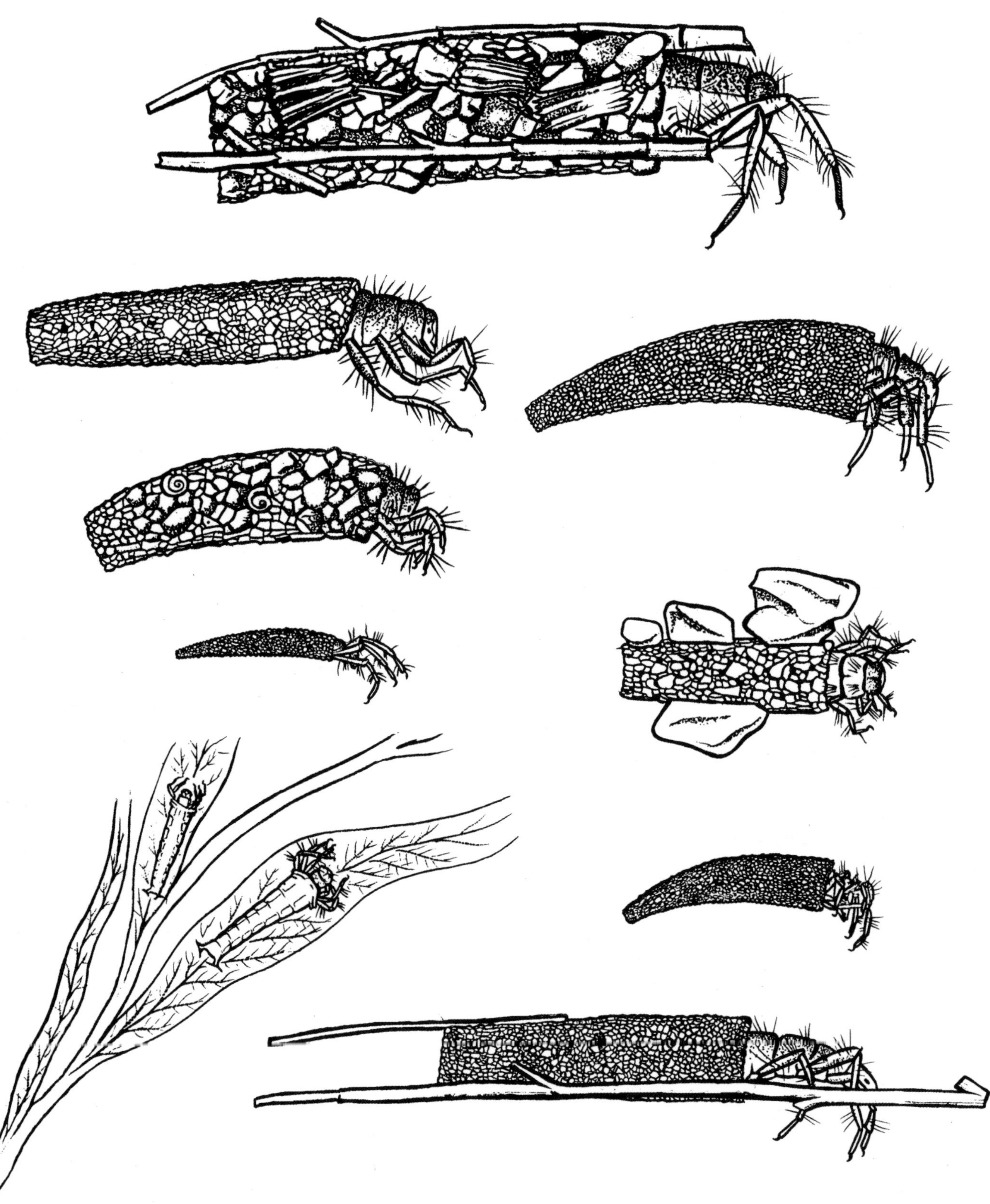

VARIATIONS OF CADDIS LARVAE CASES: *(clockwise from the top)*
The caperer, the silver sedge, the medium sedge, the Welshman's button, the brown sedge, the grannom (on weed), the silverhorn/grousewing etc, the large cinnamon sedge, and the cinnamon sedge.

THE MEDIUM SEDGE (*Goera pilosa*). The larva of this caddis adorns its case with unusually large pieces of stone cemented along each side. This species prefers swift streams, and it may be trying to counteract the force of the current by adding these large stones! The case itself is 5/8" (16mm) long by 3/16" (4mm) wide.

THE GRANNOM (*Brachycentrus subnubilus*). On the river Wharfe, where I fish, the grannom larva makes its case from a material which has the appearance of rubberised tissue paper. The colour is dark red/brown, and is quite smooth and tough. This material is a natural secretion. The case is small, thin and evenly tapering about 1/2" (12mm) long by 1/10" (2-3mm) wide. The grannom case is usually attached at its posterior to the substrate.

THE SILVER SEDGE (*Odontocerum albicorne*). The larva of this species makes a very plain, smooth case of sand grains. It tapers towards the rear and is also curved slightly, about 3/4" (20mm) long by 3/16" (4mm) wide at front end.

The black sedge, brown silverhorn, black silverhorn and grousewing (*Leptoceridae spp.*). All these members of the family Leptoceridae have cases which are about 1/2" to 5/8" (12 to 16mm) long, quite thin, tapering and often curved. The usual construction material is tiny sand particles but larger pieces of stone or grit or any odd piece of detritus may also be incorporated.

The case-making caddis larvae in this list can all be imitated using variations of the two patterns which follow, particularly the larger, more robust types.

THE PEEPING CADDIS

Cased caddis larvae often figure very highly in the diet of trout and grayling. Indeed, there are times when cased caddis are eaten in such significant numbers that they become of interest to us fly fishermen. My own observations have lead me to believe this to be from September to the end of the grayling season (end of February). The reason for this specialised feeding may be very simple to explain. In late spring and summer, the underwater larder is well-stocked with the larvae and pupae of many insect orders. These are all soft bodied and I imagine that fish can digest them very quickly. At this time of plenty, fish may well prefer to take 30 or 40 of these small food items rather than pick up one or two larger meals wrapped up in a hard, gritty indigestible overcoat.

As autumn runs into winter, and the second brood of the Baetid nymphs have all finally emerged, the stream itself begins to change. The weeds have nearly all died back and the stream bed must appear deserted and barren to the resident fish. They are forced to forage or lose condition.

Caddis larvae now figure highly in the diet, both cased and uncased. The uncased, free-living types seek sanctuary in nooks and crannies under stones for overwintering thus making the cased types the easier prey.

For the river flyfisher, the first good spate of autumn after weeks of drought can provide perfect conditions for using an imitation of the cased caddis. The scouring currents of a heavy river not only clear away the algae and trailing silkweed of summer, they also lift and trundle along many cased caddis larvae. This is a known fact - the uncontrolled downstream migration.

Nature counterbalances this effect since the adult female caddis will always fly upstream to lay her eggs. Spates will always provide good caddis larvae fishing, especially as the water level drops and clears.

HANS VAN KLINKEN'S LEADHEAD

The Leadhead first came to my attention in 1988 when Hans van Klinken, the talented Dutch flydresser, made his first visit to Yorkshire. He made a tremendous impact on both fish and fishermen with what to us Yorkshiremen were unorthodox and outsized flies. Wherever Hans went, he made large catches of fish both with the Leadhead and his now famous Klinkhamer Special (see page 155).

Hans fishes his Leadhead in a variety of ways:

from dead drift using a well-oiled yard strike indicator, to lengthy 'across and down' casts with good mends when necessary. He also takes fish by simply twitching the Leadhead back upstream. This last method puzzles me a little even allowing for the occasional stupidity of fish.

Further proof of this pattern's effectiveness came in 1989. It was February, the week before the end of the grayling season. The England World Team wanted to visit Yorkshire to have some practice on rainfed rivers - preparatory to the World Championships. Some of us were to guide for them.

Unfortunately the weather decided to do its damnedest. The heavens opened midweek and we were faced with a cold, high river, on the Saturday. Despite the adverse conditions it wasn't long before someone had a fish - yes, on the Leadhead - followed by several more. Pretty soon, the Leadhead was much in demand.

The trick with these cased caddis patterns is to have the right amount of weight incorporated into them. Ideally, they should be fished square across with only the slightest amount of swing. The caddis should trip, tap, skip along the bottom. Even when you are fishing it correctly, you should still expect a few snaggings on the bottom, despite the fact that the pattern is designed to fish hook point up.

As you can imagine, building in the right amount of ballast is very much a hit and miss affair, and those who have coarse fished will appreciate just how critical weight below the float can be. I personally don't like adding split shot to the leader unless I am forced - we are supposed to be *fly* fishermen not *coarse* fishermen! I've already made a tremendous concession by including a split shot in the dressing.

If, while I'm fishing, I don't feel the 'pluck and pull' from the bottom, I don't worry too much so long as the fly is fishing deep. I've known grayling take this pattern as it was rising through mid-water.

You may wish to tie a series incorporating different shot weights, say BB No.2 and No.4. And if you want to tie yourself a really deep diver you should consider incorporating an SSG. Bear in mind, of course, you will have to use the legal non-toxic shot.

Finally, don't be put off by the size and appearance of these two flies, particularly the very shaggy Leadhead. Fished at the appropriate times they can be deadly.

SOME CASED CADDIS SPECIES APPROPRIATE TO THIS PATTERN

British species:
LIMNEPHILIDAE
Cinnamon Sedge *Limnephillis lunatus.*
Large Cinnamon Sedge *Potomophlax latipennis .*
Caperer *Halesus radiatus.*
Brown Sedge *Anabolia nervosa.*

SERICOSTOMATIDAE
Welshman's Button *Sericostoma personatum.*
Medium Sedge *Goera pilosa.*
Grannom *Brachycentrus subnubilus.*

ODONTOCERIDAE
Silver Sedge *Odontocerum albicorne.*

LEPTOCERIDAE
Black Sedge, Silverhorns *Athripsodes spp.*
Grousewing *Mystacides spp.*

Some American species:
LIMNEPHILIDAE
Dot Wing Sedge *Frenesia spp.*
Snow Sedge *Psychoglyha spp.*
Giant Orange Sedge *Dicosmorcus spp.*
Smoke Wing Sedge *Apatania spp.*
ODONTOCERIDAE
Dark Blue Sedge *Psilotreta spp.*

A complete list of North American tube cased caddis larvae suitable for being imitated by the pattern under discussion is far too extensive. The above list is just a small sample of them.

THREE PEEPING CADDIS and *(Bottom)* HANS VAN KLINKEN'S LEADHEAD
(Top two) Typical Limnephilids (Cinnamon Sedges, etc).
The small one is the Grannom, with the distinct green larva.

NOTES ON MATERIALS AND DRESSING

I recommend using one of the modern Kevlar or Kevlar-type tying threads. Regular 6/0 and 8/0 threads are not man enough for the job. When it comes to the fur for simulating the caddis case, you can let you imagination loose. I've used rabbit, hare, grey squirel and opossum and combinations of them. It all comes down to the colour and texture you want. Generally, it is hare and rabbit which is used.

Don't skimp when you load the dubbing into the spinning loop and make sure also that you spin it tight, hence the need for a strong thread. When it comes to hackle choice, you can use whatever hackle you wish. I've watched Hans tie his Leadhead using a partridge hackle which was quite long in barb length and taken from the rump.

I prefer to use a shorter barbed partridge hackle but I don't use the very best, these I reserve exclusively for my Partridge and Orange Spiders. I have also used partridge hackles dyed very dark brown and hackles from a red grouse.

Do remember to make sure that the split of the shot is facing forward so that the shot is trapped. It's most annoying to lose the shot when you're into fish.

When imitating the small cased caddis larva such as the grannom or silverhorn, you will have to bring everything down in proportion: very small shot, very little hackle showing and a neat, thin, closely-cropped case.

PEEPING CADDIS DRESSING

Hook: Medium or heavy wire 2x to 3x longshank hook (must be turned down eye). Suggest Partridge 'Capt. Hamilton' Nymph Code H1A size 6 to 14.
Thread: Fine Kevlar type or Kevlar blend, any brand. Colour: mid brown.
Cement: Dave's Flexament (USA) or Floo Glue (UK), both thinned.
Weight: Non-toxic split shot, size to suit conditions (depth, flow etc).
Case: Heavily applied and tightly dubbed fur from wild rabbit or hare's mask or a mixture of both, guard hairs included.
Legs: Partridge hackle (natural brown or grey or dyed black) or grouse hackle, fairly short in barb length.
Head: Man-made fibre such as Antron. Wool knitting yarn will not make a lasting head. Colours of yarn: cream, yellow, very pale green, dirty olive yellow, etc.

HANS VAN KLINKEN LEADHEAD

As for Peeping Caddis, except for:
Case: dubbed rather less tightly, more shaggily. Sometimes velcro-ed but never sculpted.
Legs: Choose a softer hackle and one much longer in barb length.
Tag: 3 or 4 turns of fluorescent lime green Flexibody strip around end of hook shank (part way past bend).

Tying the Peeping Caddis

Fig 1
Make sure the hook is very tightly gripped with the shank horizontal. Take a 4"(100mm)length of 8 to 10lbs BS mono and crimp on your split shot at mid-position.

Fig 2
Catch on the tying thread just behind the eye, then run it up the shank in touching turns about one quarter of the way up the shank. Now offer up the split shot on the mono strand. Position the shot on top of the shank over the eye of the hook and slightly forward of it. The split should be facing downwards at this stage. While holding this position, firmly bind one leg of the nylon mono to the hook shank, working towards the eye. When at the eye, make several tight turns of thread.

Fig 3
Now take hold of the other leg of nylon mono and pull it back over the shot and bind it down securely. The shot will now have its split facing forward. Trim off any excess nylon mono. Run the thread up to the start of the bend and let the bobbin holder hang.

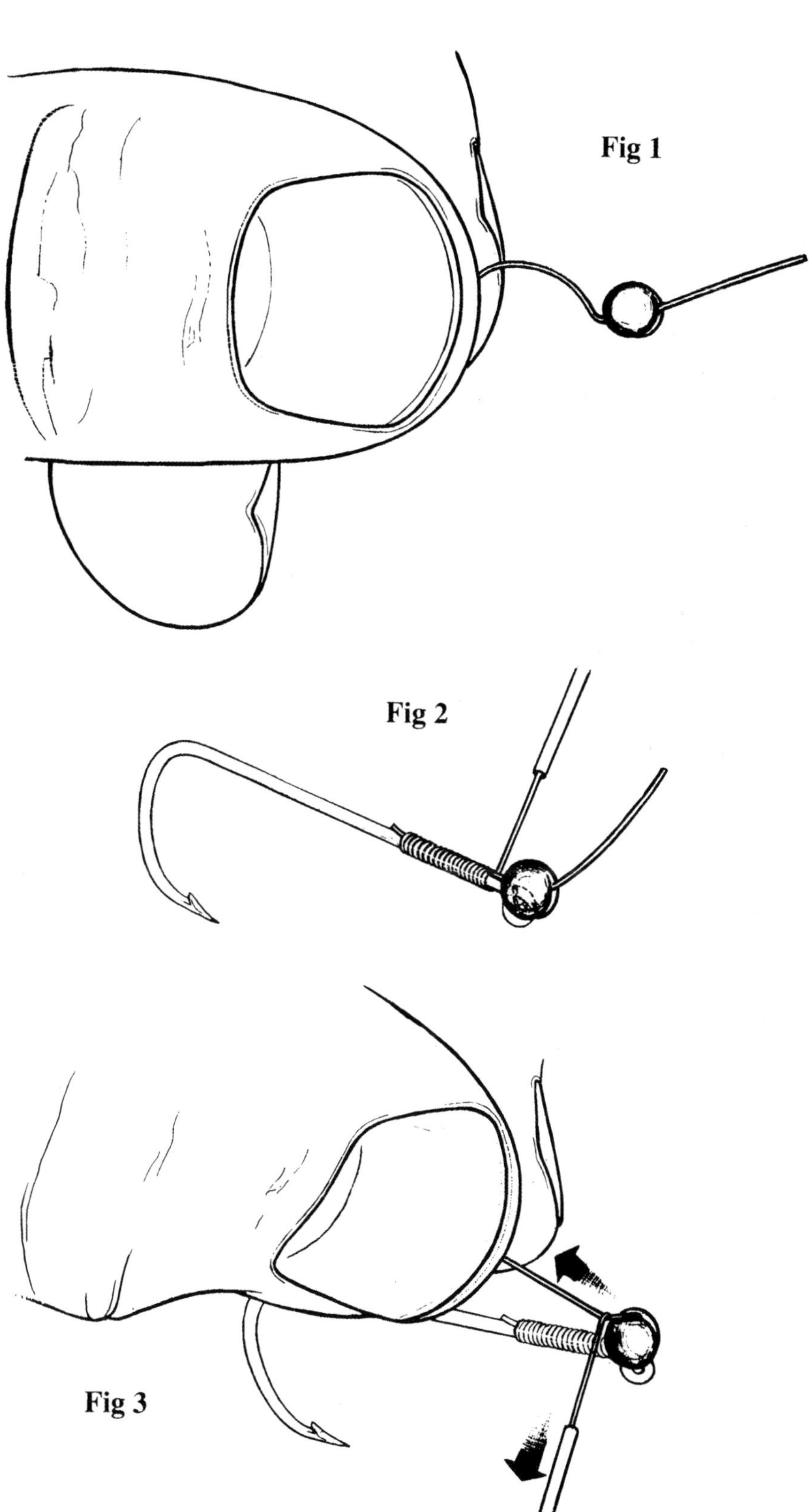

Fig 4
Cut off a 1" (25mm) length of Antron yarn and hold the end over a cigarette lighter or match flame. The man-made fibres will fuse, bubble and turn dark brown, whereupon you immediately withdraw it from the flame - you may inadvertently set it alight, so watch out. Don't touch it while still soft or your finger will be burnt! In seconds, however, it will be set and cool.

Fig 5
Next offer this piece of Antron up on top of the shank with the burnt tip (the dark glossy head of the larva) protruding over the eye of the hook. The amount it protrudes is a matter of personal preference.The real larva rarely protrudes very much, just sufficient to allow its legs to function as it laboriously crawls along.

Fig 6
When happy with its position, bind it securely in place, on top of the shank, binding down the waste end about a quarter way along the shank, then trim off any excess Antron yarn.

Fig 7
The next item to be tied in is the partridge hackle. Tie this in by the tip right where your first thread-wraps tying down the Antron yarn are situated.

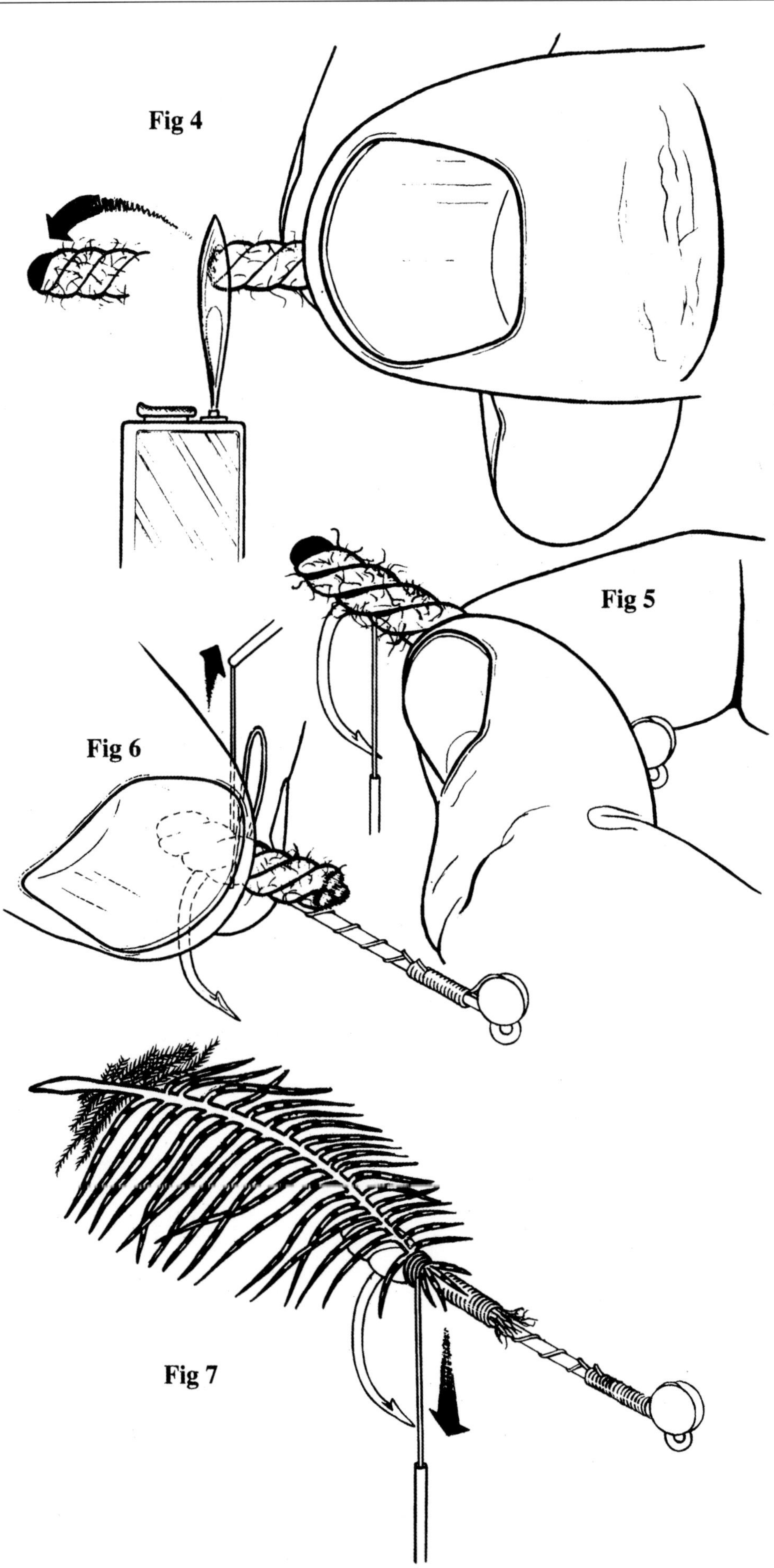

Fig 8
Wind on the hackle making about two or three full turns working backwards. Then tie off the butt end and trim off the waste.

Fig 9
To form the larva's case, the entire shank from the back edge of the hackle to the split shot is covered in a natural fur dubbing - base fur, guard hairs - the lot. Make a good long spinning loop right at the back of the hackle and hook on the dubbing whirl. Then lay the fur dubbing in between the loop, spreading it along the full length.

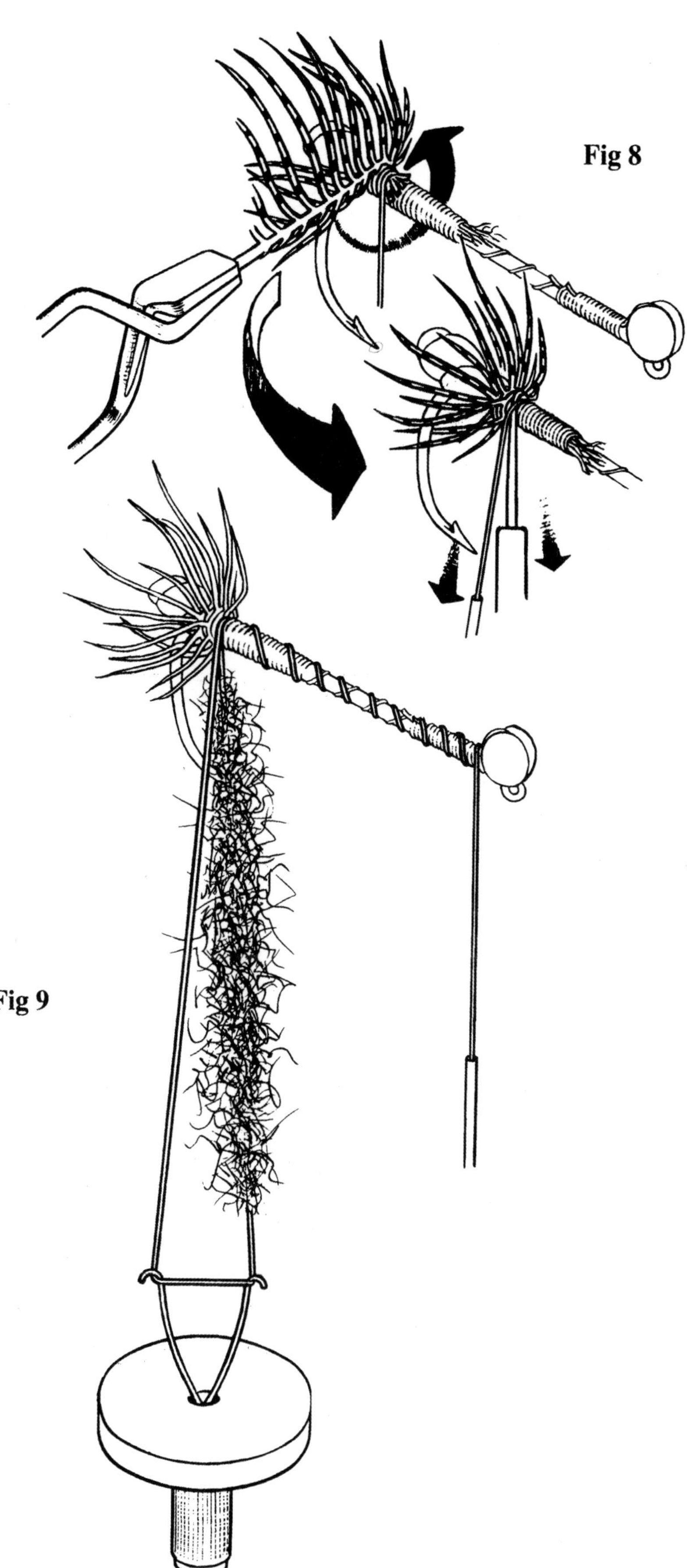

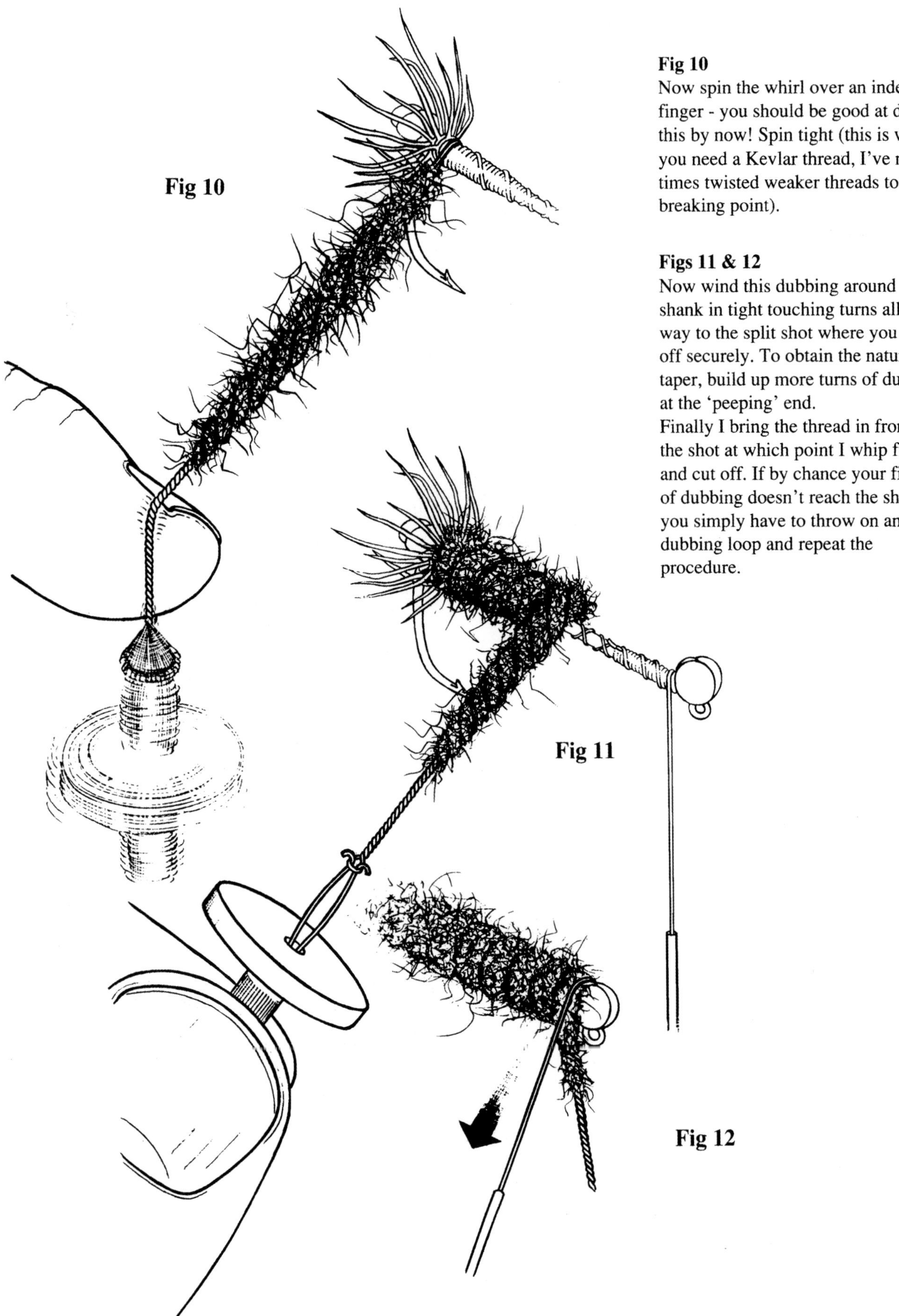

Fig 10
Now spin the whirl over an index finger - you should be good at doing this by now! Spin tight (this is why you need a Kevlar thread, I've many times twisted weaker threads to breaking point).

Figs 11 & 12
Now wind this dubbing around the shank in tight touching turns all the way to the split shot where you tie it off securely. To obtain the natural taper, build up more turns of dubbing at the 'peeping' end.
Finally I bring the thread in front of the shot at which point I whip finish and cut off. If by chance your first lot of dubbing doesn't reach the shot, you simply have to throw on another dubbing loop and repeat the procedure.

Fig 13
The final job is to scrub up the fur dubbing. Using a velcro teaser go all around and along the 'case'.

Fig 14
After which you simply sculpt to a nice even taper with your fine scissors.

Fig 15
Finished!

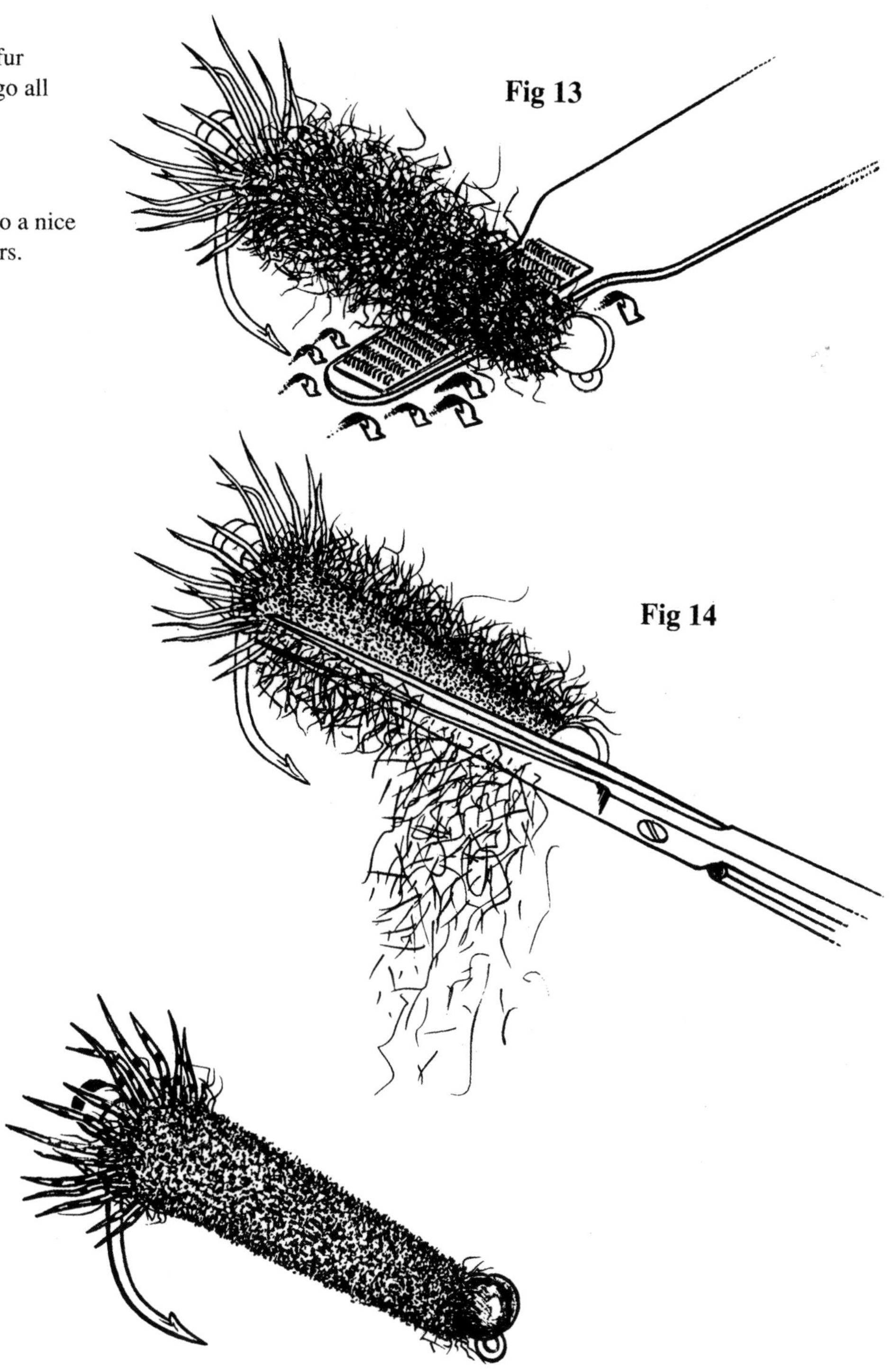

Fig 13

Fig 14

Fig 15

Tying the Hans van Klinken Leadhead

Hans' Leadhead differs only in minor detail as far as the tying is concerned. The mounting of the split shot is identical. He uses a partridge hackle which is much longer in barb length than I use on my pattern. His fur dubbing is left uncut and quite rough.

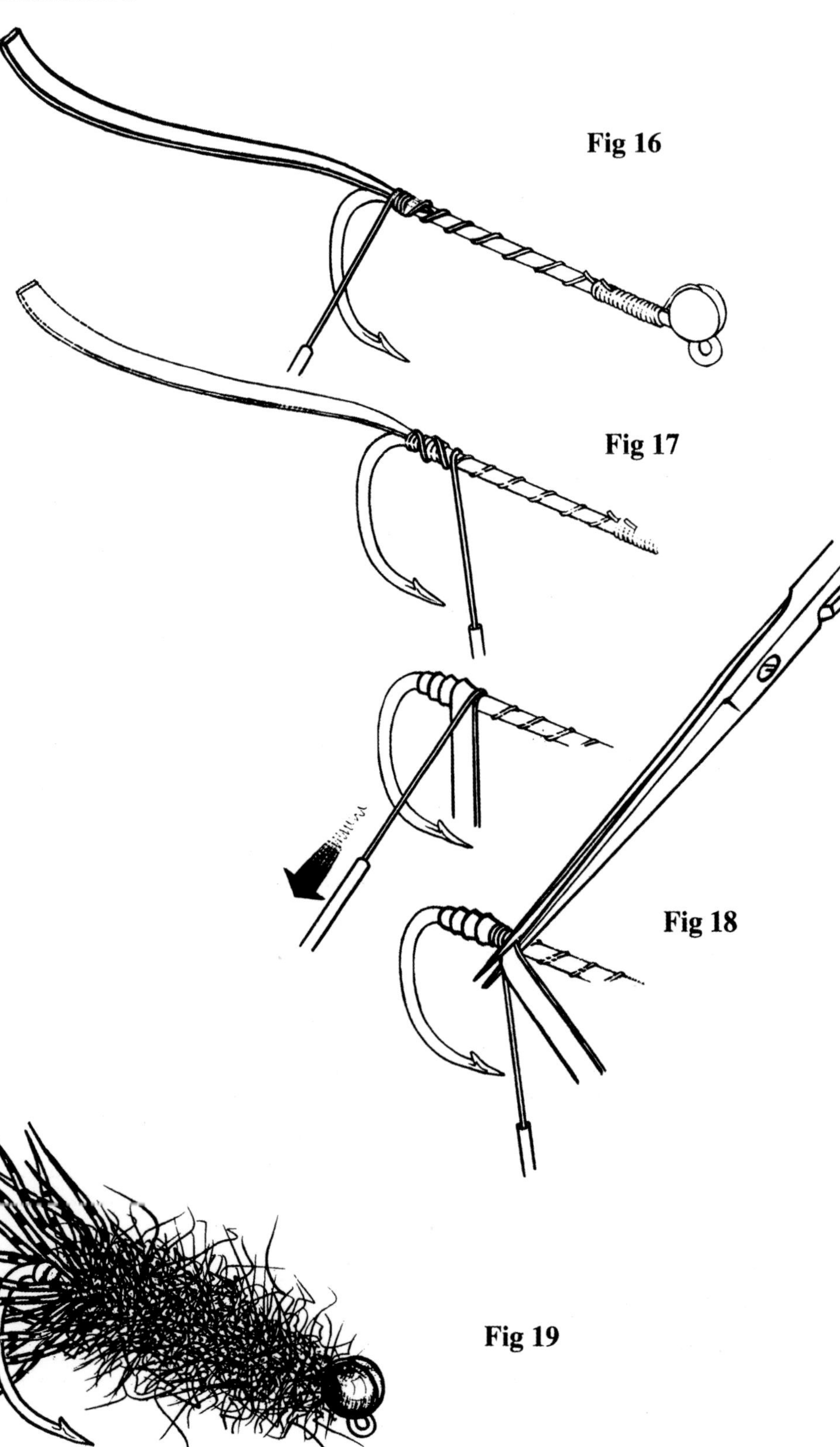

Fig 16
The one big difference is that Hans ties in a tag right at the end of the shank, it can even go slightly round the bend. The tag can be yarn or floss, but a narrow strip of Flexibody is his favourite. I cut off a strip about 1/8" (3mm) wide which is tapered to a point for tying in. Tie it in by this fine tip, watch out that your thread doesn't slice through it.

Fig 17
Then I take my thread back up the shank the distance I want the tag to be.

Fig 18
Make four or five tight, quarter overlapping turns, then tie off and snip off the waste Flexibody.

Fig 19
The hackle is next tied in and wound on and the case formed exactly as previously explained. Hans' pattern is, if anything, a little quicker to tie and I've seen him knock one out in a minute.

13. The Klinkhamer Special

This brilliant semi-dry fly pattern was devised by Hans van Klinken. Hans fished various rivers in Yorkshire in August 1988 and had great success catching grayling with this huge creation.

His day on my club water, on the river Ure, was vividly recounted by the member who accompanied him. The river was low and clear, conditions which usually make the fish shy and very pernickety.

Hans, with his outsized fly, apparently released upwards of 35 fish, the majority of which were grayling; the best, I was reliably told, approaching 2lbs. Now, 35 fish on our club water - on any northern freestone stream - on the fly, is a great day indeed. Half that score is considered good sport. Ure grayling can be particularly frustrating and I would have been highly sceptical had it not been for the fact that the report came from a reliable source.

I had another reason to banish my fears of fisherman's exaggeration, for I had previously been told of this wonder fly by John Roberts. John had fished with Hans in Germany where they had had tremendous sport using this fly almost exclusively.

Haven't we all been influenced down the ages by authors insisting on: 'smaller sizes when fishing for grayling', or 'tiny drys which must sit high on their hackle points', etc, etc? Very sound advice in my opinion and a sheet anchor for any grayling fly fisherman.

Why then, in such difficult conditions, did so many fish apparently abandon the rule book and throw themselves at a fly which has a parachute hackle span of over 3/4" (19mm)? What exactly does the 'Klinkhamer Special' represent? Hans' reply is unequivocal - a hatching caddis. A perfectly reasonable supposition, at the appropriate time. However, its effectiveness goes beyond caddisflies - hatching or otherwise.

It is, in my view, the way this pattern sits *in* the water which makes it unique and suggestive of a whole host of struggling, half-drowned, juicy insects. It is surely taken for the many larger terrestrials which fall onto rivers every season. Candidates which readily come to mind are soldier beetles, oak flies, cowdung flies, blow flies, horse flies, ichneuman flies, social and solitary wasps, hover flies, and many of the social bees. They all kick or vibrate their wings when trapped in the glue-like meniscus - and the meniscus always tends to be thicker during hot weather. Their desperate actions make patterns on the surface and it is my opinion that the Klinkhamer, with its many-fibred parachute hackle, may give a passable impression of one of these large struggling terrestrials.

In high summer, trout and grayling rely quite heavily on terrestrial food items and, while apparent fasting through the heat of the day seems to occur, it is also well known that, given the opportunity, a good mouthful, feebly kicking and passing directly overhead, is rarely refused.

This pattern has gone a long way to overcoming that perennial problem: hooking grayling on the floating fly. My own performance with the conventional dry fly is not good and the Grey Lady often has me completely beaten. Was it Charles Ritz who said that a flyfisherman should congratulate himself if he hooks one in five grayling risen? Now for the good news. The Klinkhamer Special evens up the score. In fact, from my own experience, Charles Ritz's one-in-five is reversed - one missed, four landed!

My friend and grayling fanatic Bernard Benson has had tremendous results with this pattern too. He also has come up with a quirky little theory to explain why grayling are so difficult to hook on conventional drys.

It goes like this. Grayling, as we all know, are not designed for taking surface food. Their protruding upper lip makes them better suited to bottom feeding, even though they do regularly rise to flies on the surface. When rising to conventional dry flies, they charge up from the stream bed, dropping back with the current and tilting backwards - past the vertical - as they near the surface. This backward tilt is essential because of the fish's prominent upper lip.

As the grayling's mouth approaches the fly, a tiny pressure front is pushed ahead (remember the grayling is coming up at speed). Its lips open only at the instant the meniscus is reached by which time the pressure front has developed into a small raised mound of water immediately underneath the dry fly. The dry fly, of course, is tethered to the end of your leader. So, as the pressure mound rises, the dry fly slides away, down this tiny bank of water. The angler reacts instantly to the rise, but there is no resistance - another missed fish.

The problem seems not to exist with the big Klinkhamer. It appears that grayling do not have to contort themselves nearly so much when hitting this fly and it's possible that contact is made below the meniscus. As Bernard says: 'It's like giving them a jug handle to get hold of'.

Hans van Klinken is a true grayling specialist and has pursued them throughout Western Europe, taking many huge specimens on this fly (best 61cm, 2.2kg) on his many forays into central and northern Norway, and Sweden. It was Norwegian grayling for which this pattern was originally designed.

Whilst preparing a large specimen for a camp meal, Hans carried out a quick stomach check and found his fish had been feeding heavily on large caddis pupae right at the point of hatching. Their strongly curved abdomen and emerging wings finally gave rise to the Klinkhamer Special.

In my view this is one of best ever all-round floating flies for bringing fish up, in a no-hatch situation, and its effectiveness goes beyond grayling and brown trout. Hans has taken many grilse, seatrout and arctic char in Norway on this fly, using the same size as he does for grayling.

Hans developed this fly on the banks of the river Glomma in Norway in 1985. In some very interesting notes he recently sent me, he states that the Klinkhamer works best when there is no hatch in progress, on bright sunny days, fished in rapids and riffle water. On dark or rainy days it also works on slower water. He states that tied with a dark tan poly dubbing body it is a real killer when the mayfly (*E. danica*) is hatching.

He also sent me a clipping from a Norwegian newspaper. The article relates one of Hans' typical forays on one of the lesser known west coast streams, where Hans caught (with the Klinkhamer) 15 salmon and grilse in 5 hours. The newspaper is dated 14 July 1988. The same year he caught 73 seatrout in a sea pool of a small Norwegian river in broad daylight. Some fly, some fisherman!

NOTES ON MATERIALS AND TYING

The hook must be quite long and curved in the shank and, most importantly, light in wire gauge. Hans recommends Partridge GRS12ST, or K12ST which are classified as long shank caddis hooks. However, it is necessary to carry out a slight re-bending operation before starting to tie. This is absolutely essential for the fly to sit correctly in the surface - a point missed by several authors. (see Fig 1).

Re-bending at room temperature is possible, with great care, but it can induce concentrated stress points which can lead to a sudden breakage. Localised annealing (softening) is therefore preferable and, with such fine wire, the tip of a butane cigarette lighter is sufficient to create a tiny zone of softened wire.

The tying thread should be ultra-fine. The parachute hackle for this pattern is tied off at the base of the polypropylene 'wing', not around the hook shank as on a conventional hackle, the base of the poly wing being used as a tying post. If, say, the usual 6/0 thread is used it is all too easy to find that the bottom turn of hackle is forced up much too high from the thorax when performing the final whips and tying off, making the fly look as though it is wearing a vicar's dog collar below the hackle. So, Hans and I strongly recommend Danville's 'Spider Web', since with this thread so little space is used up.

The crimped polypropylene yarn used for the wing is readily available from many mail order catalogues. It is easy to work with, makes a highly visible wing and, of course, has a natural water-shedding action. On white flecked water such as rapids it is better to use a coloured wing; and dyed pink poly yarn it is highly visible.

There is also another bonus when tying this fly - you can at last make use of all those hundreds of large hackles, too large for the usual conventional dry flies. You can now pluck away at your cape well beyond that familiar bald patch. Also, all those old cheap capes can now be resurrected as some of their hackles will be ideal. The most popular hackle colours appear to be in the ginger range from light to quite dark, in fact Hans' original recipe recommends the colour chestnut.

The abdomen dubbing is Fly-Rite Extra Fine Poly.

Note: Hans re-shapes the hooks cold, bending them with steady finger and thumb pressure. His objection to using heat is the localised loss of anti-corrosion coating. Hans also uses Blue dun as a hackle and occasionally black herls (peacock wing) for the abdomen but states that when using herl you must over rib with fine silver wire in the opposite direction, to help combat teeth shredding.

KLINKHAMER SPECIAL DRESSING

Hook: Light wire long curved-shank hook. Suggest Partridge Long Shank Sedge/Caddis Hook Code K12ST, or GRS12ST (re-shaped - see Fig 1) sizes 8-14.
Thread: Midge 8/0 (any pale colour) or Danville's Spider Web (untinted).
Cement: Dave's Flexament (USA) or Floo Gloo (UK).
Abdomen: Fine synthetic dubbing, almost any light brown, tan olive, brown-olive, etc. Hans van Klinken, the originator, specifies Fly Rite Extra Fine Poly in the following colours: No.19 light tan, No.20 dark tan, No.32 rusty olive, No.39 medium brown dun. Hans also uses black feather barbs from a peacock wing, which require a rib with fine silver wire.
Thorax: Bronze peacock herl.
Wing: Poly yarn. Colour: white or light grey, pink for the Pinkhamer.
Hackle: Dry-fly-quality cock (not necessarily genetic).
Colours: light ginger, cree, grizzle, grizzle dyed light ginger, and blue dun (natural or dyed).

KLINKHAMER SPECIALS

(Top) Black Peacock wing herl abdomen *(Middle)* Dark Tan Pinkhamer *(Bottom)* Standard 'LT' Klinkhamer (Light Tan).

Tying the Klinkhamer Special

Fig 1
Bend down the first quarter of the shank, say 20° to 30°. It will help if the hook is gripped in the vice while performing this. Play only the tip of the lighter flame on the wire having the snipe nosed pliers to hand so that no time is lost. It isn't necessary to make the wire glow red.

Now re-position the hook in the vice with the re-bent portion near the eye horizontal. Catch on the tying thread just behind the eye and run it in open turns down the shank, well around the bend and back again. Stop right where the shank was re-bent and let the bobbin holder hang.

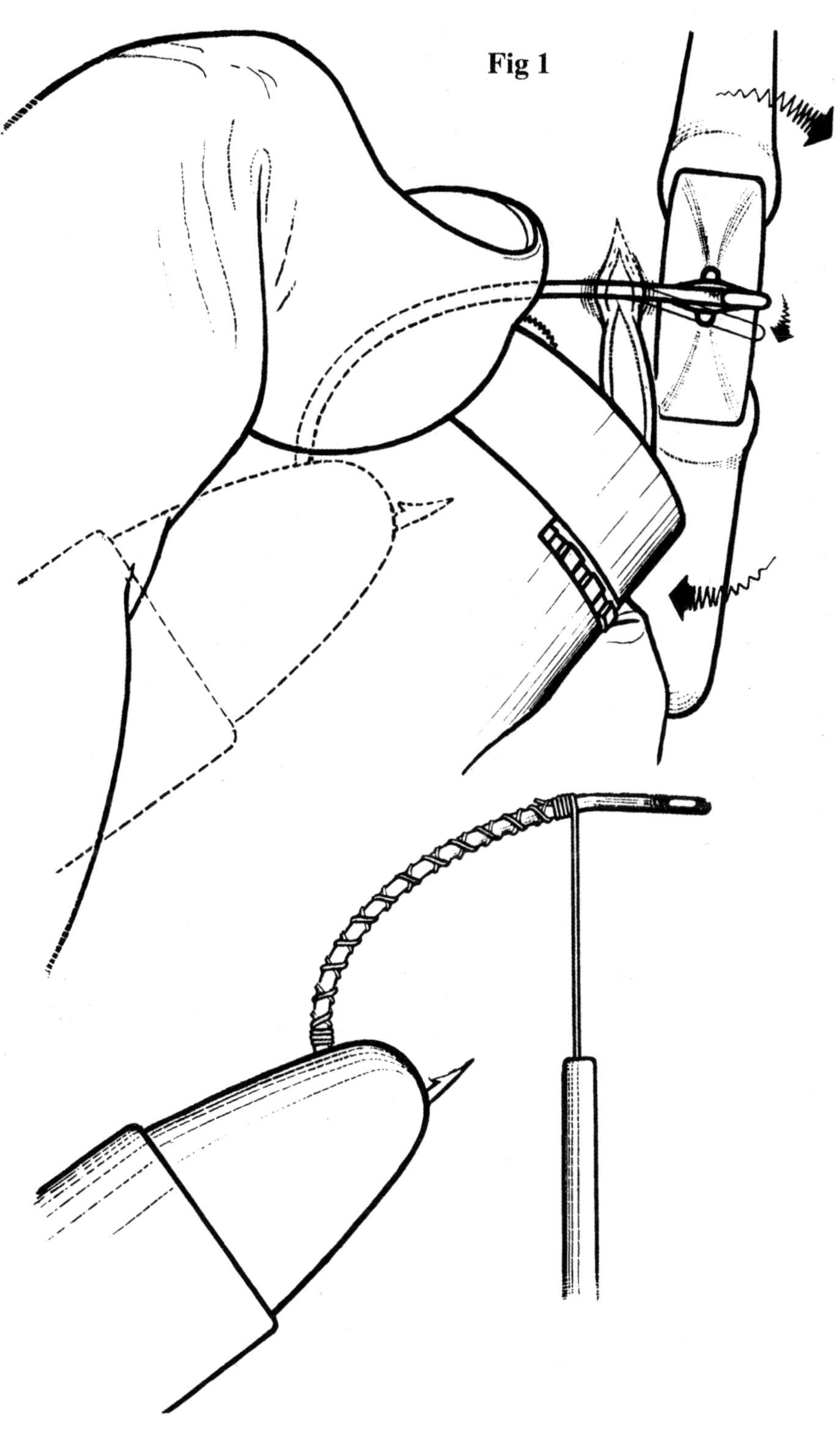

Fig 2
Cut off a 1½" (40mm) length of poly yarn and tie it to the top of the shank using several successive 'pinch and loops'. The yarn should lie in line with the shank and the tying-in position should be slightly forward of the re-bend point.

Fig 3
Next, securely bind down the rear portion of the poly yarn all the way along the hook shank, keeping the yarn on top. Continue this binding down procedure around the bend to where you judge the end of the abdomen to be.

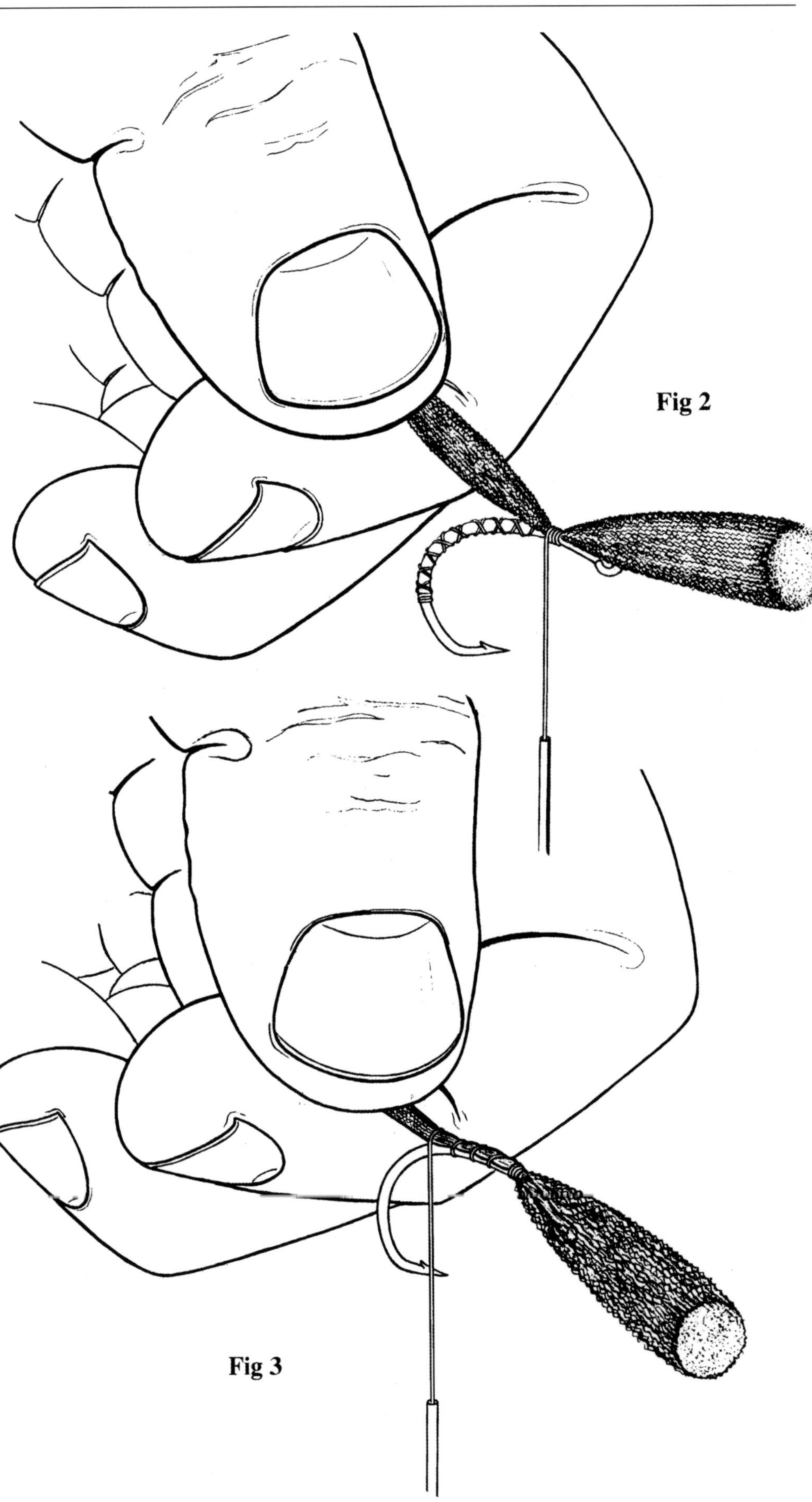

Fig 2

Fig 3

Fig 4

Trim off any remaining poly yarn on the slant and return the tying thread to the tying-in point. Raise the front portion of the poly yarn - the wing - and make several snug turns of tying thread in front of it. Also make several tight turns of tying thread around the base of this wing tuft itself. This has a twofold effect: it gathers together all the individual fibres at the base, causing them to flare out attractively; it also helps to form a foundation or wrapping post for the parachute hackle. The wing should now be vertical with a slight diverging flare. It will be cut to the required length when the fly is finished. Let the bobbin holder hang.

Fig 5

The hackle is next to be tied in. Select a hackle with a barb length of 1/3 to 1/2 the overall hook length and strip off all the basal fluff. Tie it in at the base of the wing with the barbs lying horizontal, dull side uppermost. The hackle should project beyond the eye of the hook. When firmly tied in, continue winding the tying thread to a point well around the bend, binding down the hackle stalk. When you arrive at the point where the abdomen will finish, trim off remaining hackle stalk and let the bobbin holder hang.

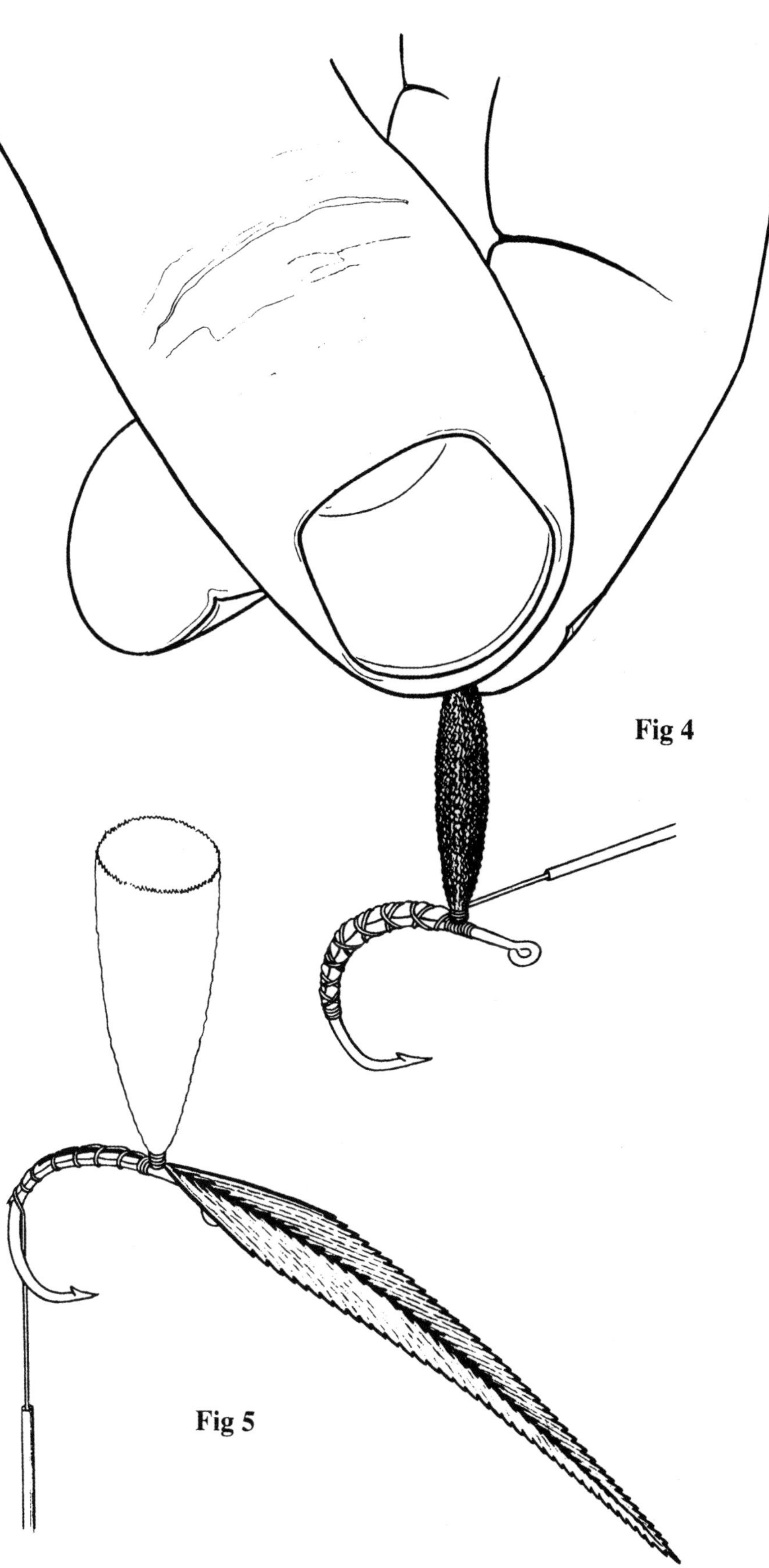
Fig 4

Fig 5

Fig 6
When securely tied, the entire hackle should be raised by kinking it upwards with the thumbnail. This will keep the hackle out of the way while other manoeuvres are taking place.

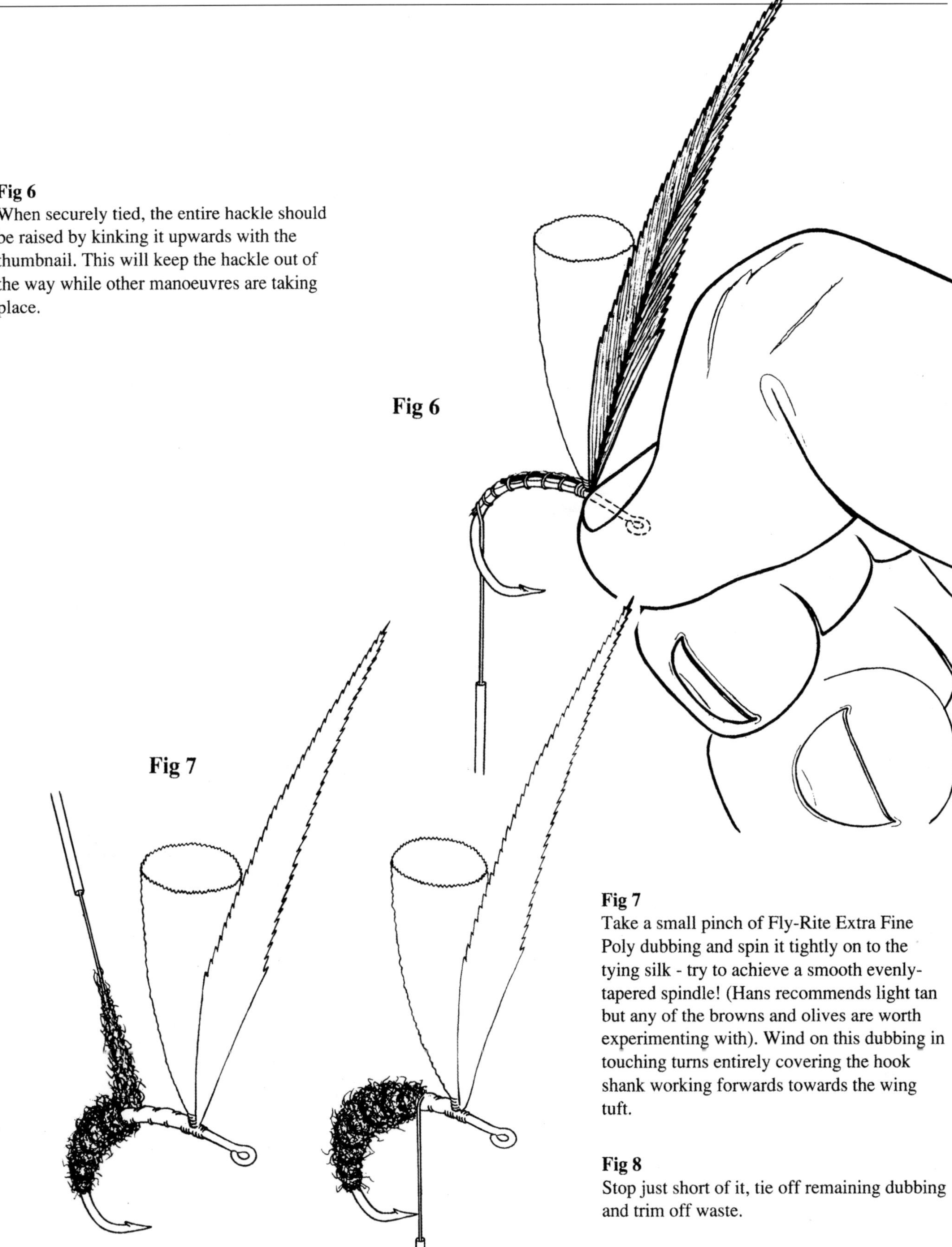

Fig 7
Take a small pinch of Fly-Rite Extra Fine Poly dubbing and spin it tightly on to the tying silk - try to achieve a smooth evenly-tapered spindle! (Hans recommends light tan but any of the browns and olives are worth experimenting with). Wind on this dubbing in touching turns entirely covering the hook shank working forwards towards the wing tuft.

Fig 8
Stop just short of it, tie off remaining dubbing and trim off waste.

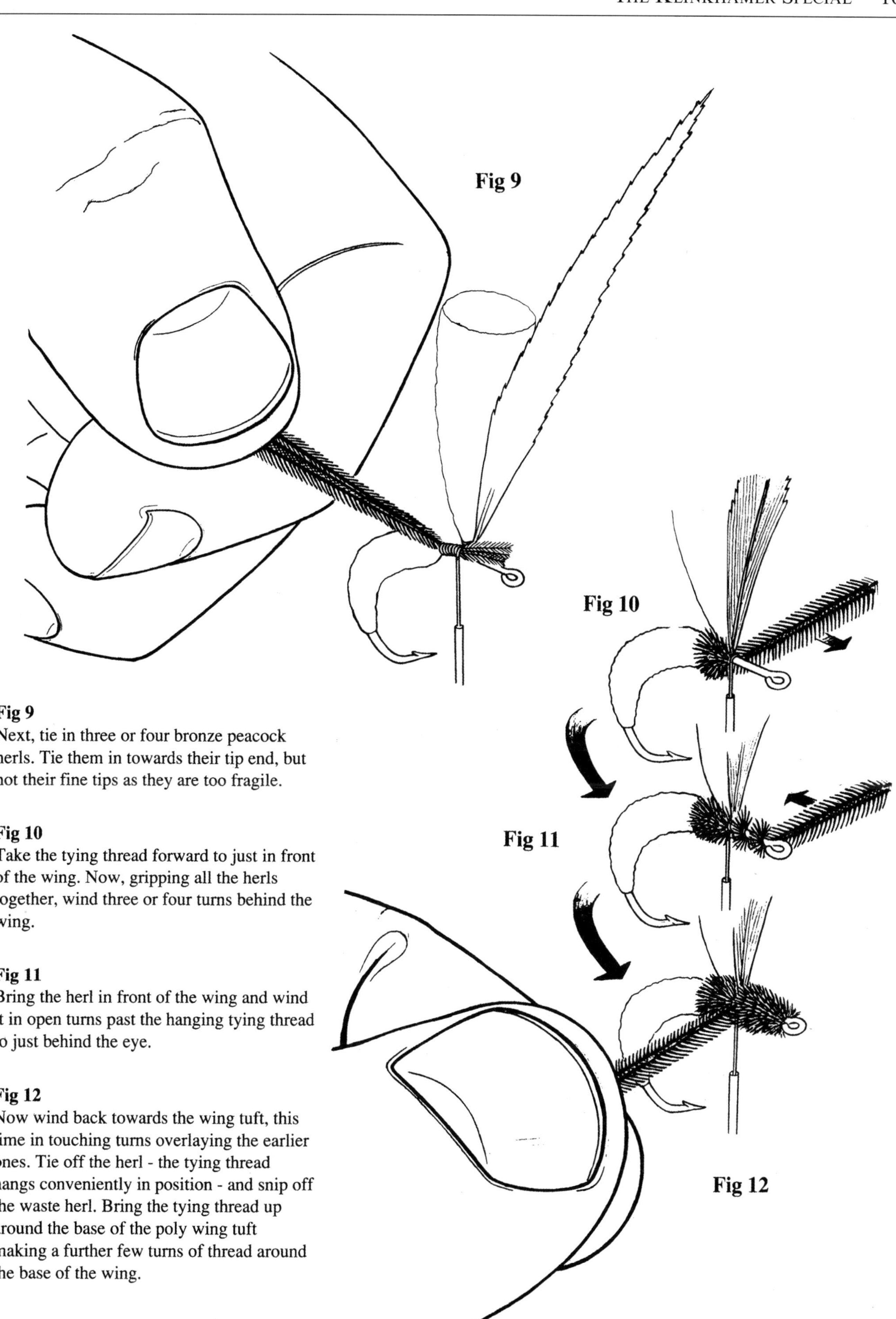

Fig 9
Next, tie in three or four bronze peacock herls. Tie them in towards their tip end, but not their fine tips as they are too fragile.

Fig 10
Take the tying thread forward to just in front of the wing. Now, gripping all the herls together, wind three or four turns behind the wing.

Fig 11
Bring the herl in front of the wing and wind it in open turns past the hanging tying thread to just behind the eye.

Fig 12
Now wind back towards the wing tuft, this time in touching turns overlaying the earlier ones. Tie off the herl - the tying thread hangs conveniently in position - and snip off the waste herl. Bring the tying thread up around the base of the poly wing tuft making a further few turns of thread around the base of the wing.

Figs 13 & 14
Press the hackle back down to lie flat again. Clip on the hackle pliers and wind the hackle tightly around the 'post'. Each turn of hackle should be wound underneath the previous one. Three or four turns are sufficient (Hans recommends six turns).

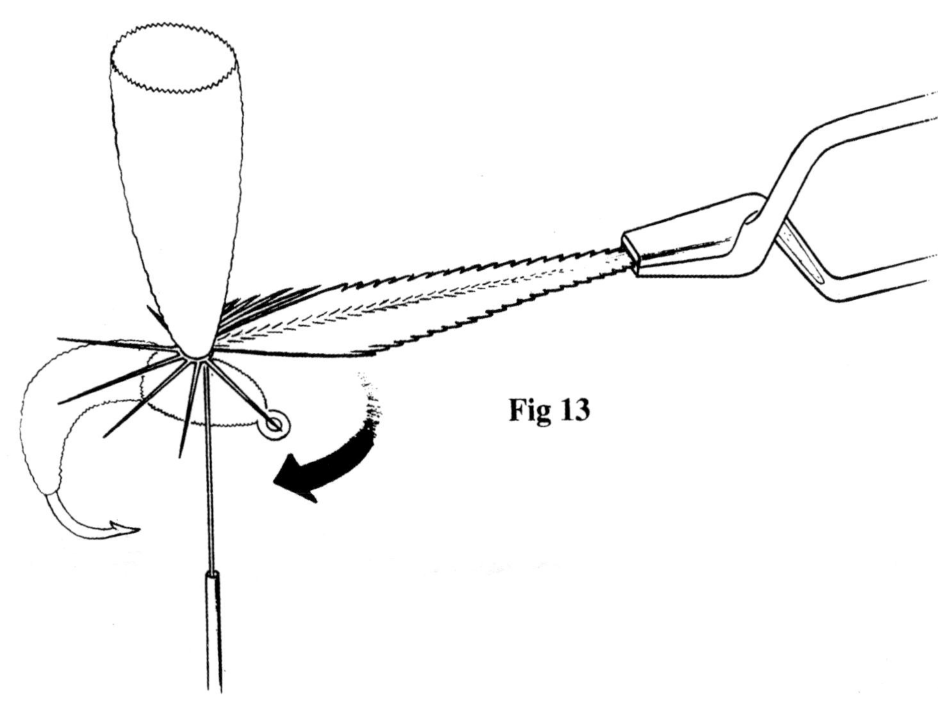

Fig 13

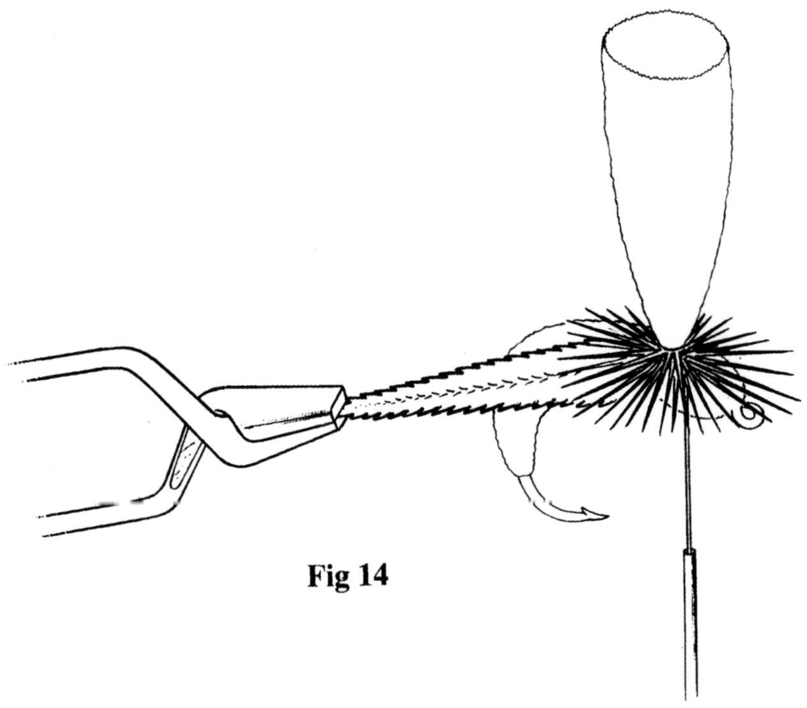

Fig 14

Fig 15
Holding the hackle tip low and taut over the thorax, take two or three tight turns of tying thread around the base of the poly wing, binding the tip of the hackle to it. Finally perform a whip finish, again around the wing and hackle tip. If you like, reposition the fly so that the poly wing is horizontal.

Snip off the waste end of hackle (making sure not to remove any of the radiating hackle barbs) and the tying thread, not too close to the whipping, leaving a tiny tag. With the side of your dubbing needle, apply a drop of head cement to the whippings. Finally, cut the poly yarn wing to length. It should be about the same length as the abdomen.

Fig 16
There, it's finished. An easy tie, but take care to get all the components nicely proportioned. And keep the finishing whips down to a minimum otherwise you end up with an ugly gap between the underside of the hackle and the thorax.

Note: Hans says the tuft wing must float, but the abdomen must sink - quickly! It doesn't matter if the parachute hackle sinks too. In fact it is lethal when partly submerged like this. A real iceberg of a fly! The best floatant for the tuft wing is Dilly Wax, specially developed for poly yarns and poly dubs. Apply the Dilly Wax only to the poly tuft wing and thoroughly wet the abdomen before starting fishing.

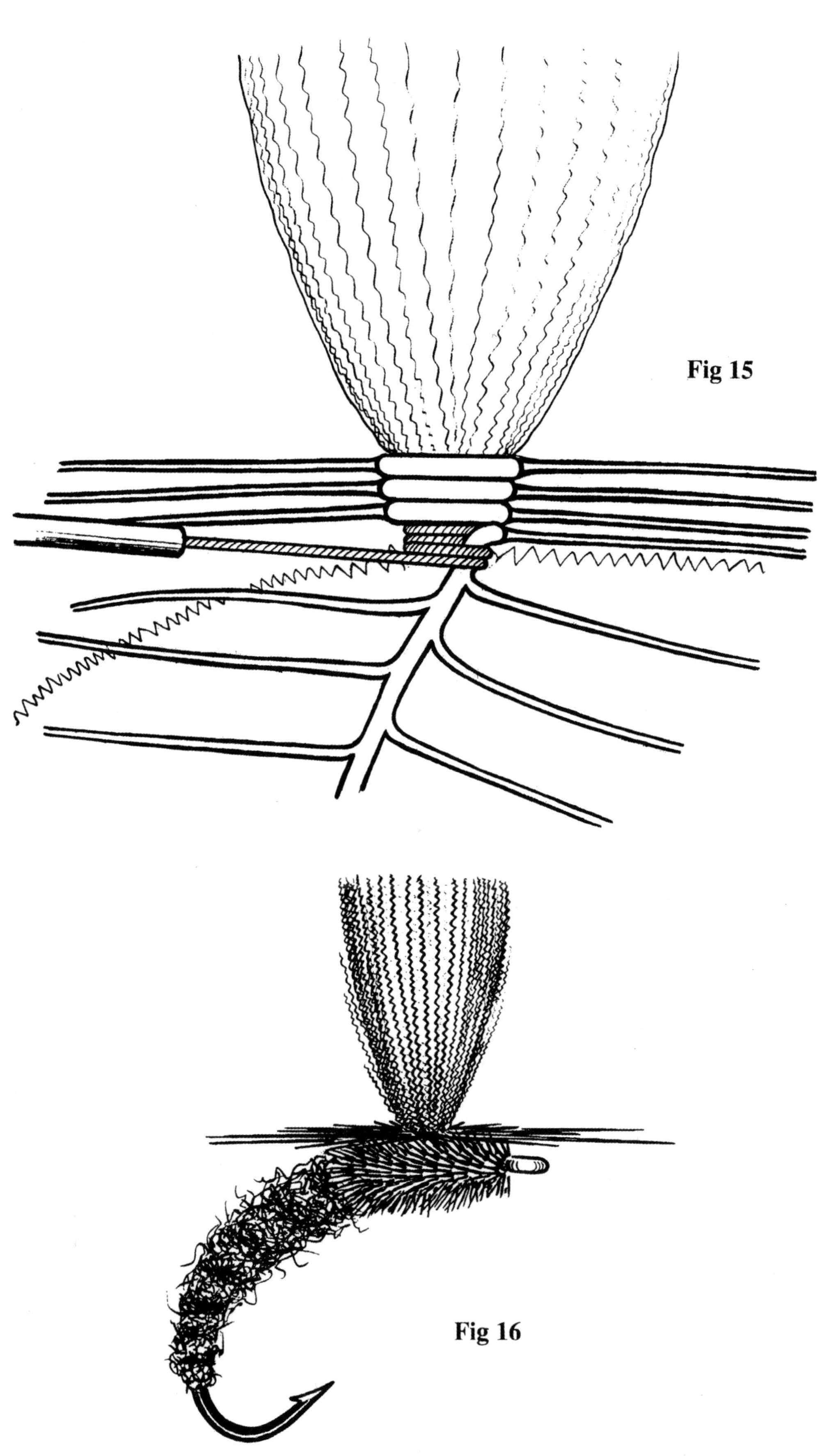

Fig 15

Fig 16

VOLJC-MOSER DRY CADDIS
(Top) Grannom *(Left)* Cinnamon Sedge *(Right)* Caperer

14. The Voljc-Moser Dry Caddis

This dry caddis is a good-looking, easy-to-tie fly. It is, in fact, an amalgam of two dressings which are little known outside their respective countries of origin.

At the Chatsworth Angling Fair in May 1989, we were all entertained to some wonderful casting demonstrations by Roman Moser. I was demonstrating flytying on the Partridge stand and had the opportunity to question Roman in the evening about the caddis patterns he uses on his home river, the Traun in Austria.

What immediately caught my attention when he opened his fly box was the most life-like way the legs had been created - roughly-dubbed, chopped deer hair, mixed with a tiny amount of fine synthetic dubbing as a binder. The overall effect was of random long and short 'legs' sticking out every which way. Roman dubs this chopped deer hair forward of the wings, over the full thorax, making his caddis flies excellent floaters.

Later that same year, I found myself sharing the tying bench with Darrel Martin, one of America's top flytyers. I already knew of his meticulous tying skills and was eager to watch him perform again.

Darrel did not let the gathered crowd down. He tied a dry caddis (pretty ordinary stuff you may be thinking). However, when it came to putting on the wing, what I saw was the most realistic, ingenious, yet simple caddis wing I had ever seen.

I had in fact read of this clever wing construction in Taff Price's book, *Fly Patterns - An International Guide*, a copy of which I had bought the previous year. However, while Taff's book does clearly state that various feathers are stuck on to nylon stockings (tights UK, panty hose USA) using a clear glue (suitable for PVC) his instructions are fairly brief. As a result, I let it all wash over me without bothering to investigate further. My nonchalance came to an abrupt end though, when I saw Darrel put on this wing. It was a revelation! So simple and utterly realistic.

This wing construction is attributed to the Slovenian flytyer, Dr Bodizar Voljc and, as far as I can trace, it was first introduced into the UK by Taff.

The pattern which I am about to describe combines the shaggy deer hair body of the Moser caddis with the Voljc wing - it's a mongrel.

My own fishing introduction to this pattern was dramatic and instantaneously successful. It occurred during a midsummer visit to my club stretch on the River Ure. The wind had strengthened gradually all day so that, by evening, it was quite gusty. The bridge pool was showing a ruffled surface with a wind blowing towards the opposite bank and slightly upstream - perfect for scuttling a dry caddis downstream through the wavelets.

My first cast produced no response, but the second provoked a violent slashing attack. Luckily, I had the rod tip high, so the fish hit a soft cushion and impaled itself. A minute later, I was releasing a fine 1¼lb brownie. The very next cast, my guard was down. So was my rod tip. The explosive take this time delivered the dull thud that spells disaster - a clean tippet break!

The one thing which will immediately strike you, when fishing this pattern, is its life-like, low profile. It is absolutely perfect for a scuttling caddis: those which keep their wings folded over their body without making a single flutter. They 'run' quite effectively over the surface until they are spotted by a prowling trout. Fish this pattern with confidence but be ready for smash takes!

NOTES ON MATERIALS AND TYING

Although my illustrations may suggest that this is a lengthy tying, the opposite is the case - you can knock them out like shelling peas! The only thing you have to resign yourself to is that you do need to spend some time making up the frames of nylon-backed feathers.

However, once you have made up three frames (say, one each of dark partridge hackles, red/brown hen hackles and any light speckled hackle such as mallard breast or flank) you will have enough to last you for several seasons. You can, of course, let your imagination run riot and, if you know of anyone who keeps rare breeds of poultry, there is always the possibility of obtaining some really caddis coloured feathers. I have a friend who recently presented me with the corpse of a Wellsummer hen, a family pet, which had died of old age. Its feather now fool trout.

Whatever feather you use, there are three basic considerations: 1) The feathers must be webby and soft. 2) The thinner the centre quill the better. 3) The broader the feather the better. Sections cut from large whole feathers can also be used, but I've not found them quite as durable as the full feather, complete with central quill.

As to nylon hose, you have to 'kill' the stretch by brushing all over with cellulose dope. The brand of cellulose dope I use is Humbrol. As far as I can tell, it's the same dope I used as a lad, when making gliders of balsa and tissue paper. The smell awoke old memories. You don't necessarily need to brush on the dope. I sometimes turn the embroidery frame over so that the taut hose side comes into contact with an outspread sheet of newspaper. Then I simply pour on a small amount and spread it about with a piece of kitchen paper towel. It takes only a few seconds to dry, then you can start to stick on the feathers.

So far I've used two adhesives for sticking on the feathers - Loctite Clear Glue Extra Strong and Bostic All Purpose clear adhesive. Choose a clear glue which is suitable for PVC.

For the shaggy deer hair body, you'll need to make yourself a small amount of 'Moser Dub'. Don't mix in too much of the fine 'binder' - the ultra-fine synthetic poly dubbing.

Actually, all you require of this binder dubbing, according to Roman, is 15%, the balance being randomly chopped deer hair. Here again, Roman recommends that the hairs are cut off to a maximum of 4/5" (20mm) in length. So here's a use for your Muddler trimmings! Then, it is simply a question of mixing the two thoroughly together.

I have come up with a much craftier way of

VOLJC-MOSER CADDIS DRESSING

Hook: Medium or fine wire standard shank dry fly hook. Suggest Partridge 'Hooper' 4x Fine Dry Fly Hook Code E1A sizes 8-20, or Partridge 'Capt. Hamilton' Dry Fly Hook Code L3A sizes 8-20, or Partridge 'Roman Moser' Barbless Dry Fly Hook Code CS27GRS sizes 10-18.
Thread: Regular 6/0 or Midge 8/0, eg. Unithread, Danville's, etc. Colour to match natural, usually tan, brown, olive or grey.
Cement: Dave's Flexament (USA) or Floo Gloo (UK).
Body (Moser version): Chopped tan/brown deer hair mixed with fine brown polydub: 80/90% deer hair, 20/10% polydub. Or lightly waxed with petroleum jelly (see Notes), no polydub.
Body (Voljc version): Dry-fly-quality cock hackle wound straight on to hook shank. Colour to match natural you wish to copy.
Wing: Whole neck, saddle or flank hackle glued to 10 or 15 denier nylon tight gauze (panty hose, USA). Colour of feather to match wing of natural you wish to copy. Suggest domestic poultry, partridge, grouse, hen pheasant, mallard, etc.
Glue: Loctite Clear Glue Extra Strong or Bostic All Purpose Clear Adhesive. Also try slightly thinned Pliobond (USA).
Shoulder hackle (optional): Good quality dry fly hackle, colour to suit natural you wish to copy.
Antennae (optional): Finely tapering animal hair or whiskers or stripped fine end of hackle stalk.

making chopped deer hair controllable. Simply spread a small amount of petroleum jelly or paste floatant over the palm of your hands, then work your hands thoroughly through your bag of chopped deer hair. This makes the hair waxy and it will hang together.

For spinning the dubbing loop I strongly recommend using the genuine Darrel Martin Dubbing Whirl, now available in the UK. I first saw this cunning little gadget at the Chatsworth Angling Fair of 1987 where Darrel himself demonstrated its many uses. The secret of its success seems to lie in the correct choice of wire gauge for the legs. It is such a simple idea.

The front collar hackle should be the best quality you can afford. There is a tendency among some flytyers to think that the hackle quality on a caddis pattern isn't really all that important.

I disagree. I think that a superior grade hackle is just as important on a dry caddis as on an Ephemeroptera dun, even though you have more overall points in contact with the water surface on this caddis pattern. My own view is that the antennae aren't really necessary.

Making the Voljc Wings

Fig 1
Push the inner ring of a small embroidery frame down the leg of a pair of nylon tights. Then gather up the nylon mesh all around the frame. Keep it nice and taut. Then slip the outer ring over and close it tightly with the clamping screw. Trim off the rest of the nylon hose all around the frame .

Fig 2
Apply cellulose dope to the nylon hose using a small paint brush. You will find that it is dry in less than 30 seconds.

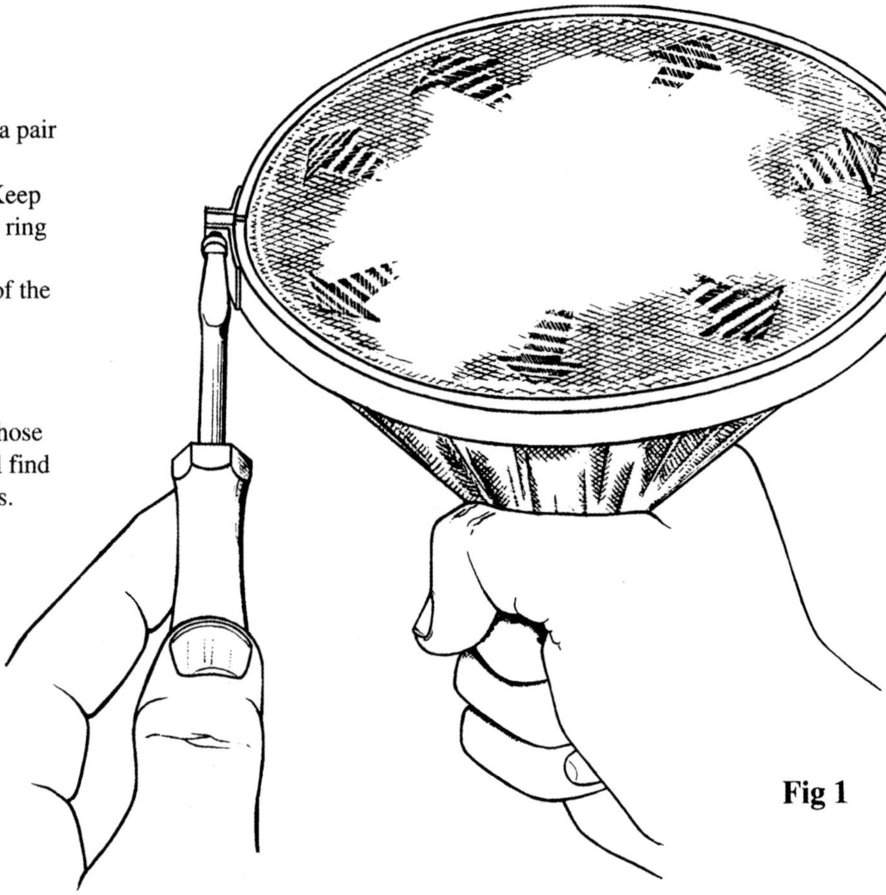

Fig 1

Fig 2

Fig 3

Now take your selected feathers and strip away all the basal fluff and just a few of the lower fibres. When you have, say, 36 feathers prepared thus, you are ready to start sticking them on. Take the first feather and very lightly draw it between finger and thumb to form a nice oval or elliptical shape. Then squeeze on to the underside of the feather a drop of adhesive, applying it near the stripped quill end. As you touch the glue down, draw the tube nozzle towards the tip of the feather to work the glue along without actually touching it with a finger.

Fig 4

Now, very quickly - time is of the essence - turn the feather over and press it down on to the nylon hose. As you press, stroke your finger along the feather, working from base to tip. Then slide your scissor blade underneath the bare quill and snip it off.

Fig 5

Now bring your finger up underneath the frame and wipe off all the excess glue. This is vital.

Form neat rows to fill the frame as efficiently as possible.

Fig 6

When you have your frame full of feathers, run the scissors all around the inside of the inner frame. Very often, some of the dope sticks the nylon hose to the frame and you must avoid any snagging of the nylon strands. So, cutting it out is a safer bet.

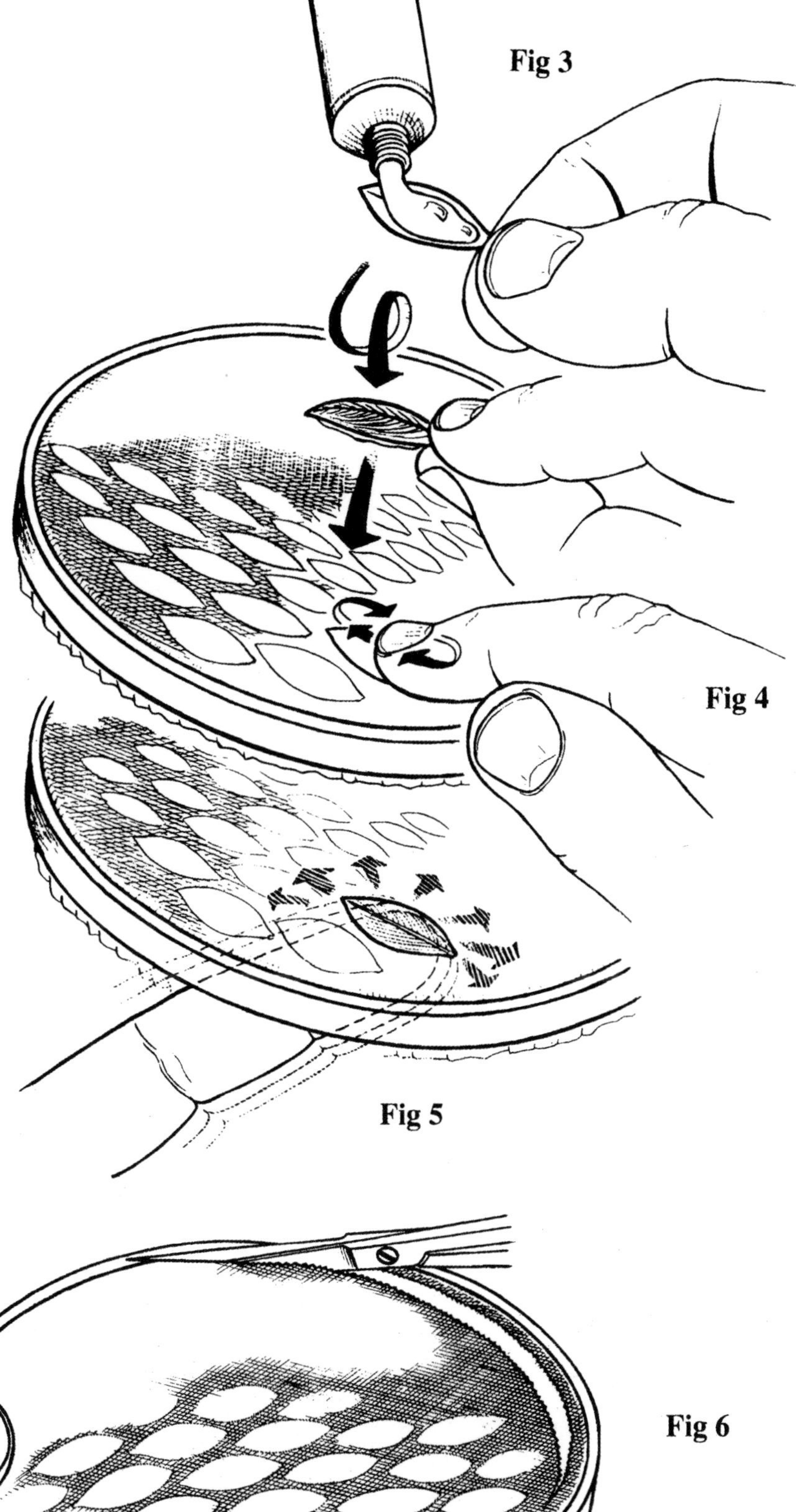

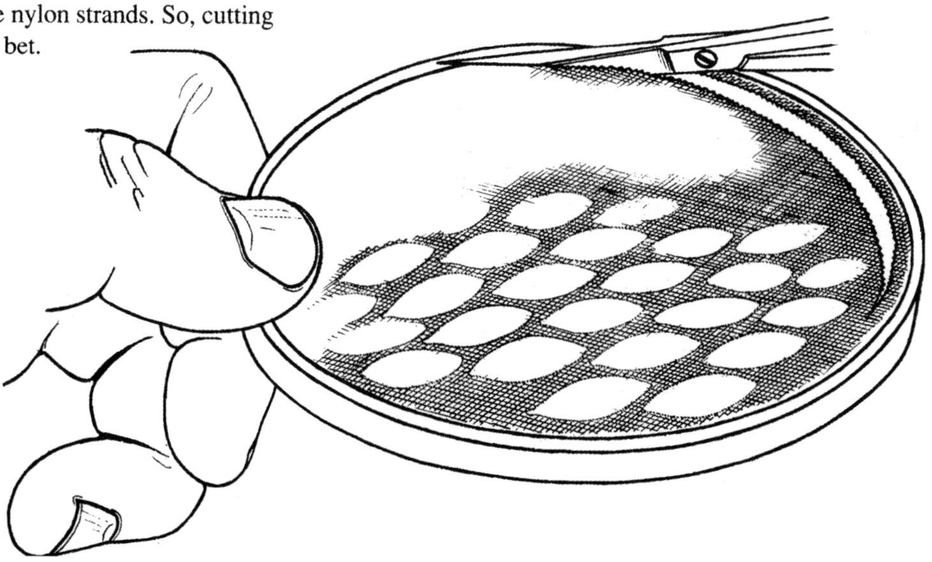

Tying the Voljc-Moser Caddis

Fig 7
Grip the hook firmly in the vice with the shank horizontal. Catch on the tying thread just back from the eye and run it down the shank in open turns to where the bend starts. Now make the dubbing loop. Place one or two fingers behind the hanging thread, then bring the bobbin holder over the shank trapping the initial hanging part. Then 'lock' the loop by taking the thread around it, followed by two or three further tight turns over the locked loop. Wrap the thread in open turns to the eye and let the bobbin holder hang.

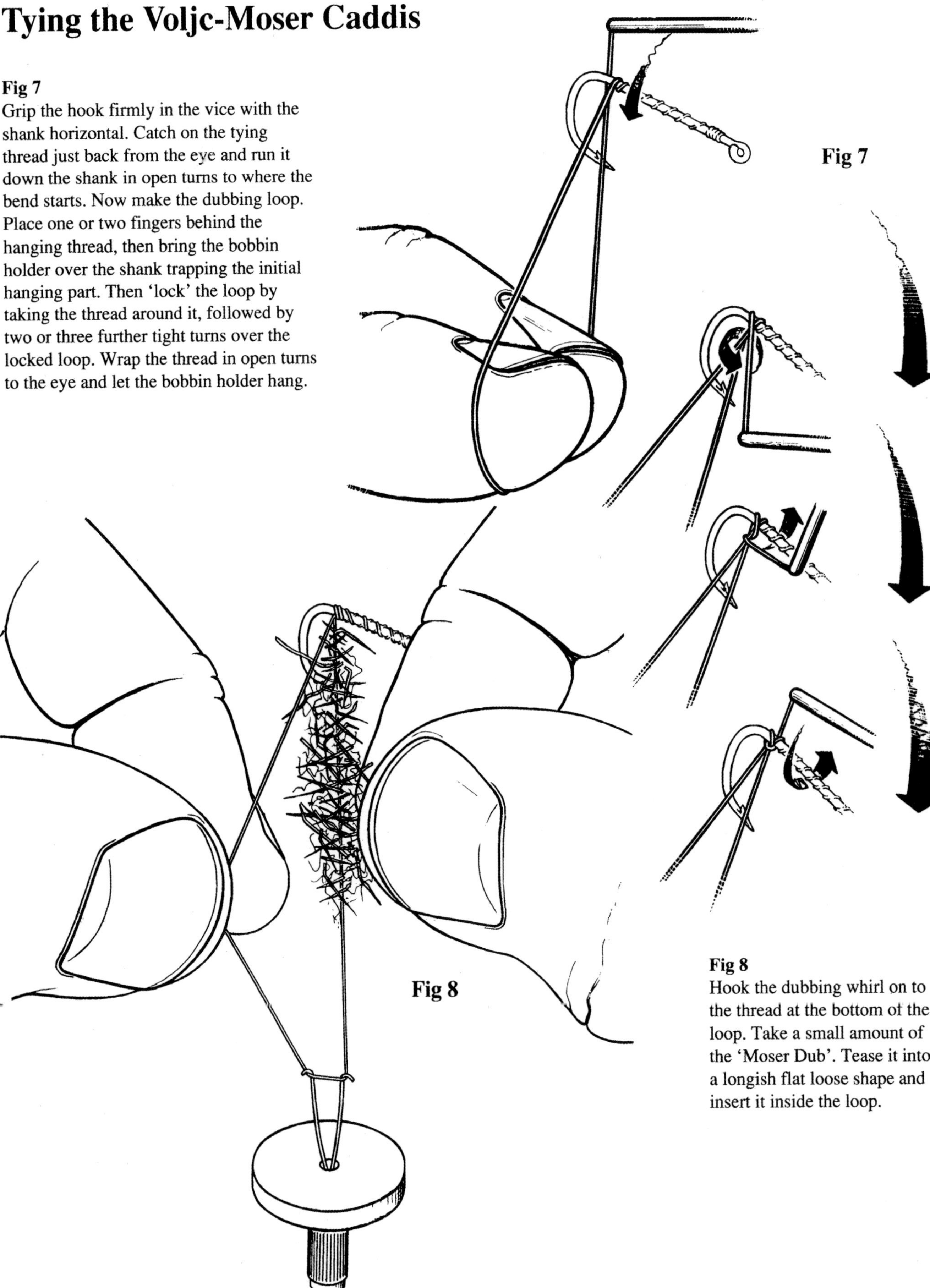

Fig 7

Fig 8

Fig 8
Hook the dubbing whirl on to the thread at the bottom of the loop. Take a small amount of the 'Moser Dub'. Tease it into a longish flat loose shape and insert it inside the loop.

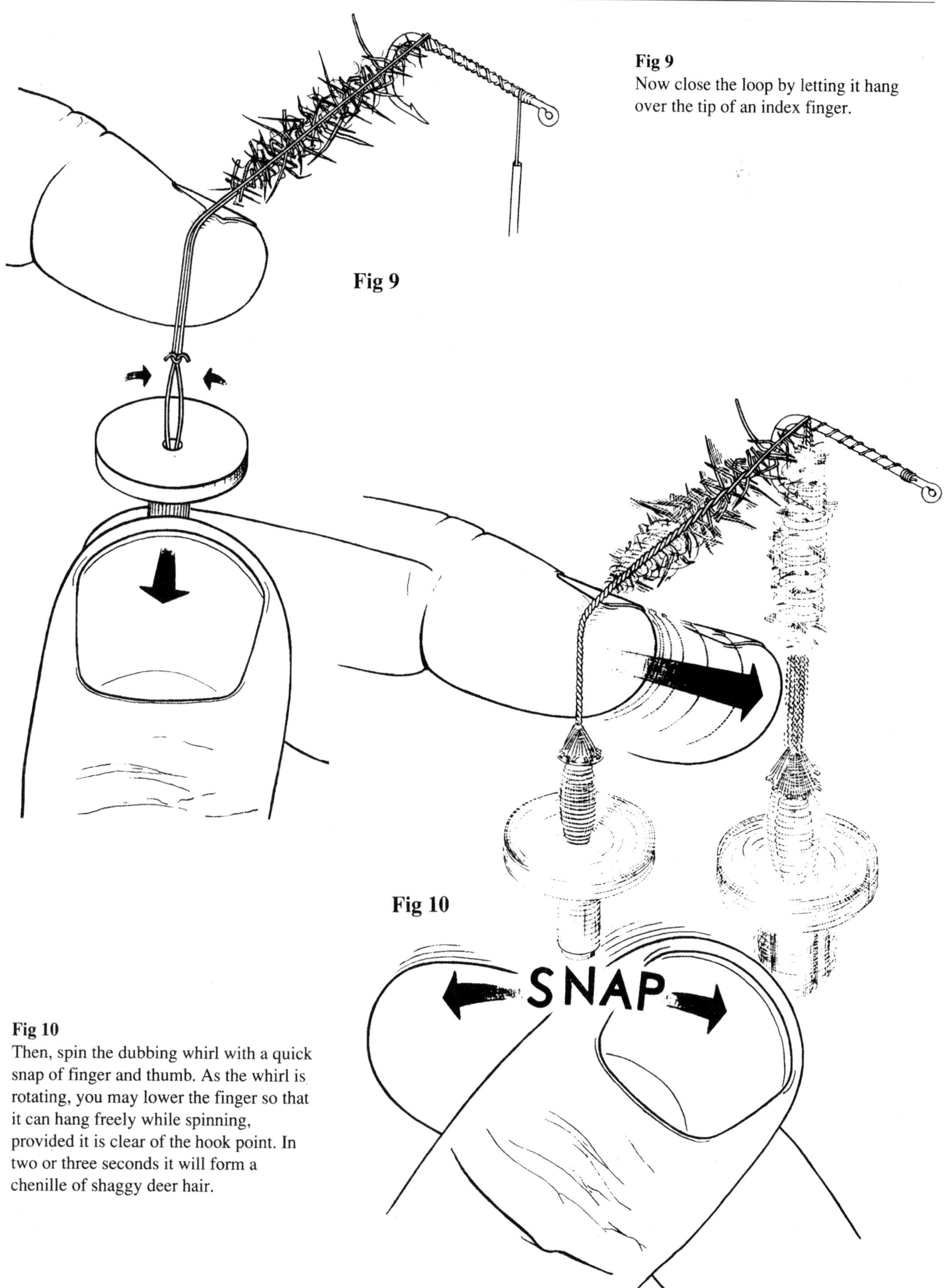

Fig 9

Fig 9
Now close the loop by letting it hang over the tip of an index finger.

Fig 10

Fig 10
Then, spin the dubbing whirl with a quick snap of finger and thumb. As the whirl is rotating, you may lower the finger so that it can hang freely while spinning, provided it is clear of the hook point. In two or three seconds it will form a chenille of shaggy deer hair.

Fig 11
Now, wrap the chenille of deer hair in touching turns around the hook shank, working towards the eye ensuring that you do not trap down any of the protruding hairs. When you reach a position 1/10" (2-3mm) from the eye, tie off. Trim off the excess dubbing loop.

Fig 12
Trim the top by making a slightly sloping cut about 15° tapering from front (low) to back (high). Two further cuts will be necessary, on each side, at an angle of about 60°, sloping towards the top of the body. The purpose of this 'haircut' is to make a seat on which the wing will sit.

Fig 13
Now cut out the wing around the full perimeter of the feather.

Fig 14
Carefully fold the feather exactly on the centre quill with the nylon mesh on the underside.

Fig 15
Gripping the folded feather firmly, cut it to the correct shape of a caddis wing.

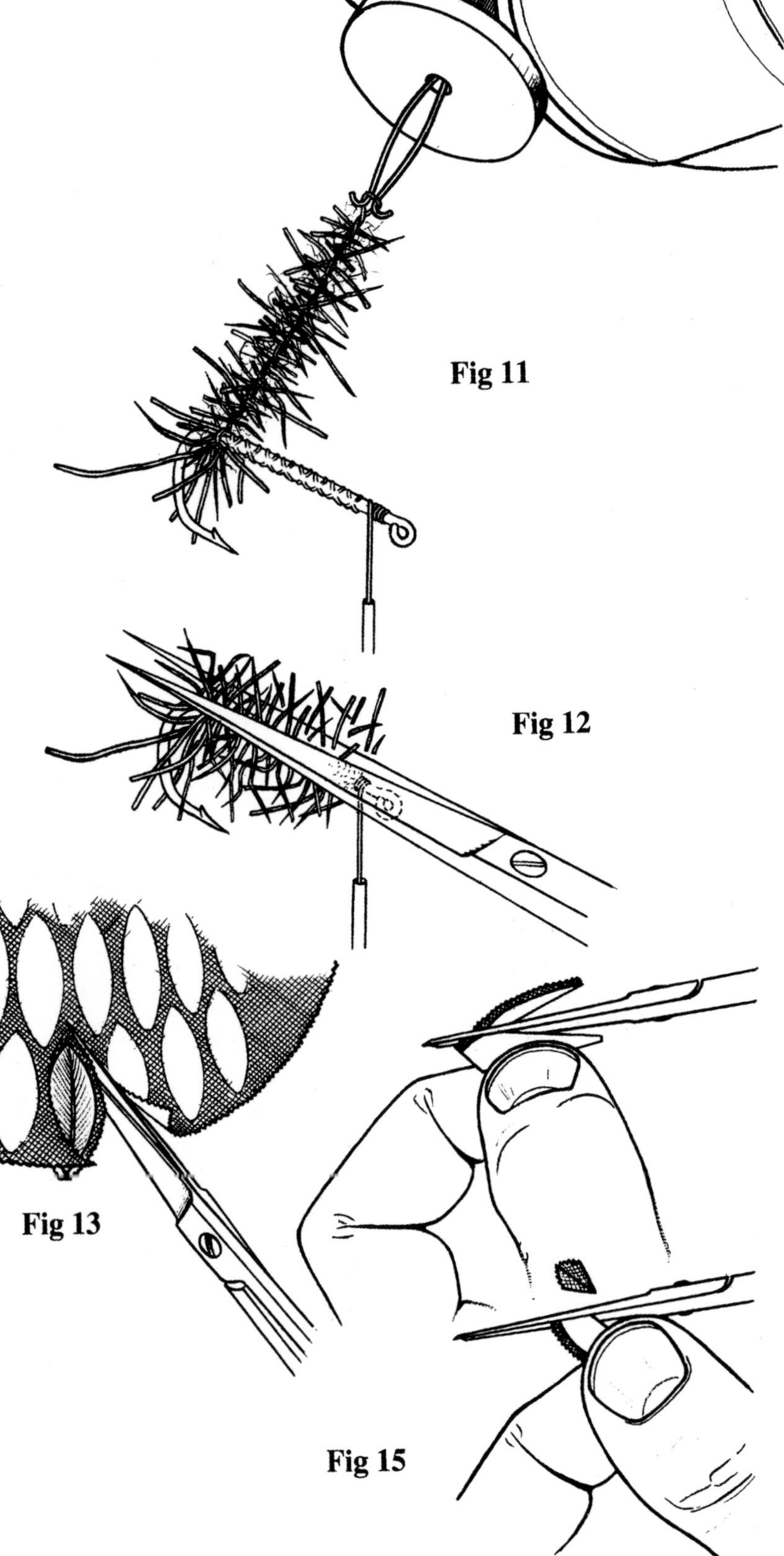

Fig 11

Fig 12

Fig 13

Fig 14

Fig 15

Fig 16
Now apply a tiny amount of the same clear glue to the back edge, the top only of the trimmed tips of deer hair. Then immediately position the shaped and folded wing above the body. Check its position for the correct amount of overhang at the back, then simply sit it on top of the body, pressing it in contact with the glue on the tips of hairs.

Fig 17
With the wing held firmly in place between finger and thumb, bind it securely to the hook shank. Four 'pinch and loops' should suffice.

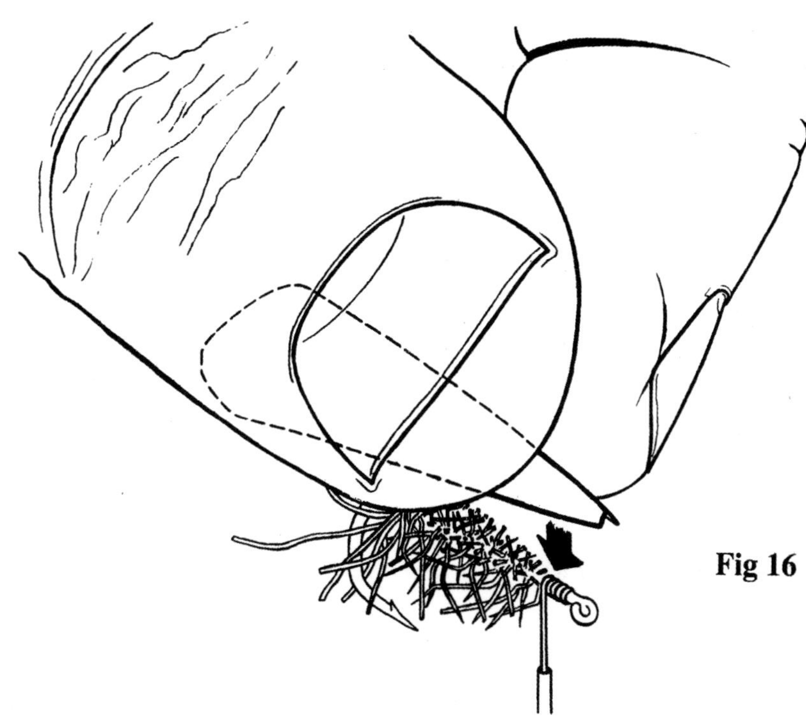

Fig 16

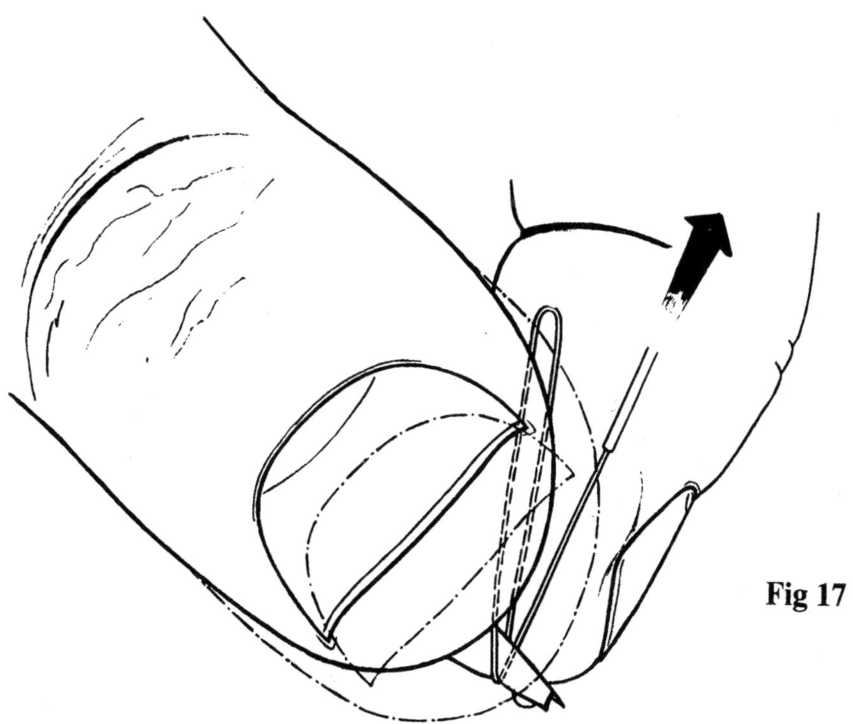

Fig 17

Fig 18

Now for the antennae - but heed my earlier warning! Put them on as a pair, one on either side and slightly to the top of the shank, make a couple of turns of thread to secure. If their length is not correct, simply pull on either the fine tips or the butts. Then add two more tight turns and trim off the waste butts. To raise them slightly make a turn of thread underneath them.

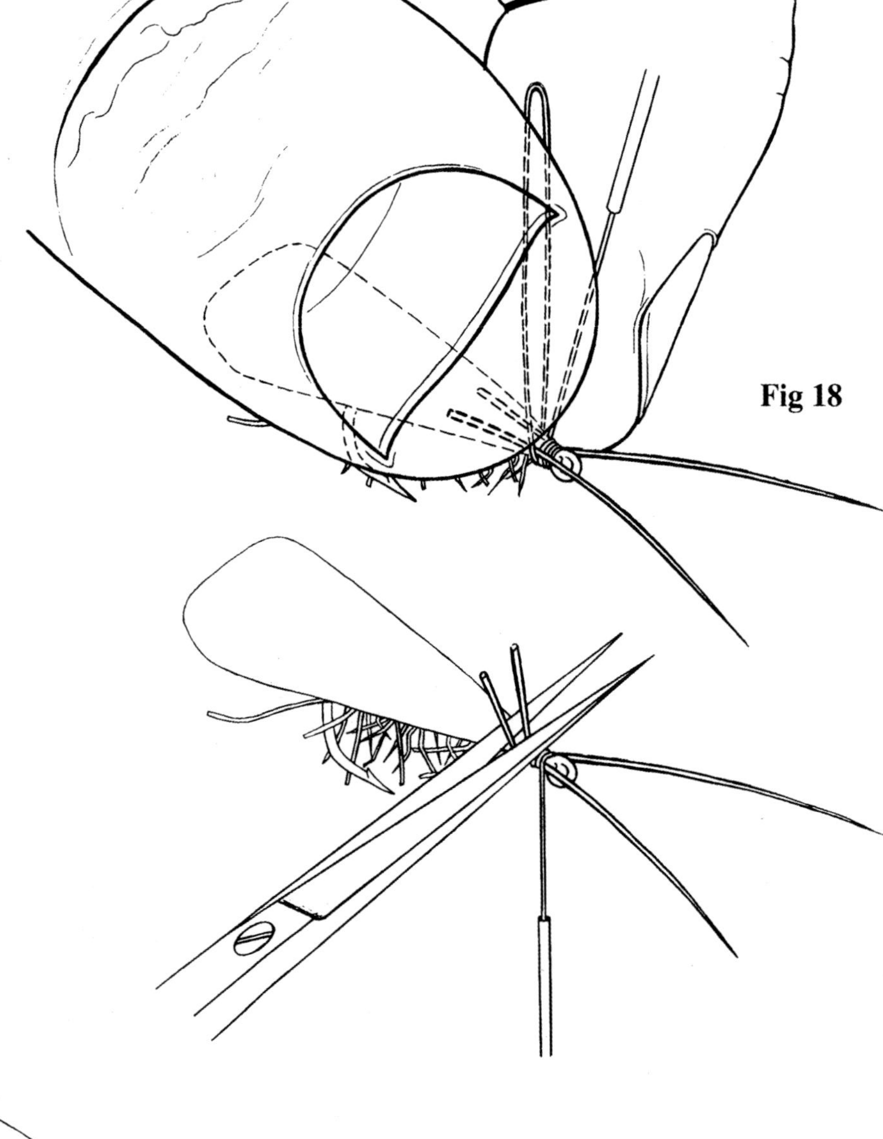

Fig 18

Fig 19

Finally, the front hackle. Check the barbs for correct length. Strip off all the lower inferior barbs and the basal fluff. Offer it up to the side nearest you. The hackle feather should project out beyond the eye with the underside facing you. Tie it in this position very securely, working backwards towards the bend. Let the bobbin holder hang. Do not trim off the waste quill yet.

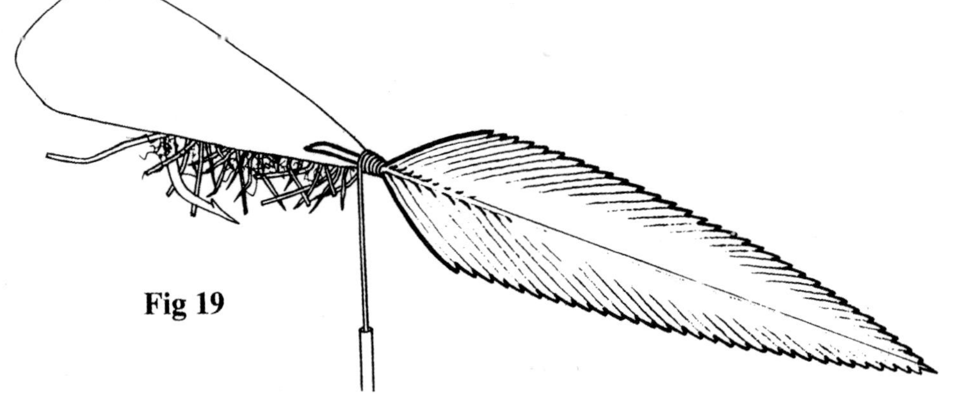

Fig 19

Fig 20
With the front edge of your thumb nail, kink the hackle out at right angles, pushing into the first binding.

Fig 21
Clip on the hackle pliers. Apply tension to the hackle and wrap it around the hook shank, working backwards. At the point where the bobbin holder is hanging, bring the tying thread over the hackle tip and pull the thread firmly down to the hook shank thus trapping the hackle tip. Make two more turns and follow this with the conventional three or four turn whip finish. Trim off the waste tip of hackle and tying thread. Finally slip your scissors under the quill end and snip it off flush with the whip finish. Apply a drop of head cement to the whips.

Fig 22
Before committing this caddis, in fact any dry fly, to fishing, I always make 'dry runs' on a polished surface to ensure that the fly sits correctly without rolling. Sometimes, a rogue hackle barb will tip the finished fly over to one side. With this particular pattern, you have also to watch out for awkward deerhair ends too. A judicious snip here or there with the scissors will cure the problem, giving you a dry caddis unsurpassed for correct profile and action. A very deadly fly.

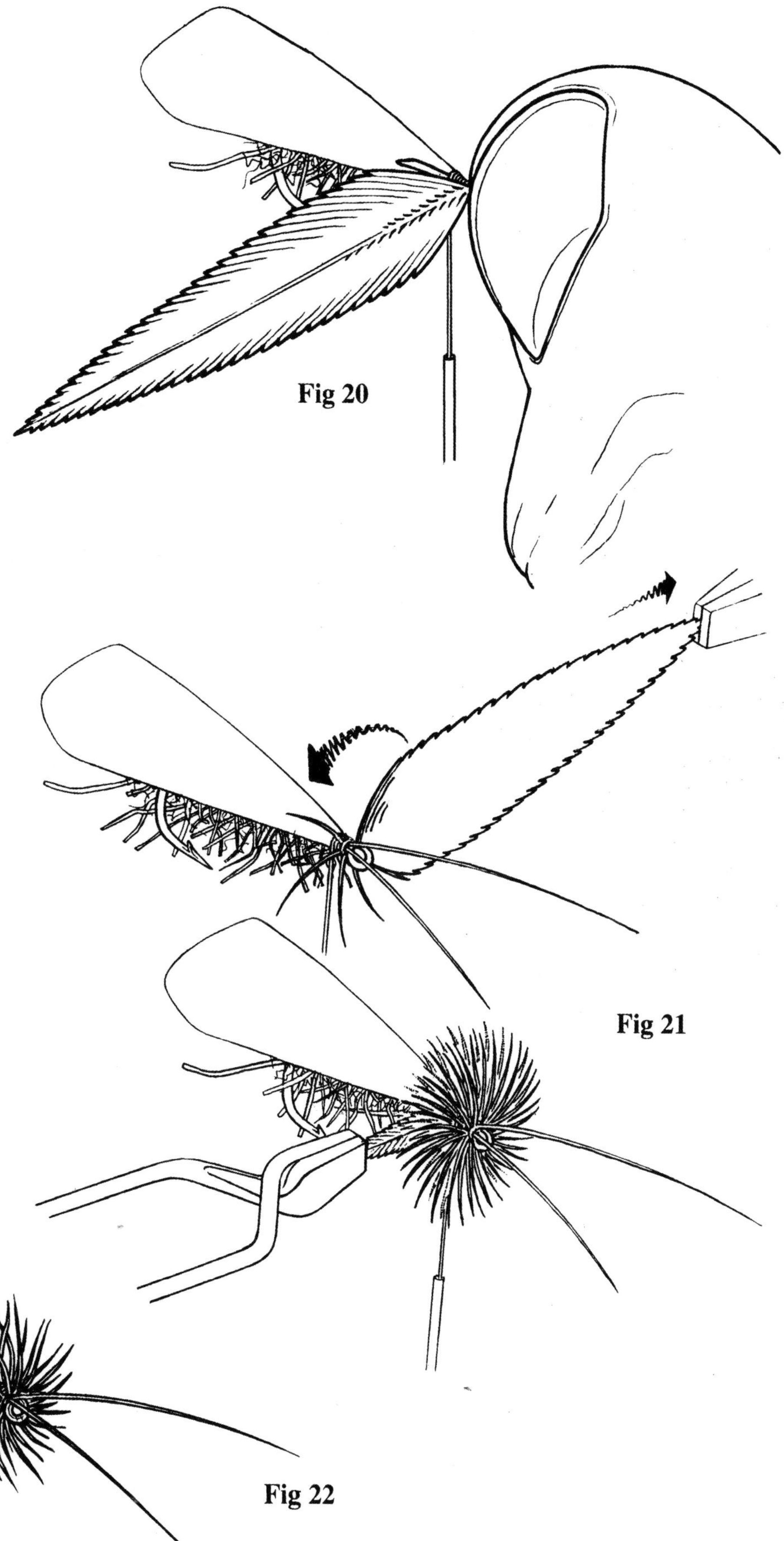

Fig 20

Fig 21

Fig 22

POPA CADDIS
Note the straggly Deer-hair legs.

15. The POPA Caddis

or the Post-OviPositing Adult Caddis!

Caddisflies, in all stages of their life cycle, are a very important food organism for fish. In freestone streams of swift broken currents, they are often the principal food item. It has been recorded that they constitute up to 80% by volume of a trout's food intake throughout the year!

This pattern imitates the adult female caddis as she swims and drifts back to the surface after ovipositing (egg-laying). It has tremendous fish-catching potential and fills a gap which, up to now, has rarely been exploited - and then only by accident using one of the old winged 'wet sedges'.

A slow downstream retrieve with the occasional pause, or an erratic, twitched retrieve is the way to fish it. I fish it either singly at the end of a 9' tapered leader, or on a dropper, with my pupa artificial on the point. Watch your leader strength - the takes are usually savage!

I had several years of flyfishing experience behind me before I read of the phenomenon of egg-laying by total submergence of the winged adult female insect. I do recall, though, that it was a discussion concerning the Ephemeroptera - the upwing flies - and specifically the Baetidae. At last, I had a reason to believe in the old fashioned Red Spinner fished as a sub-surface wet fly. What at the time seemed totally unbelievable was how such a flimsy, frail creature could push downwards into the thick meniscus, puncture it, then make its way underwater by walking down some fixed object, against its own natural buoyancy, finally to lay its eggs at some chosen site.

When I learned of this apparent suicidal behaviour of ovipositing Baetids, I should have delved deeper into the ovipositing behaviour of other aquatic insects. I didn't, and that mistake cost me several years of missed sport with our friend the caddisfly. I thought they all laid their eggs by dipping the tips of their abdomens into the stream as they fluttered over it or, as I had often seen, by dotting the surface randomly, releasing eggs with every touch of the abdomen.

The two books which have been an absolute revelation to me are by American angler-entomologists and both deal with caddisflies exclusively. In *The Caddis and the Angler* by Larry Solomon and Eric Leiser (Stackpole, 1977) I was surprised to read that several caddis families lay their eggs underwater, just as the Baetid mayflies do. Moreover, some caddisflies, once through the meniscus, actually *swim* to the stream bed. On reaching the stream bed, the female caddis looks for a rock or stone and proceeds to discharge her cargo of eggs.

After this you would think that the female caddis would be exhausted and spent, and go drifting off at the whim of the current - like the red spinner - helpless prey for any fish. Not so, the females of some of these underwater ovipositing caddisflies actually swim back to the surface and re-emerge. This is quite sensational news for the fisherman and flytyer.

I had more than a casual interest when I read this information since amongst the caddis which oviposit underwater and re-emerge are the abundant Rhyacophilidae and Hydropsychedae. The species *Rhyacophila dorsalis* is particularly abundant in the fast rivers and streams that I fish in the north of England.

From Gary Lafontaine's brilliant book,

Caddisflies (Winchester Press, 1987) I learnt about a typical diving caddis: 'Their longest period on the surface was when they tried to dive through the rubbery meniscus, flying as high as twenty feet up and hurtling down to hit with a fearful impact...'

I have never personally witnessed this aerial high dive but there is good evidence to suggest that some British caddis can be just as reckless as their American cousins.

Caddis Larvae by Norman E. Hickin (Hutchinson, 1967) records that a Miss R. M. Badcock observed a *Hydropsyche angustipennis* 'bend the tips of its antennae into the water after it had alighted on a projecting stone in an upland stream. It then suddenly flew up two or three feet and, after it had zigzagged a few yards, it dived vertically into the stream. Miss Badcock was able to follow its course by its silvery appearance as it swam to the under surface of an inclined submerged stone...' Here was evidence that at least one British caddisfly species does dive through the surface and swims to the stream bed to oviposit.

Gary Lafontaine gives an interesting account of the return journey of the two divers: the Rhyacophila and the Hydropsyche. Of the Hydropsyche: '...the adult females, returning to the stream to oviposit, act like a well co-ordinated horde. They dive underwater, swim to the bottom and paste strings of eggs on solid objects. They do not swim back to the surface when this is done, however. They simply release their grip on the substrate and drift slowly upwards.

When they reach the meniscus, they wiggle and push to break through, and, once they are on the surface, they ride along in an apparent state of exhaustion, some flopping feebly and some sprawling inert...'

The Rhyacophila behave similarly and once they have released their eggs we are told that '...they ride for long distances, making no effort to swim, and they rise very slowly to the surface. It also takes them quite a bit of time to push through the surface film...' Solomon and Leiser, in *The Caddis and the Angler*, suggest that these diving caddis are tough old birds, informing us that some female Hydropsyche not only make it back to fresh air but they re-mate after initial ovipositing. These ovipositing females time their return journey to coincide with the emergence of the pupae! Could it be an ingenious way of protecting the species, a kind of confusion strategy? Is this the reason why a few winged adults are often found in a stomach crammed full of pupae?

As a caddis hatch builds up, usually in conditions of failing light, trout will become increasingly excited. The habitat of Rhyacophila and Hydropsyche is brisk, streamy water so the trout have to be opportunistic feeders. In such a situation, even though the pupa may be favoured by virtue of sheer numbers, it is highly likely that feebly-kicking winged females, drifting towards the surface, will also end up going down the gullets of trout.

The pattern I am about to describe has taken many trout and grayling during times of caddis activity and mostly they took the fly as it was being drawn towards the surface. On more than one occasion, I was able to discern, in the failing light, a trout rush up from the depths, open-mouthed, to intercept the fly.

NOTES ON MATERIALS AND TYING

The most important single feature of this pattern is the wing. I wanted a material which would hold its shape when thoroughly wet, so quill feather slips were out (too much separation of feather barbs). Another requirement was that the wings should be soft and flexible.

Whenever I have studied winged caddisflies in autopsies, the first thing that strikes me is the softness of the wings and their semi-translucence. So, the first material which came to mind for the wings of this pattern was the old faithful, Raffene.

Flytyers usually see Raffene when it is dry, and in this state it certainly does not appear to recommend itself since it is far too shiny and caddis wings are matt and dull. Once wet, though, the change is almost magical. The shine goes and it becomes soft, semi-translucent with an almost slimy feel to it.

For the abdomen material, I prefer the modern synthetic dubbings, and the crinkly types with 'highlight' reflective filaments are ideal.

POPA CADDIS DRESSING

Hook: Medium or heavy wire, straight or curved shank, standard length hook. Suggest Partridge 'John Veniard' grub/shrimp hook Code K4A sizes 8-18, or Partridge 'Hooper' 1x short 4x fine dry fly hook code E6A sizes 8-16.
Thread: Midge 8/0 olive or light brown or Danville's Spider Web (tinted olive or light brown with waterproof pen).
Cement: Dave's Flexament (USA) or Floo Gloo (UK).
Abdomen: Fine synthetic dubbing for sizes 14-18.
Colour: olive, brown, tan, snuff, etc. Coarser synthetic dubbing for sizes 8-12, eg. Davy Wotton Finesse Masterclass blends MC 1,2,8,11,15.
Rib (abdomen only): Fine gold wire.
Thorax: Chopped deer hair, natural dark grey/brown or dyed brown or snuff colour.
Wing: Raffene (Swiss Straw, USA) in various browns, pale gold, cinnamon, etc.
Antennae: Animal hair with very fine tip, any dark colour.

I pondered for a while over what material to use for simulating the dangling legs. Knotted pheasant tail barbs, as used on my pupa, would obviously work well, but they are a bit time-consuming to make. Dyed partridge hackle barbs were also tried, tied-in beard fashion. The result wasn't bad but they lacked definition. Also, for once, I wanted a plain, not mottled material. I finally settled for a small pinch of Moser Dub, the coarsest type with thick deer hair fibres. Only a very small amount should be used, say seven or eight individual strands of deer hair.

I have included antennae. I think that on sub-surface patterns, they add realism, and I mean fish-fooling realism as opposed to cosmetic prettying. For material, it really boils down to whether you want them to last. Animal whiskers, such as rabbit or hare, dyed light brown, are very strong and finely tapered. Another good option is fine moose hair from the mane - the advantage here is that you get loads of suitable hairs in a small patch. Barbs from wood duck and dyed mallard look very realistic but just don't have the necessary strength.

Tying the Popa Caddis

Grip the hook firmly in the vice. If using a curved shank hook, grip it so that the part immediately behind the eye is horizontal. Catch on the tying thread just back from the eye, making six or seven tight touching turns. Let the bobbin holder hang. Cut off a 2" (50mm) length of fine gold wire (No.27) or finer. Bind it against the far side of the hook shank. Stop when you reach a position well round the bend.

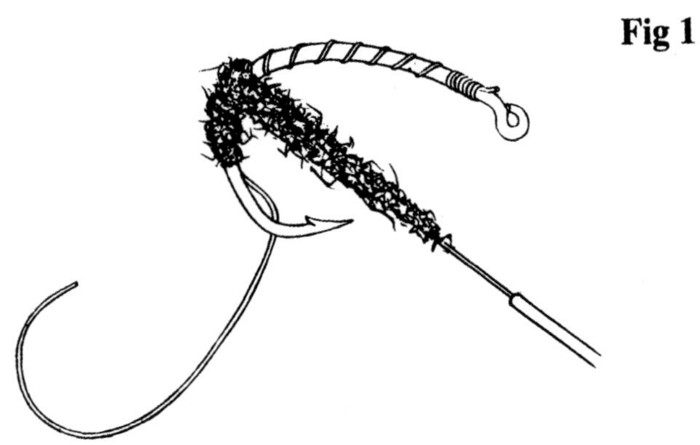

Fig 1

Fig 1
Take a small pinch of fine synthetic dubbing, tease it out into a spindle, offer it up to the tying thread and spin it on. Wrap on this dubbing spindle in touching turns to the thorax about 1/3 back from the eye. Let bobbin holder hang.

Fig 2
Now grip the ribbing wire and spiral it through the dubbing making seven or eight turns. Tie off the ribbing wire. Waggle the waste end of wire until it fractures.

Fig 2

Fig 3
Form a dubbing loop (see pages 172-3). Now take a very small amount of coarse Moser Dub, ensuring that there are at least 8 to 10 good stout deer hairs mixed within it. Trap this within the dubbing loop, let the whirl hang over an index finger, and spin the whirl. Having produced a short spindle of shaggy dubbing, now press all the projecting deer hairs back to one side of the now tightly twisted dubbing loop.

Fig 4
One edge of the dubbing should be reasonably smooth, and the other edge should have all the ends of deer hair protruding.

Fig 5
Now wind this forward to just short of the hook eye. As each turn is wound on, stroke and coax the deer hairs to slope downwards and backwards. Tie off the dubbing loop. Some of the hairs may reach beyond the bend which is perfectly acceptable. Trim off any hairs above the shank.

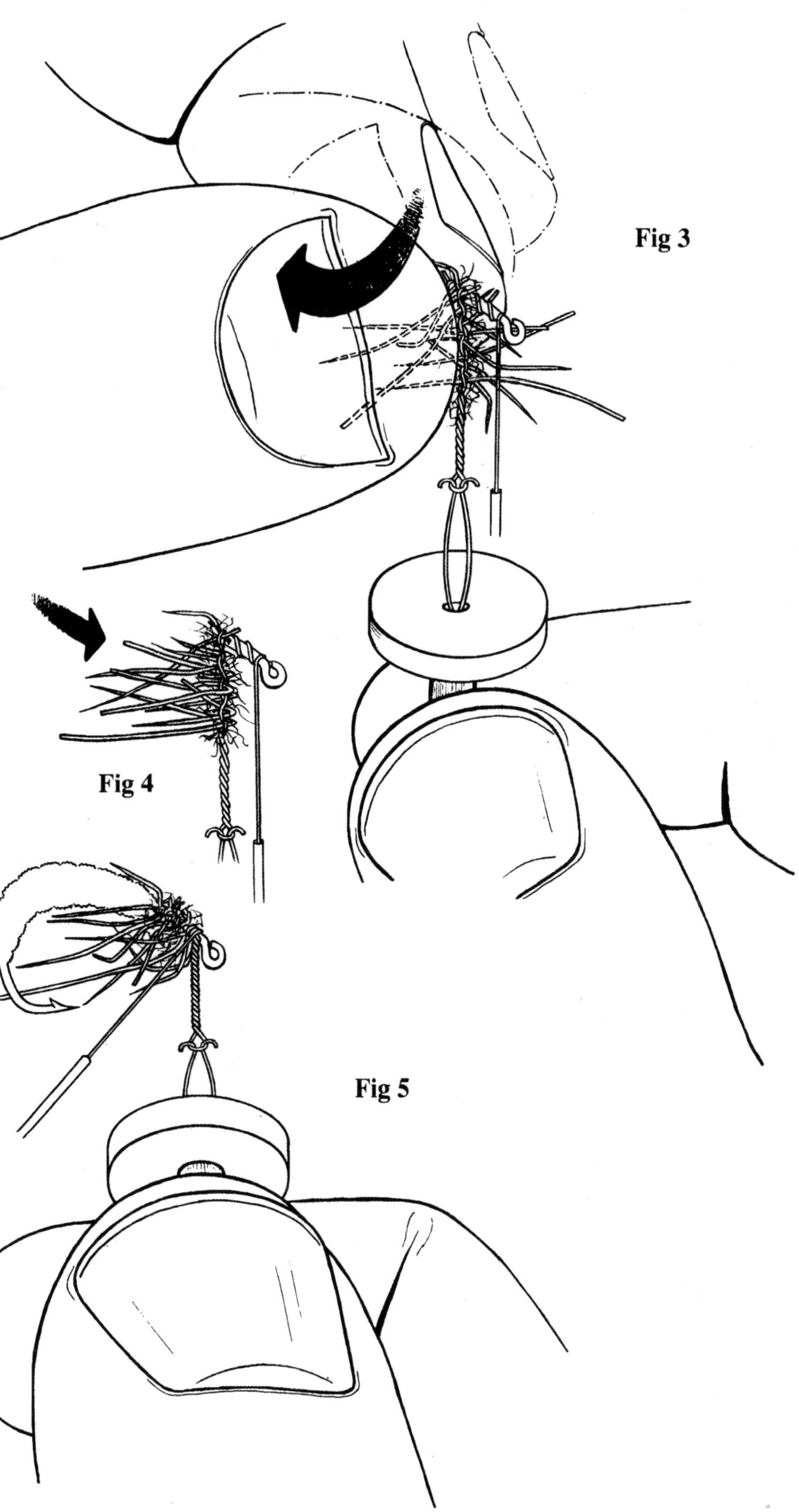

Fig 6
Now for the wings. Take a 2" (50mm) length of Raffene, the colour to match the wings of the natural. Open it out to its full width then cut along the length to produce a piece approximately 3/8" to 1/2" (8-12mm) wide depending on hook size. Repeatedly stroke out this piece firmly to iron out any creases. Now fold it along its centre so that you have a piece 3/16" to 1/4" (4-6mm) wide by 2" (50mm) long. Again apply strong finger and thumb pressure and firmly stroke it out making a good clean crease.

Fig 7
The next fold is half way along its length so that the piece is now approximately 1" (25mm) long with a fold at the front, the two ends showing a distinct 'vee' configuration.

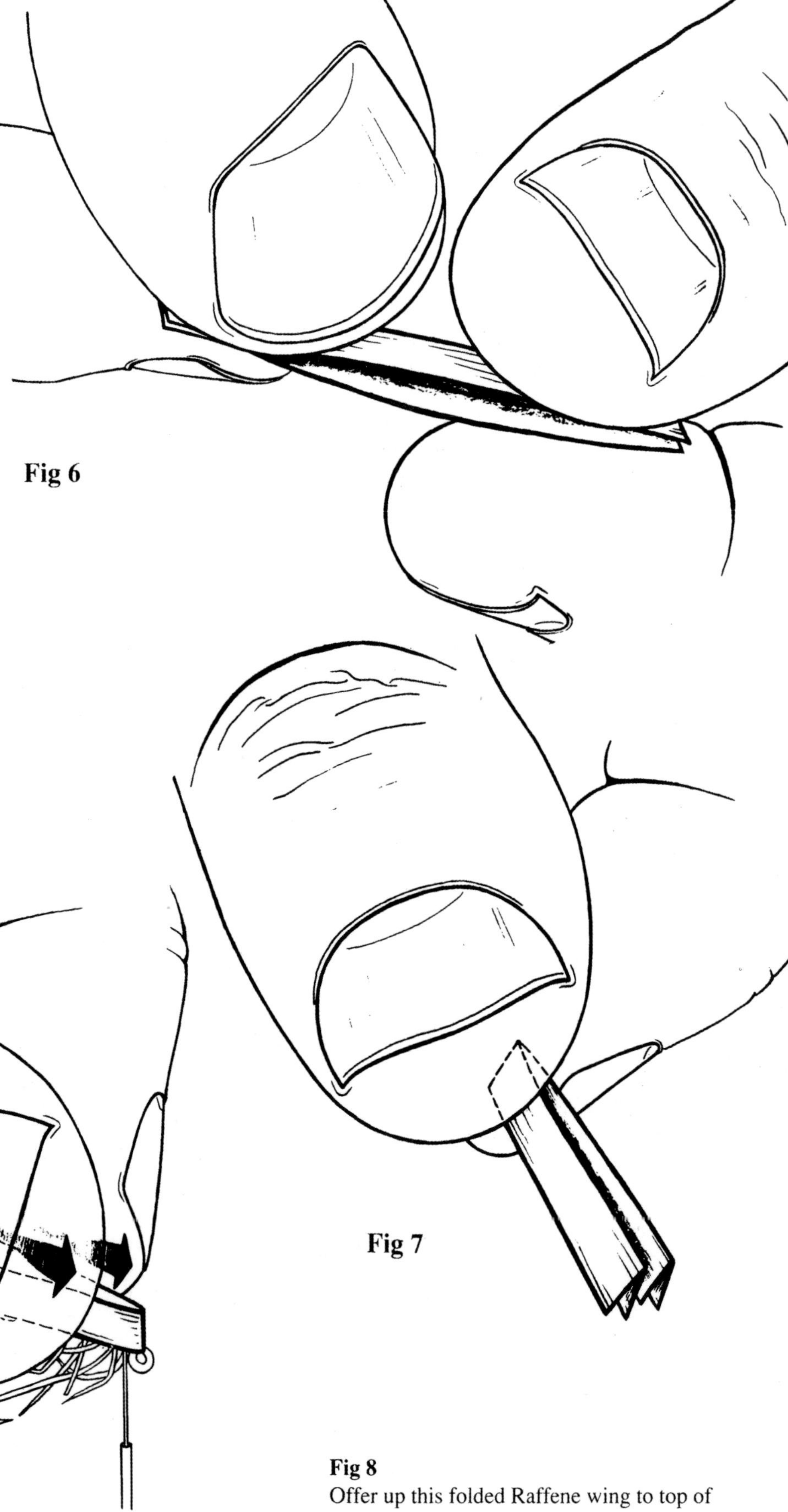

Fig 6

Fig 7

Fig 8

Fig 8
Offer up this folded Raffene wing to top of hook shank.

Fig 9

Now, move your finger and thumb further forward until they virtually cover the front fold. Then tie in, using a 'pinch and loop' as you would for a wet fly feather slip wing, tightening the thread down. This first full turn of thread should be about 1mm back from the front crease. While still applying finger and thumb pressure add three or four more tight 'pinch and loops'. Now you can release your grip. The folded Raffene should be nicely positioned on top and slightly down each side of the hook shank. Add two more tight turns followed by a single half-hitch, then let the bobbin holder hang. I add the half-hitch at this stage because dry Raffene is a springy material. Without the half-hitch, the Raffene can 'recover', if you are relying on the weight of the bobbin holder alone, rendering the bindings slightly loose.

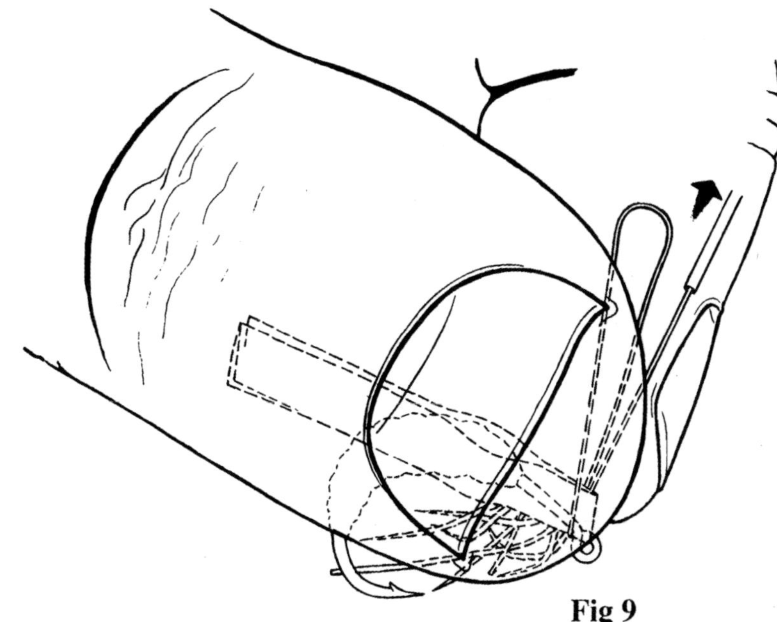

Fig 9

Fig 10

Finally, trim the ends of the Raffene to the correct length and shape of the caddis wing.

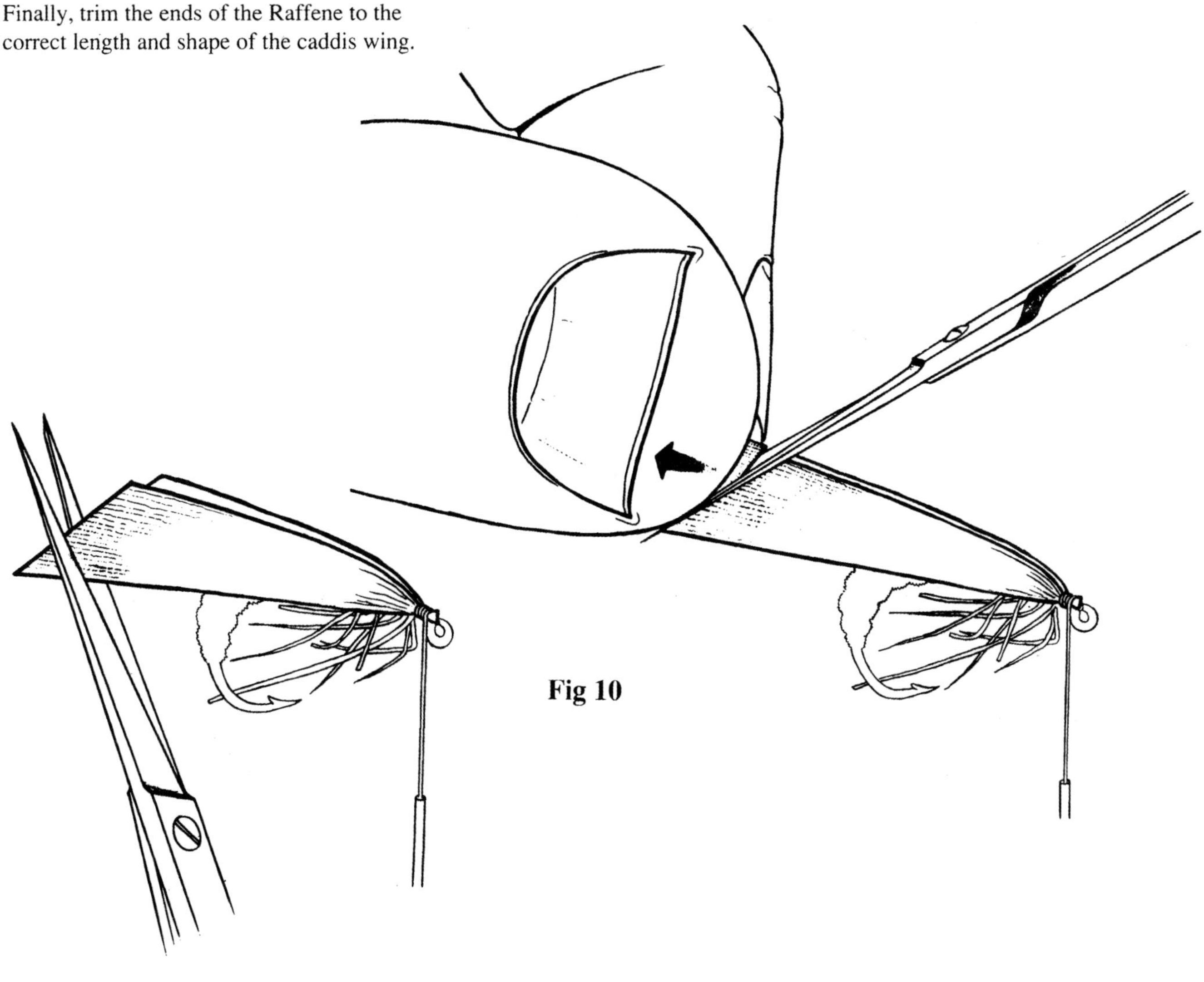

Fig 10

Fig 11
For the antennae, I like moose mane. Tweak out two long, straight hairs and either offer them up together with their tips even, or singly. The fine tips should project back just beyond the wing. Then manoeuvre both so that they are in line with one another. Three or four tight turns of thread, applied 'pinch and loop' again, will secure them. If they both finally angle outwards when viewed from above, that's okay.

Fig 12
Apply the usual whip finish and trim off the tying thread and the waste butts of the antennae hairs. If you are using a white Kevlar-type thread, stain the head with a brown waterproof felt pen. Finally, touch the bindings with head cement.

Fig 13
There you are, quite a different caddis to the ones you are used to seeing. As soon as the head cement is hard, drop it into a dish of water, leave for half a minute, then swish the dish about. If you have a few preserved adult caddis of about the same size, drop them in too. I think you will agree that the likeness is very passable. Believe me, trout and grayling think so.

Note: The pattern depicted here is unweighted and relies on the materials used to take it below the surface. However, in strong currents weighted patterns are sometimes more successful than the unweighted version. Six or seven turns of fine lead wire, or the equivalent in wine bottle foil, is adequate. Wrap on this lead ballast first, then proceed as per the instructions.

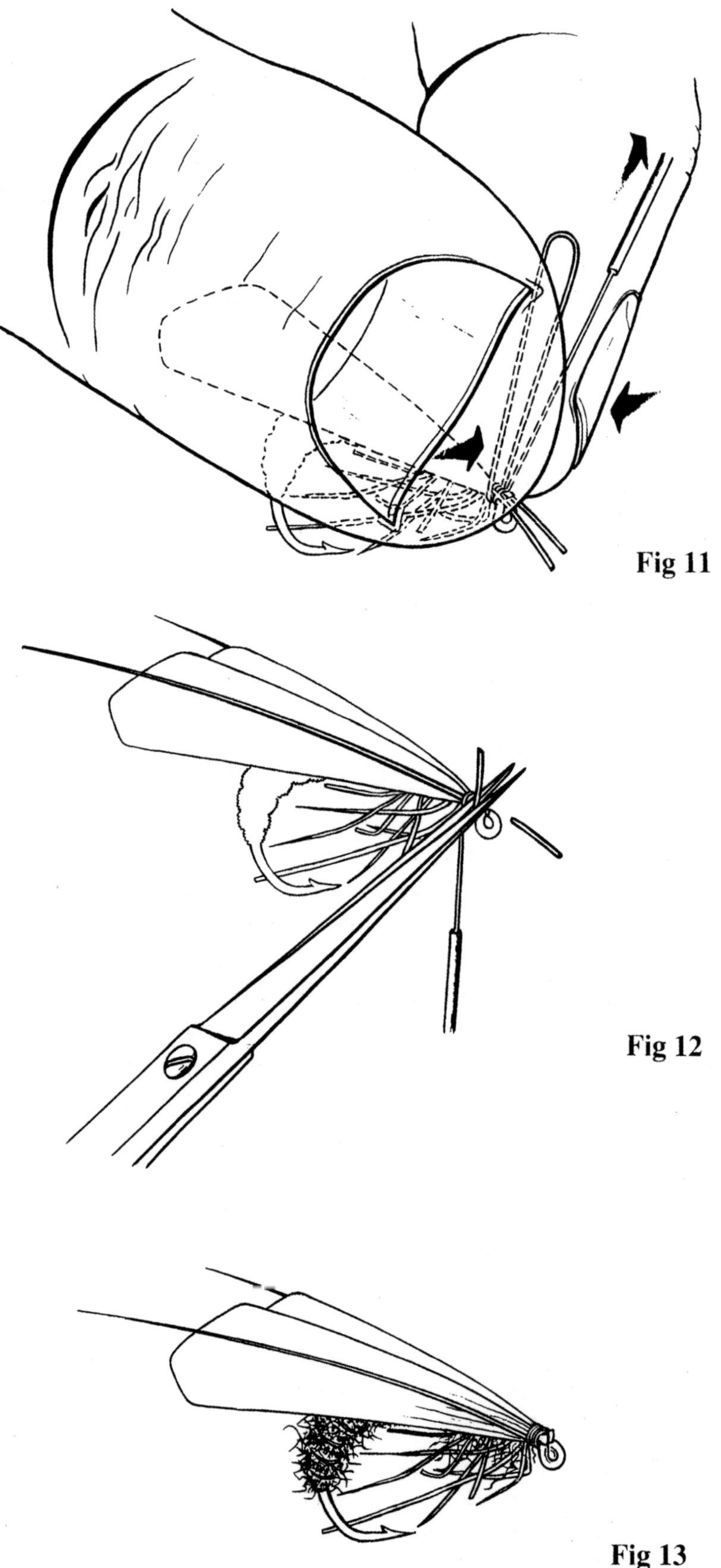

16. The Spent Willow and Needle Fly

This pattern has been on and off my drawing board for several years. The breakthrough for realism, effectiveness and ease of tying came when I turned to Raffene for the wings. After the success of my Post-ovipositing (Popa) caddis, I saw no reason why the same material wouldn't prove just as effective for imitating the spent wings of the needle flies. I think I have it about right now to pass it on - it is a real October special.

The small stoneflies of the genus Leuctra are common and widespread throughout most of the natural trout regions of Britain. A stony or rocky substrate is the preferred habitat, which means that the freestone rainfed rivers of the South West, Wales, and those northern rivers flowing east and west out of the Pennines, all hold healthy populations of these stoneflies. The same applies to Scotland with its mile upon mile of rocky upland streams and rivers. Many provide ideal stonefly habitat. The genus Leuctra is also well distributed throughout North America.

Here in Yorkshire, the river Nidd from Pately Bridge downstream, teems with millions of these thin Leuctra needle flies. The Nidd would be called a tailwater were it situated in the USA since its main fishing starts below an impoundment, Gouthwaite Reservoir.

Below the tail race and for the following 15 or so miles, down to Harrogate, the river flows in a series of short riffles interspersed with small pools and glides. It is a small river, 10-20 yards across, and for the most part it is shallow. Despite this, the river bed is always difficult to discern. Even in low, summer conditions, the water is always tinged with colour, described as being 'lingy' by old Yorkshire anglers. The stream bed is also dark, composed of rock, stones and slabs many of which are moss-covered, making a good micro-habitat for stonefly nymphs. A further feature of the substrate, which is regarded as being desirable for nymphs of the Leuctra stoneflies, is silt. The Nidd has plenty of silty areas, in fact many of the large stones and rocks are set firmly in fine silt.

However, the river Nidd has another feature which may be unique in Yorkshire Dales rivers - it has an almost continuous regiment of alders on both banks. In places, the effect is of a river flowing through a veritable tunnel of branches. It is, I believe, these old trees above all else which make the Nidd such a prime needle fly river as they provide ample shelter from predators, particularly swallows and martins.

In the UK there are six species of Leuctra stoneflies. They all look basically the same - both adults and nymphs - and they can only be positively identified by trained entomologists. As far as we anglers and flytyers are concerned, they can all be regarded as one, and by making size variations only, the whole range of these flies can be represented. They are small, however, with some male adults being a mere 3/16" (4mm) long. An adult female willow fly, on the other hand, may reach 1/2" (12mm).

The name 'needle' is very appropriate since at rest the smallest species could be mistaken easily for pine needles. However, the name did not originate from their likeness to pine needles. It is said by Courtney Williams to have derived from their closeness to the colour of Spanish sewing needles. You would be forgiven for thinking that the adults have no wings since they stow them so neatly. Instead of being laid flat on top of their abdomens, like all the larger stoneflies, the needle flies wrap their wings very snuggly around their abdomens, giving the appearance of a continuous sheath tapering to a point. The colour of all these adult stoneflies is a dark brown with just a faint hint of dark maroon.

Small stoneflies spend much of their time at rest, wings sheathed, and well camouflaged. If disturbed, they tend to scuttle away rather than take to the wing. A warm autumn afternoon, with still air and bright sunlight shafting through the overhead canopy of branches, often stirs them into flight at which time mating and egg-laying may occur. Mating is generally thought not to occur on the wing. Egg-laying is achieved by 'dipping'. The ripe female, with eggs already starting to exude from the end of her oviduct, flutters over the water's surface, touching down with the tip of her abdomen as she flies about. With each dip of her tail, eggs are discharged.

After egg-laying, many females expire before making it to the bankside. They die in the fully spent attitude, fixed in the surface film. During busy egg-laying periods, I have seen many of these little corpses float past me, their four wings symmetrically spread like so many tiny crucifixes. Both trout and grayling are fond of this late season bounty. I can recall several occasions in October when the weather has been still, warm and sunny - typical Indian Summer days - when certain riffles have come alive with grayling intercepting the spent females or trying to nab others in the act of egg-laying.

The Spent Willow fly, as a pattern, is not new, and I am not trying to claim any originality. However, my pattern has been tied 'from life' without reference to past patterns.

Because this is a spent pattern, many flyfishers would consider that it is best fished dry. However, from my own experience, I believe that it is just as effective when fished wet, just below the surface. I nearly always fish it so, knotting it on the top dropper of my 3-fly leader. The trick when fishing it in this manner is to strive to make it ride the current dead drift. In a popply riffle a small degree of swing can be tolerated, but in glides or smooth necks of pools, the pattern must be fished dead drift or else it will skate. Cast upstream preferably using a reach cast. When the flies have alighted and sunk, simply track the rod tip around, moving it from upstream to pointing directly downstream. The idea is to keep intimate contact with the flies throughout the drift; any rogue bows or bellies are carefully mended out as the drift progresses.

On a recent visit to the river Ure in mid October, on a stretch more noted for trout than grayling, I had the rod almost taken out of my hands, so savage were the offers to this fly. Of the seven trout I fooled, five took the Spent Willow.

SOME NATURALS APPROPRIATE TO THIS PATTERN

BRITISH SPECIES:
Leuctra geniculata, L. inermis, L. hippopus, L. nigra, L. fusca, L. moselyi.
BRITISH FISHING NAMES:
Willow Fly, Needle Fly (Dark Needle, Light Needle, Dark Spanish Needle).

NORTH AMERICAN SPECIES:
Leuctra grandis, L. occidentalis, L. sara.
NORTH AMERICAN FISHING NAME: Needle Fly.

NOTES ON MATERIALS AND TYING

The quill for the abdomen is from peacock herl taken from within the actual eye of a good quality peacock eye feather. However, you may be unlucky when you acquire your eye feathers, some produce very thin quills when stripped. Some do not have the all-important lighter stripe down the side - I know as I seem to have cornered the market of duff peacock eyes! You may have problems sloughing the 'flew' off the quill. This is easy: simply trap the herl between the ball of your index finger and your thumb nail, then draw your

SPENT WILLOW AND NEEDLE FLY DRESSINGS

Hook: Medium or fine wire standard shank dry fly hook. Suggest Partridge 'Hooper' L/S 4x Fine Dry Fly hook code E1A, size 16 (Spent Willow), sizes 18 and 20 (Spent Needle); or Partridge 'Capt. Hamilton Dry Fly Hook codes L3A or L4A, size 16 (Spent Willow), sizes 18 and 20 (Spent Needle).
Thread: Danville's Spider Web, tinted dark brown (waterproof felt pen).
Cement: Dave's Flexament (USA) or Floo Gloo (UK), both thinned.
Abdomen: Striped peacock herl from the eye of a good quality eye feather.
Thorax: Fine synthetic dubbing very dark olive brown, eg. Davy Wotton Finesse Masterclass blend 50/50 MC 4 and MC 8.
Legs: Hen hackle or inferior quality cock (henny), dyed or natural dark brown or very dark olive brown.
Wings: Brown Raffene (Swiss Straw).
Antennae: Brown guard hairs from a mink tail or similar.

thumb nail along the herl, maintaining pressure as you progress. Alternatively, rub off the flew using a fairly hard eraser. Another method is to place the herls in a dish of bleach solution. I don't care for the latter method as the amount of bleach in the solution is critical. It's a hit and miss affair, trying to get the solution just right so that the flew is dissolved away. Too much bleach and the quill will be weakened severely.

There are quite a few synthetic raffias, or swiss straw, on the market but the very best in my opinion is Raffene. This is my first choice for the wings. When you cut off the sliver of Raffene for the wings, make the cut at a shallow angle, you don't want it to be a step wedge, the shape of a slice of cake!

Remember also to allow sufficient length - it has to make two wings! Before you cut your wings, dunk your opened out strip of Raffene into very thinned Flexament. Allow to dry then dunk again. This strengthens the wings considerably.

Keep the abdomen very slim. You will notice that I have shown a slight swelling out as it approaches the thorax.

Please don't overdo this, it's only meant to be slightly thicker, so don't go making it like Billy Bunter!

Also, do please keep the amount of dubbing to a minimum. There should only be a slight covering of fur at the thorax.

Tying the Spent Willow Fly

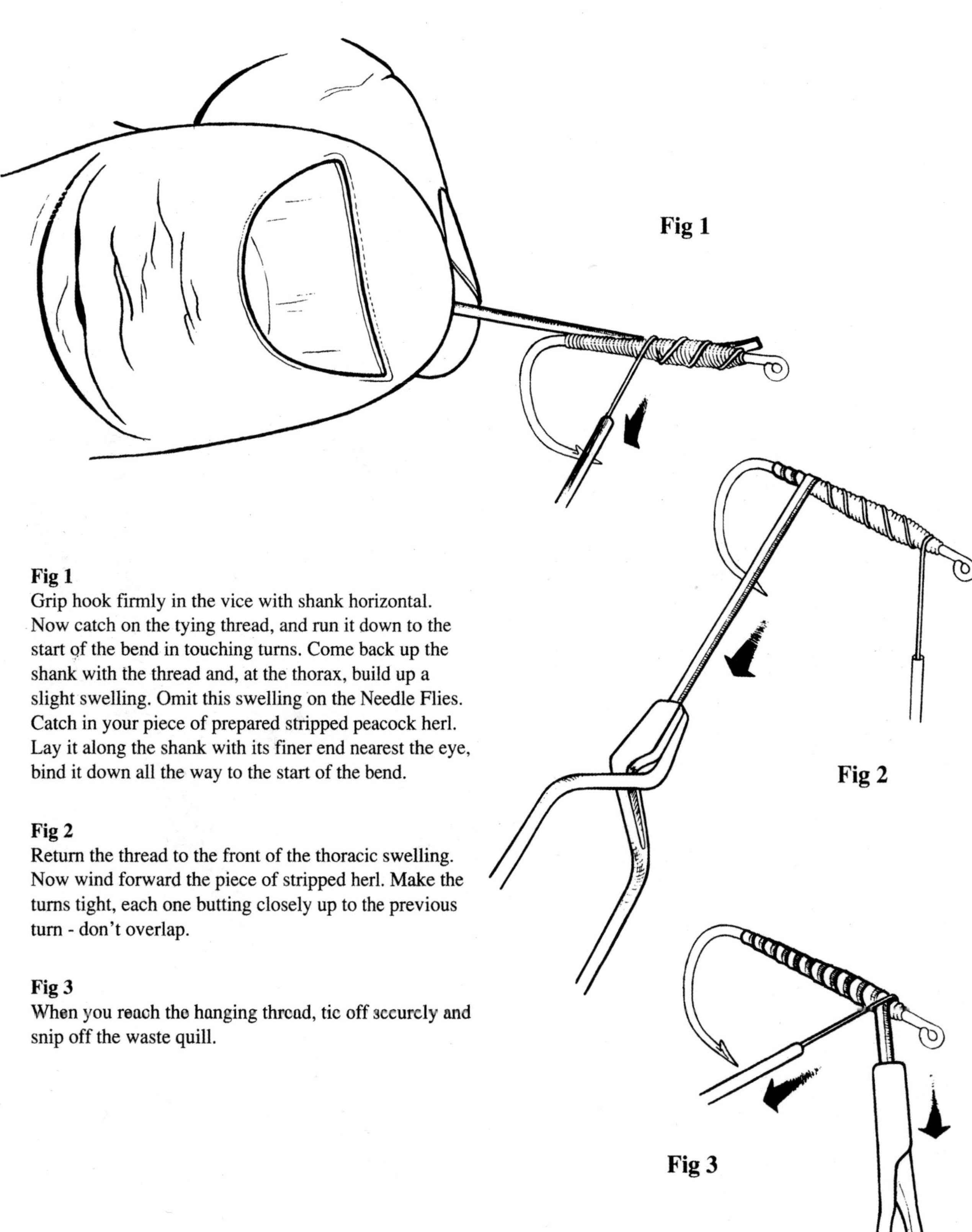

Fig 1
Grip hook firmly in the vice with shank horizontal. Now catch on the tying thread, and run it down to the start of the bend in touching turns. Come back up the shank with the thread and, at the thorax, build up a slight swelling. Omit this swelling on the Needle Flies. Catch in your piece of prepared stripped peacock herl. Lay it along the shank with its finer end nearest the eye, bind it down all the way to the start of the bend.

Fig 2
Return the thread to the front of the thoracic swelling. Now wind forward the piece of stripped herl. Make the turns tight, each one butting closely up to the previous turn - don't overlap.

Fig 3
When you reach the hanging thread, tie off securely and snip off the waste quill.

SPENT WILLOW AND NEEDLE FLIES
(Top two) Willow Flies.
(Lower three) Needle Flies.

Fig 4
Next offer up your hen hackle and tie it in.

Fig 5
Tie it to the side of the body with the tip of the hackle protruding beyond the bend.

Fig 6
Now make your two wings. Remember to cut them at a shallow angle,

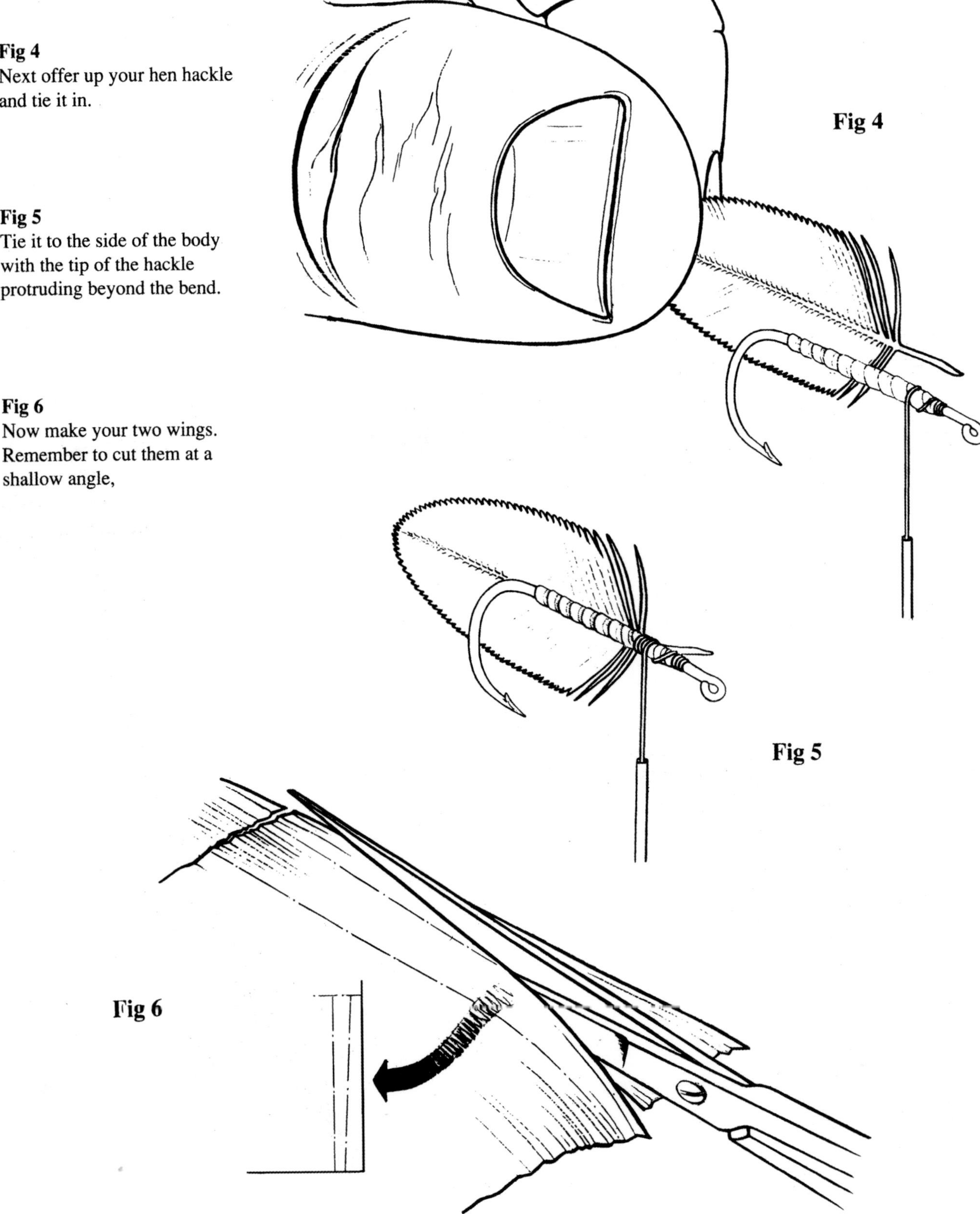

Fig 7
Then fold in the centre so as to produce a pair of wings in a vee configuration, at about a 45° angle.

Fig 8
Offer one wing up at a time. I tie in the far side pair first and I make sure that the turns of thread go over both front and rear wings by making the turns of thread right in the centre of the vee. Then work the thread forwards and backwards. Offer up and tie in the pair of nearside wings on top of the far side ones, exactly as you did for the latter.

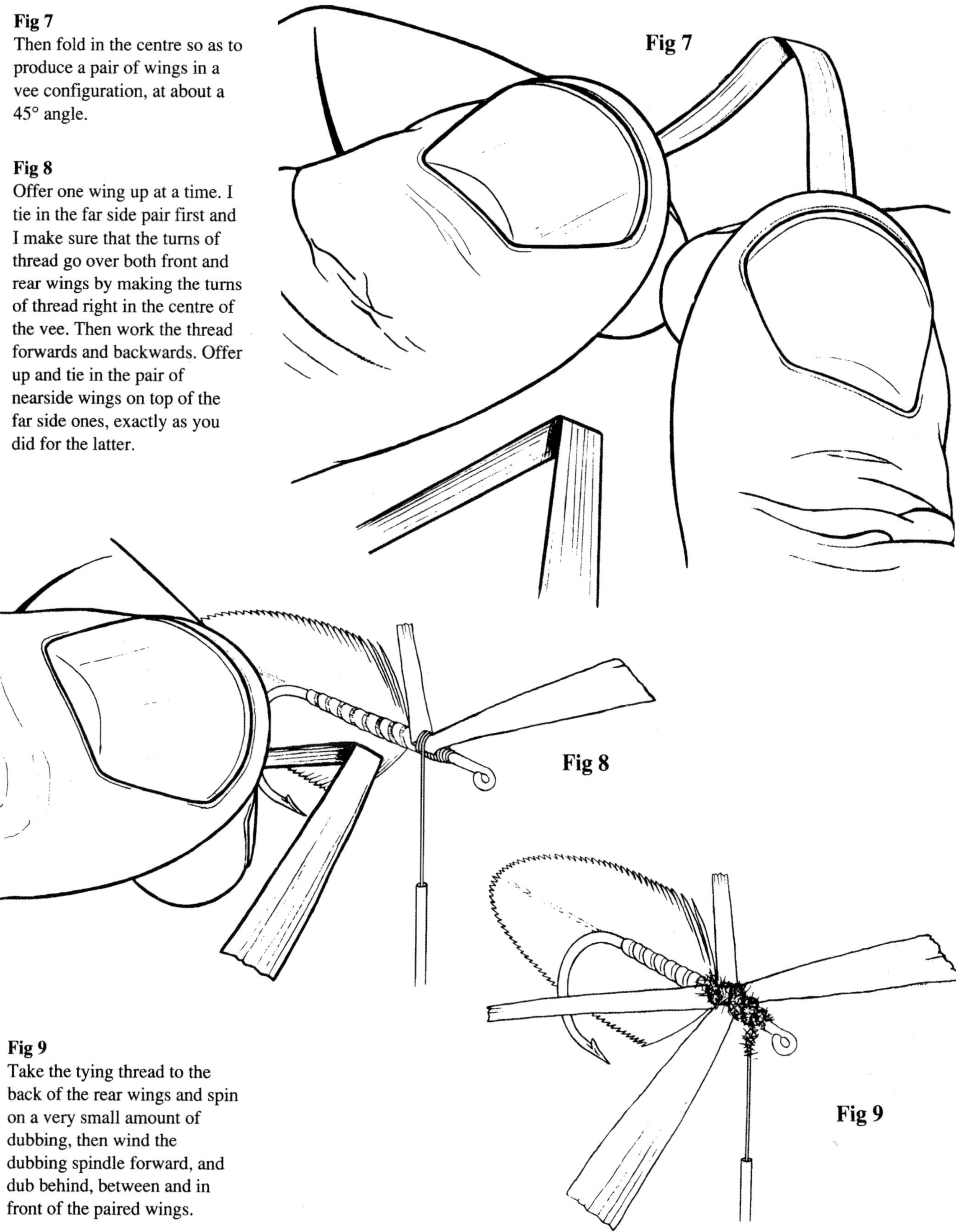

Fig 9
Take the tying thread to the back of the rear wings and spin on a very small amount of dubbing, then wind the dubbing spindle forward, and dub behind, between and in front of the paired wings.

Fig 10
Now clip your hackle pliers on to the hackle tip and wind the hackle forward, making one full turn behind, between and in front of the wings. Tie the butt end down very securely and snip off the waste end.

Fig 11
The last tying stage now is to tie in the two antennae. Tie them in on top of the shank and slightly to the side - make sure both are the same length, protruding about 3/4 body length and diverging to make a vee. Snip off waste ends.

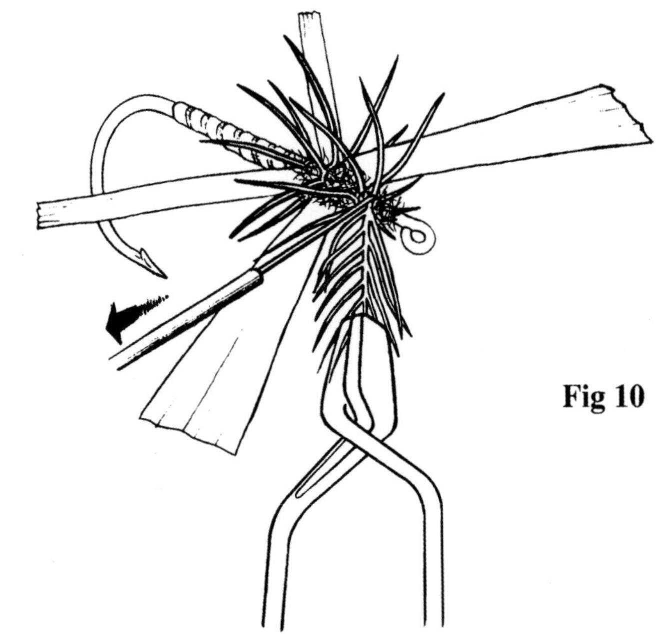
Fig 10

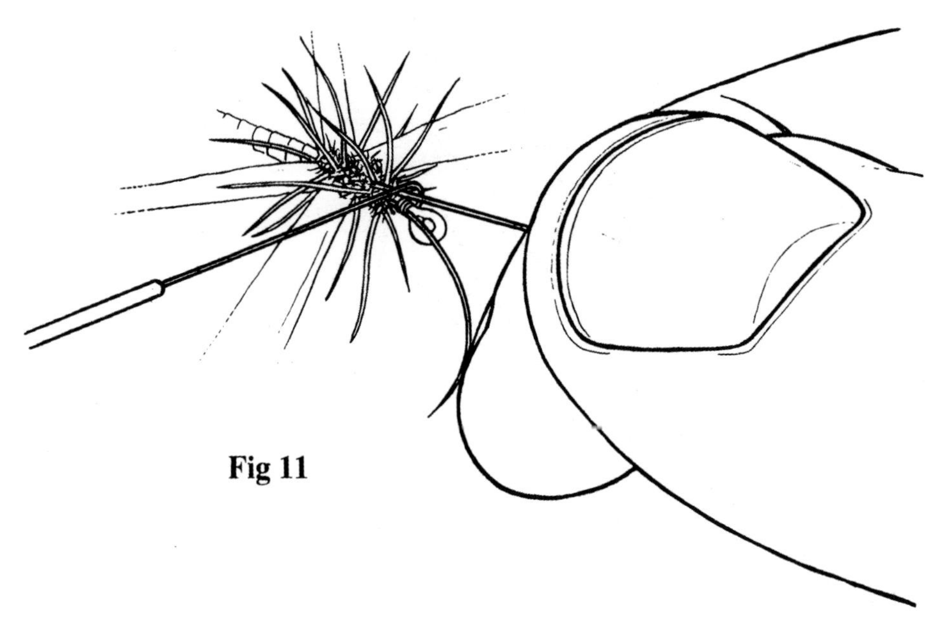
Fig 11

Fig 12
Finish the fly by building up a nice round neat head as you whip finish and tie off. Touch with head cement. All you have to do now for a perfect Spent Willow or Needle Fly is to snip off those hackle barbs protruding above the fly.

Fig 13
Then just shape up the Raffene wing tips with a couple of sloping cuts to each wing.

Fig 12

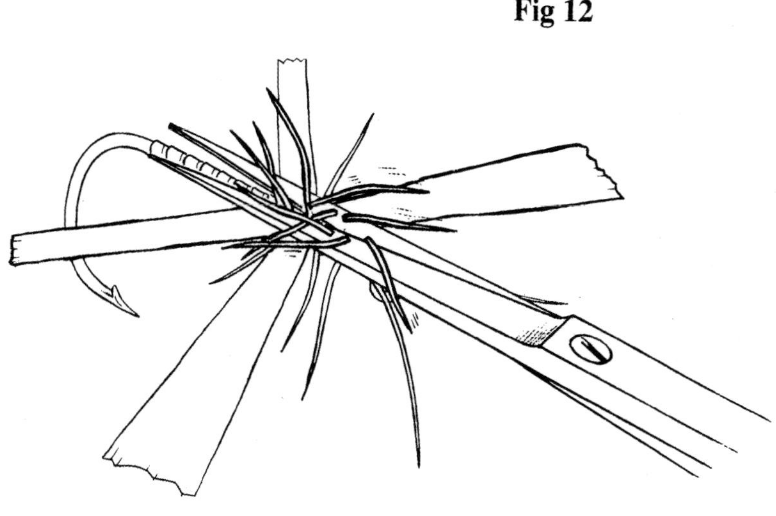

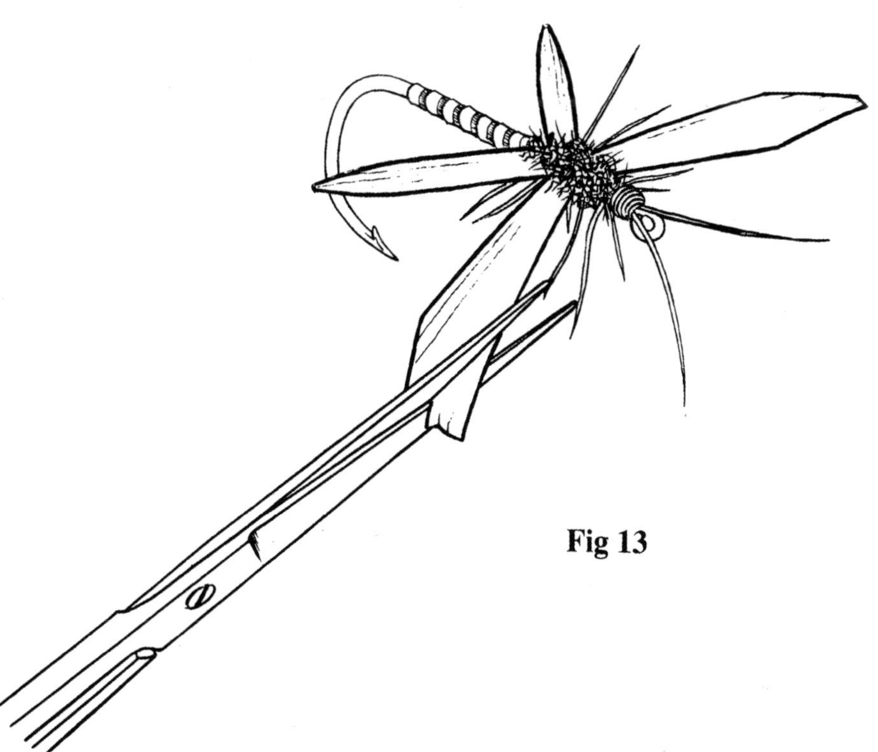

Fig 13

Fig 14

There it is, a quick yet lifelike pattern, the only fiddle being the cutting and folding of the wings.

Incidentally, the fly illustrated is arranged with the wider wings at the front. Yet strictly speaking, they should be reversed, since on the natural, the hind wings are a bit wider and shorter than the front wings. So you have a choice. You can have the front wings wider or the rear wings wider. It doesn't seem to matter much to the fish.

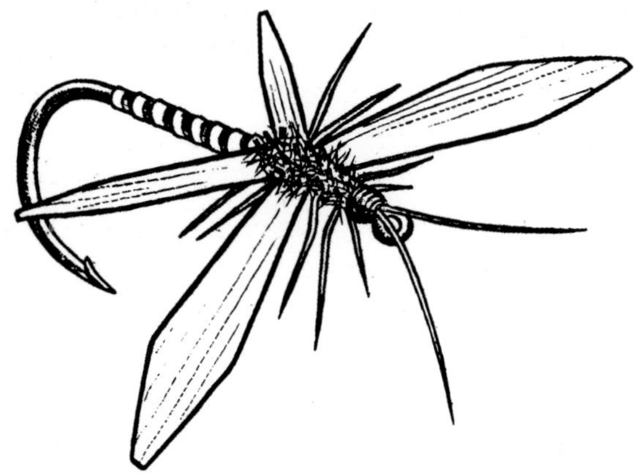

Fig 14

17. The Large Stonefly Nymph

I have often pondered the fact that in the UK, there is scant history of stonefly fishing with the artificial, nor do we have standard patterns to cover both nymphs and adults. I'm referring here particularly to the larger species of stoneflies, those with a body length of 5/8" (15mm) and longer.

There seems to be no good reason why this should be, when one considers how rich in large stoneflies our upland rivers were in the days before nitrates, phosphates, dairy effluent, silage spills and all the other junk we have since poured into them.

Although stoneflies may not now be present in quite the same numbers, their distribution in the UK remains widespread. The only region of the British Isles where stoneflies (small as well as large) are scarce is the flatter counties east of the Humber Estuary-Bristol Channel line. This area is particularly unsuitable, with very few species recorded.

Nevertheless, you would still think it possible to lay your hands on an artificial stonefly from some old collection. Unfortunately, it is not so easy and old collections, often in their original leather wallets, usually comprise neat rows of spiders and winged wets. You search in vain to find a stonefly pattern!

Don't get me wrong, I'm not suggesting that old stonefly patterns have never existed. On the contrary, Courtney Williams' *Dictionary of Trout Flies* informs us that the stonefly is given an airing in Dame Juliana Berners' *A Treatise of Fysshyng with an Angle* (1496). If that reference is seen as being somewhat quaint or even suspect, there can be no doubt about the stonefly's inclusion in Alfred Ronald's masterpiece *The Fly Fisher's Entomology* (1836). Not only does he give the dressing (No.12) but he illustrates both the natural and the artificial.

However, my own quest has been to unearth a pattern - a physical artifact - for the *nymph*. Even a written recipe for a dressing would do! All the old dressings, including the Ronald's pattern, are for copying the winged adult.

So far, I have drawn a blank and I have come to the conclusion that patterns to copy the nymphs of our large stoneflies have probably never existed and, if they ever did, they were probably parochial, short-lived and never written down. There were possibly many reasons why our flydressing ancestors never attempted to copy these large gawky creatures. Not having suitable materials was certainly not one of them, and long shank hooks, although crude by today's standards, were available. So one must look further.

In those early days, the trout angler had a varied repertoire and the phrase 'fly only' was unheard of. There was no guarantee, therefore, that the wielder of the fly rod would have an artificial fly at the other end!

The fly rod was, in fact, a universal implement and the leash of flies would be changed without hesitation to a single hook cast, on which would be mounted a well-scoured brandling or, a gilt tail. Even a quill minnow or, better still, a live one would be tossed into any likely looking hole using the same fly rod.

The fly rod and flyline of the nineteenth and early twentieth century was used for 'fishing the creeper' - the stonefly nymph - a large one, alive and kicking! This was a very popular method, used in season on our northern rivers and is the reason why, I'm sure, my quest to find an artificial stonefly nymph is doomed.

The current population status of the large UK stoneflies varies considerably region to region. The river Wharfe's population has been decimated in my own lifetime. I well remember a school youth hostelling holiday in 1951. We walked from Bolton Abbey to the hamlet of Buckden (not in one day!) and I was constantly holding up progress, forever being chided for spending more time in the river than on the footpath. I was busy turning over stones in the fast shallows, catching the large 'creepers'. I remember the river teemed with them, under every stone, often several per stone. Today, you would be hard pressed to fill a match box!

The heaviest concentration these days, if that's the correct word, seems to be at Grassington. The river Ure, another large stonefly stronghold of the past, has a similar tale to tell - very few left. I have found the odd specimen of *Perlodes microcephala* on our club's stretch at Masham. I have also found them further up Wensleydale at Redmire and higher still at Bainbridge. However, the vast quantities of the past have gone.

If the stonefly nymph has been neglected in the UK, the opposite is the case in the United States. It is not easy to establish just when stonefly nymph patterns first appeared in the States and it is highly likely that some patterns were in use well before they appeared in print. For instance, I can well imagine that Edward Hewitt would have quickly realised their value, and some copies of *Field and Stream* for the year 1933 contain articles by him entitled 'Nymph fly fishing'. It is obvious from these articles Hewitt was impressed by the effectiveness of nymph fishing and that he was championing it in America.

We also learn that in 1933 he had only been nymph fishing a few years. He even mentions visits to England to fish the Test and Itchen, the latter at the invitation of a Mr Skues, a visit which seemed to impress him. Whilst Hewitt's articles deal with nymph fishing in general, there is an illustration of a large stonefly nymph and mention of a size 10 long shank hook.

However, it is apparent when reading these articles that the dry fly was the favourite method, and the use of the nymph was in its infancy but was already arousing much interest. In fact, flyfishing as a whole was much less popular in those days than spinning or bait casting. So the enthusiasm for nymph fishing in the States developed over a relatively short period of time. Today, in the States, the large weighted stonefly nymph is high in the popularity chart, with thousands of flytyers devising their own individual patterns. Scores of new patterns are published every year, using new materials and new techniques.

I found it fascinating to look at these large artificials during my recent visit to West Yellowstone and the patterns being demonstrated by the experts at the FFF Conclave. The patterns in the shops were simple, impressionistic ties, conveying only overall size, body outline and colour as triggers. Appendages were simple: goose biot antennae and tails. Some had a turn or two of wispy grizzle hackle wound at the thorax and that was more or less it. One thing which struck me about these commercial patterns was the robustness, they looked as tough as old boots.

Then I went to fish the mighty Madison below Quake Lake and it became obvious why these large stonefly nymphs were tied this way: they had to be capable of taking a pounding. I was looking at a roller coaster of a river with a bed like some gigantic continuous ball mill.

Conventional wisdom has it that in turbulent water like this, the trout only see a blurred outline or only get a fleeting glimpse of the nymph and therefore have to be quick off the mark or the meal is lost.

Well, I'll go along with that if we are talking about the maelstrom water chutes of the Madison. But large stoneflies are to be found in less turbulent water, and in very large numbers. I found lots of stonefly nymphs in the Gallatin, in water similar to some stretches I fish in the Dales at home. And don't let anyone tell you that trout can't detect minute detail in fast riffle water

LARGE STONEFLY NYMPHS

(Clockwise from top) Perla species (drifting/foetal position) - Perla species (crawling) - Dinocras species (drifting/swimming, 'soft' legs) - Isoperla species (Yellow Sally) - Dinocras species (crawling)

SOME NATURALS APPROPRIATE TO THIS PATTERN

British and European/Scandinavian species:
(plus approx. body length of mature female nymph)

Isoperla grammatica 5/8" (15mm)
Perlodes microcephala 1" (26mm)
Diura bicaudata 9/16" (17mm)
Dinocras cephalotes 1 1/8" (30mm)
Perla bipunctata 1 1/8" (30mm)

British fishing names:
Of the five large stoneflies, only one, *Isoperla grammatica*, has been given a popular fishing name - the Yellow Sally. The remaining four species have only their Latin names. They are known collectively by flyfishers of the UK as Medium and Large Stoneflies. In the northern counties of England the nymphs are called 'Creepers', in Scotland 'Gadgers'.

Some North American species:
(plus approx. body length of mature female nymph)
Pteronarcys californica 1 1/2" (40mm)
Pteronarcys dorsata 2" (52mm)
Acroneuria californica 1 1/4" (32mm)
Acroneuria lycoris 1" (25mm)
Acroneuria nigrita 7/8" (21mm)
Acroneuria pacifica 1" (25mm)
Acronuria ruralis 3/4" (20mm)
Perla immarginata 7/8" (21mm)
Perla capitata 1" (25mm)
Isoperla signata 3/4" (19mm)
Isoperla marmona 5/8" (15mm)

North American fishing names:
Giant Salmon Fly
Giant Black Stonefly
Golden Stonefly
Great Brown Stonefly
Black Willow Fly
Brown Willow Fly
Yellow Legged Stonefly
Orange Stonefly
Great Stonefly
Light Brown Stonefly
Western Yellow Stonefly

because they can. I have caught trout from fast riffles which had been feeding on the tiniest of nymphs imaginable, very early instar Baetis nymphs not long out of the egg. Those tiny nymphs were being picked off quite meticulously, one at a time. So, I'm all in favour of adding as much detail to my stonefly nymphs as possible.

Notes on Materials and Tying

This style of tying can be used on a wide size range and it is quite possible to tie it as small as size 18 should you wish to tie the nymphs of the willow and needle flies. Remember, though, when tying these *small* stonefly nymphs you are limited as to how much lead you can use, since their abdomens are little thicker than the actual hook wire! So put your lead ballast on the thoracic section only. Similarly, each leg will be just one hackle barb, not a clump, as I've illustrated. It may also be better on such small nymphs to use 0.005" thick dyed polythene instead of the thicker Flexibody.

At the other end of the scale, the very large stonefly nymphs of the Western States of North America, including the two huge black stoneflies of the Pteronarcys genera, are tailor-made for this style of tying and the flytyer can be very liberal with the lead. You'll need to, anyway, as these patterns are destined to be hurled into racing rivers like the Madison, Deschuttes and Big Hole and will therefore be required to sink quickly. These nymphs are over 2" (50mm) long excluding antennae and tails, so don't be afraid to lay on the lead. For good reason the casting of these missiles is known as 'chuck and duck'.

I don't like the effect goose biots give when used for antennae and tails. To my eye, they are too wide at the base, particularly when used as antennae. However, many successful patterns use them and robustness is one reason why they are so popular. For tails and antennae I much prefer stout animal hairs such as skunk and moose. The grey moose hairs, suitably dyed, I like very much. For tails of the largest nymphs I want more definition than one hair can give, so I tie in two or even three on either side. Then when all the tying is completed, I draw the hairs together by running a bead of flexible cement or flexible superglue along their full length, then stroke out from base to tip with finger and thumb.

The underbody dubbing on the abdomen serves various purposes. Firstly, it is a useful padding to achieve the required abdomen width.

LARGE STONEFLY NYMPH DRESSING

Hook: Medium or heavy wire 2x to 3x longshank (re-shaped to produce swimming attitude if necessary). Suggest Partridge 'Capt. Hamilton' Nymph code H1A sizes 2 to 18; or Partridge 'Roman Moser' Barbless Streamer hook code CS29GRs sizes 2 to 8; or Partridge 'Keith Fulser' Thundercreek hook code CS5 sizes 4 to 8; or Partridge 'Taff Price' Swimming Nymph code K6ST sizes 8 to 14.
Weight: Strip of wine bottle lead foil (for small to medium sizes). Lead wire (for large sizes).
Cement: Dave's Flexament (USA) or Floo Gloo (UK).
Thread: Danville's Spider Web for the smallest sizes. Midge 8/0 for medium sizes. Regular 6/0 or 3/0 for larger sizes.
Tails: Single or groups of stout animal hair. Groups cemented together to produce tails for the largest sizes, eg. moose mane or body hair, dark or grey. Grey hairs can also be dyed, as can stripped hackle stem (dyed after stripping).
Abdomen: Polythene 0.008" (0.2mm) thick, or Flexibody, wrapped over base of fine synthetic dubbing, the colour of natural's ventral side. Dark 'ribbing' effect on some abdomens can be created by colouring one edge of the Flexibody strip with a permanent marker pen.
Abdomen Tint: Felt tip waterproof pens in suitable shades for dorsal surface.
Wing buds, pronotum and head: Abdomen material, folded for wing buds, single layer pulled over for pronotum, pulled back for head.
Thorax (and under head): Fine synthetic dubbing to match ventral colour of natural you wish to copy. Eg Davy Wotton Finesse Masterclass blends MC12 and MC 13, or blends of both.
Legs: Three prepared, suitably coloured, game bird hackles, eg. dyed or natural partridge, grouse, pheasant, guinea fowl, etc.
Antennae: Tapering animal hair (eg. moose) or stripped hackle stem, dyed.

Secondly, since the overbody is a translucent material (Flexibody or polythene), the tyer can produce some beautifully life-like colour effects with a kind of inner glow. By choosing, say, a strong yellow dubbing and a dark olive Flexibody, a yellow-olive is achieved with the yellow coming from beneath the skin, as it were. It is also very easy to produce the two-colour 'counter-shading' effect, which all nymphs have.

Wrap on the dubbing underbody, then, before wrapping on the Flexibody, simply mark the upper surface of the dubbed abdomen with a felt pen. Use an old almost worn-out pen. New pens give problems when trying to achieve clean divisions of colour, especially on wick-like soft dubbing.

If, while wrapping on the Flexibody, filaments of dubbing become trapped and appear as a fuzz at each abdomen joint, don't worry. Some tyers actually strive to produce this effect and if it appears evenly at each joint, it can look good, even though the natural has a perfectly smooth abdomen. (The tracheal gills of stoneflies are on the ventral side of the thorax, usually at the bases of the six legs).

If the two folded wing buds tend to 'bag' open, simply load the tip of your dubbing needle with flexible cement, then slide the needle between the folds and wipe the cement on the inner surfaces. Then press them firmly together.

I've illustrated the completed nymph in the three most popular body shapes or attitudes:

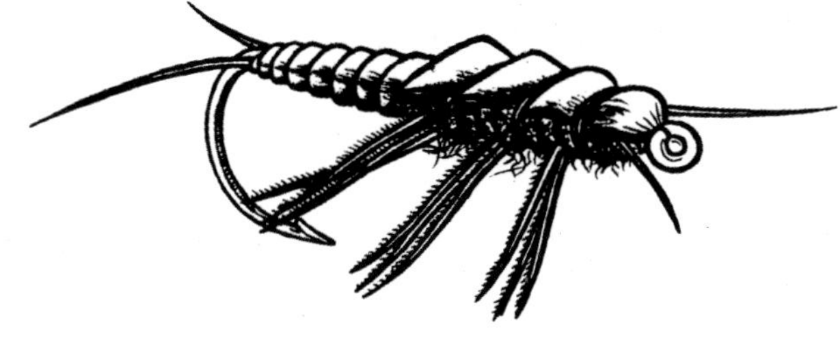

Fig A (above) shows the nymph tied on a straight-forward longshank in the attitude commonly called the 'crawling nymph'.

In **Fig B** (overleaf, top) the nymph is displaying the typical 'foetal position', an attitude some of the larger stonefly nymphs adopt when dislodged and tumbling helplessly in the current. For this style, a

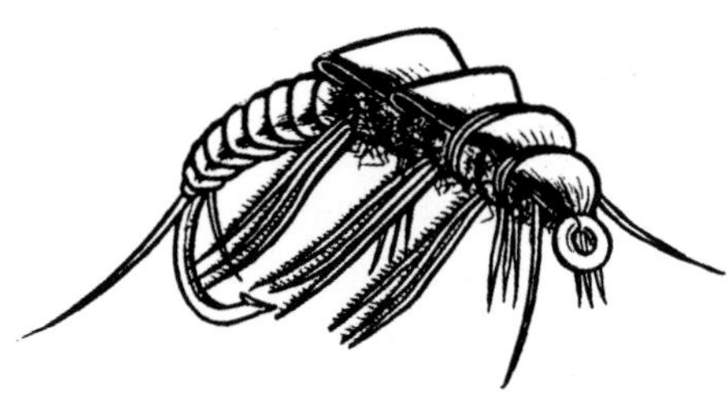

re-shaped longshank is required.

The third shape - illustrated below - (**Fig C**) is usually called the 'swimming nymph'. Hooks for this style are curved upwards near the eye. However, I curve mine sideways also, giving the nymph a sinuous writhing appearance.

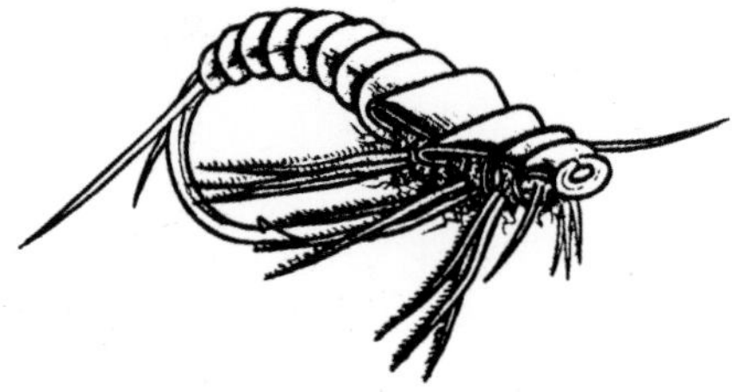

Finally, you may decide to heat kink the legs and treat them with flexible cement as illustrated at the end of this chapter (Figs 35 and 36). You will be immediately struck by the realism (Fig 37).

On the natural, the legs are very thick, rarely thrash about and are far more distinct than the antennae and tails, even when held closely tucked into the side of the body, irrespective of the nymph's attitude. However, some flyfishers dislike such close copying and prefer instead the flowing clumps of hackle barbs. So, the choice is yours.

I have been influenced by the artistry of some of the world's greatest stonefly nymph tyers, in particular, Poul Jorgensen, Bill Blackstone and last but not least, Dave Whitlock.

Tying the Large Stonefly Nymph

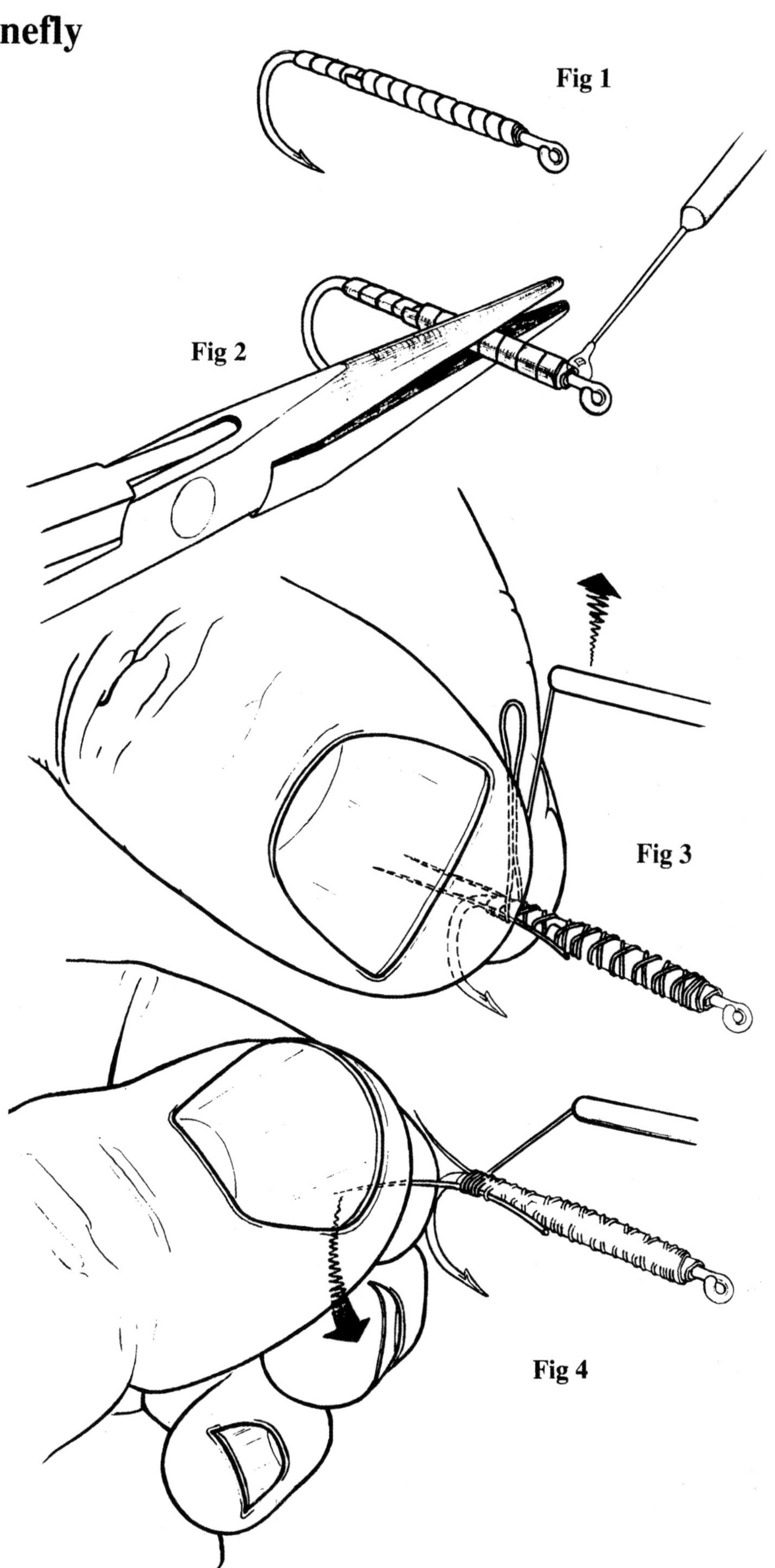

Fig 1
The first thing to fix in your mind is the nymph's proportions. Shank length divided by two = abdomen and thorax; thorax divided by four = wing buds, pronotum and head. Grip the longshank hook firmly in the vice with the shank horizontal and touch the shank with superglue. Cut off a parallel sliver of wine bottle lead foil and wrap it up and down the shank in abutting turns. The number of layers of lead will be governed by the water you intend to fish. The final layer of lead should stop short of the end of the abdomen portion.

Fig 2
Flatten this lead a little in the dorso-ventral position, then seal all over with head cement or superglue, particularly at the ends. Next, attach the tying thread and run it up and down the lead, cocooning it randomly.

Fig 3
For the tails, tweak out a couple of dyed hairs (several paired hairs for the large patterns). Offer these up on either side of the leaded shank, trap between finger and thumb and secure initially using several 'pinch and loops'.

Fig 4
Now even up the tails so that the tips align and extend by about one abdomen length. Keep both tails or sets of tails on the sides. When in position, apply more thread tension while at the same time pulling each tail in turn outwards. The effect of the thread slightly biting into the lead keeps the tails reasonably splayed.

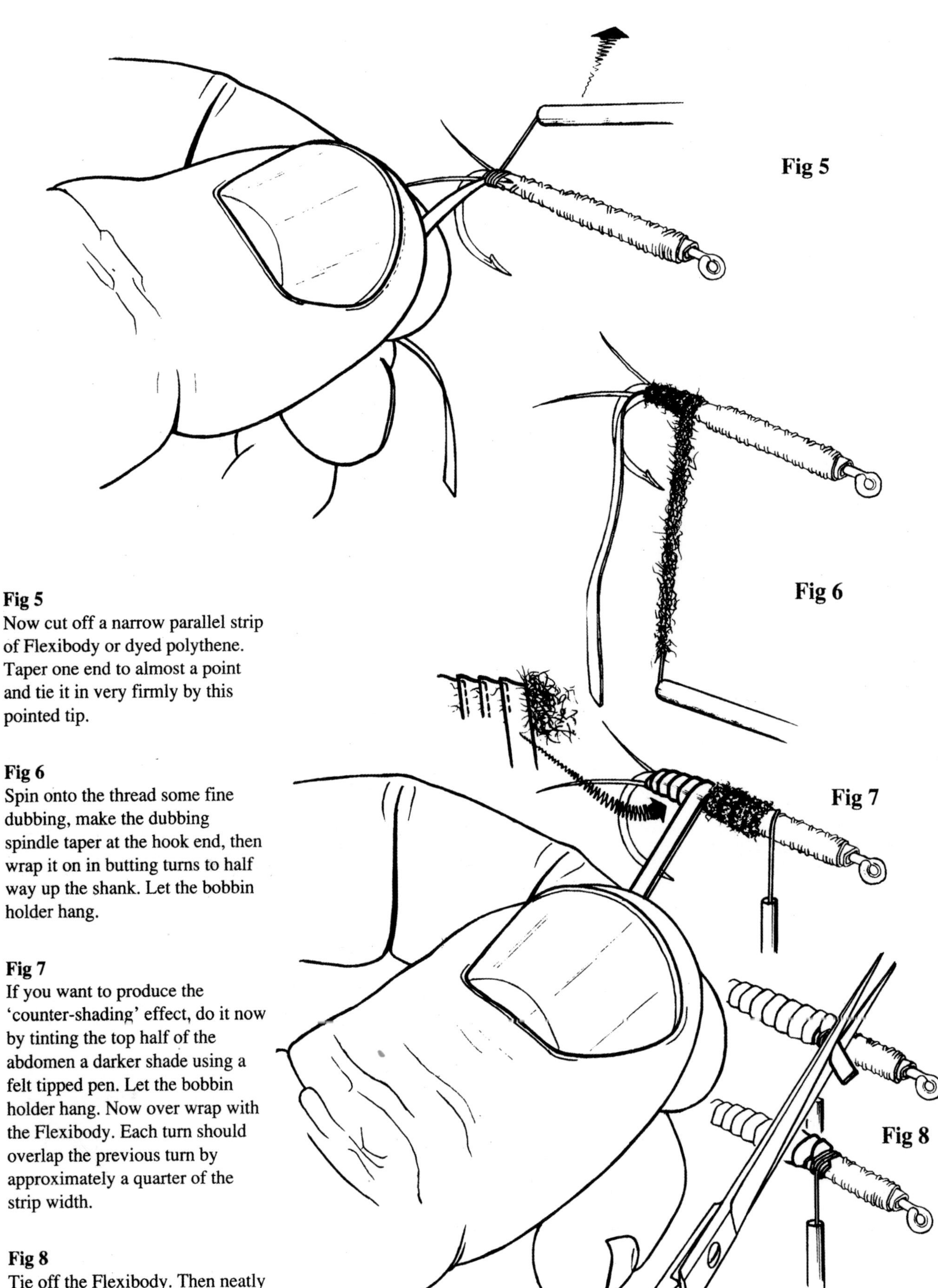

Fig 5
Now cut off a narrow parallel strip of Flexibody or dyed polythene. Taper one end to almost a point and tie it in very firmly by this pointed tip.

Fig 6
Spin onto the thread some fine dubbing, make the dubbing spindle taper at the hook end, then wrap it on in butting turns to half way up the shank. Let the bobbin holder hang.

Fig 7
If you want to produce the 'counter-shading' effect, do it now by tinting the top half of the abdomen a darker shade using a felt tipped pen. Let the bobbin holder hang. Now over wrap with the Flexibody. Each turn should overlap the previous turn by approximately a quarter of the strip width.

Fig 8
Tie off the Flexibody. Then neatly trim off the waste.

Fig 9
Now for those large wing buds. Cut off a long parallel strip of the same Flexibody $1^1/2$ times the width of the abdomen. Cut a fairly steep point on one end and tie it on top of the shank by this point. The strip should lie central, and flat. Let the bobbin holder hang.

Fig 10
Now for the legs. Take up your chosen feather. Clean up the shaft by stripping off lower barbs. Using fine-pointed scissors, snip off a section at the centre quill containing one, two, three or more pairs of barbs, the number depending on the size of the nymph.

Fig 11
Each leg clump should angle down and back at about 45°, straddling the abdomen.

Fig 12
This shows how it should appear when viewed from the front.

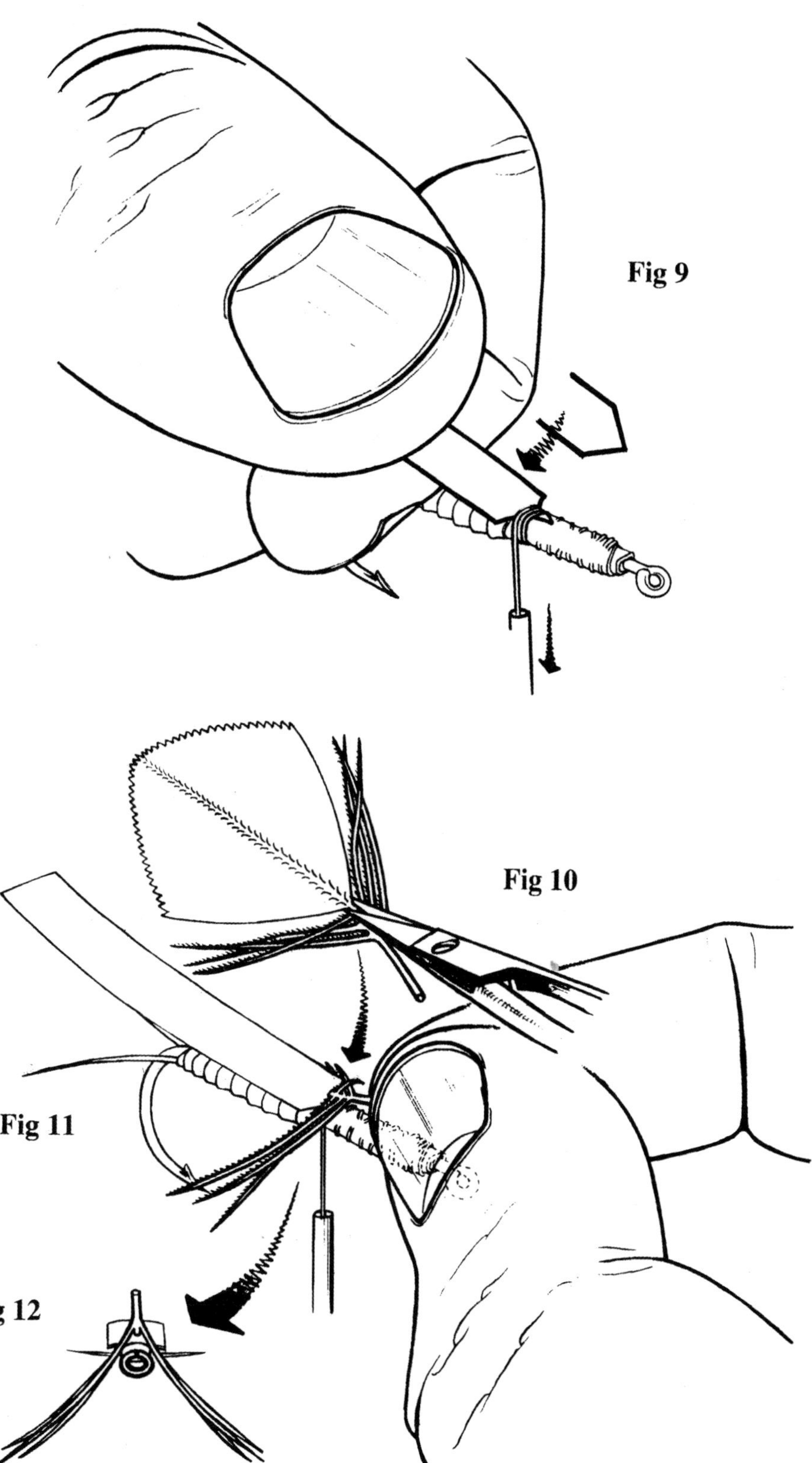

Fig 13
Grip the two leg clumps to the side of the abdomen and secure with several 'pinch and loops'.

Fig 14
Manoeuvre each leg clump so that they are tidy and distinct - then secure with a few more tight thread wraps. Snip off waste. Let bobbin holder hang.

Fig 15
Spin on a small amount of dubbing (colour to match underside of abdomen) and wrap on, progressing towards the eye, covering about one quarter of the thorax. Let the bobbin holder hang.

Fig 16
Make the first wing bud now - the hind one. Press the Flexibody against the top of the abdomen with the dubbing needle. The fold line should be level with the last abdomen segment edge.

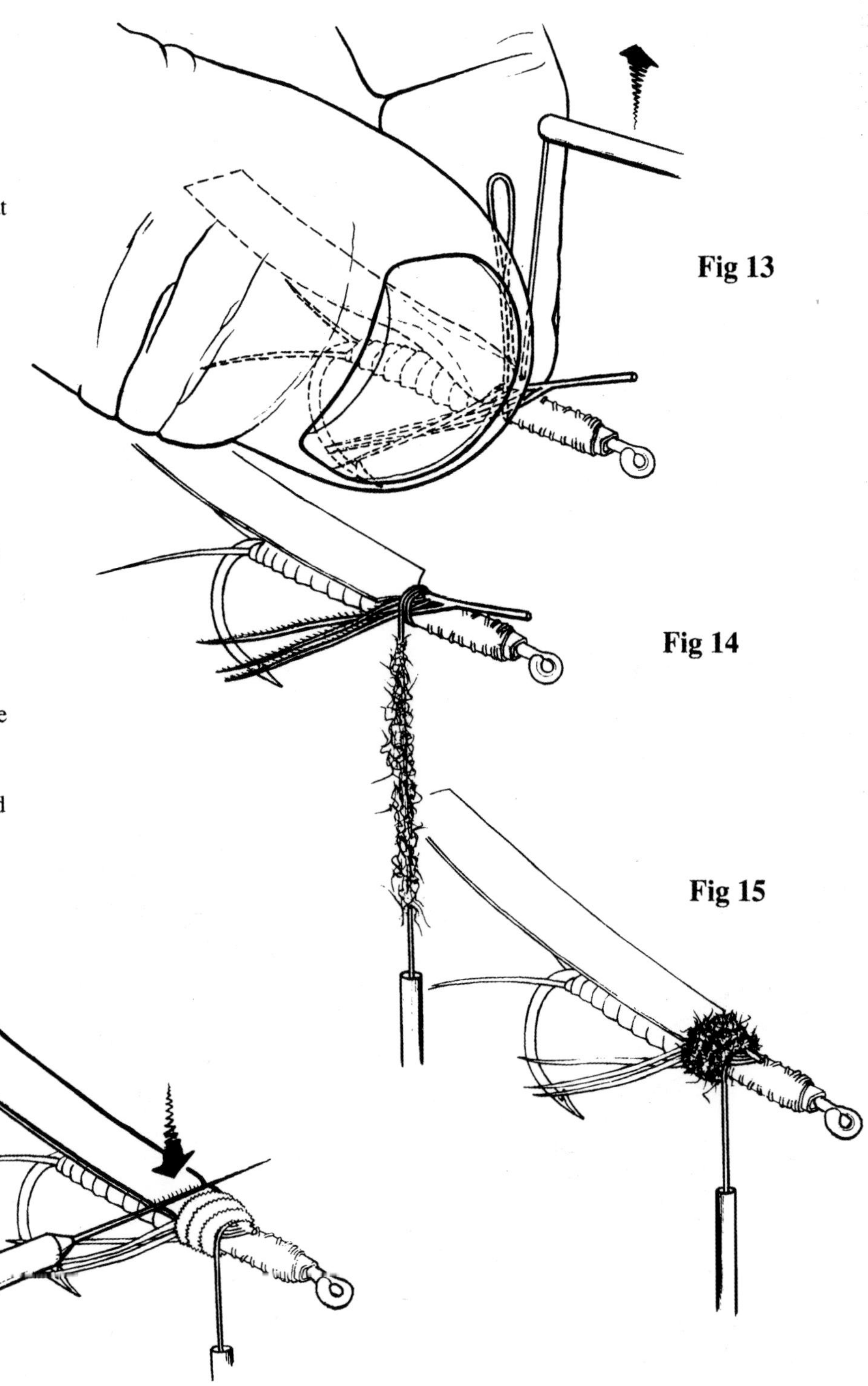

Fig 13

Fig 14

Fig 15

Fig 16

Fig 17
Maintaining pressure on the needle, fold over the Flexibody and hold in position against thorax with finger and thumb.

Fig 18
With the index finger of the other hand, press down hard on top of the wing bud, release the finger and thumb grip on the other hand and slide out the dubbing needle. While holding in this position, make several tight wraps of thread binding it down very securely. There, that's the hind wing bud done.

Fig 19
With tension still maintained on the thread, fold back the Flexibody and make two tight turns of thread over it as near to the fold as practicable. If it will flip over and stay put, omit the turns of the thread.

Fig 20
Now it's simply a question of making the second pair of legs as before.

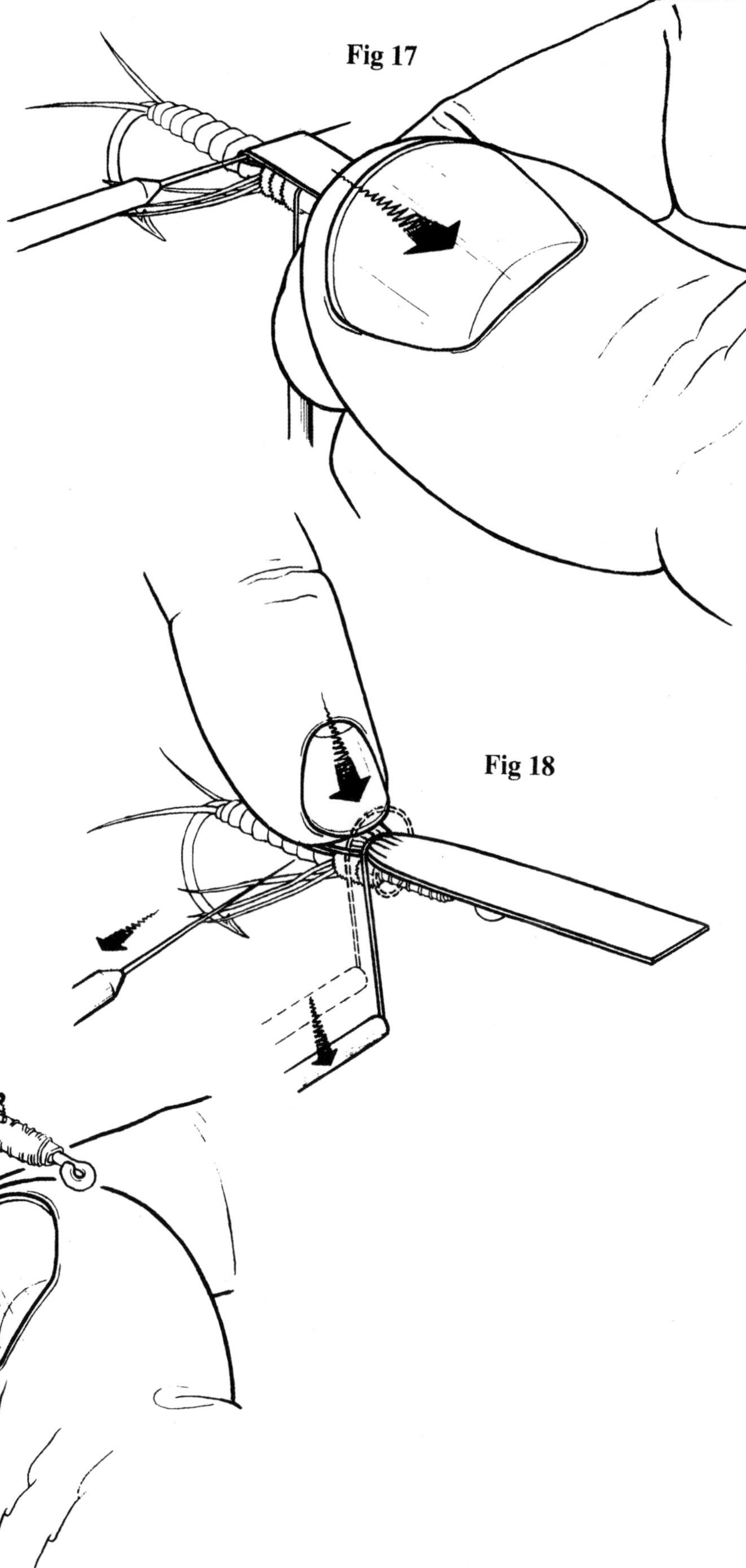

Fig 21
Secure the legs with a couple of turns of thread, then make another short spindle of dubbing.

Fig 22
Dub forward another one quarter distance. Let the bobbin holder hang. Press Flexibody down with the dubbing needle.

Fig 23
Once again, fold Flexibody over.

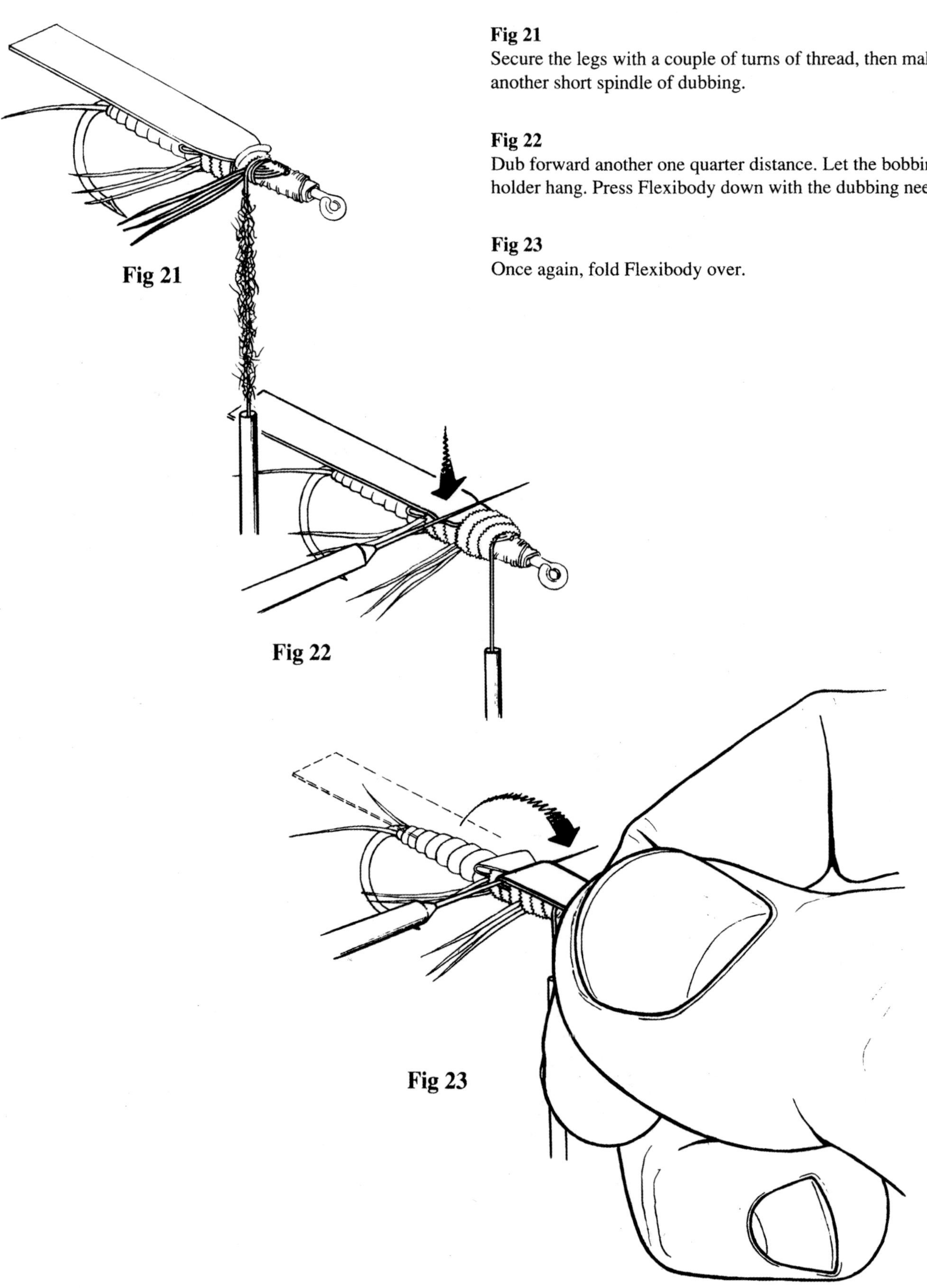

Fig 21

Fig 22

Fig 23

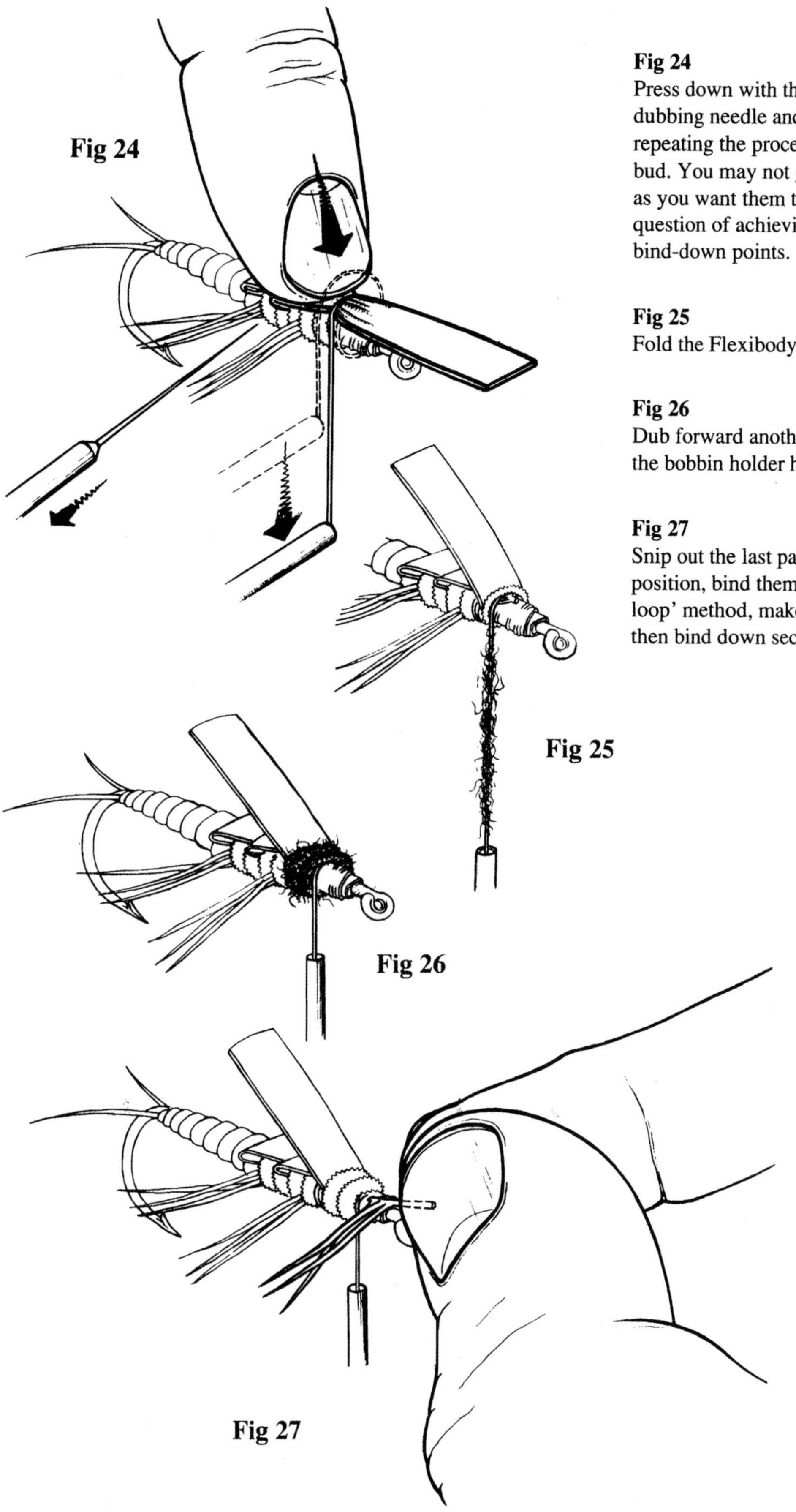

Fig 24
Press down with the index finger, slide out the dubbing needle and bind down. You are simply repeating the process for making the hind wing bud. You may not get the two wing buds exactly as you want them the first few times, it's a question of achieving the correct spacing of the bind-down points.

Fig 25
Fold the Flexibody strip back again.

Fig 26
Dub forward another one quarter distance. Let the bobbin holder hang.

Fig 27
Snip out the last pair of legs, offer them in position, bind them down with the 'pinch and loop' method, make any necessary adjustments, then bind down securely. Snip off any waste.

Fig 28
Pull over the Flexibody strip and bind down securely. This segment is called the pronotum and is a very distinct feature on the natural; as is the wide, pale-coloured band which separates the front wing bud from the pronotum and the pronotum from the head.

Fig 29
Take hold of the Flexibody strip and stretch it, at the same time binding it down very securely, working the thread towards the back of the hook eye. On reaching the eye, make several tight bindings in the same position.

Fig 30
Once again, spin on another small amount of dubbing and make two or three wraps, working back towards the pronotum. Let the bobbin holder hang.

Fig 31
The final components to go in now are the two antennae. Choose two stout, tapering hairs and position on either side of the head. The fine tips should extend beyond the eye the same length as the tails. Secure using several 'pinch and loops'. Snip off waste.

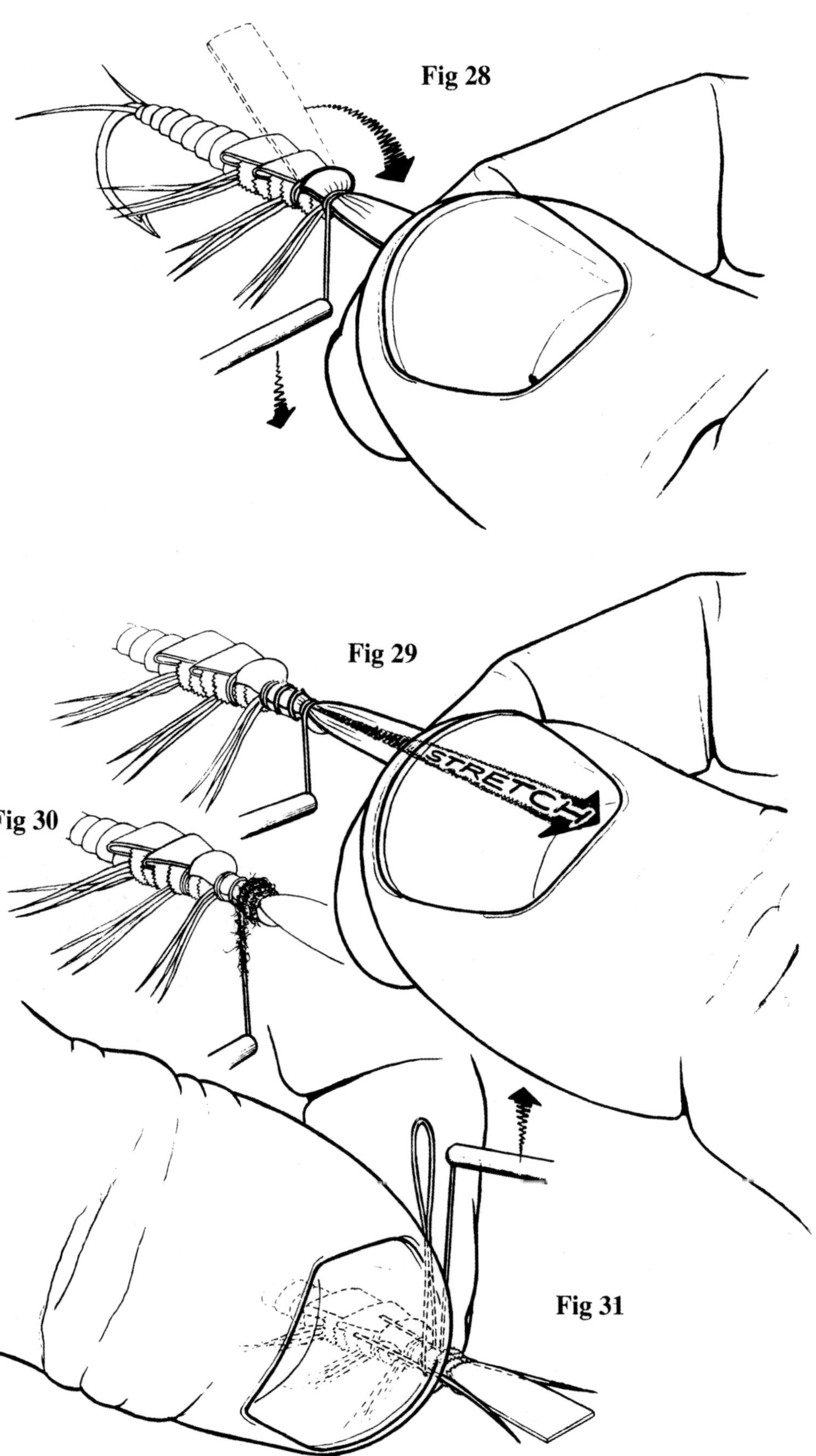

Fig 32
Make sure that each antenna is still on the side of the head. Spin on another small amount of dubbing and cover the remaining head area, working back towards the pronotum. Let the bobbin holder hang.

Fig 33
Finally, pull over the remaining tag of Flexibody and bind down securely just in front of the pronotum. Make the thread wraps distinct.

Fig 34
Trim off the waste Flexibody and the tying thread. Touch the thread wraps at both sides of the pronotum with head cement. You've just made your first Large Stonefly Nymph.

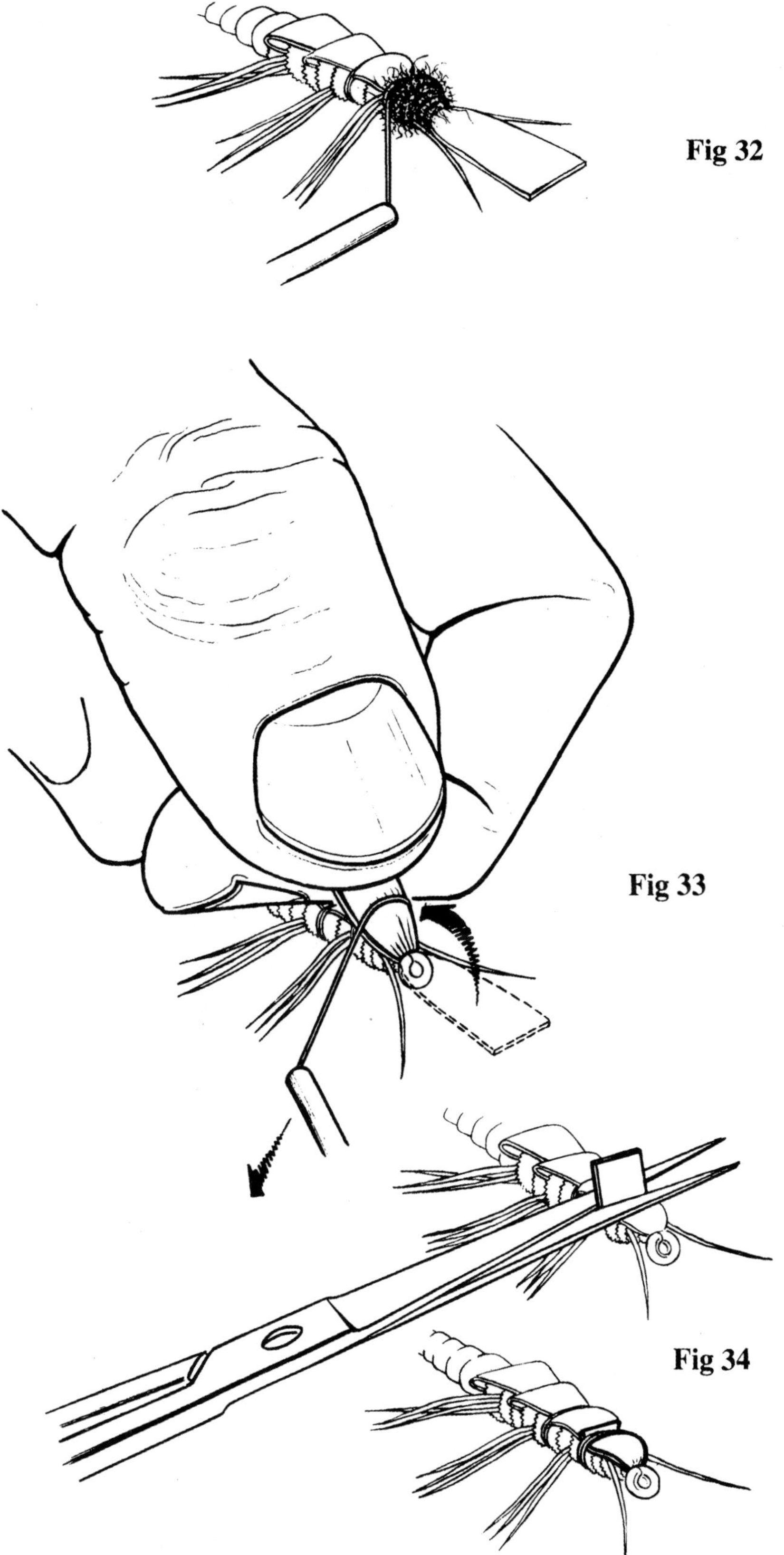
Fig 32

Fig 33

Fig 34

Figs 35 & 36
If you decide to heat kink the legs and treat them with flexible cement, you will be immediately struck by the realism.

Fig 37
These Stonefly Nymphs are excellent fish foolers and are tough enough even for the mighty Madison.

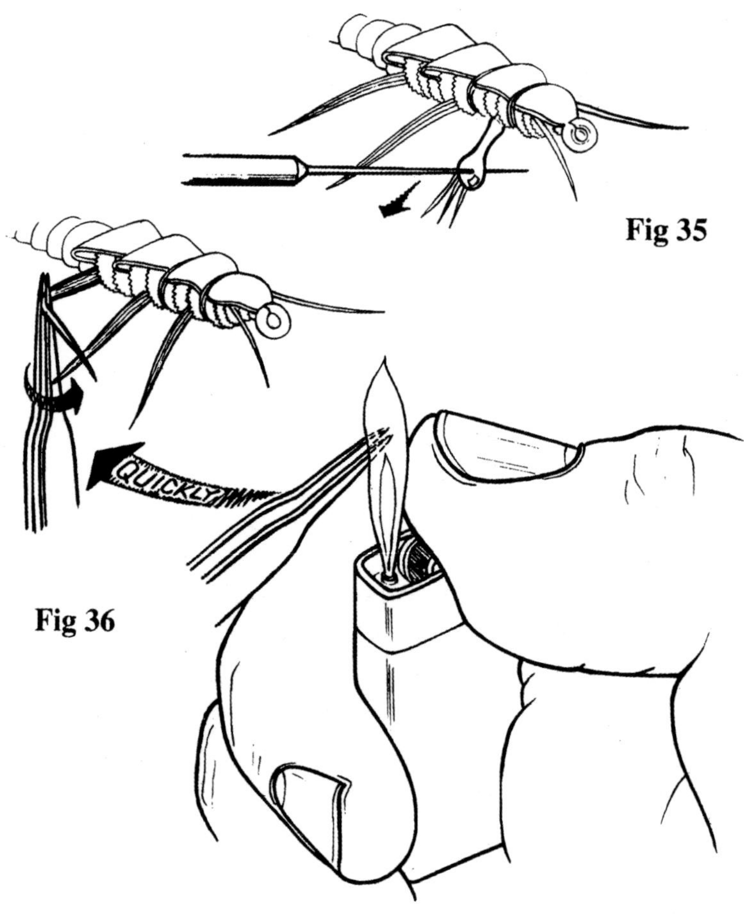

Fig 35

Fig 36

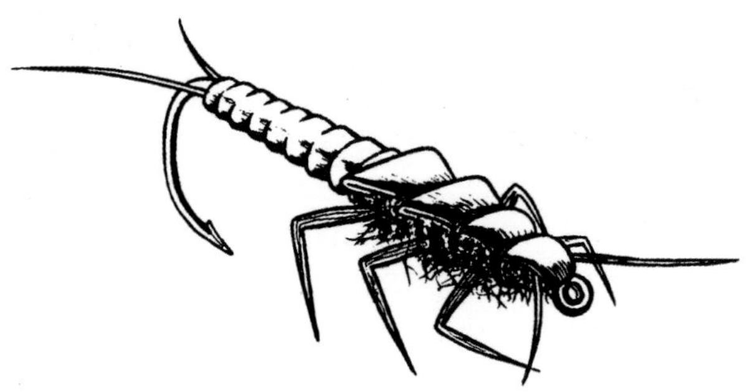

Fig 37

18. The Large Drowning Bibio

The hawthorn fly (*Bibio marci*) is one of those instantly recognisable flies, particularly so when in flight, facing the breeze with long hind legs trailing out beyond its abdomen. It is difficult to state with any accuracy when it will appear and the old rule, that it first appears on St. Mark's day (25 April), can only be a generalisation. I usually reckon that they are about in large numbers only when the grannom have finished, which is about the end of April.

The fly itself could never be regarded as having a prime place in the flyfisher's calendar since its season is so short - sometimes only a few days. However, it fills a useful niche since we are usually 'between hatches' when it arrives.

Little has been researched about this very handsome Diptera. Its life cycle and larval habitat are little understood and, as it is known *not* to have an aquatic larval stage, this seems to be a good enough reason why we, as flyfishers, should delve no further. Rotting vegetation is said to be the habitat of the larva but it is highly likely that damp soil near ponds, streams and rivers are breeding sites.

Hawthorn trees and bushes are important, probably, to its well-being, as it seems that the adults take nourishment from the hawthorn's blossom, either nectar or pollen. Many times I have observed the insect, head down, either fully in the cup of the pungent scented 'May' blossom or with its front half over the edge of it. So, if you have a local water which has a good covering of hawthorns on the windward side, you are well blessed.

Why so many hawthorn flies end their days on the river's surface as trout food is beyond me, as they seem to be quite capable fliers. Only when alighted do they seem clumsy. Whatever the reason - wind, confusion, fatigue - many find their way on to the river surface.

If the lifestyle of the hawthorn fly is rather vague, then that of the heather fly (*Bibio pomonae*) is positively obscure. Indeed my immediate library can shed no light at all on the 'Bloody Doctor', as it is known in Scotland, where its stronghold is said to be.

Nevertheless, we do have the heather fly here in Yorkshire. I have definitely identified them, bright red femurs and all. I've also seen some good trout taking them.

It was mid August and I had been invited for a day on a delightful sheet of water, Gowthwaite reservoir, by my regular fishing partner Bernard Benson. A kind of 'heat fog' swirled around the bowl of the reservoir most of the morning, eventually sparking off a rumble of thunder with an accompanying heavy downpour and lashing wind. By early afternoon the oppressiveness had cleared and it was pleasantly warm and sunny with a good stiff breeze coming off the bank.

Whether this strange, very local thunderstorm had somehow sucked up the insects from the surrounding hillsides and dumped them over the reservoir, or whether they were on some migratory flight I simply don't know. The fact is that the reservoir's surface along our bank was littered with these large red-legged, black terrestrials and the fish were 'tucking their napkins in'.

At first glance, I thought they were 'hawthorns' totally out of season - I had heard of the heather fly but dismissed it as being mainly found in Scotland - then when I lifted out a half-drowned specimen, I nearly whooped with glee - a red leg, a 'Bloody Doctor', the first I had ever seen outside the Highlands!

Notes on Materials and Tying

I suggest you use a fine black thread, say 8/0 gauge. Many material suppliers now stock fine, closed-cell foam in three or four basic colours. Popular brand names which spring to mind are Ethafoam, Polycelon, Styrofoam and Plastazote. However, many good foams are found in modern packaging so keep your eyes peeled and be a magpie!

Z-Lon (pronounced zelon) is relatively new in the UK but is destined to become highly popular. It is a fine-fibred sparkle poly. However, don't panic if you can't get hold of Z-lon because white poly yarn is an excellent alternative.

For the legs choose a feather fibre which is robust and well herled. Try black-dyed barbs from a goose wing quill, dyed turkey quill or even dyed cock pheasant tail (can be weak).

Basically it's a question of experimenting with a likely looking quill feather. Incidentally, dyeing anything jet black is not as easy as it may sound.

Many Hawthorn patterns have the two long trailing legs knotted. However, heat kinking is much quicker and it takes no time to nip round half a dozen finished flies with the hot tweezers. Also, you can judge the position where the joint should be better than you could if you knotted them.

I'm keen on the jointed leg, and in this pattern the legs, hanging down below the surface film, will be visible in the trout's window and I believe they are a first-rate trigger.

As with all my heat kinked legs I dot the joint with flexible superglue or wipe along the entire leg with flexible head cement on a dubbing needle to prevent recovery when wet.

LARGE DROWNING BIBIO DRESSINGS

The Hawthorn Fly:
Hook: Fine wire short shank dry fly hook. Suggest Partridge 'Hooper' 1x short 4x fine dry fly hook code E6A, sizes 14 and 16.
Thread: Danville's Spider Web, tinted black (felt pen).
Cement: Dave's Flexament (USA) or Floo Glue (UK), both thinned.
Abdomen: Black fine closed-cell foam, eg. Ethafoam, Plastazote, Polycelon, Styrofoam.
Thorax and head: As abdomen.
Wing: Z-lon or poly-yarn, white.
Legs: Barbs from a flight quill feather, either natural black or dyed black, eg. goose, turkey or cock pheasant tail (thicker end of barbs).

The Heather Fly
As for Hawthorn Fly above, except for:
Legs: Barbs from a white flight quill feather dyed bright red.

LARGE DROWNING BIBIOS
(Top and bottom) Heather Fly (Bloody Doctor).
(Middle) Hawthorn Fly - note 'set' of legs.

Tying the Large Drowning Bibio

Fig 1
Grip the hook securely in the vice with the shank horizontal. Catch on the tying thread at mid-shank position, then make several thread wraps thus making a short bed of tying thread.
Cut off a 1/2" (12mm) length of black closed-cell foam approximately 1/16" (2mm) square in section and tie this in on top of the shank. The foam piece should be approximately equal about the tying-in point.

Fig 2
Now bind down the foam with two or three widely-spaced turns, working towards the bend.

Fig 3
Fold back the front tag of foam, bind this down, now working forward towards the hook eye, placing the thread in the previously formed 'valleys'.

Fig 4
Trim off the waste tag, then trim the extended abdomen to length, say 3/32" (3mm) past the bend.

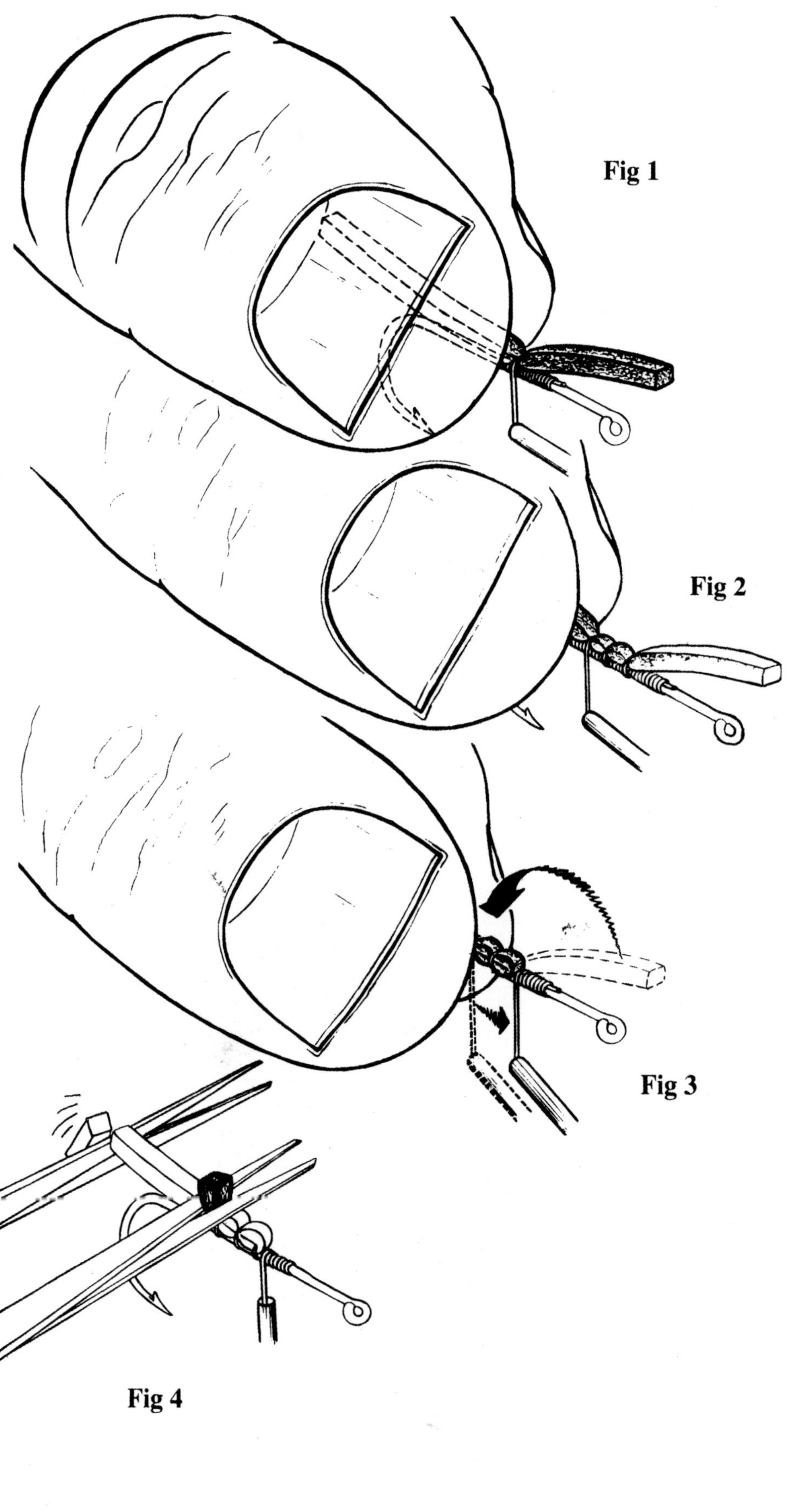

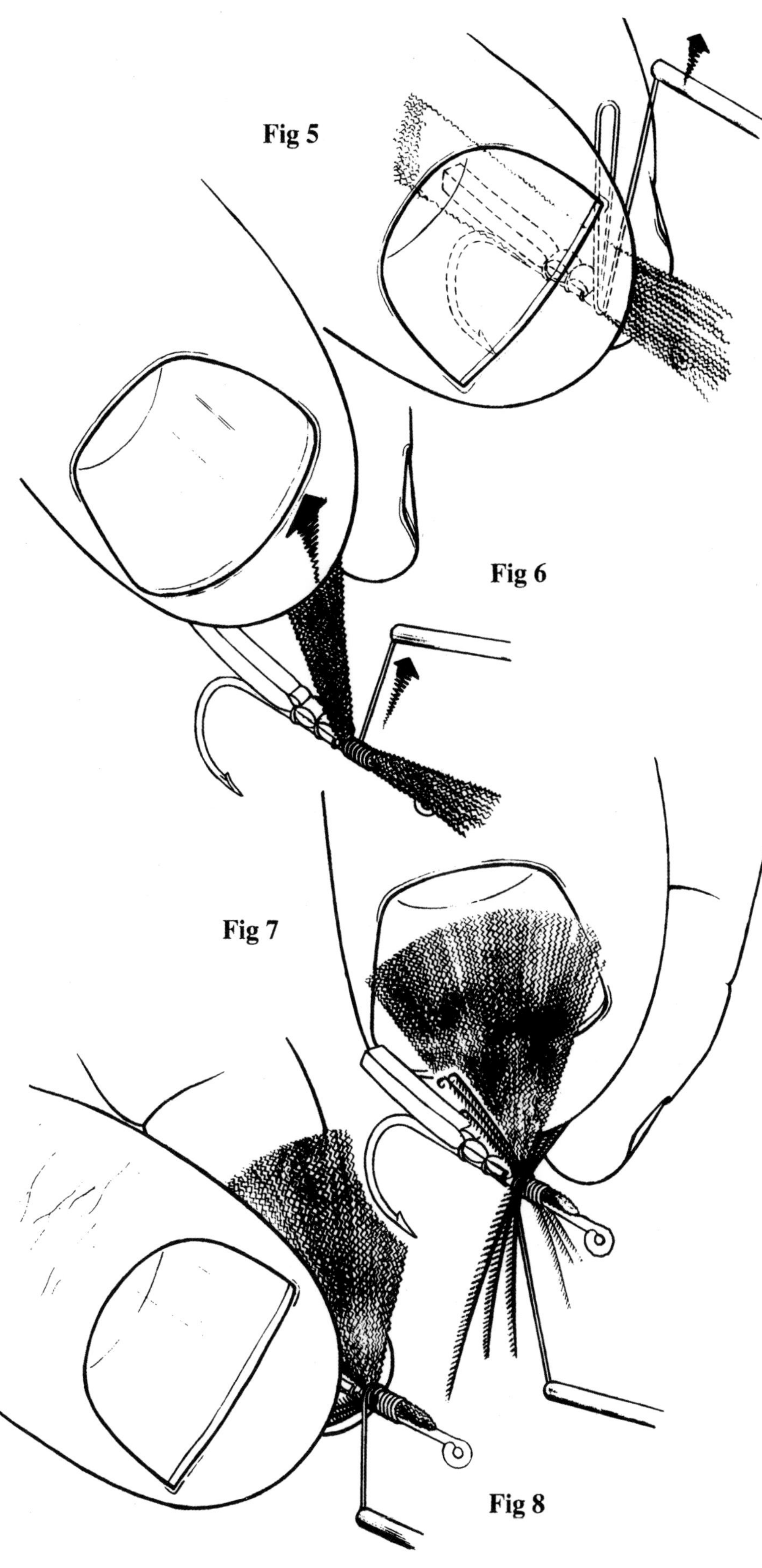

Fig 5
Now take a slim bunch of white poly yarn or Z-lon and tie it in using the 'pinch and loop' method, just clear of the front fold of the abdomen.

Fig 6
Next, holding the tuft wing almost vertical, bind it down very firmly, working towards the first fold of the abdomen. Bind it tightly into the front edge of this fold. This edge will help keep the wing near vertical.

Fig 7
Trim off the waste tag of poly yarn with a sloping cut. Next, tie in the two bunches of black feather barbs which represent the insect's long, hairy legs. Each clump should consist of three good stout barbs with one barb in each clump pulled out longer than the others. Tie each clump separately, one on either side and immediately in front of the wing tuft. Try to arrange each clump so that the long barb is the back one, ie. nearest the hook bend. Trim off the waste butt ends when secure.

Fig 8
Hold both clumps back between finger and thumb at about 45° and bind securely down, working towards the wing tuft.

Fig 9
Advance the thread to the hook eye. Let the bobbin hang.

Fig 10
Cut off a piece of the black foam approximately 3/4" (20mm) long and 1/8" (3mm) square in section. Snip off tiny corners to one front edge of the foam.

Fig 11
Now place the foam on top off the shank with this trimmed front edge slightly overhanging the hook eye, then circle the tying thread around the foam and the hook shank, far enough back to form a nice bulbous head. Pull fairly tight on the thread, the foam will compress, the trimmed corners will disappear and a nice neat head will be formed. Make several thread wraps in this position, but avoid over-tightening the thread or you will slice through the foam.

Fig 12
Having formed the insect's distinctive head, now bind the rest of the foam down with two or three widely-spaced turns of thread, working towards the wing tuft.

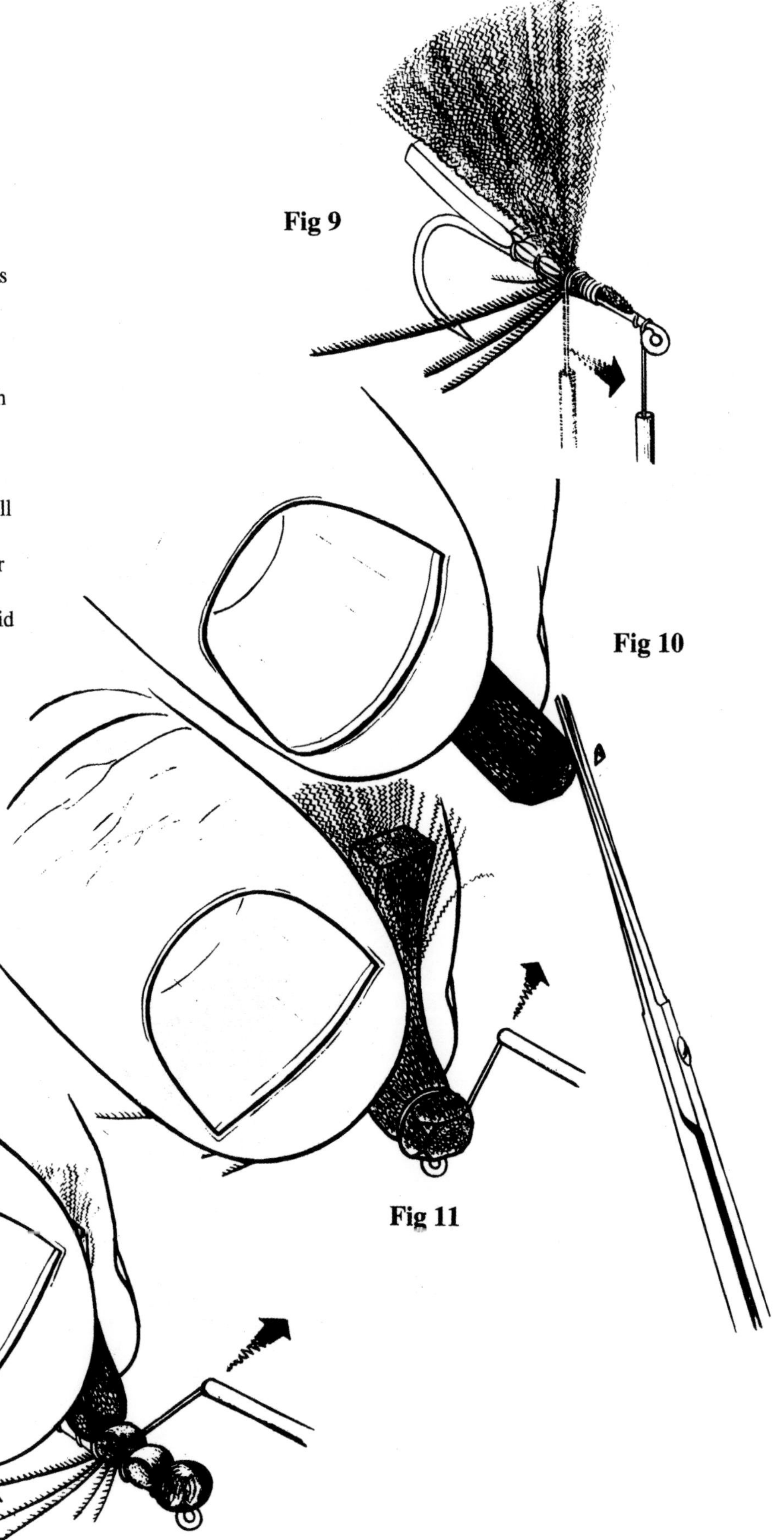

Fig 13
On reaching the wing tuft, make two or three thread wraps on the spot, then pull forward the two shorter legs of each clump, passing the tying thread between them and the two longer trailing legs. Make sufficient thread wraps here to permanently push the two pairs of shorter legs forward. If you are satisfied with the results, simply bring the tying thread forward to a position just behind the head.

Fig 14
Now pull forward the large tag of foam.

Fig 15
Tie down securely with several thread wraps behind the head, gradually increasing the tension with each wrap - avoid high tension on the first wrap.

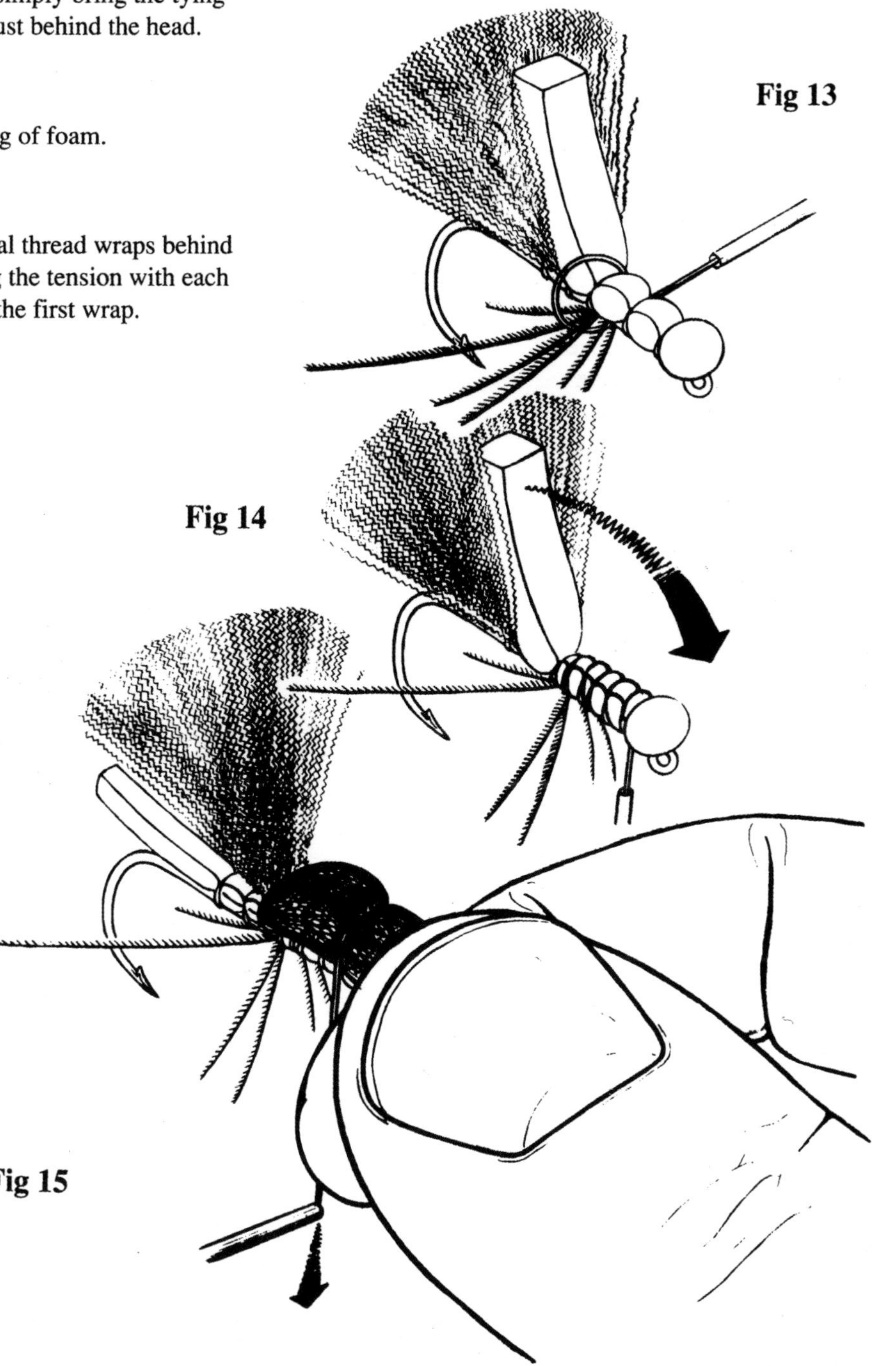

Fig 16
Snip off the waste tag of foam as closely as possible. Then neatly crush down the cut end of foam with the tying thread. Whip finish in the same position - the neck - then neatly trim off the tying thread and touch the thread wraps with head cement.

Fig 17
All that remains now is to heat kink and fix the six legs.

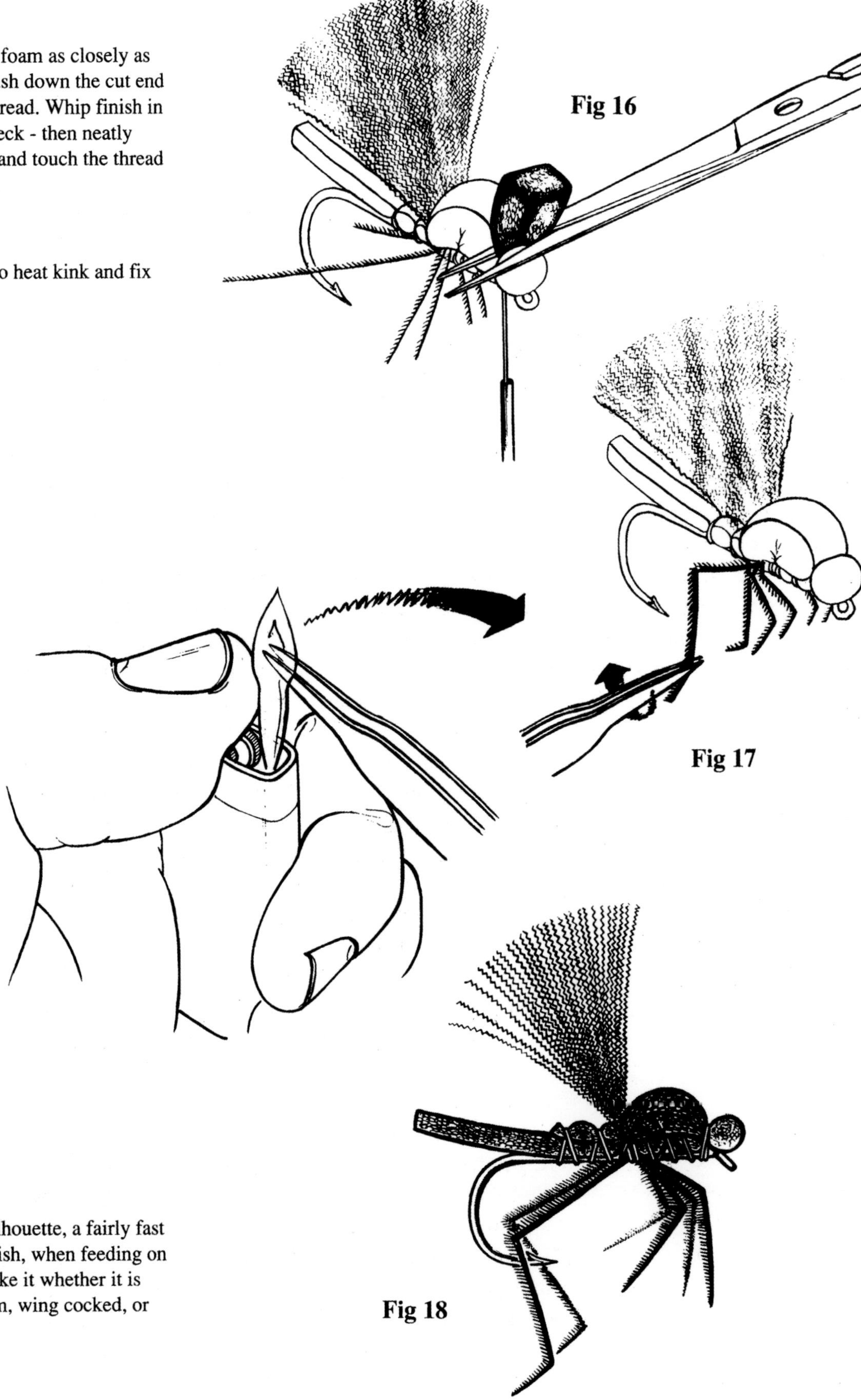

Fig 18
That's it, a very good silhouette, a fairly fast tie and a good floater. Fish, when feeding on the hawthorn fly, will take it whether it is sitting upright in the film, wing cocked, or even lying on its side.

19. The Hair and Foam Beetle

Beetle patterns have never really caught on in the UK, with the exception of the Garden Chafer (*Phyllopertha horticola*), known as the Coch-y-bonddu in Wales, or the Bracken Clock in the north. However, there are times when a small beetle pattern, well-presented, can unlock the door to success on an otherwise fishless day.

Picture the scene. It is early August, the last real rain was on the 5 June which lifted the river by just 1", and since then, hardly a drop. The river is very weedy, and the water, at 65° F, is warm. The weather is hot, bright and still, and you have to be home by 5.30pm.

Prospects of sport are limited, to say the least. Virtually nothing will stir in the shimmering heat and the only stream-born insect you're likely to see will be the odd gaudy damsel. On such a day, I would make a cautious approach to the nearest bankside cover where I would sit, watch and wait. A canopy of overhanging branches and high lush vegetation is a wonderful asset to any trout stream. Such habitats literally team with terrestrial invertebrates of every description, and beetles will be present, often in good numbers.

There are always certain current lanes, under a canopy of overhanging trees, which will become a virtual conveyor-belt of micro goodies. These are the areas to watch. Trout know of such places too, they seem to know that what's on the surface will stay there, so the rises are often slow and languid. In such places, a size 16 bright green Hair and Foam Beetle can be the best bet of the day.

Beetles (Coleoptera) are the largest order of insects on this planet and it is recorded that about 4,000 species occur in Britain alone. Most can fly but a few are flightless. Beetles occupy virtually every habitat imaginable from piles of smelly dung to sweet scented, pollen-laden flowers, rotting tree limbs to corpses of small mammals.

For flyfishers, two groups of beetles are of importance: the leaf beetles and the weevils. Many are small, 3/8" (8mm) to 1/8" (3mm) in length, nearly all have the classic oval outline and some have a patterned upper surface.

As for colour, most of them are a plain shiny black, a drab brown or, of course, green - often a vivid metallic green. Their preferred habitat is also a happy coincidence for flyfishers since many of these leaf beetles prefer trees and vegetation found close by streams and rivers. In fact, all rich rank vegetation will provide a suitable habitat. One species of green weevil, for instance, is often to be seen on stinging nettles.

Apart from beetles, there is another group of insects which also fall or hop onto the stream's surface. These are the Hemiptera. However, it is species from two sub-orders of the Hemiptera that we are most likely to find drowning in the stream's surface.

The first of these sub-orders is the Heteroptera and within this group of insects, the likeliest candidates are the capsid bugs. The common green capsid is one of the very few with an English name as well as a Latin one. The other sub-order is the Homoptera which include common froghoppers, leaf hoppers and plant hoppers. These are all quite small and manifest themselves by the well-known frothy 'cuckoo spit' made by the froghopper nymph and seen throughout the summer, usually at the leaf axil of vegetation.

Species of both these sub-orders turn up in the autopsies of summer-caught trout and grayling and, while not true beetles, for the purpose of flyfishing they can be classed as such since they display a similar crisp oval outline and six well-defined sturdy legs.

I cannot lay claim to originality for this pattern, I hasten to add. Good looking beetle patterns have been around for years in the States.

SOME NATURALS APPROPRIATE TO THIS PATTERN

Order Coleoptera
Leaf beetles: *Donica vulgaris, Donica sp., Cryptocephalus hypochaeridis, Chrysolina polita , C. menthastri, Gastrophysa viridula, Phyllodecta vitellinae, Luperus longicornis, Galerucella lineola*
Weevils: *Brachytarsus nebulosus, Apion pomonae, Phyllobius pomaceus, Polydrusus sericeus*

Sub-order Heteroptera
Capsid bug *Orthotylus virescens*
Common Green Capsid *Lygocoris pabulinus*

Sub-order Homoptera
Common Froghopper *Philaenus spumarius*

The use of fine closed-cell foam for beetles, ants and many other terrestrials probably first appeared in the fly boxes of anglers in the USA. Certainly the tackle shops of West Yellowstone were well stocked with Foam Beetle patterns when I briefly visited for the Federation of Fly Fishers Conclave in 1991.

This pattern of mine combines two well-tried materials. I simply like to add the black hair over the back. This seems to shape the pattern better, and the view from below - as the fish would see it - looks more authentic. There is a certain crispness to the edges, almost as though you were seeing the edges of the beetle's elytron, the tough shell-like front wings which cover the true hind wings when all beetles are at rest.

This pattern floats well where the drowning naturals are found: *in* the surface, not on the surface. Fish see no reason to be suspicious if the beetle is fished without drag. And my cranked legs? Well, they take about 20 seconds to produce. Look at the beetle before you crank them, then crank them. Now tell me to which one you think the trout will react favourably.

Notes on Materials and Tying

One of the prerequisites when tying this pattern is to ensure that you use strong tying thread, preferably the fine Kevlar types, since, to avoid too much bulk, it is essential to compress the initial bunch of hair very tightly to the hook shank. Further high thread tension is called for when tying off the hair when it is finally pulled over the back and head of the beetle.

As to hook sizes, I have personally found this pattern works best tied small and I would never go larger than a size 14. The foam I use to produce the main profile and, of course, for buoyancy is either Ethafoam or Plastazote. However, any very fine closed-cell foam should work well - experiment! The sheets of foam I have are approximately 1/8" (3mm) thick and, for very small beetles, the strip I cut off is only about 3/32" (2mm) wide. So the strip I tie in is 1/8" (3mm) x 3/32" (2 mm) x approx. 1 1/2" (40 mm) long. It is always tied in with the widest dimension across the shank. Do be careful when tying in and tying off any plastic foams. Too much initial tension and these modern Kevlar type threads will simply slice through the foam.

For the beetles of, say, sizes 14 and 16, fine bucktail seems to be OK for the overback and head. However, for the size 18 and smaller, it is obviously better to use a finer hair such as squirrel tail.

For the beetle's legs, I find nylon brush bristles to be ideal. Kitchen sweeping brushes and small hand brushes from a brush and pan set are preyed upon. Pull a full tuft out - but watch out for the wife! Keep your eyes peeled also when you are

HAIR AND FOAM BEETLES
(Clockwise from top) Soldier Beetle - Weevil - Leaf beetle - Ground Beetle (underside) - note the fluorescent 'sight' spots.

being dragged around the shops, for likely sources of leg material. Keep your eyes peeled for brushes with bristles of bright green, black, mid and gingery brown and both bright and dull red.

One final point. Because this is essentially a wide dressing which is all seated *above* the hook shank, you may find that rotation or hook bend displacement takes place. To help combat this I find that an application of waterproof superglue such as Zap-A-Gap on the hook shank before binding down the clump of hair will help. Once the hair clump is tied in I don't like flooding it with head cement, because on the very small sizes, this can add too much weight into the dressing, and then the tiny amount of foam cannot support the beetle, so it becomes a very slow sinker. Remember also that if you use a white Kevlar thread, as I do, you must finally tint the thread - the underside of the beetle - when you've finished the tying. Here a Pantone pen comes into use yet again.

As I mentioned earlier, this pattern floats in the surface film which, of course, makes it fairly difficult to see and follow in the current. The Americans have found a way around this, so I will pass on their little tip. When you finally pull the bunch of hair over the head and tie it off, tie in a little tuft of white or fluorescent poly yarn. Just a tiny amount - a tuft - renders the pattern highly visible and it is on the upper surface, so the fish cannot be put off by it.

There's another method, much quicker and easier - dab on a little dot of fluorescent T-shirt paint. Fluorescent yellow shows up tremendously in bright sunlight.

HAIR AND FOAM BEETLE DRESSING

Hook: Medium or fine wire standard shank dry fly hook. Suggest Partridge 'Hooper' L/S 4x fine dry fly hook code E1A, sizes 14-22; or Partridge 'Capt. Hamilton' dry fly hook code L3A.
Thread: Fine Kevlar type or Kevlar blend. Any brand (tinted to match foam with felt pen).
Cement: Dave's Flexament (USA) or Floo Gloo (UK).
Abdomen and head: Fine closed-cell foam, eg. Ethafoam, Plastazote, Polycelon, etc. Colour to match that of the beetle you wish to copy.
Over back and head: Fine bucktail or squirrel tail, colour to match foam colour.
Legs: Nylon bristles from household brushes, fine to medium thickness. Colour to match foam.

Tying the Hair and Foam Beetle

Clamp the hook very securely. The shank should be horizontal. Catch on the tying thread just behind the eye and make half a dozen or so tight butting turns. Now snip out a small clump of bucktail or squirrel tail hair. When twisted tight it should be less than a cocktail stick for a size 14 hook. Leave the hair clump as cut, do *not* align the fine tips.

Fig 1
Tie in this clump of hair on top of the shank using the 'pinch and loop' method, making sure that the hair stays on top of the shank. The fine tips should extend beyond the hook eye.

Fig 2
Now very securely bind down the hair clump all the way to the bend where you should make several very tight touching turns. Keep the hair bunch on top of the hook shank.

Fig 3
Then return the thread back to just short of the eye. Note that there should be approximately an equal amount of hair protruding at both ends of the hook.

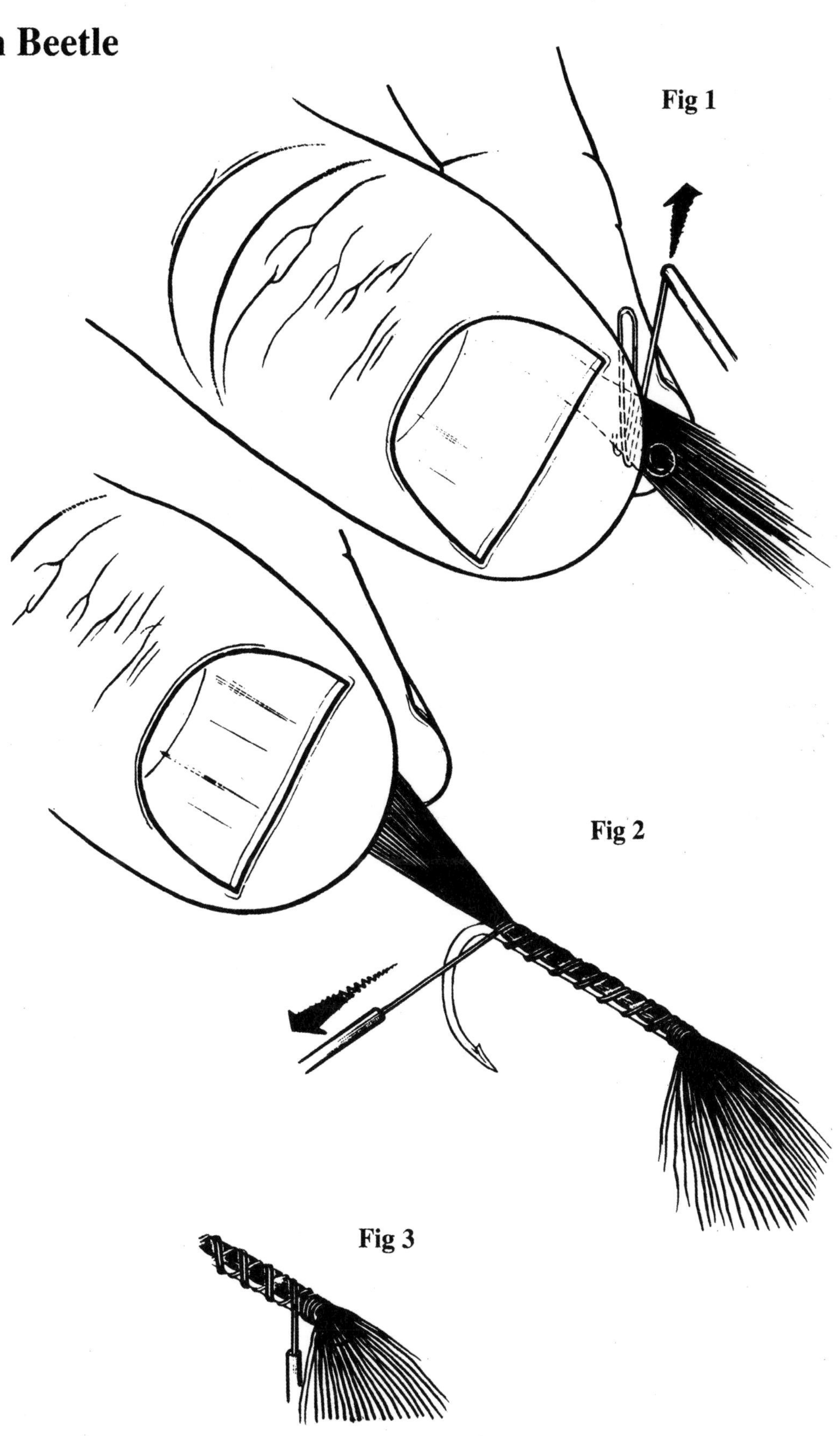

Fig 4
Next, from your piece of closed-cell foam cut a thin parallel strip, the width being governed by the hook's size. Tie in directly on top of the hair, with the front edge just behind the eye, and the rest of it extending out beyond the bend.

Fig 5
Now bind the foam down in open turns to the bend. Then return the tying thread back up the shank a short distance.

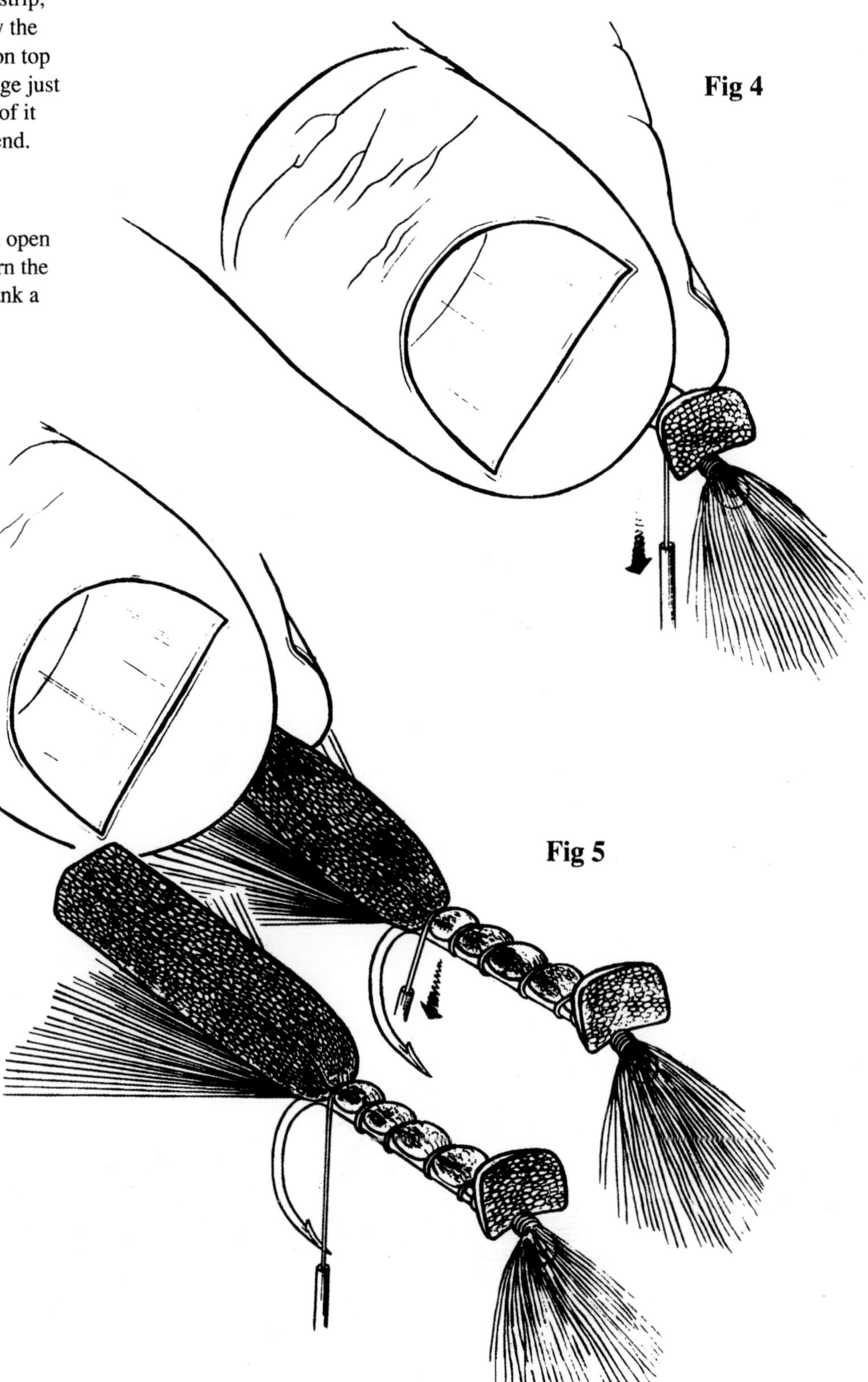

Figs 6 & 7
Tie in three nylon bristles on top of the shank using figure-of-eight bindings, each one at right angles to the shank. Touch each bristle binding with head cement. Crush down the front part of the foam. Let the bobbin holder hang.
All materials are now tied in, so it's just a question of a few finishing manoeuvres.

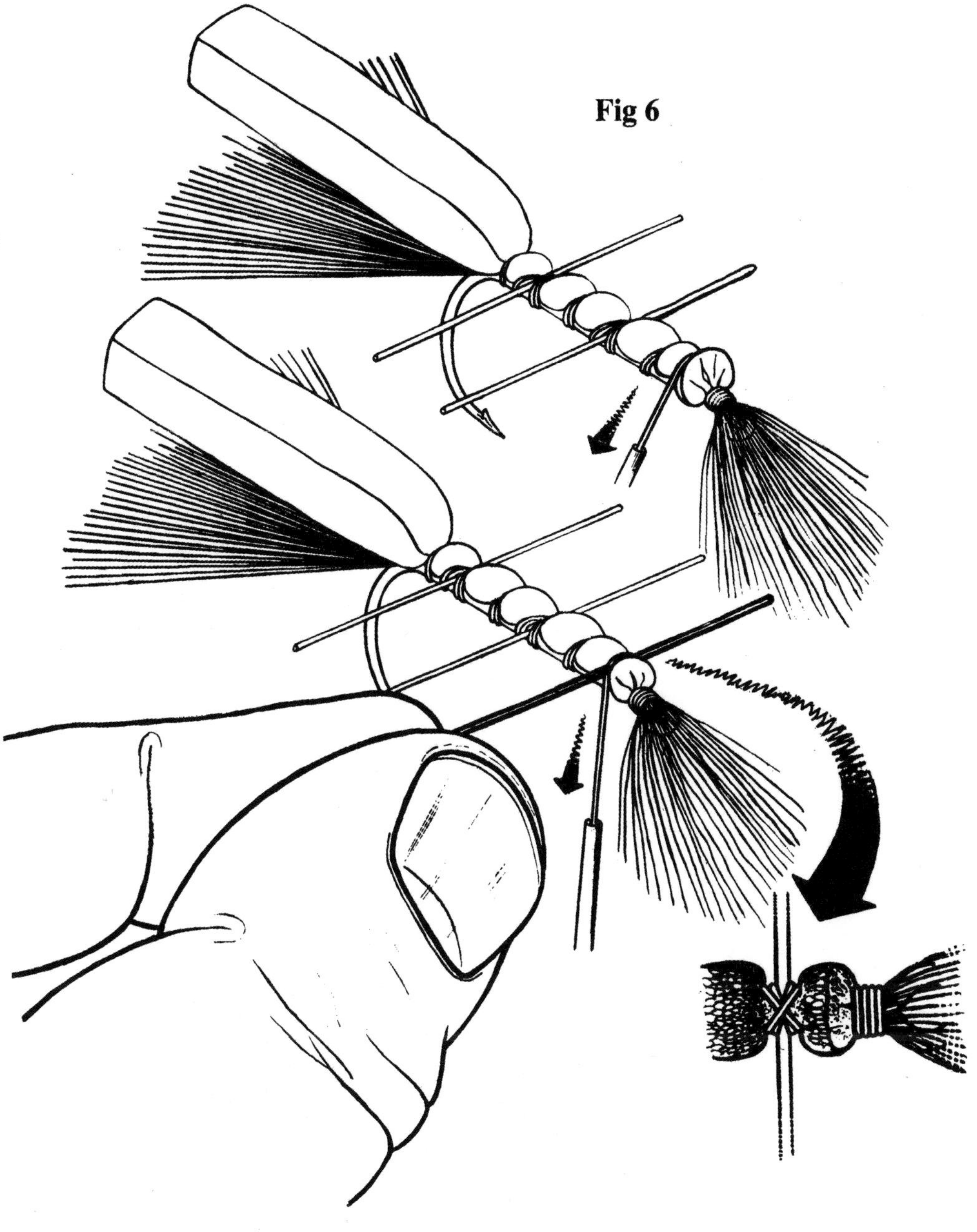

Fig 6

Fig 7

Fig 8
Pull the foam over the hook shank, forming the back of the beetle. Bind it down securely at the position where the bobbin holder is hanging - just slightly forward of the front bristle.

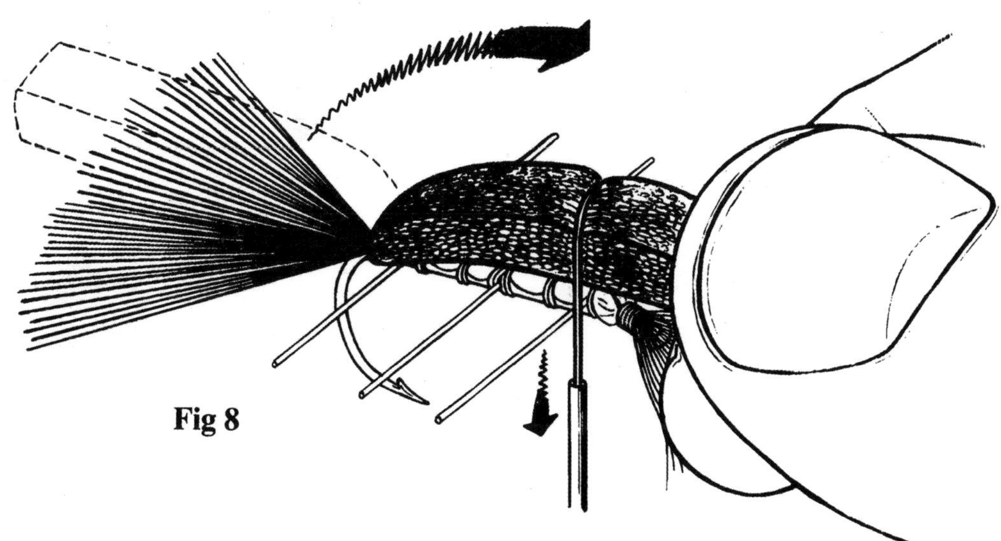

Fig 8

Fig 9
Bind the foam down, working forward to the hook eye, then return the tying thread back to the initial bind-down position, making a very short neck.

Fig 10
Now pull back the tag of foam projecting out beyond the eye and bind it down in this 'neck', thus making the pronotum. The pronotum of most beetles is usually very prominent and quite distinct, the head by comparison is quite small and insignificant.

Fig 11
Snip off the waste.

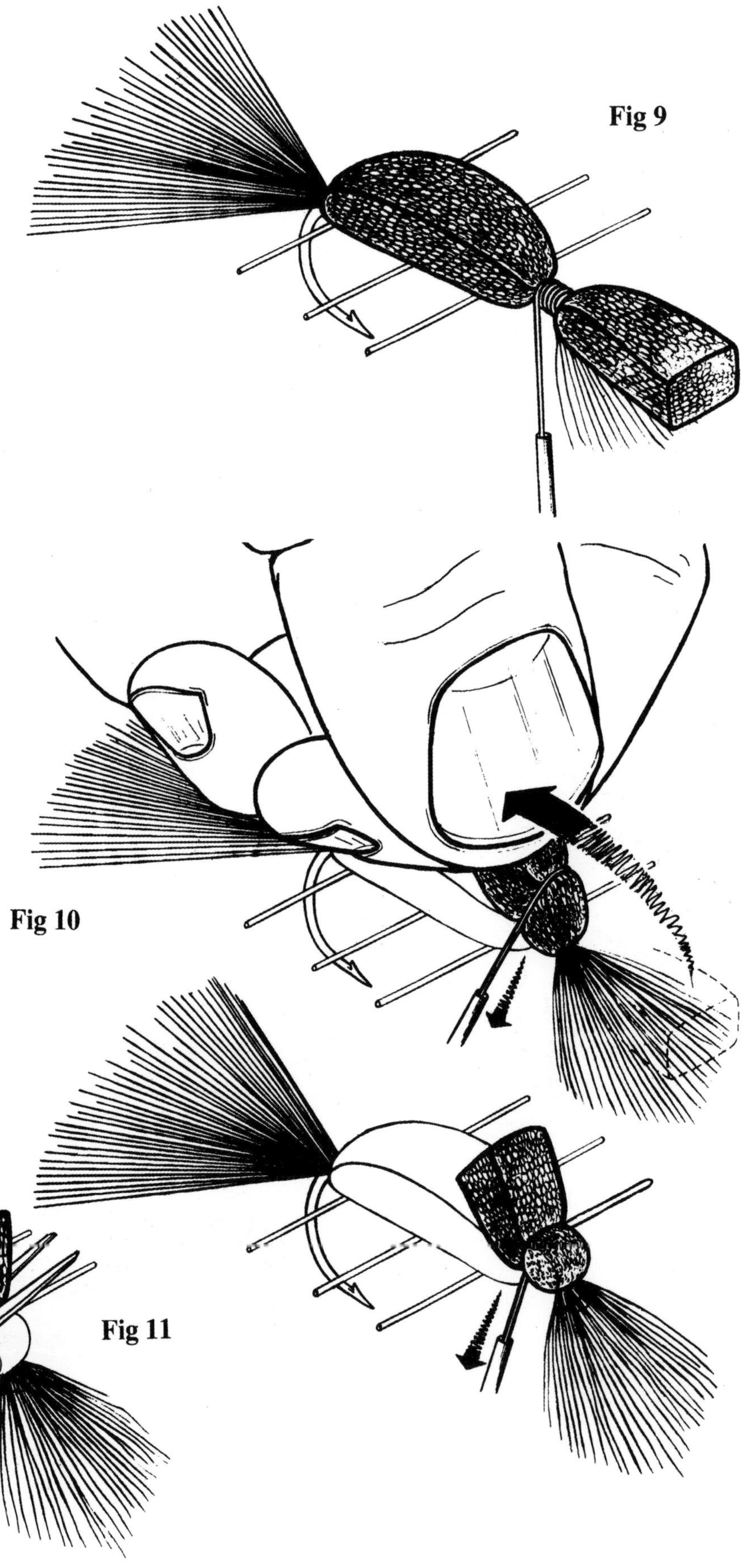

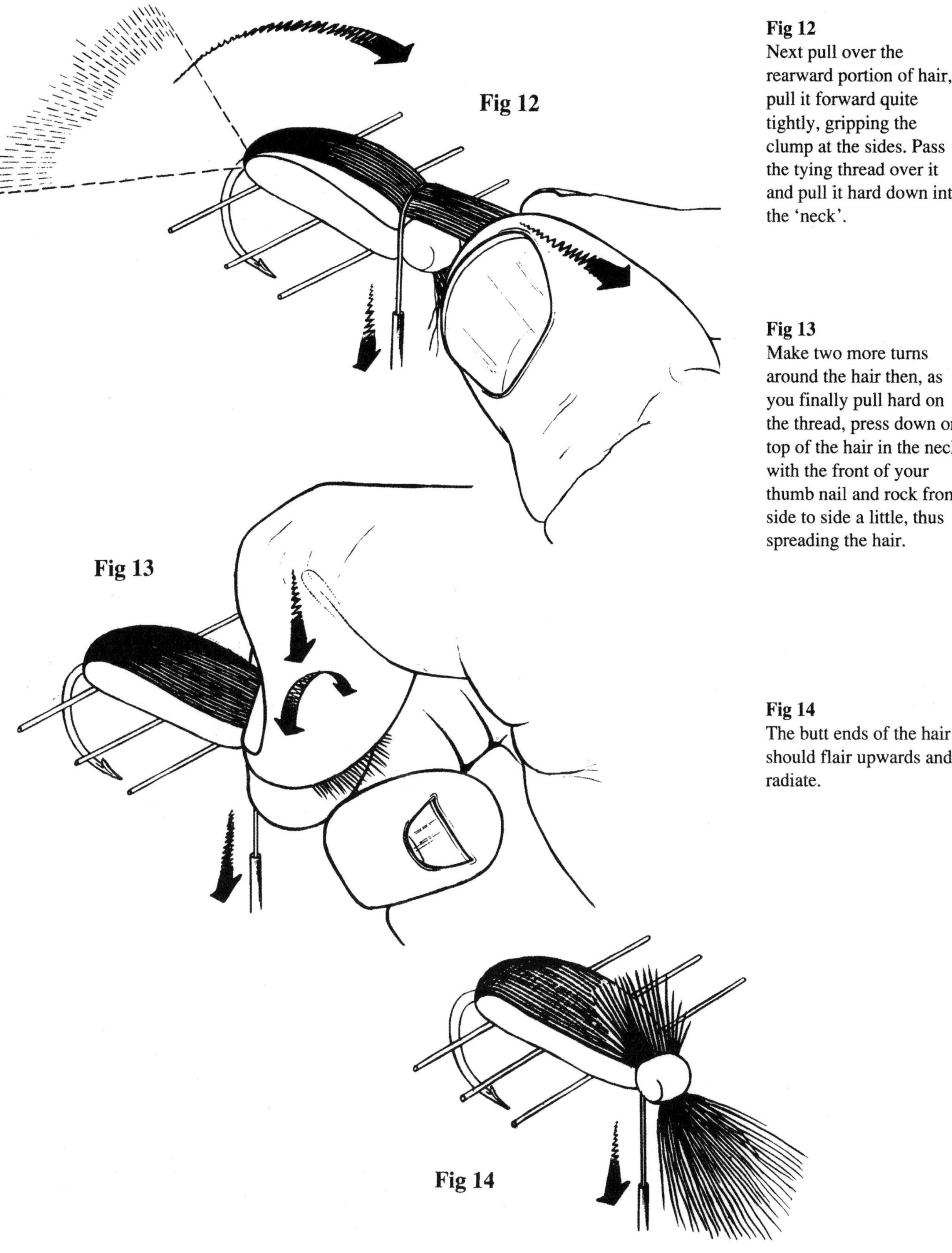

Fig 12
Next pull over the rearward portion of hair, pull it forward quite tightly, gripping the clump at the sides. Pass the tying thread over it and pull it hard down into the 'neck'.

Fig 13
Make two more turns around the hair then, as you finally pull hard on the thread, press down on top of the hair in the neck with the front of your thumb nail and rock from side to side a little, thus spreading the hair.

Fig 14
The butt ends of the hair should flair upwards and radiate.

Fig 15
Neatly trim off the excess hair.

Fig 16
Finally pull back the bunch of hair projecting out beyond the eye.

Fig 17
When doing so, allow some of the fine tips to spring forward.

Fig 18
Bind this bunch down also in the 'neck'. Ensure that you bind the bunch down very securely; the tips should flair vertically again.

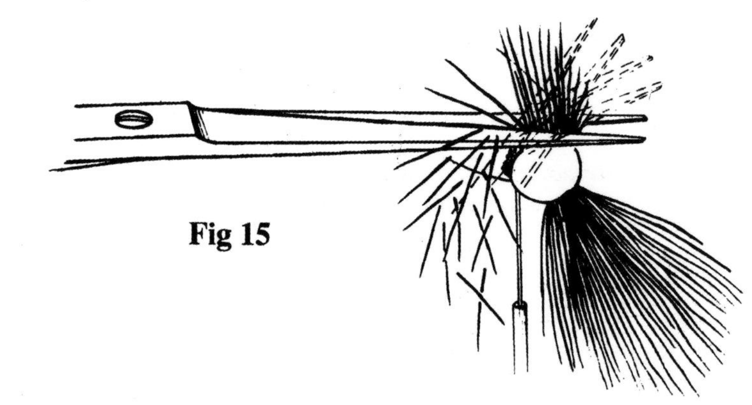

Fig 15

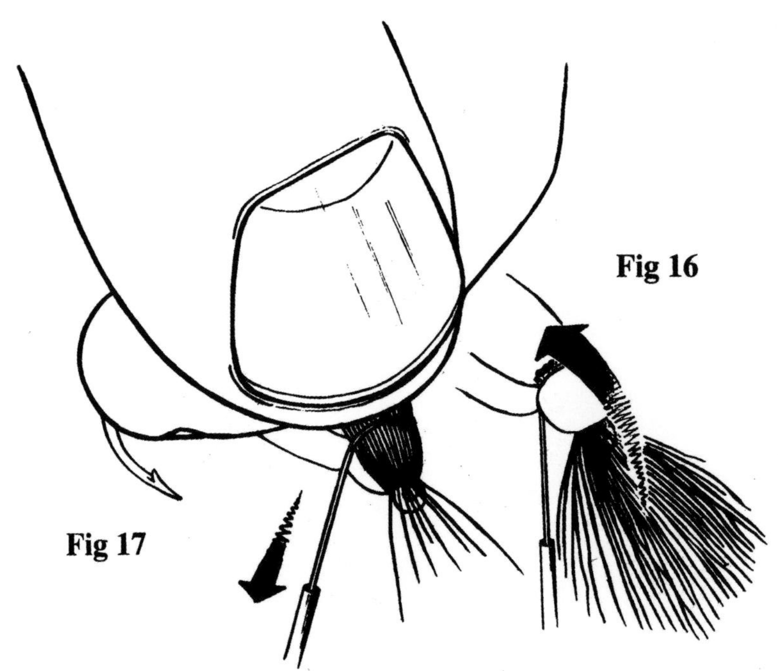

Fig 16

Fig 17

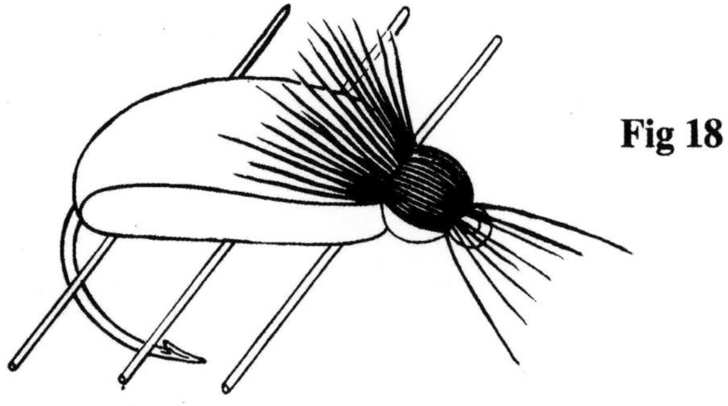

Fig 18

Fig 19
Trim off all the vertical excess tips very neatly. Whip finish in the 'neck' then finally trim off the tying thread. Remember the tip from the American flytyers about tying in a little tuft of fluorescent poly yarn. This tuft should be tied in now before trimming off the tying thread.
Now to put the finishing touches to your beetle...

Fig 20 (optional)
Trim off all those fine hair tips which you allowed to spring forward beyond the eye, leaving just two intact - one on either side - these are the antennae.

Fig 21
Shorten them if you wish.

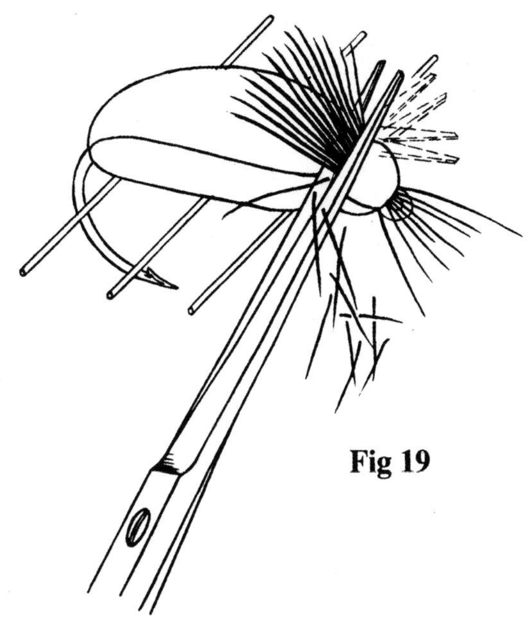

Fig 19

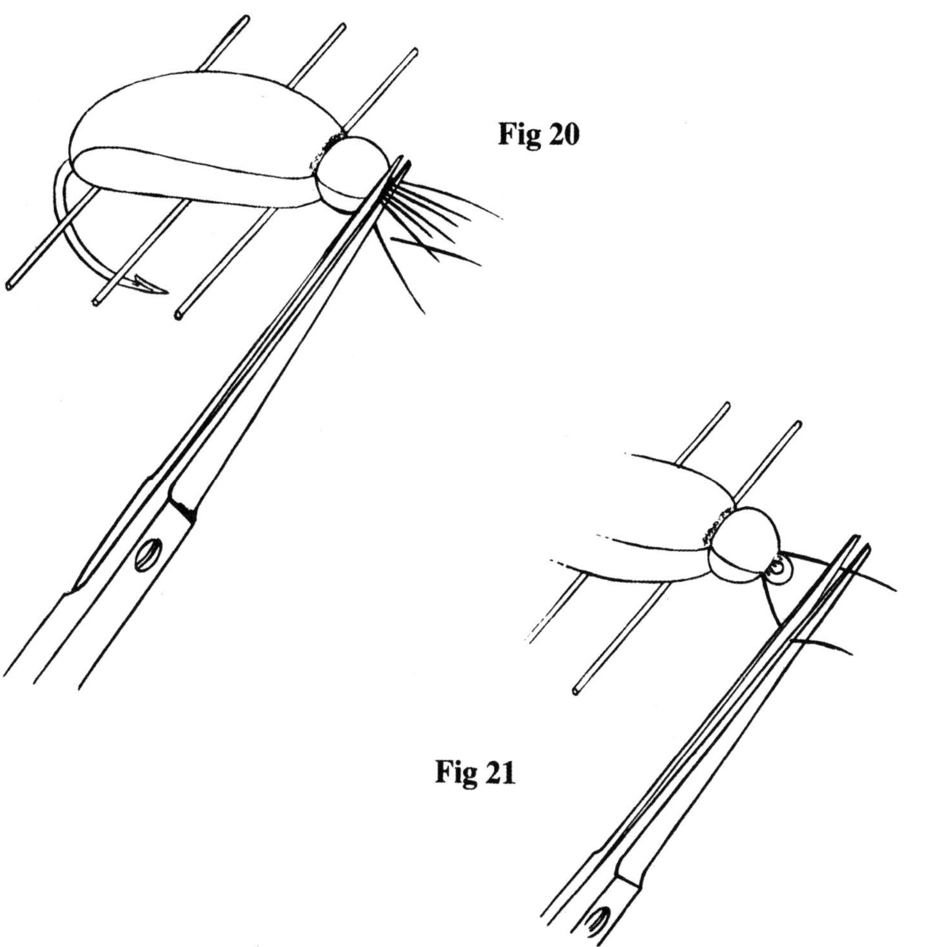

Fig 20

Fig 21

Fig 22
Shorten the leg bristles next.

Fig 23
Then warm the tips of a pair of fine pointed tweezers and, one by one, kink the legs, first pair forward, middle and rear pairs backward.

Fig 24
That's it, not only life-like but also a very effective fish fooler, and a guaranteed floater, which floats in the film where the naturals are found. Great fun to tie.

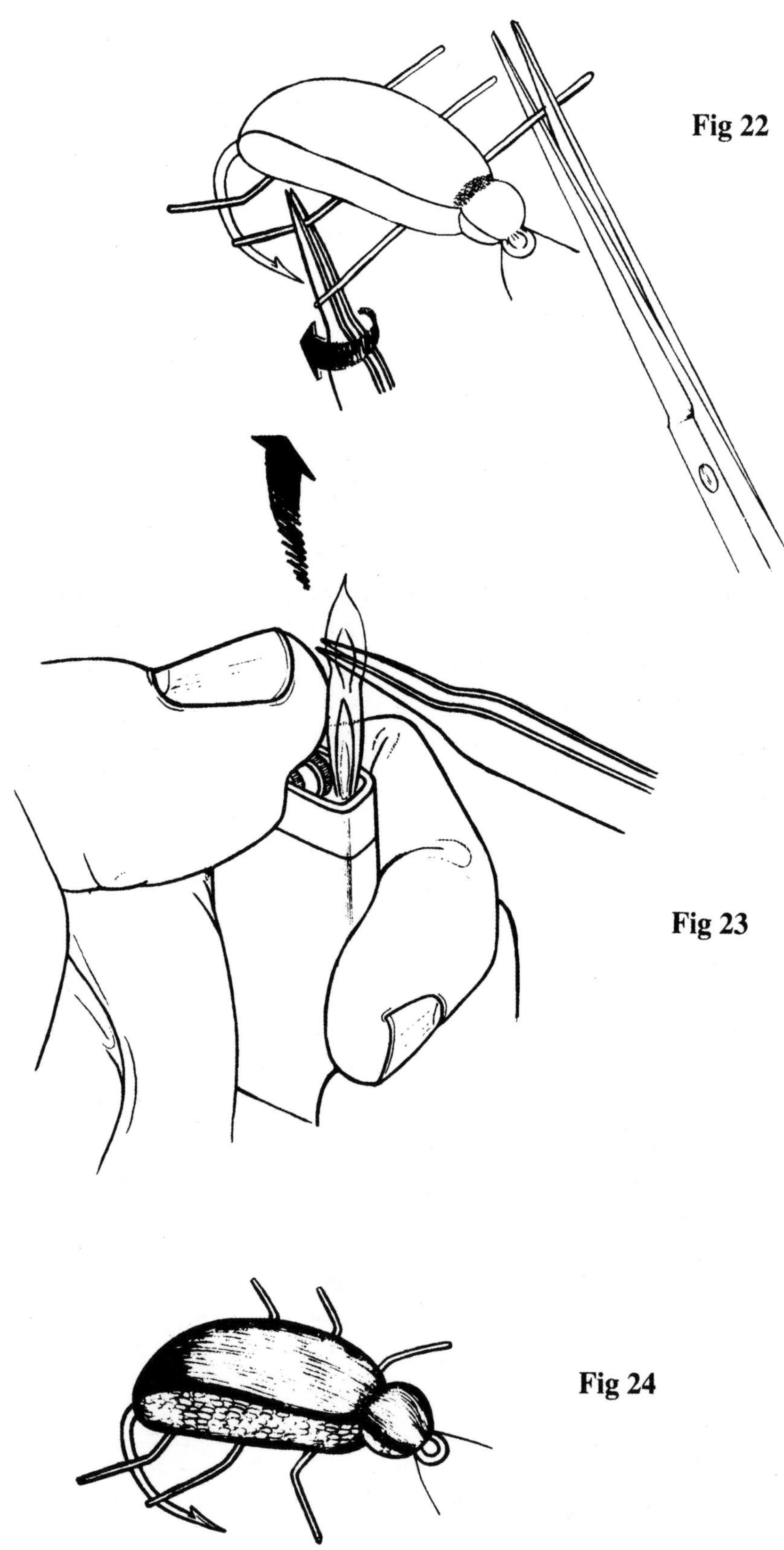

Fig 22

Fig 23

Fig 24

20. The Freshwater Shrimp

The ideal habitat for the freshwater shrimp, *Gammarus pulex*, is watercress, ranunculus and a gliding stretch of water with a pH of around seven.

As a lad in my teens, it became almost an annual custom for me and my friends to visit water like this on the Rye in Yorkshire. These trips always took place between the opening of the trout season (16 March) and the opening of the coarse fish season (1 June). It was a way of getting around the coarse fish close season and we could legitimately trot down our maggots and red worms for trout - or dace or chub - or anything else which swam! I was just as guilty as the rest of those 'trout' fishermen.

Most Sundays, four or five of us would pile into a van of doubtful lineage and dire roadworthiness, to risk the 50-mile journey once more! It was one of those Rye trips which first aroused my interest in the freshwater shrimp.

Like the rest of my fishing mates, I was a very keen coarse fisherman - it was in my family (an uncle fished for Leeds in the 'All England' for many years). However, unlike my mates, I had received the flyfishing 'jab' and its effects were now widespread throughout my body! So, these trips were something of a double pleasure to me since I could have a dabble with the fly rod too. I remember how I would agonise over which tackle to take. My resolve was always strong though, I took both!

The stretch of the Rye which we regularly fished was, unfortunately, known by other trout fishers - too many! Consequently, the brownies were becoming few and far between. At that time, I hadn't caught many trout, and I certainly hadn't broken my duck on the Rye. So the day in question is still vivid in my memory.

I wasn't flyfishing, I was maggoting; happily steering a 7" porcupine quill down the many narrow fingers of clear water in between the ranunculus beds. Small dace and grayling were yanking the 'porky' under almost every swim down. Then, as I tapped the hook home for the umpteenth time, the surface erupted and I was attached to my first Rye brownie, all 10" of it! But that wasn't the end of my good fortune. I caught yet another, further downstream, this one just made the 9" size limit. I had a brace from the Rye! Yes, of course I ate them. I had them for breakfast, that's what trout were for, as far as I was concerned. Remember this was the early 50s.

About that time, what fish ate was also becoming very interesting to me. In fact, any fish I took home, which included the occasional jack pike, eel, flounder and perch, was eagerly opened up to find out what had been its 'last supper'.

I could hardly wait to find out what my prize brace had been feeding on. The first one I caught, the ten incher, was a big disappointment - full of maggots, some still wriggling, would you believe. However, the 9" trout was a revelation. Its stomach was chock full of pale olive-grey shrimps, dozens and dozens, a solid-packed sausage as big as a boy's thumb. I soon had them in a clean dish, and poked about amongst them for hours. I was transfixed.

At that time, my flytying was very much in the embryonic stage. I didn't have any books to refer to, nor did I know of anyone who tied flies. I did, though, have a vice of sorts, an Eclipse toolmakers pin vice. I had made one or two attempts at tying a simple fly, having discovered how a hackle was wound on by dismantling a shop-bought fly. But trying to complete a fly to the stage where it looked remotely like a professionally tied one was a lengthy and frustrating exercise and I thirsted for more knowledge and skill.

There were few authorities on the subject. It was a secret society, or so it seemed, and I was on my own. I had heard of a chap at Scarborough called Eric Horsfall Turner, who tied flies, and there was that mythical character Bernard Venables who had a friend called Mr Cherry, and that seemed to be it. Dick Walker was busy catching big carp and Bob Church was probably mucking about in the Fen drains after bream!

That's how it was, about 40 years ago. Looking back now, my first Freshwater Shrimp pattern must have been a pretty awful representation, and the learning curve stretched out in front of me. The pattern developed slowly. Inevitably, however, there came a time when I was happy with it, and, more importantly, catching with it. In the intervening years, there have been long pauses when it has remained untouched.

Now the pattern has reached the stage where I no longer wish to 'improve' it any further, and, in this latest guise, I rank it as one of my all-time lethal patterns. For not only will it pick off almost a whole shoal of grayling, it will also take grayling which have been 'Sawyer bugged' to the point of 'refusal sulk' and many's the time I have seen a trout whip around and charge off downstream to grab it.

I must stress heavily, though, that one has to use it on shrimp-rich rivers, typically limestone streams and chalkstreams - in Europe or the USA. In Sawyer's river, the Wiltshire Avon, the trout and grayling are easy, almost suicidal for this pattern and it has been quite common for me to catch between 30 and 50 grayling, plus 'mistake' trout on it during an afternoon's fishing in October!

For many years, I was under the impression that there was only one UK species of the freshwater shrimp. However, some quick research revealed that we have at least five species.

Gammarus pulex is by far the most common and widespread in England. *G. lacustris* is frequently encountered in Scotland, while *G. duebeni* takes over as the common species in Ireland. The fourth species is striped, aptly named *G. tigrinus*, and is now a naturalized alien from North America! I have certainly never seen one nor have I ever heard it mentioned in angling circles. Nevertheless, it is reported to be fairly common in some parts of the UK.

Distribution of the first three species is not clearly defined and some overlapping occurs. There is also another freshwater shrimp, the fifth, which is not a member of the genus Gammarus. This is another North American alien and its latin name is rather a mouthful, *Crangonyx pseudogracilis*! Again, it is reputed to be well established here in the UK, so it is only right to mention it. Apparently, it is very similar to the Gammarids but has the distinction of being more transparent and having a blueish hue.

Gammarids are quite fussy regarding their habitat. They will thrive in rich, hard alkaline water. It must have sufficient dissolved salts of calcium carbonate to help produce the shrimps' new hard shell every time it moults. A pH of 6.5 is about the lowest they will tolerate but on the whole this is too acid for them to thrive, multiply and make good-sized colonies. An exception is *G. duebeni*, which is known to thrive in brackish water!

I have found Britain's commonest shrimp, *G. pulex*, to be quite choosy about the plants it lives amongst. They have a great fondness for those which grow in dense mats, and if they have thick fleshy stems and intertwining exposed white roots, so much the better. Ranunculus and watercress both have this growth characteristic. Watercress in particular seems to be very attractive to *G. pulex*. Pull out a handful and it often fairly rattles with them. In fact, freshwater shrimps are often called 'cress bugs' in North America.

You will not find many shrimps in fast rough water. Instead, you should look for them in the quieter areas: weedbeds at the edges of main currents, small bays, back eddies, slow flats and quiet pools - in fact any area where silt can collect

FRESHWATER SHRIMPS

(Top and middle) Two Grey Shrimps, one showing the leg detail on the underside.
(Bottom) Shrimp in the orange phase (mating?).

SOME NATURALS APPROPRIATE TO THIS PATTERN

GENERA: Gammarus, Eucrangonyx
BRITISH SPECIES:
Gammarus pulex, G. lacustris, G. duebeni, Eucrangonyx pseudogracilis
BRITISH FISHING NAMES: Freshwater shrimp, Shrimp

NORTH AMERICAN SPECIES:
Gammarus fasciatus, G. limnaeus, G. minus, Eucrangonyx pseudogracilis
NORTH AMERICAN FISHING NAMES:
Freshwater shrimp, Scud, (Grey, Olive, Yellow and Tan scuds).

and aquatic plants can get a foothold.

A common misconception is that freshwater shrimps only swim backwards. This is not so. True, they often propel themselves backwards when traversing their aquatic jungle. However, when truly swimming in open water, I find they swim forwards, head first, on their sides.

Gammarids grow to a maximum of 5/8" (16mm) in the UK. *G. Duebeni* appears to be larger than *G. pulex* and *G. lacustris*. More usually they are found between 1/4" (6mm) and 3/8" (9mm). They all have many appendages, arranged in pairs. These are (from head to tail): a pair of antennae, 3 pairs of gnathopods (mittenlike 'hands'), 5 pairs of true walking legs, 3 pairs of pleopods and 3 pairs of uropods.

If you keep a few freshwater shrimps in your cold water aquarium, you will soon realize that they are nocturnal creatures. They dislike strong sunlight and, when it is bright, they hide away. So, a dull day or late evening may be the best time to use your artificial, although I have found it works well most times of day.

NOTES ON MATERIALS AND TYING

There was a time when I preferred straight shanked hooks for my shrimps, producing the distinctive hump by lashing the lead wire ballast backwards and forwards, on top of the shank, in ever-decreasing lengths, the method recommended by the late Dick Walker. The reasoning behind this method was to avoid gape-obstructing bulk and also to ensure that the pattern fished point up.

My opinion regarding a suitable hook for shrimps has now been changed forever after using the Partridge code K4A Grub/Shrimp hook and I can't really see myself going back to a straight shank again. Even with the lead ballast wound on in the conventional way, plus dubbing and appendages, I cannot fault its hooking-to-holding ratio. I confidently recommend the K4A.

Another major change I have made is to the material I use for the so-called 'shell back'. For years I was wedded to polythene, both clear and dyed, and many of my small imitative patterns contained some polythene somewhere in their make-up. However, the advent of Flexibody has rendered my stock of dyed polythene nearly redundant. Flexibody does not have a slippery surface, a most annoying characteristic of polythene. This improvement offers a tremendous advantage to the flydresser when ribbing the shrimp with another equally slippery material - nylon mono. The problem when using polythene was trying to get that all-important first rib to 'hold' and it was always a source of great frustration as time after time, it would simply slip off the end. This problem does not exist with Flexibody.

For general hook covering and 'padding' you can, if you wish, use any suitably coloured fine natural fur dubbing - I did so for many years. However, most natural furs tend to darken considerably when wet, a point always to bear in mind when you want to create any pale pattern. I now prefer to use the modern synthetic dubbings. The high-glint Finesse darkens very little when wet - it is my current favourite.

One thing I have not changed is my allegiance to partridge hackle barbs for my Shrimps' various appendages. What I have changed significantly though, is the way I tie in these appendages. This new method is foolproof and guarantees perfect results every time. The old method of mixing together stripped partridge hackle barbs with fine

FRESHWATER SHRIMP DRESSINGS

THE GREY SHRIMP
Hook: Curved shank medium or heavy wire. Suggest Partridge 'John Veniard' Grub/Shrimp hook code K4A sizes 10-18, usually 12 and 14.
Weight: Narrow strip of wine bottle lead foil.
Thread: Midge 8/0 (light grey) or Danvilles's Spider Web (untinted).
Cement: Dave's Flexament (USA) or Floo Gloo (UK).
Tails: Several barbs from brown-grey partridge hackle.
Body: Fine synthetic dubbing, medium grey-olive, eg. Davy Wotton Finesse Masterclass blend MC14.
Shellback: Clear thick polythene 0.008" (0.2mm), or clear Flexibody.
Rib: Any pale or clear nylon mono 4-6lb BS.
Legs: Barbs of brown-grey partridge.
Antennae: As tails but smaller clump.

THE MATING SHRIMP
As for Grey Shrimp (above), except for:
Tails: Grey partridge dyed ginger-orange.
Body: Fine synthetic dubbing, ginger-orange, eg. Davy Wotton Finesse Masterclass blend MC15.
Rib: Sometimes on this shrimp, I use a fine gold wire (brass) for the rib instead of the clear mono.
Legs: Grey partridge dyed ginger-orange.
Antennae: As tails but smaller clump.

dubbing gave quite acceptable-looking results but was never foolproof and a certain knack was required to ensure that plenty of barbs protruded.

My Shrimp remains much as it was since my last update six or seven years ago and, while my latest method of producing the life-like appendages accounts for the fly spending a little more time in the vice, I think you will agree that the end result justifies it.

Tying the Freshwater Shrimp

Fig 1
Grip the hook so that the straight part near the eye is almost horizontal. Load the shank with lead. A 1/16" (2mm) wide sliver of wine bottle foil does the job well and lies nice and smooth. The amount of lead ballasting will be dictated by the rivers you fish. Catch on the tying thread just behind the eye and run it back and forth over the lead to cocoon it. Take the tying thread to a position well around the bend. Let the bobbin holder hang. Next, tie in a small clump of partridge hackle barbs, five or six. The tip ends should project beyond the tie-down point by approximately 1/3 to 1/2 the hook length.

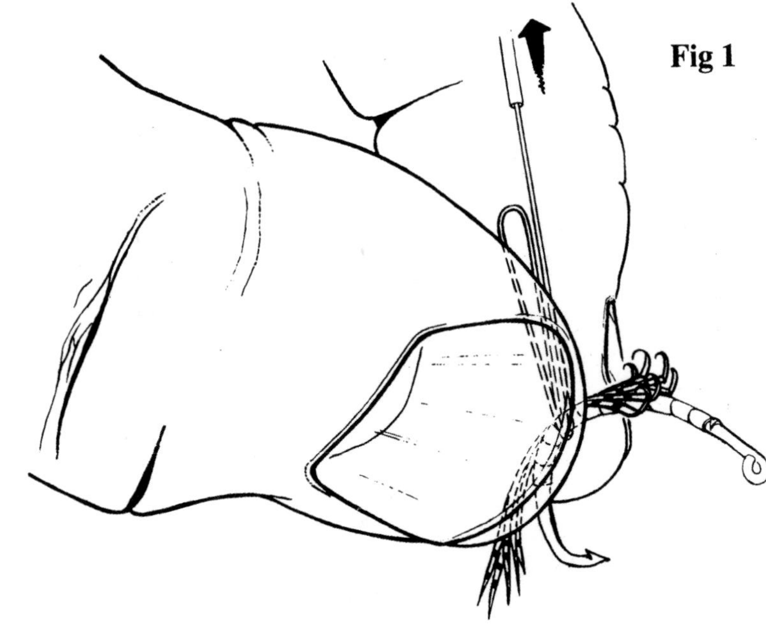

Fig 1

Fig 2
Now take the tying thread back up the shank tying down the tail butts as you go. At midshank let the bobbin holder hang.

Fig 2

Fig 3
Next offer up a 4" (100mm) length of 3-4lb BS mono, choosing a transparent or near transparent brand. Tie in the mono very securely. If this rib slips out as you start winding it on, you'll be really vexed. I usually dent it with my teeth to stop it slipping.

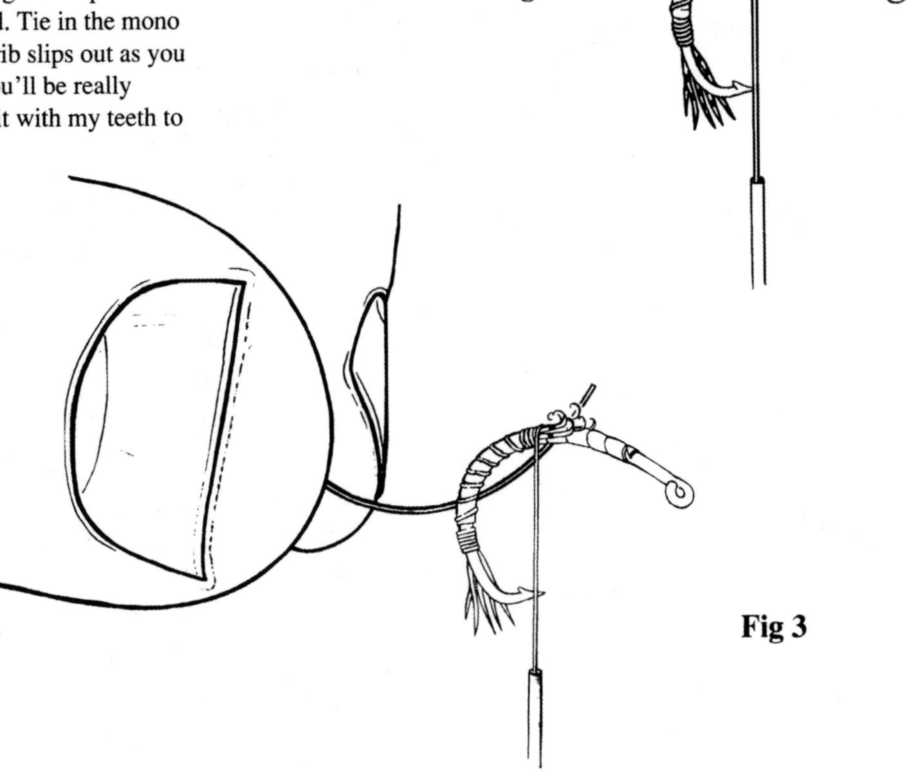

Fig 3

Fig 4
Bind it down all the way to where the tails are tied in.

Fig 5
Now cut out the shellback shape from your sheet of Flexibody. This shape should be a pointed oval, like a long American football, pointed more at one end (the tying-in tip) than the other. It should be just longer than the distance from tail tying-in point to eye, measured around the bend.

Fig 6
It must also be wide enough to cover the back, coming part way down both sides - a wrap around effect.

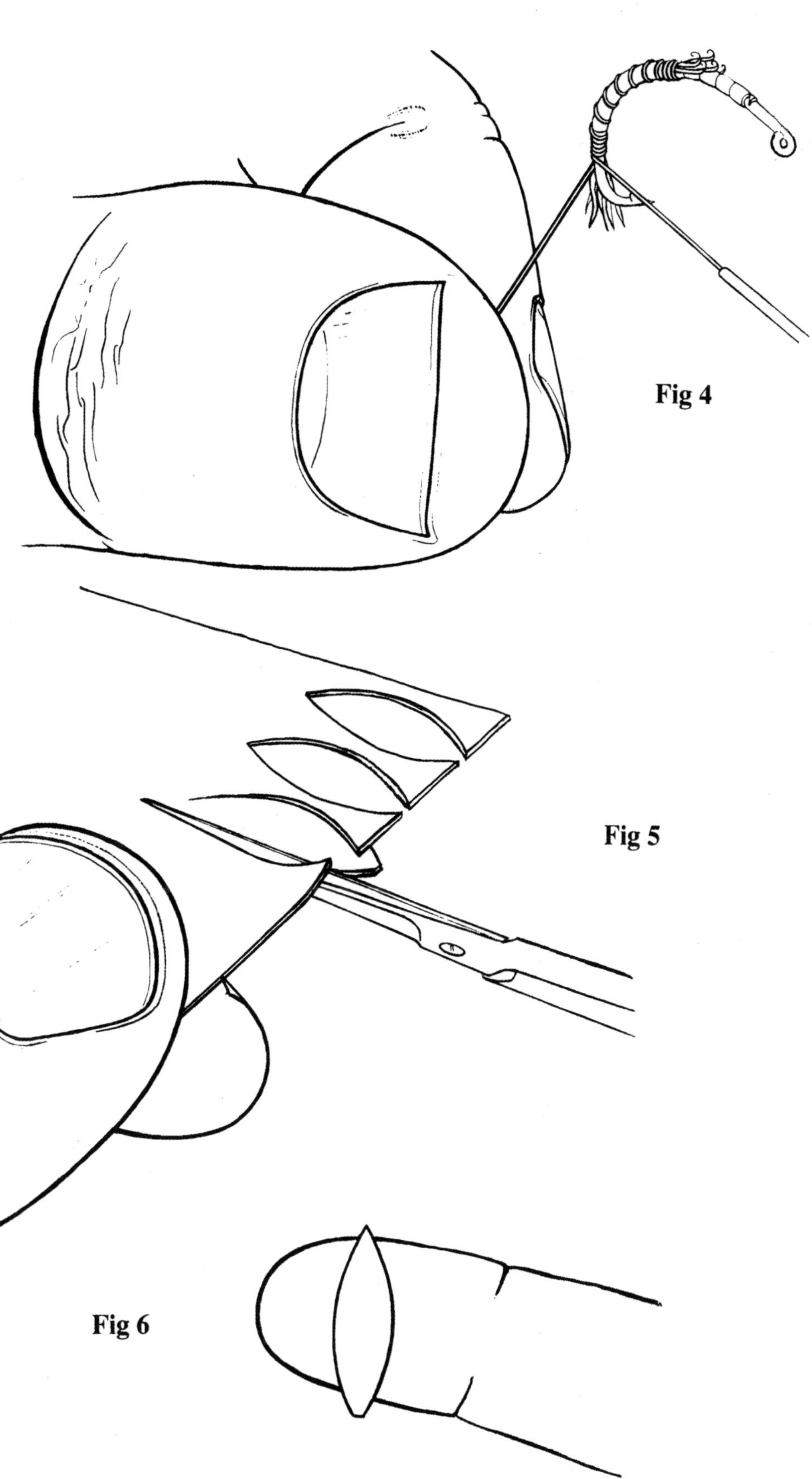
Fig 4

Fig 5

Fig 6

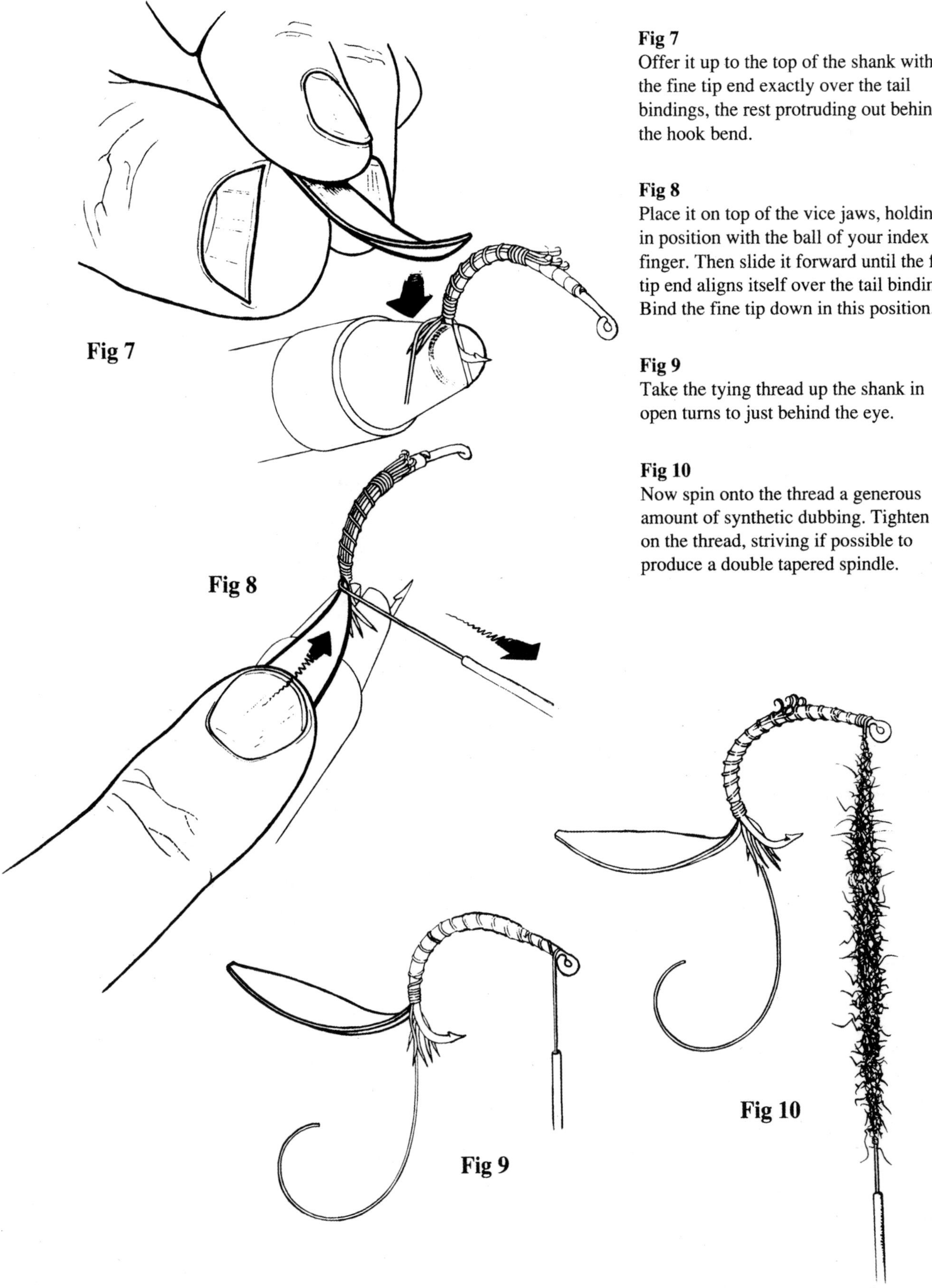

Fig 7

Fig 8

Fig 9

Fig 10

Fig 7
Offer it up to the top of the shank with the fine tip end exactly over the tail bindings, the rest protruding out behind the hook bend.

Fig 8
Place it on top of the vice jaws, holding it in position with the ball of your index finger. Then slide it forward until the fine tip end aligns itself over the tail bindings. Bind the fine tip down in this position.

Fig 9
Take the tying thread up the shank in open turns to just behind the eye.

Fig 10
Now spin onto the thread a generous amount of synthetic dubbing. Tighten this on the thread, striving if possible to produce a double tapered spindle.

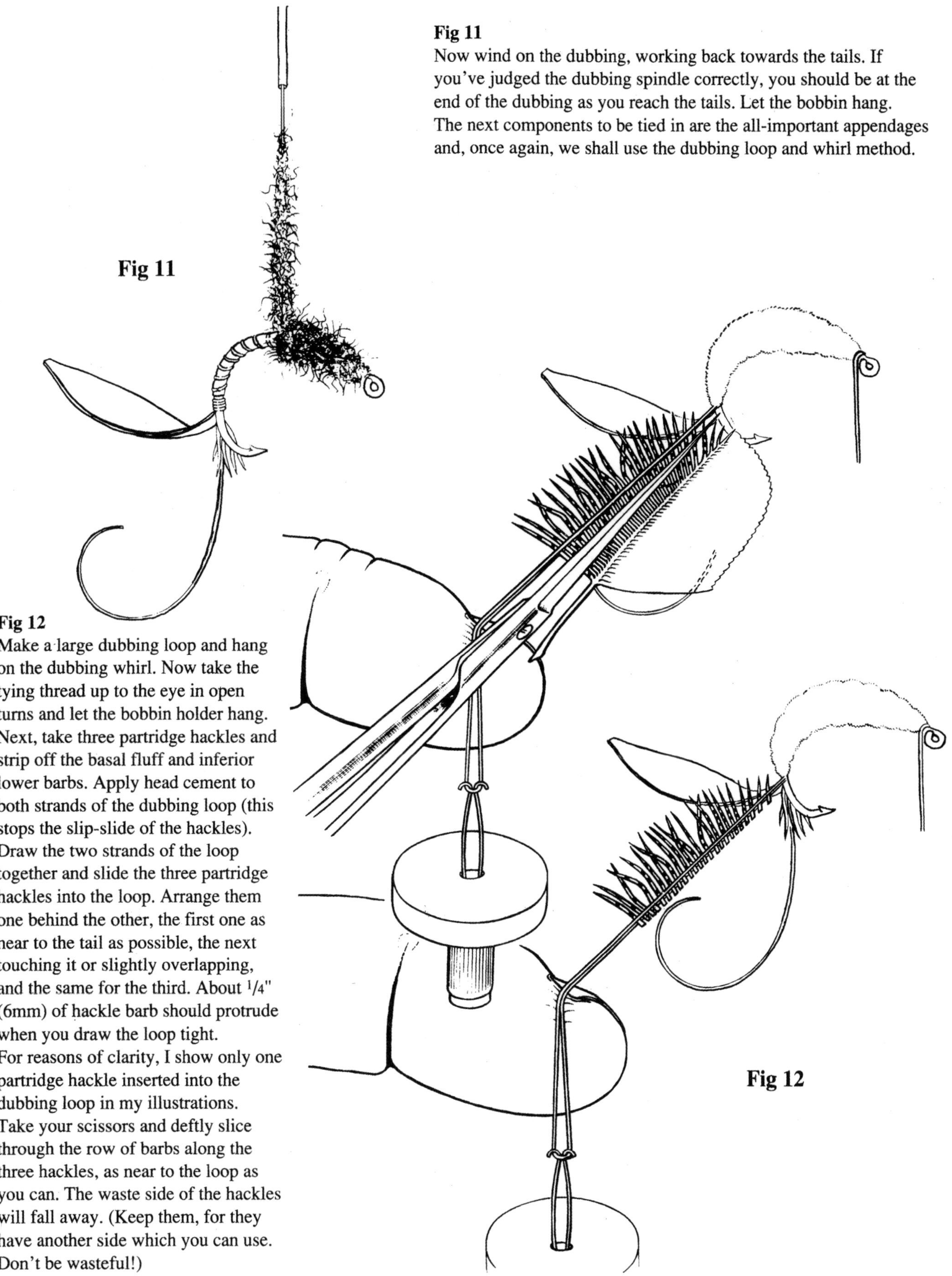

Fig 11
Now wind on the dubbing, working back towards the tails. If you've judged the dubbing spindle correctly, you should be at the end of the dubbing as you reach the tails. Let the bobbin hang. The next components to be tied in are the all-important appendages and, once again, we shall use the dubbing loop and whirl method.

Fig 12
Make a large dubbing loop and hang on the dubbing whirl. Now take the tying thread up to the eye in open turns and let the bobbin holder hang. Next, take three partridge hackles and strip off the basal fluff and inferior lower barbs. Apply head cement to both strands of the dubbing loop (this stops the slip-slide of the hackles). Draw the two strands of the loop together and slide the three partridge hackles into the loop. Arrange them one behind the other, the first one as near to the tail as possible, the next touching it or slightly overlapping, and the same for the third. About 1/4" (6mm) of hackle barb should protrude when you draw the loop tight.
For reasons of clarity, I show only one partridge hackle inserted into the dubbing loop in my illustrations.
Take your scissors and deftly slice through the row of barbs along the three hackles, as near to the loop as you can. The waste side of the hackles will fall away. (Keep them, for they have another side which you can use. Don't be wasteful!)

Fig 13

Next, without moving a muscle, spin the whirl. As it spins move your index finger up and down the spiralling threads, this helps the twists to travel. When it is twisted, with all the barbs entrapped, stop the whirl.

Fig 14

Wind on this 'flue brush' of hackle barbs from the tail end all the way to the head. It should be wound in even, open turns and pulled in hard enough to bite deeply into the body dubbing - this will make all the hackle barbs stand out sharply.

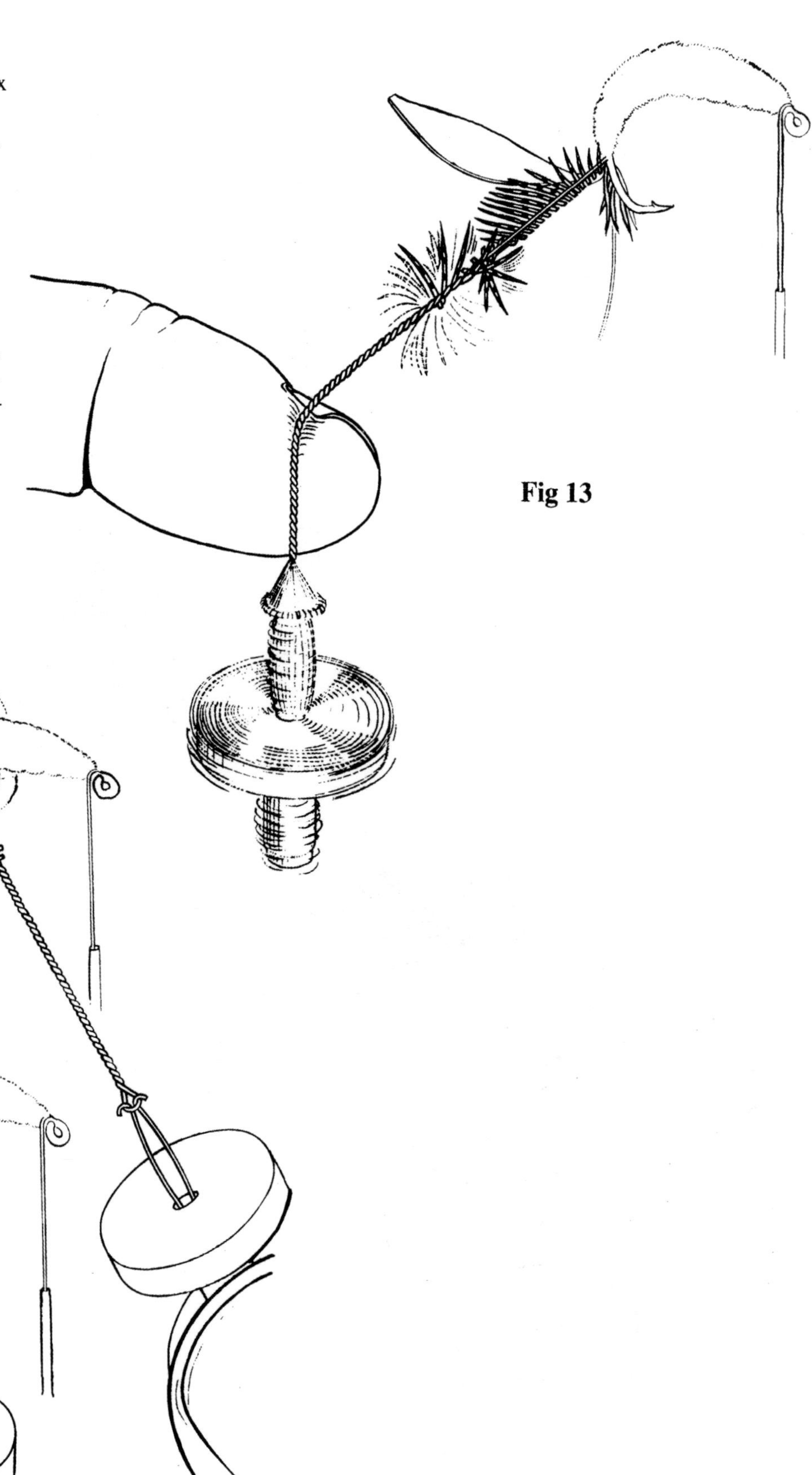

Fig 13

Fig 14

Figs 15 & 16
If you find your dubbing loop 'runs out' before you reach the hook eye, then simply let the whirl hang, allow it to untwist, insert another hackle (same method as before) and spin tight. Then continue winding up the shank to the finishing point. Inserting two or three hackles in the one loop and trimming them requires a little practice.

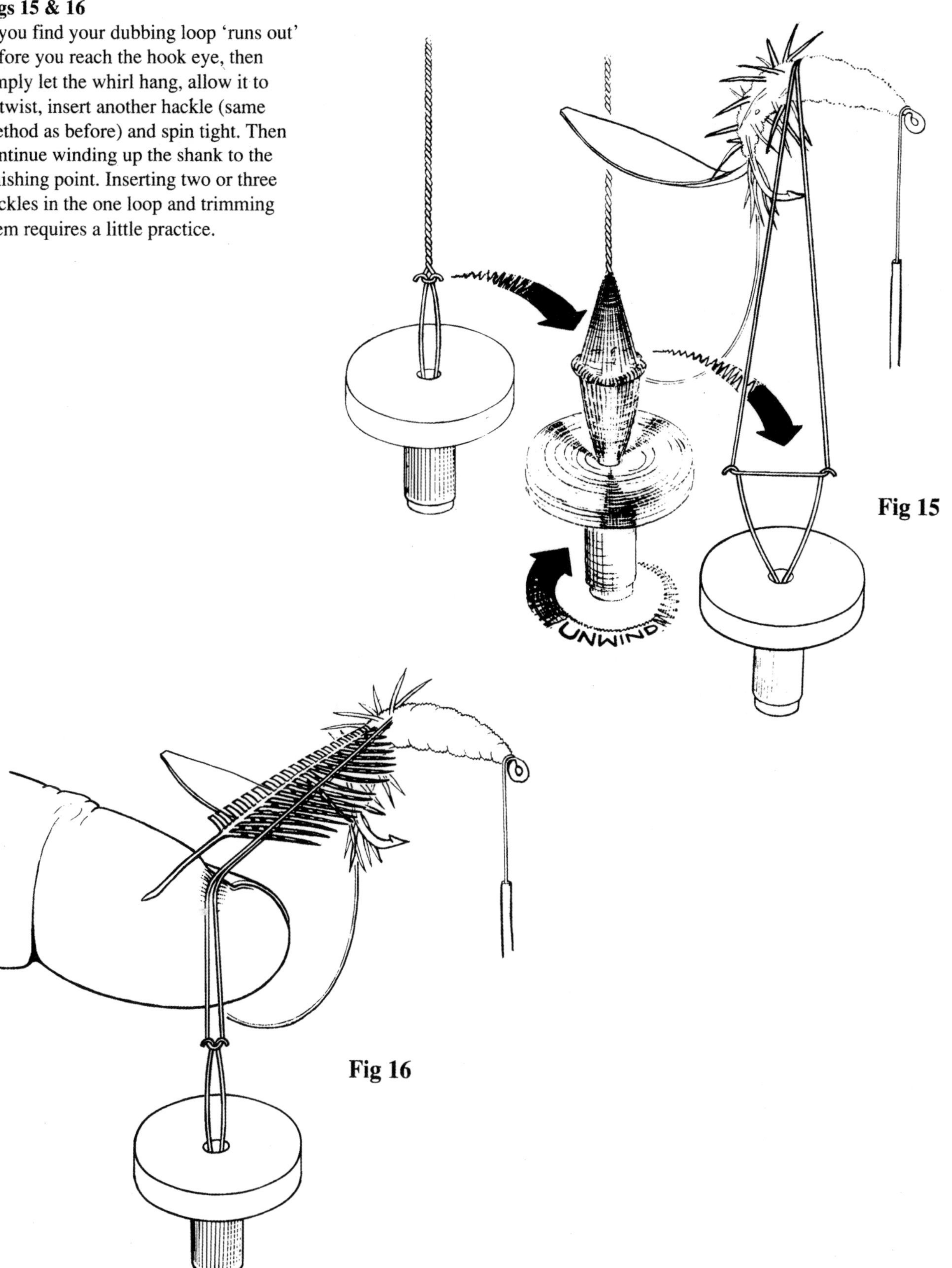

Fig 15

Fig 16

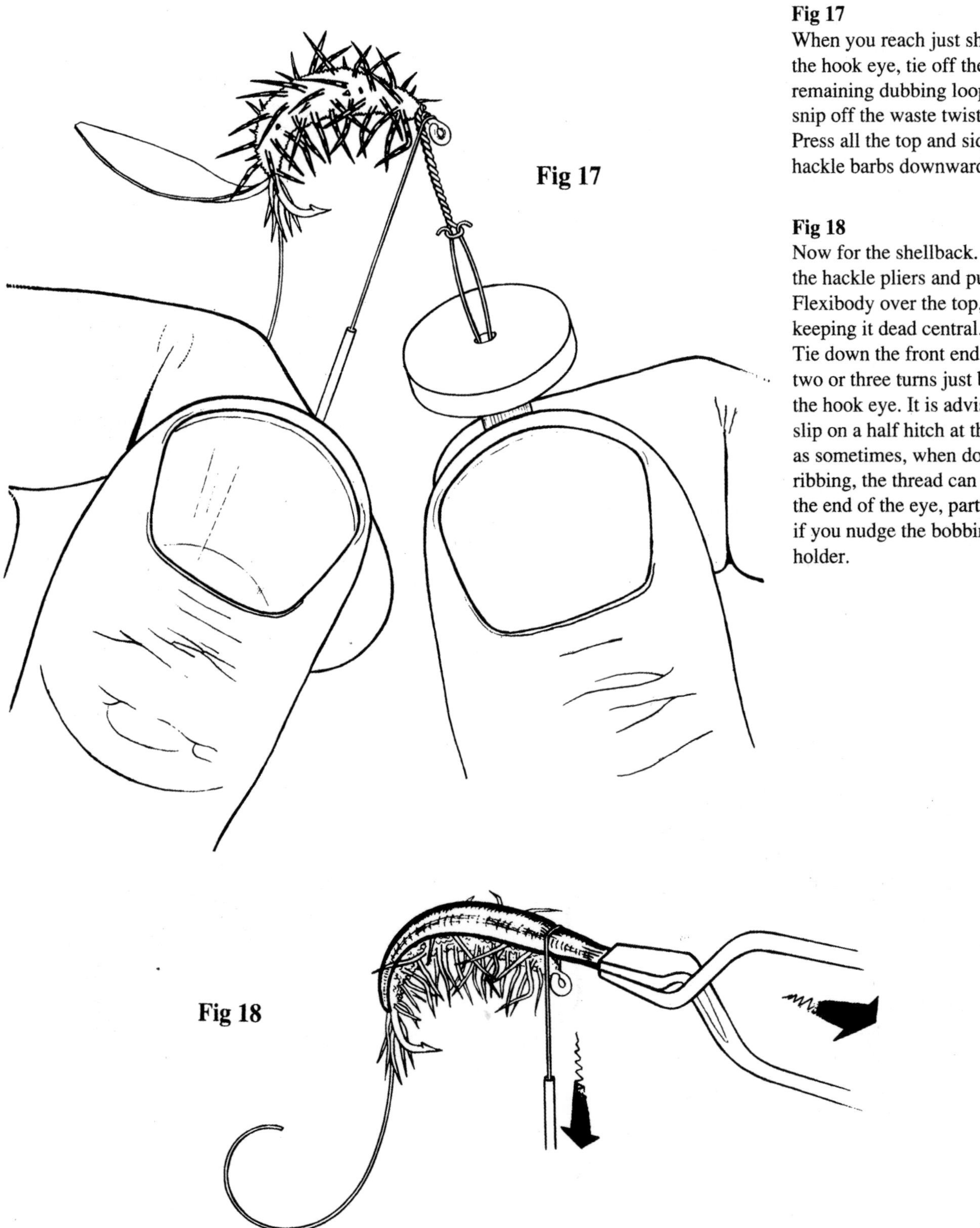

Fig 17
When you reach just short of the hook eye, tie off the remaining dubbing loop and snip off the waste twisted loop. Press all the top and side hackle barbs downwards.

Fig 18
Now for the shellback. Clip on the hackle pliers and pull the Flexibody over the top, keeping it dead central.
Tie down the front end with two or three turns just behind the hook eye. It is advisable to slip on a half hitch at this stage as sometimes, when doing the ribbing, the thread can slip off the end of the eye, particularly if you nudge the bobbin holder.

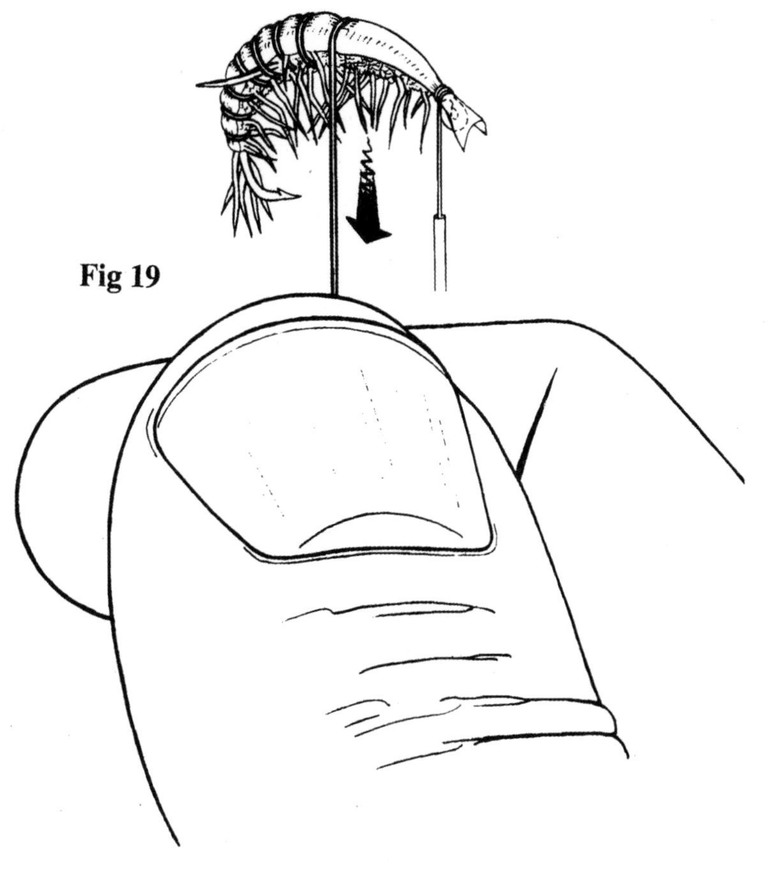

Fig 19

Fig 19
Spiral the nylon mono all the way up the shrimp from tail to hook eye. Make the rib spacing neat and even and, as you progress along, ensure that you pull each rib into the shellback deep enough to produce distinct indentations. Keep the Flexibody shape central on the hook and try not to fold down and trap any of the partridge barbs - the legs! At the hook eye tie off the nylon mono with five or six tight thread wraps. Trim off the waste mono and the tag of left-over shellback.

Fig 20
At this stage, I sometimes tie in a little beard of the same partridge hackle barbs. Tear off a small clump (say five or six barbs) and tie them in on the underside with the tips projecting back towards the hook point. Don't bother with this stage if your shrimp already has enough legs.

Fig 21
Fan out the legs by rocking from side to side with your thumb nail.
Your shrimp will only look really finished if it sports a few forward facing partridge barbs, the antennae.

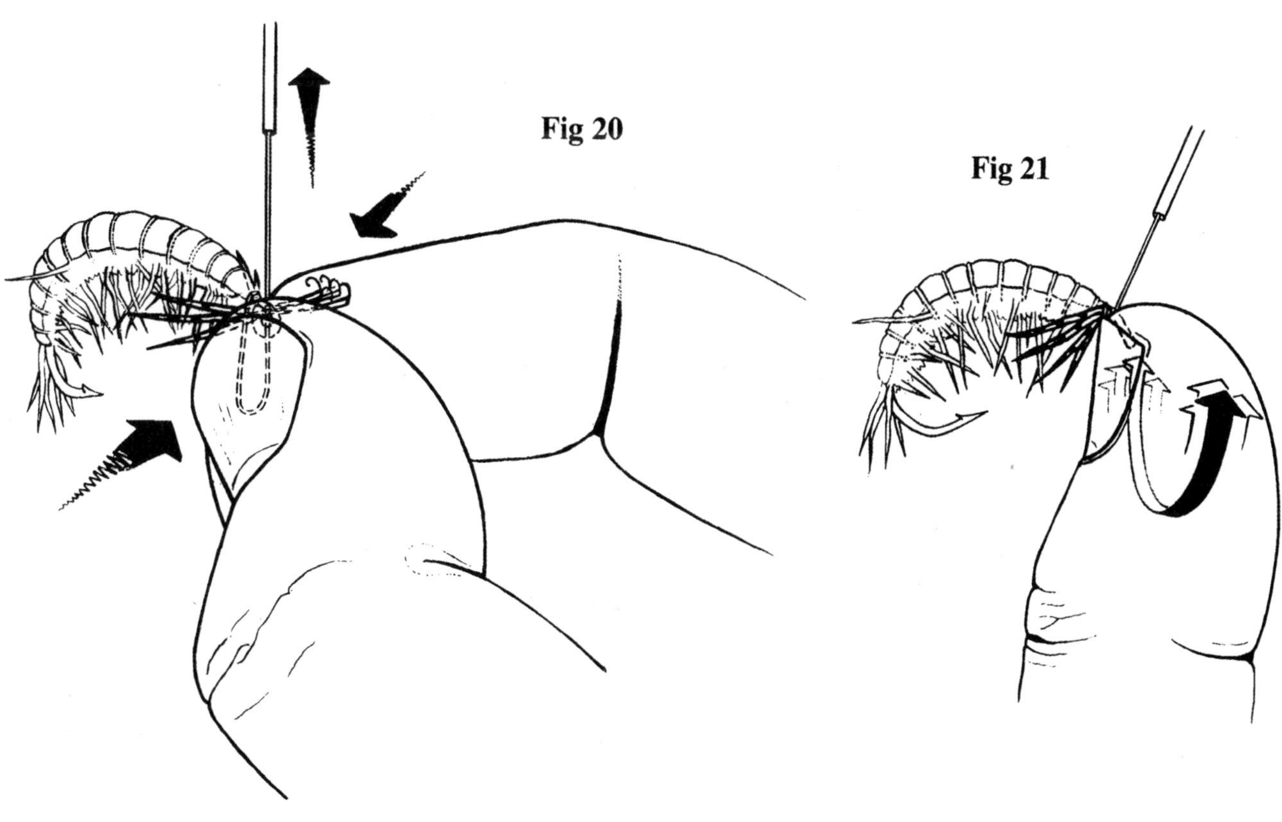

Fig 20

Fig 21

Fig 22

Take a small clump of partridge barbs, say four or five, and tie them in on top of the shank. If a couple of the barbs slip down the side, so much the better. They should project about 1/3 of the hook length. Add on a couple more tight turns, then complete with a whip finish. Trim off the tying thread, apply head cement to the whippings and you've finished!

Fig 23

These instructions may suggest a very complicated dressing. However, this is not the case and once the route is learned, the shrimp is very easily tied. It is a proven catcher of fish and, at the risk of sounding conceited, it is the most realistic imitation I know.

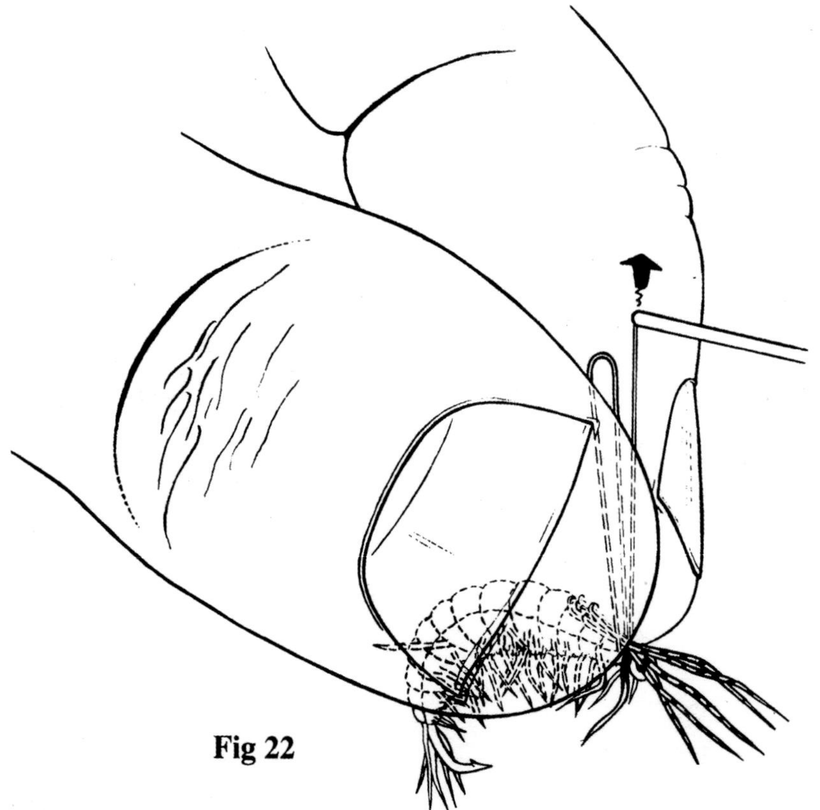

Fig 22

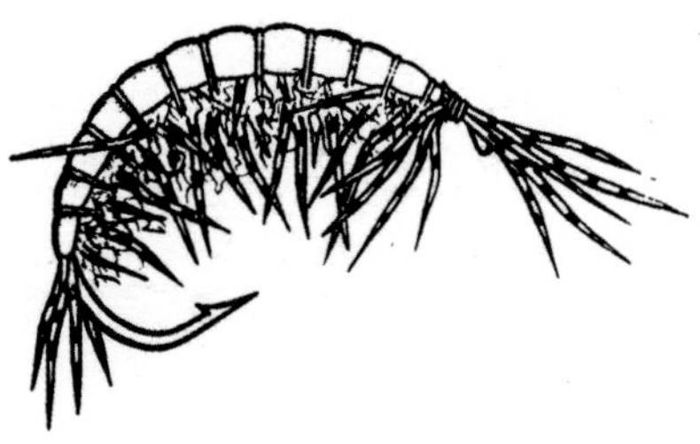

Fig 23